GREEN

ARCHITECTURE NOW!

2

IMPRINT

PROJECT MANAGEMENT
Florian Kobler, Cologne

COLLABORATION
Harriet Graham, Turin
Inga Hallsson, Cologne

PRODUCTION
Frauke Kaiser, Cologne

DESIGN
Sense/Net Art Direction
Andy Disl and
Birgit Eichwede, Cologne
www.sense-net.de

GERMAN TRANSLATION
Kristina Brigitta Köper, Berlin

FRENCH TRANSLATION
Claire Debard, Freiburg

PRINTED IN ITALY
ISBN 978–3–8365–3589–2

© 2012 TASCHEN GMBH
Hohenzollernring 53
D–50672 Cologne
www.taschen.com

GREEN
ARCHITECTURE NOW!

GRÜNE *Architektur heute!*
L'architecture VERTE *d'aujourd'hui !*
Philip Jodidio

2

TASCHEN

CONTENTS

INTRODUCTION

SUSTAINABLY GREEN

And did those feet in ancient time
Walk upon England's mountains green:
And was the holy Lamb of God,
On England's pleasant pastures seen!
And did the Countenance Divine,
Shine forth upon our clouded hills?
And was Jerusalem builded here,
Among these dark Satanic Mills?

"And did those feet in ancient time"
William Blake, 1804

At the turn of the 19th century, William Blake famously lashed out at the beginnings of the Industrial Revolution. Years before, in 1791, the steam-powered Albion Flour Mills in Southwark near Blake's residence had burnt in suspicious circumstances. "And all the Arts of Life they changed into the Arts of Death in Albion…" he wrote in "Jerusalem" (Chapter 3), which recounts the fall of Albion, the oldest name of Britain. The mechanisms of "modernity" and its trail of environmental and social destruction were already in motion, but it was not until the second half of the 20th century that real consciousness about environmental issues began to come to the fore.

And what does architecture have to do with all this? A modern response may be warranted. In the United States, 80% of greenhouse gas emissions come from buildings, and in New York City, they use 94% of the power.[1] Obviously industrial methods have allowed increasing populations to benefit from conditions of comfort that Blake's time did not afford. It is simple, however, to see how "traditional" forms of construction, making use of wood, or hand-carved stone, without modern transport links bringing materials from the other side of the world, would have produced far less damage to the environment than the average contemporary house. The use of locally sourced materials, and even passive solar design which seeks to avoid excessive heat gain (or loss), are aspects of "green" architecture that go back almost as far as the history of building.

SILENT SPRING
Modern interest in the protection of the environment can easily be traced back to Rachel Carson's *Silent Spring* (1962) that documented the detrimental effects of pesticides on the environment and is sometimes credited with being at the origin of the environmental protection movement. The dramatic oil price increases in the 1970s surely spurred interest in renewable energy sources and energy effi-

1
*Zhang Lei, Three Courtyard
Community Center, Yangzhou,
China, 2009*

ciency, but, in the United States, it was not until 1989 that the American Institute of Architects (AIA) formed its Committee on the Environment. The US Green Building Council (USGBC) was founded in 1993, launching their Leadership in Energy and Environmental Design (LEED) program five years later. Other countries led the way, or followed suit, but it can safely be said that concerted interest in the environmental impact of architecture dates from the early 1990s.

BETTER DEAD THAN GREEN

With the considerable debate about "global warming" and continually rising energy costs, it would seem that the environmental aspect of architecture has become one of its central features. And yet the enthusiasm for "sustainable" architecture may also be directly related to the state of the economy. When things go badly, as they have in most developed countries since 2008, is it not a natural reaction to just get on with the business of building without too many extra "green" expenditures? As the French daily *Le Monde* pointed out in its December 27, 2011 edition,[2] David Cameron promised as recently as the spring of 2010 that his government would be the "greenest ever." Just 18 months later, he decided to retroactively halve the subventions granted for small photovoltaic installations. In the first nine months of 2011, 78 000 solar panel systems had been put in place in the UK, at least partially because the government was offering to pay 43.3 pence per kilowatt hour generated using photovoltaic panels. In other words, things were going so swimmingly that there did not seem any point in actually paying the promised subvention. Seen against the background of the UK's rather pallid economy, events like these prompted the *Guardian* to write: "It's official: the government's ambition to be the greenest ever is dead, choked by the exhaust fumes and chimneystack smog belched out in the desperate attempt to restart the economy's engine."[3] Shades of the "dark Satanic mills."

BETTER GREEN THAN POOR

It may be fair to ask today, though, if the forces acting on architecture are not obliging it to become progressively more and more sustainable. One reason architecture contributes so mightily to carbon emissions is its voracious appetite for materials, often produced far away or at great cost to the environment. If energy costs soar because fossil fuels are dwindling and nuclear power has been exposed for the great danger it always was, sustainability offers a recipe for reducing power costs, a weighty argument in a civilization that adulates rapid profits. Of course the world is full of architects, clients, and even builders who want to do the right thing, to protect the planet for future generations, but when it comes right down to hard facts, saving money is an argument that will dictate far more decisions than saintliness.

50° IN THE SUN

Although government policies, judged too "costly" for times of economic difficulty, and overall international policies to curb greenhouse gas emissions and other forms of pollution have clearly suffered in the downturn(s) since 2008, it can be argued that "green" architecture is here to stay. In a sense, sustainable buildings have always existed around the world, and those that are the least sophisticated are often the most "green." Orienting a building so that it gets daylight but does not overheat in summer is a basic, obvious choice for any architect or owner.

2
Gulf Coast Community Design Studio,
Broussard House, Biloxi, Mississippi,
USA, 2008

2

Making use of simple, locally obtained materials should also be dictated by common sense. Privileging renewable resources such as carefully harvested wood is an obvious way to protect future generations and allow them to continue to do what is possible today. And yet, common sense is far from being the rule in contemporary architecture. Obviously encouraged by the forces of the marketplace, which put an emphasis on rapid gain, but was also thrown into overdrive by a culture of instant gratification, unsustainable and, indeed, destructive forms of architecture continue to thrive. Cities populated with glass towers have risen from the sands of the Persian Gulf where summer temperatures can reach 50° centigrade, but who is to tell the inhabitants of Abu Dhabi that they cannot reach for the skies when they clearly have the money to do so?

WATCH OUT FOR ETHANOL

The focus placed on sustainability has another, usually unwritten subtext. Clearly, since "green" is fashionable, architects, developers, and clients are prone to put forward their environmental credentials, even when passive strategies that have always been used are "recycled" for current consumption. Worse, a number of products, which need not be enumerated here, are far less environmentally friendly than they are made out to be. Citing a non-architectural example may give the tone for this aspect of today's "sustainability." It has been known for years that so-called biofuels are not a miraculous solution to the problems posed by fossil fuels. In 2008, a *Washington Post* editorial stated: "Separate studies released this month by Princeton University and the Nature Conservancy reveal that biofuels are not a silver bullet in the battle against global warming. In fact, they could make things worse. Corn and sugar cane are common sources of ethanol. Aside from emitting fewer greenhouse gases than coal or oil when burned as fuel, these biofuel crops remove carbon from the atmosphere while they are growing—thus making them nearly carbon-neutral. But the studies show that ethanol may be even more dangerous for the environment than fossil fuels are."[4]

A LABEL TO SELL PRODUCTS

An interview published online with Terry Riley, the former curator for architecture and design at the Museum of Modern Art in New York and curator of the 2011 Hong Kong and Shenzhen architecture biennale, translates such doubts into the language of today's green enthusiasm in architecture. When asked why the biennale turned down sustainability as a theme, he responded: "We rejected the word 'sustainability' in considering the theme for this biennale. It is too important to be used, as it currently is, as a label to sell products, most of which are inherently unsustainable. As a practice today, sustainability also focuses on numbers. We chose to emphasize vitality, which, I believe, incorporates sustainability as well as a number of other less quantifiable issues. This attitude guided all the decisions we made about the biennale."[5]

When searching for examples of "green" or "sustainable" architecture, an obvious question concerns the definition of these words. Sustainable development was defined by the United Nations World Commission on Environment and Development in the Brundtland Report (1987) as "those paths of social, economic, and political progress that meet the needs of the present without compromising the ability of future generations to meet their own needs." A year after the Earth Summit in Rio de Janeiro, in June 1993, the World Congress of Architects stated more simply: "Sustainability means meeting our needs today without compromising the ability of future generations to meet their own needs."[6]

DON'T WORRY, BE HAPPY

Obviously, the organizations that certify the sustainability of architecture across the world, in the image of the United States Green Building Council and its LEED standard, approach the issue of responsible construction in a more complex and complete way. The Holcim Foundation, created by a Swiss cement supplier, identifies five key areas of sustainability: 1) innovation and transferability; 2) ethical standards and social equity; 3) environmental quality and resource efficiency; 4) economic performance and compatibility; and 5) contextual and aesthetic impact.[7] This list of goals surely has a relation to the UN or Earth Summit mode that clearly links social issues to the overall question of sustainability. Architectural organizations such as USGBC grant their LEED certification on a points basis, derived from a series of qualifications that are 1) sustainable sites; 2) water efficiency; 3) energy and atmosphere; 4) materials and resources; 5) indoor environmental quality; 4) innovation in design; and 5) regional priority credits. Building types are recognized in different ways according to a clear, but rather complex system. The issues raised by USGBC ultimately have a social bias in the sense that the points examined improve the quality of life within a building and well beyond its walls, but such elements signaled out by Holcim as "ethical standards and social equality" are not overtly present. The relative complexity and variety of rating systems underlines some of the inherent ambiguity of any effort to attain sustainability beyond the most obvious and basic rules that governed almost all construction until the time of cement, steel, glass, air conditioning, and stone shipped around the world to clad the icons of corporate vanity. When all those squeaky-clean technologies like biofuels, or even photovoltaic panels that contain various heavy metals, turn out to have a dark side, some questions, or even skepticism may be justified. In the meantime, best to not worry and be happy.

It is all well and good to recall that architecture, for much of its history, was not a major source of environmental degradation. Sure, deforestation is seen as a cause of the collapse of civilization on Easter Island, but, elsewhere, smaller populations and a lack of technological infrastructure assured that buildings would not be the end of us, at least until the Albion Flour Mills came along in Southwark. But is it still possible in more or less "advanced" countries to build in an ecologically sound way? Or might this be an Arcadian nostalgia that has little reality on the ground?

TAKING THE DOG OUT FOR A TROT

The example of "Patty's House" (Broussard House, Biloxi, Mississippi, USA, 2008, page 172), an effort of several organizations to improve the lot of citizens who lost their homes during Hurricane Katrina in 2005, is an interesting one. BaSIC Initiative, which began its existence as a program to assist poor indigenous farmers in central Mexico, is now a collaboration of faculty and students from Portland State University and University of Texas at Austin, School of Architecture. BaSIC collaborated with the Hamer Center for Community Design at Pennsylvania State University, the Design Corps, Gulf Coast Community Design Studio (GCCDS), and such other organizations at the East Biloxi Coordination, Relieve, and Redevelopment Agency to bring together financing and the collaboration of 12 architecture students from different universities. The group of students and faculty worked for six weeks designing and building the house. One of the goals of the Hamer

Center was to create a LEED-certified house. The goal is supported by some grant funding to pay for improved materials and systems. The house was LEED certified in spring of 2009, the first single-family residence in Mississippi to earn the rating.

The plan of the house resembles the southern vernacular residence-type called the dogtrot, which separates the living space from the sleeping space with an open covered area, increasing the effectiveness of natural ventilation and creating a covered outdoor living area. Lifted nearly four meters off the ground to meet advised flood standards, the house was made with concrete and pressure-treated wood. Concrete columns rise up a bit over two meters, giving way at that height to wood columns and bracing.[8] This house surely bears an architectural resemblance to local residences, and in that it follows a typology developed through years of storm-related flooding, and knowledge of the local climate in general. The rather intense collaboration of various organizations to bring about what seems to be a simple project shows that it is possible to base future development on the knowledge of the past, and on the good will of people who are trying to make homeowners comfortable and ecologically responsible. Concrete was used in the Broussard House, but only where necessary, and its LEED certification attests to the care that has been taken in procuring and using materials.

BAMBOO AND RED CEDAR

Half a world away, the Vietnamese architect Vo Trong Nghia has designed a pure bamboo structure called Bamboo Wing (Dai Lai, Vinh Phuc Province, Vietnam, 2009, page 384). He points out proudly that "no steel or other man-made structural materials" have been employed for this 1600-square-meter meeting space, whose form was inspired by bird wings. This and other buildings by Vo Trong Nghia have a soaring modernity that somehow belies the extensive use of traditional building materials such as bamboo. Indeed, the rapid growth rate of bamboo makes it an excellent candidate to be considered the ultimate "renewable resource" where construction, at least on a relatively modest scale, is concerned. The fact that the site of Bamboo Wing is a relatively undisturbed natural environment also contributes to the confirmation that sophisticated materials are not really indispensible for modern architecture.

Kengo Kuma, one of the most significant Japanese architects, has long been interested in the traditions of his own country, without ever falling into the inherent traps of "pastiche" or pure imitation of the past. His Yusuhara Wooden Bridge Museum (Yusuhara-cho, Takaoka-gun, Kochi, Japan, 2010, page 264) is a grade bridge-like wooden building housing space for a workshop and an artist-in-residence program. Although he used laminated timber as opposed to the solid wood that was favored in the past, he makes reference in this project to cantile-vering techniques seen in the older architecture of China and Japan. Locally harvested red cedar was used for the project, further underlining its sustainability. Again, much as Vo Trong Nghia, Kengo Kuma makes use of regional architectural traditions to create a thoroughly modern and yet largely sustainable building. The point is not to go back to the past, but to make use of tradition to rediscover ways of building that are more in harmony not only with nature, but also with the well-being of users and local populations.

3
Vo Trong Nghia, Bamboo Wing,
Dai Lai, Vinh Phuc Province,
Vietnam, 2009

3

HANDMADE IN CHINA

It is not as though only Asian offices are engaged in the successful traditionally inspired exploration of sustainable architecture, but there are clearly many recent examples of such use—which incidentally may on occasion be inspired as much by relatively low construction costs as they are by any systemic desire to protect the environment. The Gaoligong Museum of Handcraft Paper (Tengchong, Yunnan, China, 2009–10, page 334) by TAO (Trace Architecture Office) is a very elegant example of such constructive use of the past. This small (361-square-meter) museum is located next to the village of Xinzhuang, near Gaoligong Mountain in Yunnan, a world ecological preserve. Conceived with the goal of highlighting the local heritage of handmade paper, the structure was built by local craftsmen, including farmers, and makes use of paper, bamboo, local volcanic stone, and a traditional timber structural system. Again, this is no imitation of the architectural past; it is, rather, very modern in its conception and execution. It can and will be argued that tradition is one of the best ways to attain a true equilibrium with the natural and physical world. The methods employed in the Gaoligong Museum of Handcraft Paper were not born of the needs of a multinational corporation to make profits next month; rather, generations of intelligence are exploited here in a truly sustainable fashion. The bells and whistles of contemporary life may not be as much in evidence as some would hope, but those often largely useless added features are probably more outmoded than bamboo and volcanic stone as elements of contemporary construction.

SHRINKING FOOTPRINTS

The point of this volume is certainly not to excoriate modern materials and methods, but perhaps to point out that the past, too, can offer lessons of great value in the light of growing concern over resources and the environment. There is quite clearly another school of thinking which relies both on passive and active methods to control the use of energy, and to reduce the "carbon footprint" of architecture. This school calls on the most modern materials and thinking to make contemporary design compatible with the continued health of the planet. Some of the structures published here are veritable showcases of modern technology and these frequently pursue the goal of making a house or a building "energy positive"—that is to say, contributing to the energy supply of a community rather than merely drawing it down. Werner Sobek, the famous German engineer and author of many ecologically sound modern structures, recently contributed to the design of a project he calls F87 (Berlin, Germany, 2011, page 330). Winner of a competition for an "Efficiency House Plus with Electromobility" organized by the German Federal Ministry of Transport, Building, and Urban Development, the 130-square-meter F87 building should produce enough electricity to power the electrical vehicle of its owners, as well as meeting its own energy needs. Further, the building was created to generate a minimal environment impact, both on the occasion of its construction and for its future demolition.

HOLD YOUR BREATH

The Korean practice Unsangdong may have gone even further than Sobek in the accumulation of green technologies in a single house (E+ Green Home, Jeon Dae, Cheo In, Po Gok, Yong In, Kyeong Gi, South Korea, 2010–11, page 368). This larger (344-square-meter) house uses a green roof to minimize energy loss and solar gain while maximizing the reuse of rainwater. A sophisticated external insulation system

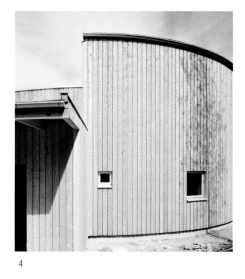

4
*Kjellgren Kaminsky, Villa Nyberg,
Borlänge, Sweden, 2010*

4

(StoTherm), thermally treated wood, building-integrated photovoltaics, high-efficiency solar thermal collectors, a wind turbine, and a geothermal heat pump made this the first PHI (Passive House Institute)–certified residence in South Korea. The Passivhaus standard was created after 1988 by Professors Bo Adamson of Lund University (Sweden) and Wolfgang Feist from the Institut für Wohnen und Umwelt (German Institute for Housing and the Environment). There are approximately 25 000 Passivhaus-certified structures in Europe, with a goal, something like that of the LEED system, to list and identify the factors that improve energy efficiency and reduce the ecological footprint of architecture. Total primary energy consumption of a certified Passivhaus must not exceed 120 kWh/m^2 per year and finally, more intriguingly, a certified building cannot leak more than six tenths of its air volume per hour. The Villa Nyberg (Borlänge, Sweden, 2010, page 248) by the Göteborg architects Kjellgren Kaminsky, for example, set a Swedish record for air tightness (0.038 l/sm^2 at 50 Pa. The Swedish passive-house standard is 0.3 and the previous record was 0.07). The Villa Nyberg is essentially round, reducing wall area and avoiding thermal or "cold" bridges. This house has an estimated heating energy consumption of just 25 kWh/m^2 per year.

Another willfully "green" house is Dick van Gameren's Villa 4.0 ('t Gooi, the Netherlands, 2010–11, page 156), a 540-square-meter structure that includes a low-temperature floor-heating system, a solar boiler, natural ventilation, a high-efficiency wood-burning stove in the kitchen, and all artificial lighting is LED-based. Somewhat less actively "sustainable" than the houses of Werner Sobek or Unsangdong, the Villa 4.0 appears to be closer to the reality of today's green architecture. By layering several different means to save energy, Van Gameren's realization surely improves on the operating costs of "normal" houses—suggesting that today's new "normal" may well exist in 't Gooi.

THE CORPORATE FACE OF RESPONSIBILITY

The principles of reduced energy consumption and overall sustainability are, of course, also applied to larger structures, and some corporate buildings have actually taken the lead in this area. One logical sponsor of an environmentally sound office is the Indian wind turbine manufacturer Suzlon. The Suzlon One Earth Global Headquarters (Pune, Maharashtra, India, 2008–10, page 21) by Christopher Charles Benninger Architects is a 55 741-square-meter complex that uses numerous "low-energy" materials, natural ventilation systems, photovoltaic panels, and, naturally, windmills. Physically attractive, the Suzlon Headquarters has a LEED Platinum certification, the highest rating given by the USGBC.

The Green Office (Meudon, France, 2009–11, page 44) by the architects Ateliers 115 seeks to go even further than Suzlon by consuming 62 kWh/m^2 versus 64 kWh/m^2 generated per year with photovoltaic panels and a cogeneration (CHP) system. In other words, within any statistics or symbols, the Green Office is energy positive. It should be able to actually feed electricity into the local grid. No air conditioning is used, but the Paris climate does not really call for it. Materials were selected for their environmental sustainability, while double-glazing and thick insulation also play a role in the overall efficiency of the structure. At 21 700 square meters, the Green Office is both large and innovative, though its external appearance may not set it apart from other corporate structures. One point of *Green Architecture Now 2* is that environmentally sound construction and usage practices surely do not go against good design. There is no real need for contemporary buildings

5
Dick van Gameren, Villa 4.0, 't Gooi,
The Netherlands, 2010–11

to look as though they are "green"—the real facts of interest will concern costs for many clients and their own feeling that they are being responsible citizens. In other terms, sustainability has gone mainstream and no longer needs to show its "green" color to every passerby. This is an important development that should be heralded and encouraged.

SKIING FAST ON THE INCINERATOR

The noted Danish architect Bjarke Ingels (BIG) has spoken out repeatedly in favor of what he calls "hedonistic sustainability"—in other words architecture that gives pleasure in its own responsible design. After early years when some felt that "green" buildings had to look odd to make their point, the various rating agencies gave a more technocratic and perhaps austere image to sustainability. Do not worry about looks and thrills when the real point is not to ship granite from Zimbabwe to Los Angeles. Ingels does not hesitate to take an opposite tack with designs such as his grand €460 million Amager Bakke Waste-to-Energy Plant (Copenhagen, Denmark, 2009–, page 72) that may well boast a ski slope on its 32 000-square-meter roof. "We want to do more than just create a beautiful skin around the factory," say the architects. "We want to add functionality!… We propose a new breed of waste-to-energy plant, one that is economically, environmentally, and socially profitable." Bjarke Ingels seems to go one step further than the sort of general acceptability that has now clothed the "green" architect; he wants to make sustainability fun and "profitable" in a broad manner.

Though Bjarke Ingels has a "big" reputation, it might be possible to point out that "hedonistic sustainability" may be less of a discovery than his ski slope on an incinerator implies. The Greek office K-Studio completed the Bar Bouni beach restaurant in 2011 (Pilos, Costa Navarino, Greece, page 236). Set on a wooden platform on a beach, with the waves breaking beneath it, this structure is based on natural wood columns and an "inverted field of hanging fabric sheets" forming a canopy. No need for a 32 000-square-meter ski slope on top of the building, all the "hedonistic sustainability" you can handle is right there on the beach. So, in a sense, sustainability also depends on location and function, with the simplest, most efficient solutions often being those that have been practiced over time. Wood, cloth, sand, and the breaking waves do not cost €460 million either. This is, of course, a facetious interpretation of the perfectly valid ideas expressed by Ingels, but modesty does not seem to be part of his game plan. What if real sustainability had more to do with modesty than with ever grander and more technological schemes?

KINGDOM COME

Some might be surprised to find the likes of Adrian Smith and Gordon Gill in a book about green architecture. Smith is, after all, the author of the Burj Khalifa (Dubai, UAE, 2004–09), the tallest building in the world at 830 meters. Even more astonishing, the pair has another super-tall structure in the works, the Kingdom Tower (Jeddah, Saudi Arabia), due to be over one kilometer high. Adrian Smith and other noted architects such as Norman Foster have long argued that there is a case to be made for the inherent sustainability of tall structures as opposed to an equivalent amount of low buildings. It is certain that in terms of infrastructure, ranging from roads to the power grid, a single tall building might well finally be greener than a large number of small structures. At the much more "normal" height of 240 meters, Adrian Smith and

6
*Gigon/Guyer, Prime Tower, Zurich,
Switzerland, 2008–11*

6

Gordon Gill won an international competition to design a tower for the Federation of Korean Industries in Seoul (South Korea, 2010–13, page 318). The specially designed skin of the building is "designed to help reduce the internal heating and cooling loads of the tower and collect energy by integrating photovoltaic panels into the spandrel areas of the southwest and northwest façades, which receive a significant amount of direct sunlight per day." According to the architects: "By angling the spandrel panels 30° upward toward the sun, the design team maximized the amount of energy collected, generating enough power to help maintain the electrical systems throughout the tower core and the office space. Just below the spandrel panels, the vision panels are angled 15° downward toward the ground, minimizing the amount of direct sun radiation and glare." While the case for building a kilometer-high tower in Jeddah may not be strong on any grounds other than the associated prestige, the Federation of Korean Industries building is being erected in an already dense city, where space is at a premium. Few would argue here that bamboo and volcanic stone would do the trick, and it must be accepted that contemporary architecture can resort to technological means to improve the carbon footprint of new structures. Such buildings will be built as long as resources allow, and it is surely better to seek to make them as sustainable as knowledge allows.

GREEN TOWER, GREEN STAR

On a smaller scale, the Swiss architects Gigon/Guyer have shown in their recent Zurich project (Prime Tower, Zurich, Switzerland, 2008–11, page 164) that a green high-rise, in this case 36-stories or 126-meters high, can live up to very high environmental standards. The LEED Gold-certified tower uses a ground-water heat-exchange pump, waste-heat recovery from the building and refrigeration devices, coupled heating/cooling with heat and ice storage, and partially operable windows. LEED standards, which are adapted to various building types, clearly take into account the need for tall buildings. On the basis of the assumption that towers will continue to be built and that they would be better off "green," let us mention another project: 1 Bligh (Sydney, Australia, 2009–11, page 29) by ingenhoven architects is meant to be Australia's "most ecological high-rise office tower." The building received the highest score in the Australian Green Star rating system, a 6 Star (World Leadership) certification. It is the first office tower in Sydney to receive this rating from the Green Building Council of Australia (GBCA). At 30 stories and 42 700 square meters, it is a substantial edifice that is not without architectural merit. Natural ventilation, wastewater treatment on the premises, a double-skin façade, and a combined electrical generation system that handles heating and cooling are amongst the features of the building.

Examples such as these towers, which are certainly of purely architectural interest, indeed have their place in a book on "green" architecture because they are proof of the mainstream viability of sustainable design. Tower design has produced a remarkable number of oddly shaped concoctions, which is surely proof that architects struggle with this kind of construction to find real originality. Of the buildings published here, the Prime Tower in Zurich would seem to be the most interesting in formal terms, in part because it stands out from its industrial neighborhood in a visibly iconic fashion. Large companies are not on the whole noted for their altruism, so sustainability must make sense on an economic basis. Those concerned will surely forgive a hint of cynicism in this remark, but it is meant as good news. If "green" and money are not in opposition, the world has a better chance of having sustainable buildings and cities. If companies can save money even as they gar-

7
Olafur Eliasson, Dufttunnel,
Wolfsburg, Germany, 2004

7

ner points as good urban citizens, then the movement toward sustainable contemporary architecture has become unstoppable. There are too many of these buildings rising for the factors that actually reduce energy consumption to be merely fashionable "gadgets." Photovoltaics and other technology will continue to make progress, and factors such as the understanding that passive measures must always be employed with the goal to reduce the electricity bill will combine to reinforce energy savings and hence the ultimate amount of pollution created by buildings.

THE ART OF MAKING SCENTS

Those who are familiar with the *Architecture Now* series of books know that they often include works by artists as well as the more obviously architectural achievements of today's creative leaders. Olafur Eliasson is something of an exception in the world of art because he has shown an active and continued interest in architecture. He co-designed the 2007 Serpentine Pavilion in Kensington Gardens (London) with the Norwegian architect Kjetil Thorsen for example. More recently, Eliasson designed the façade of Harpa, the new concert hall in Reykjavik in collaboration with the architect Henning Larsen. The Studio Olafur Eliasson in Berlin "now consists of a team of about 45 people, from craftsmen and specialized technicians to architects, artists, archivists and art historians, cooks, and administrators."[9] Two works by Eliasson are published here, his Dufttunnel (Wolfsburg, Germany, 2004, page 146) and the Flower Archway (Botanical Garden, Culiacán, Sinaloa, Mexico, 2005–08, page 152). The first piece could be described either as a tunnel or a bridge. Visitors are surrounded by 2160 potted plants on stainless-steel tubular rings that rotate around them. Few objects are more banal or immobile than potted plants, and usually they are also synonymous with a certain degree of bad taste, of which Eliasson cannot really be accused. A certain amount of humor, but also a commentary on mobility, and on architectural forms, is implied in this work. Planted with six types of flowers according to the season, the Dufttunnel (meaning "scented tunnel") also challenges the senses, and clearly poses the issue of the presence of "nature" in art and architecture. Displaced and reinvented by the artist, the potted plant becomes part of an inventive work. The Flower Archway approaches the potential relations between art and architecture in a quite different way. A five-segment latticework archway is covered by plants to the extent that it almost disappears into a web of living branches. The latticework piece is subsumed into its natural setting at the same time as it gives it its own shape. Both the Dufttunnel and the Flower Archway pose the problem of where "nature" begins and where "art" or architecture take over. By bringing together plants and forms that are on a sufficiently large scale for visitors to walk into or under them, Eliasson demonstrates the transformative power of art, and also its ability to question basic assumptions.

One basic assumption of builders might be that nature and architecture are fundamentally different and cannot be harmonized in a substantive way. Architects, too, challenge this kind of idea as one project published here, called Stacking Green (Ho Chi Minh City, Vietnam, 2011, page 392) by Vo Trong Nghia, demonstrates. The front and back façades of this small house are entirely composed of layers of concrete planters. Together with a rooftop garden, the house provides some relief from the noise, heat, and pollution of the city. Referring to the traditional Vietnamese courtyard house in his description, the architect does not suggest that he is creating a work of art here, but rather that he is using "nature" or potted vegetation to counter the ills of urban life. Natural ventilation or this "bioclimatic" principle definitely allow Stacking

8
Peter Zumthor, Steilneset, Vardø,
Finnmark, Norway, 2006–11

8

Green to be considered more "sustainable" than a house where nature is nowhere present, but raises the question of where the limits are between green and not green.

PATHS OF PROGRESS

An architect who is clearly sensitive to art is the Swiss Pritkzer Prize–winner Peter Zumthor. In a most unusual project, the Steilneset Memorial (Vardø, Finnmark, Norway, 2006–11, top), Zumthor has created a 125-meter-long structure made largely of wood and sailcloth in homage to the victims of the 17th-century Finnmark witch trials. Flanked by a black glass cube containing the work *The Damned, the Possessed, and the Beloved* by the late Louise Bourgeois, the main memorial building sits on Norway's rocky northern coast, its 91 windows each with a hanging light bearing witness to victims of barbaric treatment. The whole project is the result of collaboration between Zumthor and Bourgeois and is part of the ongoing effort to mark places along the National Tourist Routes of Norway with significant works of art and architecture. "And this is exactly what we can experience here at Steilneset, far to the north and in the easternmost part of Norway—spectacular art in magnificent and rugged natural surroundings," stated Queen Sonja of Norway at the inauguration of the memorial in her remarks on June 23, 2011. She went on to state: "Steilneset is a symbol of the intolerance of the period, but can also serve to remind us of the prejudices, injustices, and persecution that exist today."[10] Inspired partially by diagonal wooden racks used for drying fish in the region, the Steilneset Memorial might bring to mind the types of architecture that never posed a problem of pollution or "sustainability." This is architecture with a message but also a type of construction that is, for the main memorial, very close to answering the question of just what makes a building environmentally "sustainable." It was created with respect—the respect of the architect for this place, this story, and his collaboration with one of the great artists of the time. This respect makes the elaborate mechanisms of a LEED rating almost beside the point. "And all the Arts of Life they changed into the Arts of Death in Albion…" wrote Blake. In Vardø, the Arts of Death are conjured forth and banished by an act of respect. The meaning of this act goes far beyond the issue of "sustainability" in the purely architectural sense, perhaps approaching the 1987 United Nations definition that evoked "paths of social, economic, and political progress."

INHERENTLY FRAGILE

Projects have been selected for this book with a willful avoidance of purely technological definitions of sustainability. Which is to say that LEED Platinum is great, but that a certain lightness might also qualify a building as being closer to a sustainable state than the accumulation of blank, polluting, and polluted façades that march down most city streets. The Fragile Lab (Antwerp, Belgium, 2005–07, page 192) by Import-Export Architecture is a 400-square-meter store and place of residence for the owners of a fashion label. Tilted steel tubular supports inspired by bamboo, a green wall inside the building, and, finally, its obvious transparency and fragility would seem to qualify it for this book. Rather than asking what makes a building "green" or sustainable, one might reverse the proposition and ask what makes architecture unsustainable and aggressively counterproductive. The simplest answer to this complex question might be "arrogance"—the arrogance of architects and builders, but also very clearly of clients, who care only for the project that they have in mind. The 1993 definition of the World

9
Import-Export Architecture, Fragile
Lab, Antwerp, Belgium, 2005–07

9

Congress of Architects immediately comes to mind: "Sustainability means meeting our needs today without compromising the ability of future generations to meet their own needs." There are a thousand ways to respond to this injunction, and organizations such as USGBC have sought to codify them to the greatest extent possible. Do not get your materials on the other side of the world, use renewable resources, protect your building from the sun, and find ways to make it consume less. If it were just a matter of feeling good about yourself, it is unfortunately obvious that many clients, architects, and builders would privilege the "biggest bang for the buck"—the most glitzy, irresponsible, "iconic" structure that money can buy. Would recognition of fundamental fragility, or the acceptance of modesty not be the keys to real sustainability in architecture?

CHECK YOUR WALLET

And what if all of a sudden energy starts to cost more and more and if incidents like the ills of the Fukushima power plant in Japan start to enter the collective consciousness, exposing the illusion of unlimited cheap power for what it is—a sham? Would that "saving the planet" could be a sufficient motivation to make architecture rigorously sustainable starting now, but, then again, maybe the market economy is actually working better than feared. From now on, energy costs will continue to rise, and the need to stop spreading it around uselessly will impose itself. So perhaps the forces of the market are, after all, bringing architecture into line, obliging those who are not worried about global warming to stop wasting materials and power because it is really beginning to cost too much to do so. What your lungs and your eyes aren't telling you, your wallet will.

[1] http://blog.archpaper.com/wordpress/archives/29467, accessed on January 12, 2012.

[2] "Face au boom des panneaux solaires, Londres coupe de moitié les subventions," *Le Monde*, December 27, 2011.

[3] "George Osborne's false economy is the death of 'greenest government ever,'" www.guardian.co.uk/environment/damian-carrington-blog/2011/nov/29/green-autumn-statement-osborne-economy-environment, accessed on January 12, 2012.

[4] "The Problem with Biofuels," *The Washington Post*, Editorial, February 27, 2008, http://www.washingtonpost.com/wp-dyn/content/article/2008/02/26/AR2008022602827.html, accessed on January 16, 2012.

[5] Nate Berg, "Why the Shenzhen and Hong Kong Biennale Rejected Sustainability as a Theme," http://www.theatlanticcities.com/arts-and-lifestyle/2011/12/why-hong-kong-shenzhen-bi-city-biennale-rejected-sustainability-theme/790/, accessed on January 12, 2012.

[6] http://www.comarchitect.org/WebHelp/9_sustainable_development_definition.htm, accessed on January 12, 2012.

[7] http://www.holcimfoundation.org/T700/HolcimFoundationorigins.htm, accessed on January 16, 2012.

[8] http://www.gccds.org/buildings/patty/patty.html, accessed on January 16, 2012.

[9] http://www.olafureliasson.net/studio.html, accessed on January 17, 2012.

[10] http://www.kongehuset.no/c27262/nyhet/vis.html?tid=92483, accessed on January 16, 2012.

EINLEITUNG

NACHHALTIG GRÜN

Und zogen diese Füße einst
Auch über Englands grüne Höh'n?
Und war Gottes heil'ges Lamm
Auf Englands Weiden einst zu sehn?
Und schien einst Gottes Angesicht
Auf unsere bewölkte Flur?
Und ward Jerusalem erbaut
Hier zwischen Satansmühlen nur?

aus *Milton*
William Blake, 1804

William Blake verfasste seinen berühmten Aufschrei gegen die beginnende Industrielle Revolution an der Wende zum 19. Jahrhundert. Einige Jahre zuvor, 1791, war die dampfbetriebene Albion-Mühle im Londoner Stadtteil Southwark – Blake wohnte nicht weit davon – unter ungeklärten Umständen in Brand geraten. „Und all die Künste des Lebens, sie wurden Todeskünste in Albion...", schrieb er in *Jerusalem* (3. Kapitel), einem poetischen Abgesang auf Albion, einem der ältesten Namen für die britischen Inseln. Schon war das Räderwerk der „Moderne" in vollem Gange, und doch sollte es bis weit in die zweite Hälfte des 20. Jahrhunderts dauern, bis ein echtes Bewusstsein für die Umwelt entstand.

Doch was hat Architektur hiermit zu tun? Vielleicht ist eine zeitgemäße Einordnung nicht fehl am Platze. 80 % aller Treibhausgase in den Vereinigten Staaten sind Gebäudeemissionen. Zugleich entfallen 94 % des gesamten Energieverbrauchs allein in New York City auf Bauten.[1] Natürlich haben wir industriellen Fertigungsmethoden zu verdanken, dass immer mehr Menschen einen Komfort genießen, den Blakes Zeiten nicht kannten. Und doch ist unmittelbar nachvollziehbar, dass „traditionelle" Bauformen, die Nutzung von Holz oder handgearbeitetem Stein – und damit der Verzicht auf moderne Logistik, die Material vom anderen Ende der Welt beschafft – wesentlich weniger schädlich für die Umwelt sind, als ein durchschnittliches Gebäude unserer Tage. Der Einsatz lokal verfügbarer Materialien oder Passivbauprinzipien, die Sonnenenergie so nutzen, dass übermäßiger Solarverlust (oder -gewinn) vermieden wird, sind im Grunde „grüne" Strategien, die fast so alt sind wie die Geschichte des Bauens selbst.

DER STUMME FRÜHLING

Das moderne Interesse am Umweltschutz lässt sich leicht zurückverfolgen auf Rachel Carsons *Der stumme Frühling* (1962), ein Buch, in dem die Biologin die umweltschädliche Wirkung von Pestiziden dokumentierte. Ihr Werk wird oft als entscheidender Impuls für die Umwelt-

10
Ken Yeang, Solaris, One North,
Singapore, Singapore, 2008

bewegung verstanden. Zweifellos trug auch der dramatische Anstieg des Ölpreises in den 1970er Jahren dazu bei, das Interesse an erneuerbaren Energien und Energieeffizienz zu wecken. Dennoch sollte es in den USA bis 1989 dauern, bis das American Institute of Architects (AIA) schließlich ein Komitee für Umweltfragen gründete. Der US-Verband für Grünes Bauen (US Green Building Council, USGBC) wurde 1993 gegründet. Fünf Jahre später initiierte der Verband sein LEED-Programm (Leadership in Energy and Environmental Design). Andere Länder waren schneller, wieder andere zogen später nach, doch mit Sicherheit lässt sich sagen, dass es erst in den 1990er Jahren zu einem wirklich konzertierten Interesse an den ökologischen Auswirkungen von Architektur kam.

LIEBER TOT ALS GRÜN

Angesichts der hitzigen Debatten zur „globalen Erwärmung" und stetig steigender Energiekosten sollte man meinen, dass Umweltfragen inzwischen eines der zentralen Themen der Architektur sind. Dennoch scheint die Begeisterung für „nachhaltige" Bauten eher in direktem Zusammenhang mit der jeweiligen Wirtschaftslage zu stehen. Stehen die Dinge schlecht, was seit 2008 für die meisten entwickelten Länder gilt, ist dann nicht verständlich, in der Bauwirtschaft erst einmal so weiterzumachen wie bisher, ohne allzu viele Sonderausgaben für „grünes" Bauen? Die französische Tageszeitung *Le Monde* erinnerte am 27. Dezember 2011 daran,[2] dass der britische Premier David Cameron erst im Frühjahr 2010 mit dem Versprechen angetreten war, seine Regierung zur „grünsten aller Zeiten" zu machen. Nur 18 Monate später beschloss er rückwirkend, die Subventionen für kleine Solaranlagen zu halbieren. In den ersten neun Monaten des Jahres 2011 waren in Großbritannien 78 000 Solaranlagen installiert worden – teilweise auch deshalb, weil die Regierung 43,3 Pence/kWh für Strom aus Solaranlagen in Aussicht gestellt hatte. Kurz gesagt, das Ganze lief so gut, dass man keinen Grund sah, die versprochenen Subventionen tatsächlich zu zahlen. Angesichts der eher schwächelnden britischen Wirtschaft sah sich der *Guardian* veranlasst zu schreiben: „Es ist offiziell: Der Anspruch der Regierung, sich als grünste aller Zeiten zu profilieren, ist gestorben, erstickt in den Abgasen und dem Rauch der wieder angeworfenen Fabrikschlote, ein verzweifelter Versuch, den Wirtschaftsmotor wieder zum Laufen zu bringen."[3] Und wieder einmal werfen die „Satansmühlen" ihre Schatten.

LIEBER GRÜN ALS ARM

Man wird jedoch fragen dürfen, ob Architektur inzwischen nicht auch durch äußere Faktoren gezwungen wird, nachhaltiger zu werden. Einer der Gründe, warum Architektur so erhebliche Emissionen erzeugt, ist ihr unersättlicher Bedarf an Materialien, die oft in weiter Ferne oder unter hohen Belastungen für die Umwelt gefertigt werden. Wenn nun die Energiekosten steigen, weil fossile Brennstoffe schwinden und Atomkraft als die große Gefahr entlarvt wurde, die sie schon immer war, ist Nachhaltigkeit tatsächlich ein Weg, Energiekosten zu senken – ein nicht unerhebliches Argument in einer Kultur, in der schnelle Profite oberste Priorität haben. Natürlich gibt es weltweit auch Architekten, Bauherren und sogar Bauunternehmer, die schlicht ethisch handeln wollen, die unseren Planeten für künftige Generationen bewahren wollen. Doch letztendlich ist Kostenersparnis ein Argument, das bei Entscheidungen oft wesentlich schwerer wiegt als gute Absichten.

50°C IN DER SONNE

Seit der Wirtschaftskrise 2008 sind nicht nur Regierungsprogramme, die in Krisenzeiten als zu „kostspielig" gelten, sondern auch internationale Vereinbarungen zur Reduzierung von Treibhausgasen und Umweltverschmutzung in den Hintergrund gedrängt worden; dennoch kann man sagen: „Grüne" Architektur wird bleiben. In gewisser Weise hat es nachhaltige Bauformen schon immer gegeben, und das in aller Welt. Oft sind es gerade die einfachsten, die am „grünsten" sind. Ein Gebäude so auszurichten, dass Tageslicht einfällt, der Bau im Sommer aber nicht überhitzt, ist eine naheliegende Grundregel für jeden Architekten und Eigentümer. Auch die Nutzung einfacher, lokaler Materialien ist etwas, das der gesunde Menschenverstand nahelegt. Wollen wir zukünftige Generationen schützen und ihnen bewahren, was heute möglich ist, drängt sich auf, erneuerbare Ressourcen zu nutzen, wie etwa Holz aus nachhaltiger Forstwirtschaft. Dennoch ist gesunder Menschenverstand alles andere als die Regel in der zeitgenössischen Architektur. Getrieben von den Interessen des Marktes, der vor allem schnelle Profite fordert, und beschleunigt durch eine Kultur, die alles sofort will, wächst und gedeiht nach wie vor eine Architektur, die nicht nachhaltig, wenn nicht gar destruktiv ist. Im Sand am Persischen Golf, wo das Thermometer im Sommer auf über 50°C steigt, wachsen Städte mit gläsernen Türmen in den Himmel. Doch wer will den Bürgern von Abu Dhabi sagen, dass sie nicht nach den Sternen greifen können, wenn sie doch offensichtlich das Geld dafür haben?

ACHTUNG, ETHANOL!

Dass Nachhaltigkeit ein so großes Thema ist, hat auch einen anderen, oft verschwiegenen Subtext. „Grün" ist angesagt, und selbstverständlich nehmen Architekten, Bauunternehmer und Bauherren dies zum Anlass, mit Umweltfreundlichkeit zu werben, auch wenn es sich um Passivstrategien handelt, die schon immer praktiziert wurden, jetzt aber für aktuelle PR-Zwecke „recycelt" werden. Schlimmer noch: Eine ganze Reihe von Produkten, die hier nicht im einzelnen aufgeführt werden können, sind wesentlich weniger umweltfreundlich, als man uns glauben machen will. Ein Beispiel, das nicht aus der Welt der Architektur stammt, mag illustrieren, wie es sich mit dieser Kehrseite des aktuellen Trends zur „Nachhaltigkeit" verhält. Bereits seit Jahren weiß man, dass Biokraftstoffe nicht das Allheilmittel für die Problematik fossiler Brennstoffe sind. 2008 schrieb die *Washington Post* in einem Kommentar: „Verschiedene Studien, die diesen Monat von der Princeton University und der Naturschutzorganisation Nature Conservancy veröffentlicht wurden, haben gezeigt, dass Biokraftstoffe nicht die Patentlösung im Kampf gegen die Erderwärmung sind. Tatsächlich könnten sie die Problematik verschärfen. Mais und Zuckerrohr sind leicht verfügbare Ethanolträger. Diese Biokraftstoffquellen verursachen bei der Verbrennung nicht nur geringere Treibhausgasemissionen, sie entziehen der Atmosphäre beim Wachstum sogar Kohlenstoff – was sie nahezu CO_2-neutral macht. Doch diese Studien zeigen auch, dass Ethanol möglicherweise eine größere Gefahr für die Umwelt sein könnte als fossile Brennstoffe."[4]

NUR EINE VERKAUFSSTRATEGIE

Ein Interview mit Terry Riley, ehemals Kurator für Architektur und Design am Museum of Modern Art in New York und heute Kurator der Architekturbiennale in Hongkong und Shenzhen, zeigt aufschlussreiche Parallelen in der aktuellen Begeisterung für alles Grüne in der Archi-

11
Christopher Charles Benninger
Architects, Suzlon One Earth, Global
Headquarters, Pune, Maharashtra,
India, 2008–10

11

tektur. Auf die Frage, warum die Biennale letztendlich gegen das Thema „Nachhaltigkeit" votierte, antwortete Riley: „Wir haben uns bei der Suche nach einem Thema für die Biennale gegen ‚Nachhaltigkeit' entschieden. So wie die Dinge liegen, muss dieser Begriff als Etikett herhalten, um Dinge zu verkaufen, die in den meisten Fällen überhaupt nicht nachhaltig sind. Hinzu kommt, dass es inzwischen gängige Praxis ist, Nachhaltigkeit auf Zahlen zu reduzieren. Wir haben und stattdessen entschieden, das Motto ‚Vitalität' in den Vordergrund zu rücken, was meiner Meinung nach nicht nur Nachhaltigkeit umfasst, sondern eine ganze Reihe weiterer Themen, die sich nicht einfach quantifizieren lassen. Diese Prämisse war Richtschnur für alle weiteren Entscheidungen, die wir für die Biennale getroffen haben."[5]

Sucht man nach Beispielen für „grüne" oder „nachhaltige" Architektur, ist die naheliegende Frage, wie man diese Begriffe definiert. Die UN-Weltkommission für Umwelt und Entwicklung beschrieb nachhaltige Entwicklung im Brundtland-Bericht (1987) als „eine Entwicklung, die die Lebensqualität der gegenwärtigen Generation sichert und gleichzeitig zukünftigen Generationen die Wahlmöglichkeit zur Gestaltung ihres Lebens erhält". Ein Jahr nach dem Weltgipfel von Rio de Janeiro, im Juni 1993, formulierte der Internationale Architekten-Kongress noch prägnanter: „Nachhaltigkeit bedeutet, heute unseren Bedürfnissen gerecht zu werden, ohne künftigen Generationen die Möglichkeit zu nehmen, auch ihren Bedürfnissen gerecht zu werden."[6]

KEINE SORGE, DAS WIRD SCHON

Natürlich legen Organisationen wie der US-Verband für Grünes Bauen (LEED-Standard) und vergleichbare Institute in anderen Ländern komplexere und konkretere Maßstäbe an, wenn es darum geht, Nachhaltigkeits-Zertifikate für Architektur zu vergeben. Die von einem Schweizer Betonhersteller gegründete Holcim Foundation definiert fünf Schlüsselkriterien für Nachhaltigkeit: 1) Innovation und Übertragbarkeit; 2) ethische Maßstäbe und sozialer Mehrwert; 3) Umweltverträglichkeit und effiziente Nutzung von Ressourcen; 4) Wirtschaftlichkeit und Angemessenheit sowie 5) kontextuelle und ästhetische Auswirkungen.[7] Eine deutliche Parallele zu den UN- und Weltgipfelerklärungen liegt hier in der klaren Verknüpfung von sozialen Aspekten und Nachhaltigkeit. Architektenverbände wie der USGBC vergeben ihre LEED-Zertifikate nach einem Punktesystem, das sich aus verschiedenen Kriterien ergibt: 1) Nachhaltigkeit der Grundstücke; 2) Wassereffizienz; 3) Energie und Atmosphäre; 4) Materialien und Ressourcen; 5) Raumklimaqualität; 4) Innovation im Entwurf sowie 5) regionalspezifische Anforderungen. Verschiedene Bautypen werden nach einem separaten, klar strukturierten, wenn auch recht komplexen System beurteilt. Auch die vom USGBC definierten Kriterien haben eine soziale Komponente, tragen sie doch zur Verbesserung der Wohn- und Arbeitsqualität in Gebäuden – und weit über dessen Grenzen hinaus – bei. Doch die von Holcim geforderten „ethischen Maßstäbe und sozialer Mehrwert" stehen hier nicht im Vordergrund. Die hohe Komplexität und Bandbreite solcher Bewertungssysteme verdeutlicht, wie problematisch es ist, Nachhaltigkeit zu bemessen, sobald man über die naheliegendsten Grundprinzipien hinaus geht, die das Bauen seit jeher geprägt haben – noch vor Beginn der Ära von Beton, Stahl, Glas, Klimaanlagen und Stein, der weltweit verschifft wird, um Großbauten von Konzernen zu schmücken. Sollte sich herausstellen, dass all diese blitzsauberen Technologien, wie Biobrennstoffe oder Photovoltaikanlagen (die Schwermetalle enthalten), tatsächlich eine dunkle Kehrseite haben, sind Fragen und Skepsis sicher gerechtfertigt. Bis dahin ist es wohl besser, sich nicht allzu viele Gedanken zu machen: Keine Sorge, das wird schon.

P 22

12
Vo Trong Nghia, Stacking Green,
Ho Chi Minh City, Vietnam, 2011

12

Es kann nicht schaden, sich in Erinnerung zu rufen, dass Architektur lange Zeit keinen maßgeblichen Anteil an der Schädigung unserer Umwelt hatte. Zwar geht man davon aus, dass die haltlose Rodung der Osterinsel für den Zusammenbruch der dortigen Zivilisation verantwortlich war, doch andernorts verhinderten geringere Bevölkerung und ein Mangel an technischer Infrastruktur, dass Bauten unser Ende besiegelten – zumindest, bis die Albion-Mühle in Southwark gebaut wurde. Die Frage lautet: Ist es heute noch möglich, in „fortschrittlichen" Ländern ökologisch verantwortbar zu bauen? Oder ist dies eine arkadische Wunschvorstellung, die wenig mit der Realität zu tun hat?

GASSENFEGER

Ein interessantes Beispiel ist „Patty's House" (Broussard House, Biloxi, Mississippi, États-Unis, 2008, Seite 172), ein Projekt verschiedener Hilfsorganisationen für Bürger von New Orleans, die ihre Häuser 2005 beim Hurrikan Katrina verloren haben. Die BaSIC Initiative etwa, ursprünglich ein Programm zur Unterstützung verarmter einheimischer Bauern in Zentralmexiko, ist heute ein Zusammenschluss der Fakultäten und Studenten der Portland State University mit der Architekturfakultät der University of Texas in Austin. BaSIC initiierte eine Kooperation mit dem Hamer Center for Community Design (Pennsylvania State University), dem Design Corps (Gulf Coast Community Design Studio, GC-CDS) und weiteren Organisationen wie der East Biloxi Coordination, Relieve oder dem Amt für Wiederaufbau. Auf diese Weise konnte die Finanzierung ermöglicht werden; ein Team aus zwölf Studenten verschiedener Universitäten entstand. Die Studenten und Fakultätsmitarbeiter arbeiteten sechs Wochen an Entwurf und Bau des Hauses. Eines der Ziele des Hamer Center war ein Haus mit LEED-Zertifizierung. Gefördert wurde das Projekt mit Zuschüssen für bessere Materialien und Konstruktionsverfahren. Im Frühjahr 2008 wurde das Haus als erstes Einfamilienhaus in Mississippi mit einem LEED-Zertifikat ausgezeichnet.

Sein Grundriss entspricht dem sogenannten Dogtrot House, einem Wohnhaustypus der Südstaaten mit einer überdachten „Gasse" zwischen Wohn- und Schlafbereich. Die Gasse optimiert nicht nur die natürliche Belüftung, sondern wird auch als überdachte Terrasse genutzt. Gemäß geltender Hochwasserschutzvorgaben wurde der Bau vier Meter über dem Boden aufgeständert, gebaut wurde mit Beton und druckimprägniertem Holz. Auf den 2 m hohen Betonstützen setzen Stützen und ein Raumfachwerk aus Holz auf.[8] Das Haus knüpft mit seiner Architektur an lokale Wohnbauten an. Damit entspricht es einer Typologie, die sich über Jahre hinweg entwickelt hat, durch Sturmfluten und geprägt vom Klima der Region. Die intensive Zusammenarbeit verschiedener Organisationen, um ein scheinbar einfaches Projekt zu realisieren, zeigt, dass zukunftsweisende Projekte möglich sind – vorausgesetzt, man ist bereit, aus den Erfahrungen der Vergangenheit zu lernen und sich zu engagieren, um Hausbesitzern nicht nur Komfort zu bieten, sondern auch ein ökologisches Bewusstsein zu wecken. Beim Broussard House wurde nur mit Beton gebaut, wo absolut erforderlich. Das LEED-Zertifikat belegt, welche Sorgfalt auf Materialwahl und -beschaffung verwendet wurde.

BAMBUS UND MAMMUTBAUM

Eine halbe Weltreise entfernt plante der vietnamesische Architekt Vo Trong Nghia seinen Bamboo Wing (Dai Lai, Vinh-Phuc-Provinz, Vietnam, 2009, Seite 384), ein Bauwerk ganz aus Bambus. Stolz weist er darauf hin, dass bei dem 1600 m² großen Bauwerk, das den Schwingen eines Vogels nachempfunden ist, „keine Stahl- oder künstlichen Baumaterialien" zum Einsatz kamen. Dieser und andere Entwürfe von Vo Trong Nghia sind von einer dynamischen Modernität, die man bei einer extensiven Verwendung traditioneller Baumaterialien wie Bambus nicht vermuten würde. Doch in der Tat macht die hohe Wachstumsrate Bambus zu einem ausgezeichneten Kandidaten für den ultimativen „nachwachsenden Rohstoff", zumindest was Bauten kleinerer Größenordnungen betrifft. Dass der Bamboo Wing in einem nahezu unverfälschten Naturumfeld liegt, spricht zweifellos dafür, dass Hightech-Baumaterialien kein Muss für moderne Architektur sind.

Kengo Kuma, einer der bedeutendsten Architekten Japans, beschäftigt sich schon seit Langem mit den Traditionen seines Heimatlandes, ohne dabei in simple Nachahmung alter Formen oder ins Pasticcio abzugleiten. Sein Yusuhara Wooden Bridge Museum (Yusuhara-cho, Takaoka-gun, Kochi, Japan, 2010, Seite 264) ist ein Brückenbau an einem Hang. Hier sind eine Werkstatt und ein Aufenthaltsprogramm für Künstler untergebracht. Kuma arbeitet mit Schichtholz statt mit Massivholz, früher seinem bevorzugten Material; zugleich nimmt er Bezug auf Kragtechniken, eine typische historische Bauform der chinesischen und japanischen Architektur. Ein nachhaltiger Akzent ist zudem die Verwendung von Riesen-Thuja aus regionaler Forstwirtschaft. Wie Vo Trong Nghia setzt auch Kengo Kuma auf regionale Architekturtraditionen. Dennoch schafft er ein durch und durch modernes, dabei weitgehend nachhaltiges Bauwerk. Entscheidend ist hier der Rückgriff auf Traditionen statt eines Rückschritts in die Vergangenheit. So finden sich neue Wege für das Bauen, die nicht nur im Einklang mit der Natur stehen, sondern auch das Wohlbefinden der Nutzer und der regionalen Bevölkerung im Blick haben.

HANDARBEIT AUS CHINA

Auch wenn nicht nur Büros in Asien erfolgreich die Chancen traditioneller Bauformen für eine nachhaltige Architektur ausloten, gibt es doch auffällig viele Beispiele dieser Art. Dies mag an den vergleichsweise geringen Baukosten liegen – vielleicht ebenso sehr wie an der Motivation, die Umwelt zu schützen. Das Gaoligong Museum für Papierhandwerk (Tengchong, Yunnan, China, 2009–10, Seite 334) von Trace Architecture Office (TAO) ist ein besonders elegantes Beispiel für einen solch konstruktiven Umgang mit der Vergangenheit. Das kleine (361 m² große) Museum liegt in der Nähe des Dorfs Xinzhuang, nicht weit vom Gaoligongshan-Gebirge in Yunnan, einem internationalen Naturschutzgebiet. Das Museum, das dem regionalen Papierhandwerk gewidmet ist, wurde von ortsansässigen Handwerkern und Bauern gebaut. Gearbeitet wurde mit Papier, Bambus, örtlichem Vulkanstein und einem traditionellen Holztragwerk. Auch dies ist keine bloße Imitation der Vergangenheit; vielmehr ist der Bau auffällig modern in Entwurf und Umsetzung. Es darf sicher behauptet werden, dass der Rückgriff auf Traditionen einer der besten Wege ist, echten Einklang zwischen natürlicher und gebauter Umwelt zu erreichen. Beim Gaoligong Museum für Papierhandwerk wurden die Baumethoden nicht von einem multinationalen Konzern diktiert, der schon im Folgemonat Profite sehen will; vielmehr wurde generationenaltes Wissen auf wirklich nachhaltige Weise genutzt. Vielleicht vermisst mancher zeitgenössische technische Finessen bei Bauten wie diesen, und doch sind zweckfreie Extras in der zeitgenössischen Bautechnik im Grunde unzeitgemäßer als Bambus und Vulkanstein.

DER FUSSABDRUCK WIRD KLEINER

In diesem Band soll es keineswegs darum gehen, moderne Baumaterialien und -techniken haltlos zu kritisieren. Doch vielleicht sollte man daran erinnern, wie viel aus der Vergangenheit gelernt werden kann, wenn es um die immer drängenderen Fragen nach Ressourcen und

13

Umwelt geht. Zweifellos gibt es auch eine andere Schule, die stärker auf die Verschränkung passiver und aktiver Bautechnik setzt, um Energie effizienter zu nutzen und den „CO_2-Fußabdruck" von Architektur zu reduzieren. Diese Schule macht sich die modernsten Materialien und Strategien zunutze, um zeitgenössische Architektur und einen auf Dauer gesunden Planeten miteinander zu vereinbaren. Einige der hier vorgestellten Bauten sind wahre Paradebeispiele modernster Technologie. Ihr Ziel ist oft die positive Energiebilanz von Wohnbauten und anderen Gebäuden – Bauten, die ihrem regionalen Stromnetz Energie zuführen, statt es nur zu nutzen. Werner Sobek, renommierter deutscher Bauingenieur und Planer zahlreicher ökologisch verantwortlicher moderner Bauten, arbeitete erst kürzlich an seinem Projekt F87 (Berlin, Deutschland, 2011, Seite 330). Das 130 m² große F87, Preisträger eines Wettbewerbs des Bundesministeriums für Verkehr, Bau und Stadtentwicklung, ist ein „Effizienzhaus Plus mit Elektromobilität", das ausreichend Energie produziert, um nicht nur den eigenen Bedarf, sondern auch den der E-Fahrzeuge der Bewohner zu decken. Der Bau wurde darüber hinaus so geplant, dass die Umweltbelastung sowohl beim Bau als auch bei einer künftigen Demontage minimal sind.

FREUEN WIR UNS NICHT ZU FRÜH

Noch weiter als Sobek ging das koreanische Büro Unsangdong bei der Bündelung grüner Technologien in einem Einfamilienhaus (E+ Green Home, Jeon Dae, Cheo In, Po Gok, Yong In, Kyeong Gi, Südkorea, 2010–11, Seite 368). Das mit 344 m² deutlich größere Haus hat ein begrüntes Dach, um Energieverluste und Solargewinn zu minimieren und die Nutzung von Regenwasser zu maximieren. Dank eines aufwendigen Dämmsystems (StoTherm), wärmebehandeltem Holz, integrierten Photovoltaik-Elementen, hocheffizienten Sonnenkollektoren, einer Windturbine und einer Erdwärmepumpe wurde das Haus vom PHI (Passivhaus Institut) als erstes Passivhaus Südkoreas zertifiziert. Begründet wurde der Passivhausstandard 1988 von Professor Bo Adamson der Universität Lund (Schweden) und Professor Wolfgang Feist vom Institut für Wohnen und Umwelt. Europaweit gibt es rund 25 000 zertifizierte Passivhäuser. Ziel des Konzepts ist, ähnlich wie beim LEED-System, die Erfassung von Faktoren, die Energieeffizienz optimieren und den ökologischen Fußabdruck von Bauten reduzieren. Der Primärenergieeinsatz eines zertifizierten Passivhauses darf nicht höher sein als 120 kWh/m² pro Jahr. Außerdem muss ein zertifiziertes Gebäude faszinierenderweise so luftdicht sein, dass die Leckage kleiner als sechs Zehntel seines Volumens pro Stunde beträgt. Die Villa Nyberg (Borlänge, Schweden, 2010, Seite 248) beispielsweise, ein Entwurf der Göteborger Architekten Kjellgren Kaminsky, hat einen schwedischen Rekord für Luftdichtheit aufgestellt (0,038 l/m² bei 50 Pascal; der schwedische Passivhausstandard liegt bei 0,3, der bisherige Rekord lag bei 0,07). Die Villa Nyberg ist ein annähernd runder Bau, wodurch Wandfläche reduziert wird und thermische beziehungsweise „Wärmebrücken" vermieden werden. Das Haus hat einen geschätzten Heizenergiebedarf von lediglich 25 kWh/m² pro Jahr.

Ein weiterer bewusst „grüner" Wohnbau ist die Villa 4.0 von Dick van Gameren ('t Gooi, Niederlande, 2010–11, Seite 156). Zur Ausstattung des 540 m² großen Baus zählen eine Niedertemperatur-Fußbodenheizung, eine Solaranlage für Warmwasser, ein natürliches Belüftungssystem und ein Hochleistungs-Holzofen in der Küche. Die künstliche Belichtung setzt konsequent auf LED-Technologie. Die Villa 4.0, wenn auch weniger aktiv auf „Nachhaltigkeit" ausgelegt als die Bauten von Werner Sobek oder Unsangdong, kommt der Realität grüner Architektur heute näher. Durch die Verzahnung energiesparender Maßnahmen auf mehreren Ebenen reduziert van Gameren mit seinem Entwurf

14
BIG, Amager Bakke Waste-to-Energy
Plant, Copenhagen, Denmark, 2009

14

zweifellos die Betriebskosten „normaler" Wohnbauten – vielleicht ein Hinweis, dass 't Gooi durchaus den Standard dafür setzt, was heute „normal" ist.

VERANTWORTLICHE KONZERNE

Natürlich sind die Senkung des Energieverbrauchs und grundlegende Nachhaltigkeit Prinzipien, die auch bei Großbauten zur Anwendung kommen – einige Firmenbauten haben sich auf diesem Gebiet als führend erwiesen. Zu den Förderern umweltbewusster Bürobauten zählt, wenig überraschend, auch ein Windturbinenhersteller, das indische Unternehmen Suzlon. Die Suzlon One Earth Global Headquarters (Pune, Maharashtra, Indien, 2008–10, Seite 21) von Christopher Charles Benninger Architects ist ein 55 741 m² großer Komplex. Hier kamen eine Vielzahl „Low-Energy"-Materialien zum Einsatz, natürliche BeLüftungssysteme, Photovoltaikpaneele und natürlich Windturbinen. Die gelungen gestaltete Suzlon-Zentrale wurde mit einem LEED-Platin-Zertifikat ausgezeichnet, der höchstmöglichen Auszeichnung des USGBC.

Das Green Office (Meudon, Frankreich, 2009–11, Seite 44), ein Entwurf des Büros Ateliers 115 hat sich auf die Fahnen geschrieben, noch einen Schritt weiterzugehen als Suzlon: Der Bau verbraucht 62 kWh/m² gegenüber 64 kWh/m² selbst generierter Energie pro Jahr, die mithilfe einer Photovoltaikanlage und Kraft-Wärme-Kopplung (KWK) erzeugt wird. Kurz gesagt, kann das Green Office eine positive Energiebilanz vorweisen und ist damit in der Lage, Energie in das lokale Netz einzuspeisen. Eine Klimaanlange, bei Pariser Witterung durchaus verzichtbar, wurde nicht installiert. Materialien wurden nach ihrer ökologischen Nachhaltigkeit gewählt, auch Isolierverglasung und ein hoher Grad an Dämmung tragen zur Energieeffizienz des Gebäudes bei. Mit einer Fläche von 21 700 m² ist das Green Office ebenso groß wie innovativ, auch wenn sich der Bau äußerlich nicht nennenswert von anderen Geschäftsbauten unterscheidet. Ein Aspekt, den *Green Architecture Now 2* zweifellos belegt, ist, dass umweltbewusstes Bauen und umweltbewusste Nutzung keineswegs im Widerspruch zu guter Gestaltung stehen. Zeitgenössische Architektur muss durchaus nicht „grün" wirken – was für viele Auftraggeber tatsächlich zählt, sind Kosten und das Bewusstsein, als verantwortliche Bürger zu handeln. Doch Nachhaltigkeit ist inzwischen längst im Mainstream angekommen und muss nicht mehr demonstrativ seine „grüne" Flagge zeigen: Eine wichtige Entwicklung, die ebenso begrüßens- wie unterstützenswert ist.

SCHUSSFAHRT AUF DER MÜLLVERBRENNUNGSANLAGE

Der renommierte dänische Architekt Bjarke Ingels (BIG) hat sich mehrfach für „hedonistische Nachhaltigkeit" ausgesprochen – eine Architektur, die nicht nur verantwortungsvoll, sondern auch ansprechend ist und Spaß macht. Nachdem jahrelang die Meinung herrschte, „grüne" Bauten müssten ihr Anliegen durch ein entsprechend sonderbares Äußeres signalisieren, haben verschiedene Ratingagenturen inzwischen dafür gesorgt, dass Nachhaltigkeit ein technokratischeres, nüchterneres Image hat. Doch letztendlich spielen Image und Extras keine große Rolle, wenn es im Kern darum geht, Granit nicht mehr von Zimbabwe nach Los Angeles zu verschiffen. Ingels hingegen scheut sich nicht, ins andere Extrem zu gehen, etwa mit Entwürfen wie dem groß angelegten, 460 Millionen Euro teuren Müllheizkraftwerk Amager Bakke (Kopenhagen, Dänemark, 2009–, Seite 72), auf dessen 32 000 m² großen Dach eine Skiabfahrt realisiert werden soll. „Wir wollen mehr, als der Fabrik nur eine ästhetische Fassade zu geben", so die Architekten. „Wir wollen einen Zugewinn an Funktionalität! ... Unser Konzept für

15

eine neue Generation von Müllheizkraftwerken ist in wirtschaftlicher, ökologischer und soziologischer Hinsicht profitabel." Bjarke Ingels begnügt sich nicht damit, als „grüner" Architekt breite Akzeptanz zu finden; er will, dass Nachhaltigkeit Spaß macht und im weitesten Sinne „profitabel" ist.

Doch auch wenn Ingels inzwischen einen „großen" Namen hat – möglicherweise ist „hedonistische Nachhaltigkeit" eine wesentlich ältere Erfindung, als seine Skiabfahrt auf der Müllverbrennungsanlage glauben machen will. Das griechische Büro K-Studio konnte sein Strandrestaurant Bar Bouni 2011 fertigstellen (Pilos, Costa Navarino, Griechenland, Seite 236). Der Bau, aufgeständert auf einer hölzernen Plattform am Strand, unter der sich die Wellen brechen, ruht auf Holzpfählen. Eine „Landschaft aus hängenden Tüchern" bildet das Dach. Hier vermisst man keine 32 000 m² große Skiabfahrt – alle „hedonistische Nachhaltigkeit", die man sich wünschen kann, liegt direkt hier, am Strand. In gewisser Weise hängt Nachhaltigkeit eben auch von Standort und Funktion ab. Oft sind die einfachsten, effizientesten Lösungen die, die schon seit Langem praktiziert werden. Holz, Tücher, Sand und Brandung kosten keine 460 Millionen Euro. Natürlich ist dies eine eher sarkastische Lesart der durchaus ernstzunehmenden Thesen Ingels', doch Bescheidenheit ist wohl kaum die Stärke seiner Strategie. Was wäre, wenn echte Nachhaltigkeit mehr mit Bescheidenheit als mit immer hochfliegenderen und technologisch aufwendigeren Projekten zu tun hätte?

TÜRME FÜR DAS KÖNIGREICH

Manche wird überraschen, Adrian Smith und Gordon Gill in einem Buch über grüne Architektur zu finden. Schließlich ist Smith Planer des Burj Khalifa (Dubai, VAE, 2004–09), des mit 830 m höchsten Gebäudes der Welt. Noch erstaunlicher ist die Tatsache, dass das Team an einem weiteren Superhochhaus arbeitet, dem Kingdom Tower (Jeddah, Saudi-Arabien), mit einer geplanten Höhe von über einem Kilometer. Adrian Smith und andere renommierte Architekten, unter ihnen Norman Foster, argumentieren seit Langem, dass Hochbauten per se nachhaltiger sind als mehrere niedrige Bauten mit äquivalenter Nutzfläche. Unbestritten ist, dass ein einzelner Hochbau im Hinblick auf Infrastruktur – vom Straßennetz bis hin zur Energieversorgung – wesentlich grüner ist, als eine größere Anzahl kleinerer Bauten. In einem internationalen Wettbewerb konnten sich Adrian Smith und Gordon Gill mit einem Turm für den Koreanischen Industrieverband in Seoul (Südkorea, 2010–13, Seite 318) durchsetzen, der eine deutlich „normalere" Bauhöhe von 240 m hat. Die speziell entwickelte Gebäudehaut wurde „konzipiert, um die Heiz- und Kühllast des Turms zu reduzieren und mittels Solarmodulen Energie zu erzeugen. Diese sind in die Brüstungsbereiche der Südwest- und Nordwestfassaden integriert, die tagsüber beträchtlicher direkter Sonneneinstrahlung ausgesetzt sind." Die Architekten schreiben: „Durch Aufrichtung der Brüstungspaneele um 30° konnte das Planungsteam die Energieausbeute maximieren und ausreichend Strom erzeugen, um die elektrischen Systeme des gesamten Gebäudekerns und der Büroflächen maßgeblich zu unterstützen. Die verglasten Sichtpaneele unmittelbar unter den Brüstungspaneelen wurden um 15° nach innen geneigt, wodurch unmittelbare Sonneneinstrahlung und Blendlicht minimiert werden konnten." Während sich für einen kilometerhohen Turm in Jeddah wohl kaum andere schlagkräftige Argumente außer dem damit verbundenen Prestige finden lassen, steht das Hochhaus für den Koreanischen Industrieverband in einer bereits dicht besiedelten Stadt, wo Bauplatz rar ist. Nur wenige würden behaupten, dass Bambus und Vulkanstein hier den Anforderungen genügt. Es gilt zu akzeptieren, dass zeitgenössische Architektur durchaus technische Hilfsmittel nutzen kann, um die CO_2-Bilanz von Neubauten zu optimieren. Bauten wie diese wird es geben, solange es Ressourcen gibt, und es ist sicher besser, sie so nachhaltig zu planen, wie es der technische Kenntnisstand ermöglicht.

GRÜNER TURM, GRÜNER STERN

Im kleineren Stil konnten die Schweizer Architekten Gigon/Guyer unlängst mit einem Projekt in Zürich zeigen (Prime Tower, Zürich, Schweiz, 2008–11, Seite 164) dass grüne Hochhausbauten – in diesem Fall mit 36 Geschossen und 126 m Höhe – sehr hohen ökologischen Standards genügen können. Besondere Merkmale des mit einem LEED-Zertifikat in Gold ausgezeichneten Turms sind Grundwassernutzung und Wärmepumpe sowie Abwärmenutzung von Gebäude und Kältemaschinen. Hinzu kommt die Wärme-Kälte-Kopplung von Wärme- und Eisspeichern und eine natürliche Belüftung über Fensterschlitze. Das LEED-Punktesystem, abgestimmt auf verschiedene Bautypologien, berücksichtigt ohne Frage die Notwendigkeit von Hochhausbauten. Geht man davon aus, dass Hochhäuser auch in Zukunft gebaut werden und entsprechend besser „grün" sein sollten, lohnt es sich, hier ein weiteres Projekt vorzustellen. Der von ingenhoven architects geplante Turm 1 Bligh (Sydney, Australien, 2009–11, Seite 29) erhebt den Anspruch, Australiens „ökologischstes Bürohochhaus" zu sein. Das Gebäude wurde mit der höchstmöglichen Punktzahl des australischen „Green Star"-Standards, einem Zertifikat der Klasse „6 Star/World Leadership" ausgezeichnet. Es ist das erste Bürohochhaus in Sydney, das diese Zertifizierung des Green Building Council of Australia (GBCA) erreichte – mit 30 Stockwerken und 42 700 m² ein beeindruckendes und architektonisch reizvolles Gebäude. Natürliche Belüftung, Brauchwasseraufbereitung vor Ort, eine zweischalige Fassade und ein Kraft-Wärme-System, das Heiz- und Kühlleistung erbringt, zählen zu den Besonderheiten des Projekts.

Beispiele wie diese Türme, die schon rein architektonisch von Interesse sind, haben ihren Platz in einem Buch über „grüne" Architektur, sind sie doch der Beleg, dass nachhaltiges Design sich auch im Mainstream bewährt. Der Typus Hochhaus hat eine erstaunliche Anzahl eigentümlicher Entwürfe hervorgebracht – ohne Frage ein Zeichen dafür, wie schwierig es für Architekten ist, in diesem Genre echte Originalität zu beweisen. Von den hier vorgestellten Türmen ist der Prime Tower in Zürich formal vielleicht am interessantesten, nicht zuletzt deshalb, weil er in seinem industriell geprägten Umfeld deutlich sichtbar hervorsticht. Großkonzerne sind nicht gerade für ihren Altruismus bekannt, weshalb Nachhaltigkeit auch wirtschaftlich sinnvoll sein muss. Man möge mir den leichten Anflug von Zynismus nachsehen, doch dieser Umstand ist tatsächlich ein Glücksfall. Wenn „grün" und „Geld" kein Antagonismus mehr sind, hat die Welt bessere Aussichten auf nachhaltige Bauten und Städte. Wenn Unternehmen Geld sparen und dabei noch Bonuspunkte als vorbildliche Bürger sammeln können, ist die Entwicklung zu einer nachhaltigeren zeitgenössischen Architektur nicht mehr aufzuhalten. Inzwischen werden zu viele solcher Bauten realisiert, als dass man sie nur als effektive Energiesparmaßnahme, als Modeerscheinung oder technische Spielerei abtun könnte. Photovoltaik und andere Technologien werden auch weiterhin Fortschritte verzeichnen; auch die Einsicht, dass Passivstrategien Kosten senken, wird dazu beitragen, Energie zu sparen und die effektive Umweltbelastung durch Gebäudeemissionen weiter zu verringern.

16

DUFTKÜNSTLER

Wer die *Architecture Now*-Reihe kennt, wird wissen, dass sie neben den offenkundigen Highlights führender Architekten häufig auch Arbeiten von Künstlern präsentiert. Olafur Eliasson ist in gewisser Weise eine Ausnahmeerscheinung in der Kunstwelt, denn schon seit Langem beweist er ein ausgeprägtes Interesse an Architektur. So entwarf er 2007 gemeinsam mit dem norwegischen Architekten Kjetil Thorsen den Sommerpavillon der Serpentine Gallery in Kensington Gardens (London). In jüngerer Zeit gestaltete Eliasson in Zusammenarbeit mit dem Architekten Henning Larsen die Fassade des Konzerthauses Harpa in Reykjavík. Das Studio Olafur Eliasson in Berlin „besteht inzwischen aus einem Team von rund 45 Mitarbeitern, darunter Handwerker und spezialisierte Techniker, Architekten, Künstler und Archivare bis hin zu Kunsthistorikern, Köchen und Verwaltungskräften".[9] Vorgestellt werden hier zwei Werke von Eliasson, sein Dufttunnel (Wolfsburg, Deutschland, 2004, Seite 146) und der Flower Archway (dt. Blumenbogen, Botanischer Garten, Culiacán, Sinaloa, Mexiko, 2005–08, Seite 152). Der erste Entwurf ist nicht nur ein Tunnel, sondern zugleich eine Brücke: 2160 Blumentöpfe umfangen die Besucher in einem röhrenförmigen Gestell aus langsam rotierenden Edelstahlringen. Kaum etwas könnte banaler oder statischer sein als eine Topfpflanze, allzu oft assoziiert man sie gar mit schlechtem Geschmack – den man Eliasson sicher nicht vorwerfen kann. In seiner Arbeit schwingt Humor mit, doch ebenso ist sie ein Kommentar zur Mobilität und architektonischen Ausdruckformen. Der Dufttunnel, im Laufe der Gartenjahrs mit sechs verschiedenen Duftpflanzen bestückt, spricht nicht nur die Sinne an, sondern auch Fragen wie den Stellenwert von „Natur" in Kunst und Architektur. Die vom Künstler in einen neuen Kontext versetzten, und damit neu erfundenen Topfpflanzen werden Teil eines fantasievollen Kunstwerks. Der Flower Archway thematisiert das Verhältnis von Kunst und Architektur auf andere Weise. Ein Bogengerüst aus fünf Segmenten verschwindet nahezu unter den Pflanzen, einem Netzwerk lebender Zweige. Einerseits wird das Gerüst von seiner natürlichen Umgebung vereinnahmt, andererseits gibt es ihm Form. Dufttunnel und Flower Archway stellen die Frage, wo „Natur" aufhört und an welcher Stelle „Kunst" oder Architektur beginnen. Eliasson kombiniert Pflanzen und Form in einem Maßstab, der Besuchern erlaubt, durch sie hindurchzulaufen: So stellt er nicht nur die transformative Kraft der Kunst unter Beweis, sondern auch deren Fähigkeit, grundlegende Annahmen zu hinterfragen.

Eine solche Grundannahme der Bauindustrie ist die Prämisse, Natur und Architektur seien so fundamental verschieden, dass sie nicht wirklich substanziell in Einklang zu bringen sind. Auch Architekten hinterfragen diese Prämisse, wie das Projekt Stacking Green (Ho Chi Minh City, Vietnam, 2011, Seite 392) von Vo Trong Nghia belegt. Die Fassaden des Wohnbaus wurden an Vorder- und Rückseite mit übereinander gestaffelten Pflanzkästen aus Beton realisiert. In Kombination mit einem Dachgarten ist dieses Haus eine Oase in der Stadt, inmitten von Lärm, Hitze und Luftverschmutzung. In seiner Projektbeschreibung stellt der Architekt Bezüge zum traditionellen vietnamesischen Hofhaus her – er erhebt nicht den Anspruch, ein Kunstwerk zu schaffen, sondern weiß die „Natur", in Form einer Kastenbepflanzung, vielmehr für die Problematik des Lebens in der Stadt zu nutzen. Dank seines „bioklimatischen" Konzepts, das im Grunde nichts anderes ist als eine natürliche Belüftung, ist Stacking Green zweifellos nachhaltiger als Häuser ohne jede Einbindung von Natur. Doch sicherlich stellt sich hier die Frage, wo die Grenze zwischen „grün" und „nicht grün" verläuft.

17
*ingenhoven architects, 1 Bligh,
Sydney, Australia, 2009–11*

17

WEGE ZUM FORTSCHRITT

Ein Architekt mit offenkundiger Affinität zur Kunst ist der Schweizer Pritzker-Preisträger Peter Zumthor. Mit seinem höchst ungewöhnlichen Projekt, der Gedenkstätte Steilneset (Vardø, Finnmark, Norwegen, 2006–11, Seite 16) schuf Zumthor eine 125 m lange Konstruktion aus Holz und Segeltuch zum Gedenken an die Opfer der Hexenprozesse des 17. Jahrhunderts in der Finnmark. Das Hauptgebäude der Gedenkstätte, flankiert von einem schwarzen Glaskubus mit der Installation *The Damned, the Possessed, and the Beloved* der Künstlerin Louise Bourgeois, liegt an Norwegens zerklüfteter Nordküste. 91 Fenster mit je einer Glühbirne erinnern an die Opfer der grausamen Hexenjagd. Das Projekt entstand als Kollaboration zwischen Zumthor und Bourgeois im Rahmen eines Programms, das bedeutende künstlerische und architektonische Werke an besonderen Orten entlang der Norwegischen Landschaftsroute realisiert. „Genau das können wir hier in Steilneset erleben, hoch oben im Norden, im östlichsten Teil Norwegens – spektakuläre Kunst in atemberaubender zerklüfteter Landschaft", erklärte Königin Sonja von Norwegen zur Eröffnung der Gedenkstätte am 23. Juni 2011. „Steilneset ist ein Symbol für die Intoleranz früherer Zeiten und kann uns doch an Vorurteile, Ungerechtigkeiten und Verfolgung erinnern, mit denen wir es auch heute zu tun haben."[10] Die Gedenkstätte in Steilneset, unter anderem inspiriert von den diagonalen Holzpfählen der Trockengestelle für Fischernetze in der Region, steht für Architekturformen, bei denen sich die Frage nach Umweltbelastung und „Nachhaltigkeit" überhaupt nie stellte. Architektur, die aus Respekt entstand – Respekt des Architekten gegenüber dem Ort und seiner Geschichte, Respekt vor der Zusammenarbeit mit einer der größten Künstlerinnen unserer Zeit. Ein solcher Respekt lässt das ausgeklügelte Punktesystem des LEED-Standards geradezu überflüssig erscheinen. „Und all die Künste des Lebens, sie wurden Todeskünste in Albion . . .", schrieb Blake. In Vardø werden die Todeskünste durch diesen Akt des Respekts heraufbeschworen und vertrieben. Ein solcher Akt geht weit über „Nachhaltigkeit" im architektonischen Sinne hinaus und hat ohne Frage mehr mit jenem „gesellschaftlichen, wirtschaftlichen und politischen Fortschritt" zu tun, den die UN 1987 auf ihre Fahnen schrieb.

VON NATUR AUS FRAGIL

Bei der Projektauswahl für diesen Band haben wir bewusst auf rein formale Kriterien für Nachhaltigkeit verzichtet. Natürlich ist ein LEED-Zertifikat in Platin wunderbar, doch eine gewisse Leichtigkeit kann ein Gebäude durchaus näher an ein nachhaltiges Ideal rücken, als die bekannten nichtssagenden, umweltbelastenden und -verschmutzten Fassaden, die unsere Straßenzüge säumen. Das Fragile Lab (Antwerpen, Belgien, 2005–07, Seite 192) von Import-Export Architecture ist ein 400 m² großes Gebäude, in dem das Ladengeschäft und die Wohnung der Designer eines Modelabels untergebracht sind. Schiefe Stahlrohrstützen, die an Bambus erinnern, eine begrünte Wand im Innern des Baus und schließlich dessen auffällige Transparenz und Fragilität sind auf den ersten Blick genug, einen Eintrag in diesem Buch zu rechtfertigen. Statt zu fragen, was ein Gebäude „grün" oder nachhaltig macht, ließe sich umgekehrt fragen: Was macht Architektur nicht nachhaltig oder auf aggressive Weise kontraproduktiv? Die naheliegendste Antwort auf diese Frage ist vielleicht „Arroganz" – die Arroganz von Architekten und Bauunternehmern, doch ganz offenkundig auch die Arroganz von Auftraggebern, für die außer ihrem Projekt nichts zählt. Unwillkürlich erinnern wir uns an die Erklärung des Internationalen Architekten-Kongresses: „Nachhaltigkeit bedeutet, heute unseren Bedürfnissen gerecht zu werden, ohne künftigen Generationen die Möglichkeit zu nehmen, auch ihren Bedürfnissen gerecht zu werden." Es gibt Tausende von Möglichkeiten, dieser Aufforderung nachzukommen, und Organisationen wie das USGBC haben versucht, die Kritierien hierfür soweit wie möglich zu kodifizieren: Lasst uns unsere Baumaterialien nicht am anderen Ende der Welt kaufen, nutzen wir erneuerbare Ressourcen, schützen wir unsere Bauten vor der Sonne, finden wir Wege, weniger zu konsumieren. Ginge es ausschließlich um die moralische Erleichterung des Gewissens, würden viele Bauherren, Architekten und Bauunternehmer stattdessen auf maximale Wertschöpfung setzen – sich für das pompöseste, unverantwortlichste, „ikonischste" Bauwerk entscheiden, das finanzierbar ist. Doch sollte nicht vielmehr das Wissen um unsere fundamentale Fragilität oder ein Ja zur Bescheidenheit der eigentliche Schlüssel zu echter Nachhaltigkeit in der Architektur sein?

WAS SAGT DIE BRIEFTASCHE?

Was, wenn Energie plötzlich mehr und mehr kostet und Tragödien wie der Unfall von Fukushima endlich in das öffentliche Bewusstsein dringen; was, wenn die Illusion unbegrenzt verfügbarer, billiger Energie als das auffliegt, was sie ist – ein großer Schwindel? Wären „Save the planet"-Parolen genug Motivation, Architektur ab sofort konsequent nachhaltiger zu planen? Doch vielleicht ist die Marktwirtschaft besser als ihr Ruf. Die Kosten für Energie steigen, und die Notwendigkeit, sie nicht länger sinnlos zu verschwenden, drängt sich auf. Vielleicht sind es also die Kräfte des Marktes, die die Architektur zur Vernunft bringen werden. Sie überzeugen auch die, die nichts auf Erderwärmung geben, Material und Energie nicht länger zu verschwenden, weil es ganz einfach zu viel kostet. Wo Lungen und Augen nicht überzeugen, wird es die Brieftasche sicher tun.

[1] http://blog.archpaper.com/wordpress/archives/29467, Zugriff am 12. Januar 2012.
[2] „Face au boom des panneaux solaires, Londres coupe de moitié les subventions", *Le Monde*, 27. Dezember 2011.
[3] „George Osborne's false economy is the death of ‚greenest government ever'", www.guardian.co.uk/environment/damian-carrington-blog/2011/nov/29/green-autumn-statement-osborne-economy-environment, Zugriff am 12. Januar 2012.
[4] „The Problem with Biofuels", *The Washington Post*, Kommentar, 27. Februar 2008, http://www.washingtonpost.com/wp-dyn/content/article/2008/02/26/AR2008022602827.html, Zugriff am 16. Januar 2012.
[5] Nate Berg, „Why the Shenzhen and Hong Kong Biennale Rejected Sustainability as a Theme", http://www.theatlanticcities.com/arts-and-lifestyle/2011/12/why-hong-kong-shenzhen-bi-city-biennale-rejected-sustainability-theme/790/, Zugriff am 12. Januar 2012.
[6] http://www.comarchitect.org/WebHelp/9_sustainable_development_definition.htm, Zugriff am 12. Januar 2012.
[7] http://www.holcimfoundation.org/T700/HolcimFoundationorigins.htm, Zugriff am 16. Januar 2012.
[8] http://www.gccds.org/buildings/patty/patty.html, Zugriff am 16. Januar 2012.
[9] http://www.olafureliasson.net/studio.html, Zugriff am 17. Januar 2012.
[10] http://www.kongehuset.no/c27262/nyhet/vis.html?tid=92483, Zugriff am 16. Januar 2012.

INTRODUCTION

DURABLEMENT VERT

Et ces pieds ont-ils aux temps anciens
Marché sur les vertes montagnes d'Angleterre ?
Et a-t-on vu le saint Agneau de Dieu
Sur les aimables pâturages d'Angleterre ?
Et le divin visage a-t-il continué
À luire sur nos collines ennuagées ?
Et Jérusalem a-t-elle été bâtie ici
Parmi ces sombres moulins de Satan ?

William Blake
Milton, 1804

Au début du XIXe siècle, William Blake fustige en termes désormais célèbres les débuts de la révolution industrielle. Quelques années plus tôt, en 1791, la minoterie à vapeur Albion (Albion Flour Mills) de Southwark, tout près du lieu de résidence de Blake, avait brûlé dans des circonstances suspectes. « Et les arts de la vie furent tous changés en arts de la mort à Albion », écrit-il dans *Jérusalem* (chapitre 3) qui relate la chute d'Albion, l'ancien nom de la Grande-Bretagne. Les mécanismes de la « modernité » et les destructions environnementales et sociales qu'elle entraîne dans son sillage étaient alors déjà en branle, mais aucune prise de conscience réelle des questions environnementales ne devait se manifester avant la deuxième moitié du XXe siècle.

Quel est le lien avec l'architecture ? On se permettra une réponse moderne : aux États-Unis, 80 % des gaz à effet de serre sont émis par les bâtiments et, à New York, ils consomment 94 % de l'énergie [1]. Les procédés industriels ont manifestement permis à des populations de plus en plus importantes de bénéficier d'un confort que l'époque de Blake ne pouvait pas se permettre. Il n'est cependant pas difficile de voir que les formes « traditionnelles » de construction qui utilisent le bois ou la pierre taillée à la main – sans recours à des moyens de transport modernes pour faire venir des matériaux de l'autre bout du monde – ont causé bien moins de dommages à l'environnement que la plupart des maisons contemporaines. L'emploi de matériaux d'origine locale, tout comme les concepts de maisons solaires passives qui cherchent à éviter tout gain excessif (ou toute perte excessive) de chaleur, sont autant d'aspects de l'architecture « verte » qui remontent presque aussi loin que l'histoire de la construction.

PRINTEMPS SILENCIEUX

On peut facilement faire remonter l'intérêt actuel pour la protection de l'environnement au *Printemps silencieux* de Rachel Carson (1962) qui détaille les effets nuisibles des pesticides sur la nature et qui est parfois considéré comme à l'origine du mouvement de protection de l'environnement. De même, si la forte hausse du prix du pétrole dans les années 1970 a certainement suscité l'intérêt pour les sources d'énergie renouvelables et l'efficacité énergétique, il faudra néanmoins attendre 1989 pour voir l'American Institute of Architects (AIA) mettre en place son Comité sur l'environnement. Le Conseil américain pour les bâtiments verts (USGBC), quant à lui, a été fondé en 1993 et a lancé son programme de leadership en énergie et design environnemental (LEED) cinq ans plus tard. D'autres pays ont ouvert la voie ou ont suivi, mais on peut dire sans risquer de se tromper que l'intérêt concerté pour l'impact de l'architecture sur l'environnement date du début des années 1990.

PLUTÔT MORT QUE VERT

Avec le débat qui fait rage sur le «réchauffement de la planète» et la hausse continue des prix de l'énergie, l'aspect environnemental semble être devenu l'une des caractéristiques principales de l'architecture. L'enthousiasme suscité par l'architecture «durable» n'en est sans doute pas moins directement lié à la situation économique: lorsqu'elle est mauvaise, comme c'est le cas depuis 2008 dans la plupart des pays développés, n'est-il pas naturel de poursuivre simplement son activité de construction sans trop de dépenses «vertes» supplémentaires? Pas plus tard qu'au printemps 2010 cependant – *Le Monde* le faisait remarquer dans son édition du 27 décembre 2011 [2] – David Cameron promettait que son gouvernement serait le «plus vert de tous». Mais à peine 18 mois plus tard, il décidait de réduire rétroactivement de moitié les subventions aux petites installations photovoltaïques. Au cours des neuf premiers mois de l'année 2011, 78 000 ensembles de panneaux solaires avaient été installés au Royaume-Uni, en partie car le gouvernement offrait 43,3 pence par kWh produit. En d'autres termes, tout allait tellement bien qu'il ne semblait y avoir aucun intérêt à payer la subvention promise. Dans le contexte d'une économie britannique plutôt terne, ces annonces feront écrire au *Guardian*: «C'est officiel: l'ambition du gouvernement d'être le plus vert de tous est morte, étouffée par les vapeurs d'échappement et les nuages de fumée crachés par les cheminées dans une tentative désespérée de relancer le moteur économique [3]. » Sans doute les ombres de ces «sombres moulins de Satan».

PLUTÔT VERT QUE PAUVRE

On est cependant en droit de se demander aujourd'hui si les forces auxquelles est soumise l'architecture ne l'obligent pas à devenir progressivement de plus en plus durable. En effet, l'une des raisons qui expliquent sa contribution massive aux émissions de dioxyde de carbone est sa voracité pour les matériaux produits dans des pays lointains ou à un coût élevé pour l'environnement. Or, si les prix de l'énergie grimpent en flèche avec la baisse des réserves de combustibles fossiles et la dénonciation des graves dangers de l'énergie nucléaire, la durabilité offre une solution pour réduire ces coûts – un argument de poids dans une civilisation qui glorifie les profits rapides. Bien sûr, le monde est plein d'architectes, de clients, et même de constructeurs désireux de faire ce qu'il faut afin de protéger la planète pour les générations futures, mais concrètement, lorsqu'il s'agit de passer aux faits, l'argument des économies dicte bien plus souvent la décision que celui de la sainteté.

50° AU SOLEIL

Pourtant, même si bien des politiques gouvernementales – jugées trop «coûteuses» en période de difficultés économiques – et des politiques internationales globales pour freiner les émissions de gaz à effet de serre et autres formes de pollution connaissent incontestablement un

18
Ken Yeang, DiGi Technology Operation
Center, Subang High Tech Park, Shah
Alam, Malaysia, 2009

18

déclin depuis 2008, l'un des arguments en faveur de l'architecture « verte » est qu'elle est faite pour durer. Dans un certain sens, les construc-tions durables ont toujours existé dans le monde et les moins sophistiquées sont souvent les plus « vertes ». Orienter un bâtiment pour qu'il reçoive la lumière du jour sans surchauffe en été est un choix évident pour n'importe quel architecte ou propriétaire de maison. De même, utiliser des matériaux simples produits sur place semble aussi relever du bon sens. Privilégier les ressources renouvelables, notamment du bois coupé en respectant certaines précautions, est également un moyen évident de protéger les générations futures pour leur permettre de continuer à faire ce qui est possible aujourd'hui. Le bon sens est pourtant loin d'être la règle en architecture contemporaine. Manifestement encouragées par les forces du marché qui accordent une importance prépondérante aux gains rapides, mais aussi poussées vers une accélération excessive par une culture de la satisfaction immédiate, les formes d'architecture non durable, et, de fait, destructives, continuent de prospérer. Des cités entières de tours en verre ont ainsi poussé comme des champignons dans les sables du golfe Persique où les températures peuvent atteindre 50 °C en été, mais qui dira aux habitants d'Abou Dhabi qu'ils ne peuvent pas toucher le ciel alors qu'ils ont visiblement l'argent pour le faire ?

ATTENTION À L'ÉTHANOL

L'accent mis sur la durabilité cache cependant une autre question souvent non formulée. En effet, avec la mode du « vert », les architectes, promoteurs et clients sont plus que jamais enclins à mettre en avant leurs références environnementales, même lorsqu'il s'agit simplement de « recycler » pour les consommateurs d'aujourd'hui des stratégies passives utilisées depuis toujours. Pire encore, bon nombre de produits, dont on ne fera pas la liste ici, sont bien moins respectueux de l'environnement qu'on ne le dit. C'est un exemple non architectural qui donne sans doute le mieux le ton pour faire comprendre cet aspect de la « durabilité » actuelle : on sait depuis des années que les biocarburants ne constituent pas la solution miracle aux problèmes posés par les carburants fossiles. En 2008, un éditorial du *Washington Post* annonçait que « des études pu-bliées séparément par l'université de Princeton et The Nature Conservancy révèlent que les biocarburants ne sont pas l'arme absolue dans la bataille contre le réchauffement planétaire. Ils pourraient même rendre les choses encore pires. Le maïs et la canne à sucre sont deux des sources les plus courantes de l'éthanol. En plus d'émettre moins de gaz à effet de serre que le charbon ou l'essence lors de leur combustion dans un moteur, ils éliminent le carbone de l'atmosphère pendant leur croissance – ce qui rend leur bilan carbone quasiment neutre. Or, les deux études montrent que l'éthanol pourrait être encore plus dangereux pour l'environnement que les combustibles fossiles [4] ».

UN LABEL POUR FAIRE VENDRE

Dans une interview publiée en ligne, Terry Riley, ancien conservateur chargé de l'architecture et du design au Musée d'art moderne de New York et actuellement conservateur de la Biennale d'architecture de Hong Kong et Shenzhen, traduit ces doutes dans le langage enthou-siaste d'aujourd'hui pour l'écologie en architecture : à la question des raisons qui ont poussé les organisateurs de la Biennale à refuser la dura-bilité comme thème, il répond : « Nous avons rejeté le terme "durabilité". Il nous a paru trop important pour être utilisé, comme c'est actuelle-ment le cas, tel un label destiné à faire vendre des produits qui, pour la plupart, ne sont fondamentalement pas durables. Dans l'usage qui en est fait aujourd'hui, la durabilité est aussi surtout une question de chiffres. Nous avons choisi de mettre en avant la vitalité qui, à mon avis, comprend la durabilité, avec bon nombre d'autres thématiques moins quantifiables. Cette position a guidé toutes nos décisions pour la Biennale[5]. »

Pour trouver des exemples d'architecture « verte » ou « durable », l'une des questions fondamentales est celle de la définition même de ces termes. Le développement durable a été défini par la Commission mondiale de l'environnement et du développement des Nations unies dans le rapport Brundtland (1987) comme « les voies du progrès social, économique et politique qui répondent aux besoins du présent sans compromettre la capacité des générations futures à répondre aux leurs ». Un an après le Sommet de la Terre de Rio de Janeiro, en juin 1993, le congrès mondial des architectes en posait les termes plus simplement : « Le développement durable implique de répondre à nos besoins aujourd'hui sans compromettre la capacité des générations futures à répondre aux leurs[6]. »

DON'T WORRY, BE HAPPY

Manifestement, les organisations qui certifient la durabilité de l'architecture dans le monde, à l'instar du United States Green Building Council et de sa norme LEED, adoptent une approche plus complexe et plus complète de la construction responsable. La Fondation Holcim, créée par un fournisseur de ciment suisse, identifie ainsi cinq domaines essentiels de durabilité : 1) innovation et transmissibilité ; 2) normes éthiques et équité sociale ; 3) qualité écologique et conservation d'énergie ; 4) performance économique et compatibilité ; 5) effet contextuel et esthétique[7]. Cette liste d'objectifs clés est sans aucun doute liée à ceux du Sommet de l'ONU ou de la Terre qui associent explicitement les questions sociales au thème global de la durabilité. Des organisations d'architecture comme l'USGBC de leur côté attribuent leur certification LEED selon un système de points dérivé d'une liste de qualifications qui sont : 1) aménagement écologique des sites ; 2) gestion efficace de l'eau ; 3) énergie et atmosphère ; 4) matériaux et ressources ; 5) qualité des environnements intérieurs ; 6) innovation du design et 7) priorité régionale. Les différents types de bâtiments sont soumis à différents processus de reconnaissance selon un système complexe, bien que clair. Les aspects mis en valeur par l'USGBC ont malgré tout un parti pris social car, si les points pris en compte améliorent la qualité de vie à l'intérieur d'un bâtiment et au-delà de ses murs, certains éléments relevés par Holcim, notamment les « normes éthiques et équité sociale », sont manifestement laissés de côté. La complexité relative et la variété des systèmes de notation soulignent donc une certaine ambiguïté inhérente à toute tentative de durabilité au-delà des règles de base les plus évidentes – qui ont prévalu pour toutes les constructions avant l'ère du ciment, de l'acier, du verre, de l'air conditionné et des pierres transportées autour du monde pour habiller les emblèmes de la vanité des entreprises. Lorsque toutes ces technologies plus propres que propres, comme les biocarburants, ou même les panneaux photovoltaïques et les métaux lourds qu'ils contiennent, révèlent un aspect plus sombre, certaines questions, voire un certain scepticisme, trouvent peut-être une justification. En attendant, le mieux est de ne pas s'inquiéter et d'être heureux.

C'est bien beau de rappeler que l'architecture n'a pas été une source majeure de dégradation de l'environnement pendant la plus grande partie de son histoire. Bien sûr, la déforestation passe pour être l'une des causes du déclin de la civilisation sur l'île de Pâques, mais à d'autres endroits, des populations moins importantes et des infrastructures technologiques insuffisantes ont garanti que la construction ne serait pas la fin de l'humanité, au moins jusqu'à celle des Albion Flour Mills à Southwark. Mais est-il encore possible aujourd'hui, dans des pays plus ou moins « avancés », de construire écologiquement rationnel ? Ou cela relève-t-il d'un rêve nostalgique d'Arcadie sans réel ancrage sur le terrain ?

19
Kengo Kuma, Yusuhara Wooden
Bridge Museum, Yusuhara-cho,
Takaoka-gun, Kochi, Japan, 2010

SORTIR LE CHIEN À L'ABRI

La « maison de Patty » ou maison Broussard (Broussard House, Biloxi, Mississippi, 2008, page 174), résultat des efforts de plusieurs organisations pour améliorer le sort des habitants de La Nouvelle-Orléans dont la maison avait été détruite par l'ouragan Katrina en 2005, est un exemple intéressant : l'initiative BaSIC, créée comme un programme d'aide aux fermiers indigènes pauvres dans le Centre du Mexique, est aujourd'hui une association d'enseignants et d'étudiants de l'université de Portland et de l'École d'architecture de l'université du Texas d'Austin. BaSIC a travaillé avec le Hamer Center for Community Design de l'université de Pennsylvanie, les studios Design Corps et Gulf Coast Community Design Studio (GCCDS) et d'autres organisations comme l'Agence d'East Biloxi de coordination, secours et réaménagement pour réunir les fonds nécessaires et s'assurer la collaboration de douze étudiants en architecture de différentes universités. Le groupe d'étudiants et d'enseignants a travaillé six semaines à la conception et à la construction de la maison. L'un des objectifs du Hamer Center était une maison certifiée LEED ; il a été obtenu par l'octroi de subventions pour acheter des matériaux et systèmes de qualité supérieure. La maison a reçu la certification LEED au printemps 2009, c'est la première maison individuelle du Mississippi à en être dotée.

Le plan de la maison ressemble à celui des habitations typiques du Sud des États-Unis appelées « dogtrot » dont l'espace séjour est séparé des chambres à coucher par un passage ouvert avec toit qui permet une meilleure ventilation naturelle et crée un espace à vivre extérieur couvert. Elle est surélevée à presque quatre mètres au-dessus du sol comme l'imposent les normes en matière d'inondation et est construite en béton et bois traité sous pression. Des colonnes en béton montent jusqu'à un peu plus de deux mètres avant de céder la place à d'autres en bois et à l'entrecroisement [8]. La maison présente une certaine ressemblance avec l'architecture locale en ce qu'elle suit une typologie basée sur l'expérience de nombreuses années d'inondations et de tempêtes et, plus généralement, sur la connaissance du climat régional. La collaboration intense entre plusieurs organisations pour réaliser ce qui semblait un projet très simple montre bien qu'il est possible de fonder les développements futurs sur la connaissance du passé et sur la bonne volonté de tous ceux qui essaient de rendre les propriétaires des maisons à l'aise et écologiquement responsables. Le béton a été utilisé pour la Broussard House, mais uniquement lorsque c'était nécessaire, et la certification LEED témoigne du soin qui a été apporté pour se procurer et utiliser les matériaux choisis.

BAMBOU ET CÈDRE ROUGE

De l'autre côté du monde, l'architecte vietnamien Vo Trong Nghia a imaginé une structure entièrement en bambou de 1600 mètres carrés baptisée « Aile de bambou » (Bamboo Wing, Dai Lai, province de Vinh Phuc, Viêtnam, 2009, page 386), pour laquelle, souligne-t-il avec fierté, « ni acier, ni aucun autre matériau de construction artificiel » n'a été utilisé et dont la forme s'inspire des ailes des oiseaux. À l'instar d'autres constructions de Vo Trong Nghia, cet espace de réunion qui s'élance vers le ciel témoigne d'une modernité étonnante compte-tenu de l'usage extensif de matériaux de construction traditionnels comme le bambou. Il faut dire que la croissance rapide du bambou en fait un candidat de choix au titre de « ressource renouvelable » suprême en ce qui concerne la construction, au moins à une échelle modeste. Le site et l'environnement naturel presque intact sur lequel se dresse Bamboo Wing confirment également que l'architecture moderne peut parfaitement se passer de matériaux plus sophistiqués.

20
Werner Sobek, F87, Berlin,
Germany, 2011

Kengo Kuma, l'un des plus éminents architectes japonais, s'intéresse depuis longtemps aux traditions de son pays, mais n'est jamais tombé dans le piège du «pastiche» ou copie conforme du passé. Son musée du Pont de bois de Yusuhara (Yusuhara-cho, Takaoka-gun, Kochi, Japon, 2010, page 266) est un bâtiment en bois à degrés de type pont qui abrite l'espace nécessaire à un atelier et un artiste en résidence. Malgré le choix du bois lamellé au lieu du bois massif que les anciens préféraient, le projet est une référence aux techniques de construction en porte-à-faux qu'on retrouve dans les architectures historiques chinoise et japonaise. Le bâtiment est en cèdre rouge coupé sur place, ce qui contribue également à sa durabilité. Là encore, à l'instar de Vo Trong Nghia, Kengo Kuma exploite les traditions architecturales régionales pour créer un bâtiment parfaitement moderne, et en même temps très largement durable. Il ne s'agit pas ici de revenir au passé, mais de partir de la tradition pour redécouvrir des modes de construction plus en harmonie, d'une part avec la nature, et d'autre part avec la satisfaction des utilisateurs et des populations locales.

DU MADE IN CHINA FAIT MAIN

Il ne faudrait pas croire que seuls des cabinets asiatiques se lancent dans l'exploration, couronnée de succès, de l'architecture durable d'inspiration traditionnelle. On en trouve néanmoins de nombreux exemples récents – qui sont d'ailleurs parfois autant déterminés par des coûts de construction relativement bas que par le désir général de protéger l'environnement. Le musée du Papier artisanal de Gaoligong (Tengchong, Yunnan, Chine, 2009–10, page 336) par TAO (Trace Architecture Office) est un exemple plein d'élégance de ce type d'exploitation constructive du passé. Ce petit musée (361 mètres carrés) est situé à proximité du village de Xinzhuang et du mont Gaoligong, dans le Yunnan, une réserve écologique mondiale. Conçu dans le but de mettre en valeur l'héritage régional du papier fait main, la structure a été construite par des artisans locaux, notamment des paysans, à partir de papier, bambou, pierre volcanique locale et d'une charpente traditionnelle en bois. Là encore, aucune imitation d'une architecture passée, mais plutôt une conception et une exécution extrêmement modernes. On peut argumenter, et d'aucuns le feront, que la tradition constitue l'un des meilleurs chemins vers un véritable équilibre entre le monde naturel et physique. Les méthodes employées pour le musée du Papier artisanal de Gaoligong ne sont pas nées des besoins d'une entreprise multinationale de réaliser des profits le plus vite possible, au contraire, c'est ici la sagesse de plusieurs générations qui est exploitée de manière parfaitement durable. Les gadgets et accessoires de la vie contemporaine ne sont peut-être pas aussi en vue qu'on pourrait le souhaiter, mais ces ajouts, souvent en grande partie inutiles, sont sans doute plus obsolètes que le bambou et la pierre volcanique en tant que matériaux de construction contemporains.

DES EMPREINTES EN BAISSE

Cet ouvrage ne se veut en aucun cas une condamnation des matériaux et méthodes modernes, mais cherche peut-être à montrer que le passé lui aussi a des leçons essentielles à donner dans le contexte des préoccupations croissantes pour les ressources et l'environnement. Il existe manifestement une autre école de pensée qui compte à la fois sur des méthodes passives et actives pour contrôler la consommation d'énergie et réduire l'«empreinte carbone» de l'architecture. Elle fait appel aux matériaux et aux réflexions les plus modernes pour rendre le design contemporain compatible avec le maintien en bonne santé de notre planète. Certaines des réalisations présentées ici sont de véritables vitrines des technologies modernes, dont l'objectif est souvent d'obtenir des maisons ou bâtiments « à énergie positive » – qui contribuent à l'approvisionnement énergétique d'une communauté, au lieu de simplement le diminuer. Le célèbre ingénieur allemand Werner Sobek, créateur de nombreuses structures modernes écologiquement rationnelles, a ainsi contribué récemment à un projet baptisé F87 (Berlin, 2011, page 330). Vainqueur d'un concours organisé par le ministère fédéral allemand des Transports, de la Construction et du Développement urbain pour la construction d'une « maison à énergie positive combinée à l'électromobilité », ce bâtiment de 130 mètres carrés devrait produire suffisamment d'électricité pour alimenter le véhicule électrique de ses habitants et répondre à leurs besoins en énergie. Il a également été conçu pour produire un impact minimal sur l'environnement, pendant sa construction comme pendant sa démolition – future.

À COUPER LE SOUFFLE

Le cabinet coréen Unsangdong va sans doute encore plus loin que Sobek avec l'accumulation de technologies vertes dans une seule maison (E+ Green Home, Jeon Dae, Cheo In, Po Gok, Yong In, Kyeong Gi, Corée-du-Sud, 2010–11, page 370) : le bâtiment de grande taille (344 mètres carrés) dispose d'un toit végétalisé pour réduire le plus possible les pertes d'énergie et l'apport solaire, tout en optimisant la réutilisation de l'eau de pluie. Avec son système d'isolation extérieure complexe (StoTherm), son bois thermo-traité, ses éléments photovoltaïques intégrés, ses capteurs thermiques solaires haute efficacité, son éolienne et sa pompe à chaleur géothermique, c'est la première maison certifiée PHI (Passivhaus Institut/Institut de la maison passive) en Corée-du-Sud. La norme « Passivhaus » a été formulée à partir de 1988 par les professeurs Bo Adamson de l'université de Lund (Suède) et Wolfgang Feist de l'Institut für Wohnen und Umwelt (Institut allemand de l'habitat et de l'environnement). On compte environ 25 000 bâtiments certifiés « Passivhaus » en Europe dont l'objectif, qui se rapproche de ceux du système LEED, est de dénombrer et d'identifier les facteurs qui permettent d'améliorer l'efficacité énergétique et de réduire l'empreinte écologique de l'architecture. La consommation d'énergie primaire totale d'une passive certifiée ne doit pas excéder 120 kWh/m² par an tandis que, plus surprenant, elle ne doit pas perdre plus de 60 pour cent de son volume d'air par heure. La villa Nyberg (Borlänge, Suède, 2010, page 250) des architectes de Göteborg Kjellgren Kaminsky, par exemple, a battu le record suédois d'étanchéité à l'air (0,038 l/sm² à 50 Pa, la norme suédoise pour les maisons passives est de 0,3 et le record précédent était de 0,07). De forme essentiellement ronde pour réduire la surface de murs et éviter les ponts thermiques ou « froids », sa consommation d'énergie de chauffage est estimée à tout juste 25 kWh/m² par an.

La Villa 4.0 ('t Gooi, Pays-Bas, 2010–11, page 158) de Dick Van Gameren est un autre exemple de maison délibérément « verte ». L'ensemble de 540 mètres carrés comprend un système de chauffage au sol basse température, un chauffe-eau solaire, une ventilation naturelle, un poêle à bois haut rendement dans la cuisine et tout son éclairage artificiel est à base de LED. Un peu moins activement « durable » que les maisons de Werner Sobek ou d'Unsangdong, elle est cependant plus proche de la réalité actuelle de l'architecture verte. En combinant plusieurs moyens différents d'économiser de l'énergie, la construction de Van Gameren apporte sans conteste une amélioration au niveau des frais de fonctionnement par rapport aux maisons « normales » – et suggère que la nouvelle « normalité » d'aujourd'hui pourrait bien se trouver à 't Gooi.

LES ENTREPRISES ET LEUR PART DE RESPONSABILITÉ

Les principes de réduction de la consommation d'énergie et de durabilité globale s'appliquent, bien sûr, également à des structures plus importantes et certaines entreprises ont pris la tête dans ce domaine. Le fabricant indien d'éoliennes Suzlon, par exemple, soutient logiquement les bureaux écologiquement rationnels. Son siège mondial Suzlon One Earth (Pune, Maharashtra, Inde, 2008–10, page 21) par Christopher Charles Benninger Architects est un complexe de 55 741 mètres carrés qui comprend de nombreux matériaux « basse énergie », des systèmes de ventilation naturelle, des panneaux photovoltaïques et, bien sûr, des éoliennes. Le bâtiment, par ailleurs assez attrayant, a reçu une certification LEED platine, la plus haute note jamais attribuée par l'USGBC.

Le Green Office (Meudon, France, 2009–11, page 46) par les architectes d'Ateliers 115 a voulu aller encore plus loin que Suzlon avec une consommation de 62 kWh/m² pour 64 kWh/m² par an générés par des panneaux photovoltaïques et un système de cogénération (PCCE). On peut donc dire que, du point de vue statistique autant que symbolique, le Green Office est à énergie positive : il devrait être en mesure d'injecter de l'électricité dans le réseau local. Il n'y a pas d'air conditionné – mais le climat parisien ne l'impose pas réellement –, les matériaux ont été choisis pour leur durabilité environnementale et le double vitrage et l'épaisseur de l'isolation contribuent à l'efficacité énergétique globale de l'ensemble. Avec 21 700 mètres carrés, le Green Office est aussi grand que novateur, même si son aspect extérieur ne diffère pas forcément des autres bâtiments commerciaux. L'un des propos de *L'architecture verte d'aujourd'hui 2* est que la construction écologiquement rationnelle et les pratiques en usage ne s'opposent en aucun cas au design de qualité. Les bâtiments contemporains n'ont pas réellement besoin d'avoir l'air « verts » – ce qui intéresse surtout beaucoup de clients, c'est le coût et le sentiment d'agir en citoyens responsables. En d'autres termes, la durabilité fait aujourd'hui partie de la normalité et n'est plus obligée d'afficher sa couleur « verte » aux passants. C'est une évolution essentielle qu'il convient de proclamer et d'encourager.

TOUT SCHUSS SUR L'INCINÉRATEUR

L'architecte danois très remarqué Bjarke Ingels (BIG) a déjà défendu à de multiples reprises ce qu'il appelle la « durabilité hédoniste » – ou l'architecture dont le design responsable procure aussi du plaisir. Après l'époque des débuts où les bâtiments « verts » se devaient pour certains d'avoir l'air étrange pour en venir à leurs fins, les différentes agences de notation ont donné une image plus technocratique, et peut-être austère, de la durabilité : que valent esthétique et émotion lorsque l'important est de ne pas faire venir du granit du Zimbabwe à Los Angeles ? Ingels n'hésite pas à prendre la direction opposée avec des créations telles que son grandiose Centre de transformation des déchets en énergie d'Amager Bakke (Copenhague, 2009–, page 74) de 460 millions d'euros, qui affiche fièrement une piste de ski sur son toit de 32 000 mètres carrés. « Nous voulons faire plus que simplement imaginer une belle enveloppe autour de l'usine, expliquent les architectes, nous voulons y ajouter une fonctionnalité nouvelle ! [...] Nous nous proposons de créer une usine de retraitement des déchets d'un genre nouveau, à la fois économiquement, écologiquement et socialement rentable. » Bjarke Ingels fait encore un pas au-delà de la reconnaissance générale dont il jouit aujourd'hui en tant qu'architecte « vert » : il veut rendre la durabilité amusante et « rentable » au sens le plus large du terme.

21
Ateliers 115, Green Office, Meudon,
France, 2009–11

21

Malgré la « big » réputation de Bjarke Ingels, on doit pouvoir mentionner que la « durabilité hédoniste » est moins une découverte que ne le suggère sa piste de ski sur un incinérateur. L'agence grecque K-Studio a, par exemple, achevé le restaurant de plage Bar Bouni (Pilos, Costa Navarino, Grèce, page 238) en 2011 : placé sur une plate-forme en bois qui domine la plage et sous laquelle les vagues viennent se briser, cette structure est constituée de colonnes de bois naturel et d'un « champ de pans de tissus suspendus » qui forme un dais. Pas besoin d'une piste de ski de 32 000 mètres carrés sur le toit du bâtiment, toute la « durabilité hédoniste » voulue est là, sur la plage. En un sens, la durabilité dépend donc de l'emplacement et de la fonction du bâtiment, les solutions les plus simples et les plus efficaces sont souvent celles dont le temps a entériné la pratique. De même, le bois, le tissu, le sable et les vagues qui se brisent sur la plage ne coûtent pas 460 millions d'euros. Bien sûr, c'est une interprétation facétieuse des idées parfaitement valables exprimées par Ingels – dont la modestie ne semble cependant pas faire partie de la stratégie. Mais : et si la véritable durabilité était plus proche de la modestie que de projets toujours plus grandioses et technologiques ?

UN MONDE MEILLEUR

D'aucuns seront surpris de trouver des créateurs tels qu'Adrian Smith et Gordon Gill dans un ouvrage consacré à l'architecture verte. Après tout, Smith est l'auteur de la Burj Khalifa (Dubaï, EAU, 2004–09), la tour la plus haute du monde avec 830 mètres. Plus étonnant encore, les deux architectes ont une autre immense structure en travaux, la « tour du Royaume » (Kingdom Tower, Djeddah, Arabie Saoudite), qui devrait faire plus d'un kilomètre. Adrian Smith et d'autres architectes de renom comme Norman Foster affirment cependant depuis longtemps qu'il y aurait beaucoup à dire en faveur de la durabilité inhérente aux structures en hauteur par rapport à un nombre équivalent de bâtiments plus bas. Il est certain qu'en termes d'infrastructure, des routes au réseau électrique, une seule tour pourrait bien s'avérer en fin de compte plus écologique qu'un grand nombre de petites structures. Adrian Smith et Gordon Gill ont également remporté, avec un immeuble d'une hauteur plus « normale » de 240 mètres, un concours international lancé par la Fédération des industries coréennes pour construire une tour à Séoul (Corée-du-Sud, 2010–13, page 320). L'enveloppe du bâtiment est spécialement « conçue pour contribuer à réduire la chaleur interne et la charge de climatisation, tout en récupérant de l'énergie grâce aux panneaux photovoltaïques intégrés aux surfaces de remplissage des façades sud-ouest et nord-ouest, exposées à un ensoleillement direct très important pendant la journée ». Selon les architectes : « En inclinant les panneaux-allèges de 30 degrés en direction du soleil, l'équipe de concepteurs a optimisé la quantité d'énergie récupérée afin de produire suffisamment d'électricité pour contribuer à faire fonctionner les systèmes électriques dans le cœur de la tour et l'espace de bureaux. Juste en dessous, les panneaux vitrés sont inclinés de 15 degrés vers le bas afin de minimiser le rayonnement solaire direct et l'éclat. » Si les arguments en faveur de la tour haute d'un kilomètre à Djeddah ne reposent pas sur des motifs plus forts que le prestige qui y est associé, le bâtiment de la Fédération des industries coréennes est érigé dans une ville déjà dense où l'espace fait plus que jamais prime. On aurait du mal à plaider ici en faveur du bambou et de la pierre volcanique, et il faut bien admettre que l'architecture contemporaine peut avoir recours à la technologie pour réduire l'empreinte carbone des nouvelles constructions. On construira ce type de bâtiments aussi longtemps que les ressources le permettront, et il vaut certainement mieux chercher à les rendre aussi durables que nos connaissances le permettent.

TOUR VERTE, ÉTOILE GREEN STAR

À une moindre échelle, les architectes suisses Gigon/Guyer ont montré avec leur récent projet à Zurich (Prime Tower, Zurich, Suisse, 2008–11, page 166) qu'une géante verte, ici 36 étages pour 126 mètres de haut, peut répondre à des exigences environnementales très élevées. La tour, labellisée LEED or, est dotée d'une pompe à échangeur de chaleur qui utilise l'eau de la nappe phréatique, de dispositifs de récupération de la chaleur du bâtiment et de refroidissement, d'un système couplé chauffage/climatisation avec stockage de chaleur et de glace, et de fenêtres qui s'ouvrent partiellement. Les normes LEED sont adaptées à différents types de constructions mais prennent claire-ment en compte le besoin de bâtiments hauts. En partant du principe que l'on construira encore des tours et qu'il vaut mieux qu'elles soient « vertes », il convient de mentionner un autre projet de ce type : 1 Bligh (Sydney, Australie, 2009–11, page 29) par ingenhoven architects se veut la « tour de bureaux la plus écologique » d'Australie. Le bâtiment a reçu la plus haute note du système australien, « Green Star », la certi-fication « 6 étoiles/ Leadership mondial ». C'est la première tour de bureaux de Sydney à être ainsi récompensée par le Green Building Council of Australia (GBCA). Avec ses 30 étages et ses 42 700 mètres carrés, c'est aussi un édifice imposant non dénué de mérite sur le plan archi-tectural : ventilation naturelle, traitement des eaux usées sur place, façade double-peau et système de production électrique combiné qui gère chauffage et climatisation sont quelques-unes de ses caractéristiques.

Des exemples tels que ces tours, dont l'intérêt est sans doute purement architectural, ont donc leur place dans un livre consacré à l'architecture « verte » car ils montrent que le design durable est aussi parfaitement viable. La construction de tours a produit un nombre im-pressionnant de formes mixtes toutes plus étranges les unes que les autres, il faut certainement y voir la preuve que les architectes ont du mal à trouver une véritable originalité avec ce type de bâtiment. Parmi les tours publiées ici, c'est la Prime Tower de Zurich qui paraîtra sans doute la plus intéressante sur le plan formel, en partie parce qu'elle se démarque dans son environnement industriel de manière visiblement emblématique. En effet, les grandes entreprises dans leur ensemble ne se font pas remarquer par leur désintéressement, la durabilité doit donc avoir du sens sur le plan économique. Les personnes visées pardonneront le caractère quelque peu cynique de cette remarque, mais il faut aussi y voir de bonnes nouvelles : si écologie et argent font bon ménage, le monde aura de meilleures chances de posséder des bâti-ments et des villes durables. Si les sociétés peuvent faire des économies en recueillant des bons points pour leur citoyenneté urbaine, c'est que le mouvement vers l'architecture contemporaine durable ne peut déjà plus être arrêté. On construit trop de bâtiments de ce type pour que les facteurs de réduction de la consommation énergétique puissent être de simples « gadgets » à la mode. Le photovoltaïque et d'autres technologies vont continuer de progresser et d'autres éléments, tels que le point de vue selon lequel les mesures passives doivent toujours avoir pour objectif de réduire les factures d'électricité, vont y être associés pour accroître les économies d'énergie, et donc réduire la quan-tité finale de pollution générée par les bâtiments.

L'ART DES PARFUMS

Les familiers de la série *L'architecture d'aujourd'hui* savent que les ouvrages qui la composent comprennent souvent les œuvres d'artistes, en plus des réalisations plus visiblement architecturales des grands créateurs actuels. Olafur Eliasson est ce qu'on peut appeler une

22
ingenhoven architects, European
Investment Bank, Luxembourg,
Luxembourg, 2004–08

22

exception dans le monde de l'art car il a toujours témoigné un intérêt actif et continu pour l'architecture. Avec l'architecte norvégien Kjetil Thorsen, il a notamment contribué à la conception du pavillon 2007 de la Serpentine Gallery dans les Kensington Gardens (Londres). Plus récemment, il a créé la façade du Harpa, la nouvelle salle de concerts de Reykjavik, en collaboration avec l'architecte Henning Larsen. Le Studio Olafur Eliasson de Berlin « se compose aujourd'hui d'une équipe de 45 personnes environ, des artisans et techniciens spécialisés aux architectes, artistes, archivistes et historiens de l'art, cuisiniers et gestionnaires[9] ». Deux réalisations d'Eliasson sont publiées ici, son Tunnel des parfums (*Dufttunnel*, Wolfsburg, Allemagne, 2004, page 150) et l'Arceau fleuri (*Flower Archway,* Jardin botanique, Culiacán, Sinaloa, Mexique, 2005–08, page 152). La première peut autant être vue comme un tunnel que comme un pont : les visiteurs y sont entourés de 2160 pots de fleurs qui tournent autour d'eux sur des anneaux tubulaires en acier inoxydable. Seuls peu d'objets sont plus banals ou immobiles que les pots de fleurs, souvent aussi associés à un certain degré de mauvais goût – ce dont on ne saurait cependant accuser Eliasson. L'œuvre implique une certaine dose d'humour, mais se veut aussi un commentaire de la mobilité et des formes architecturales. Planté de six fleurs différentes selon la saison, le *Dufttunnel* stimule les sens et pose clairement la question de la « nature » dans l'art et l'architecture. Transposés et réinventés par l'artiste, les pots de fleurs font partie intégrante d'un travail inventif. Le *Flower Archway* fleuri aborde les relations potentielles entre art et architecture par une voie très différente. Une arche treillissée en cinq segments est recouverte de plantes au point de presque disparaître sous le réseau de branchages vivants. Le treillage est subsumé sous son cadre naturel auquel il donne en même temps une forme propre. Le *Dufttunnel* et le *Flower Archway* posent tous les deux le même problème, à savoir où commence la « nature » et où l'« art » ou l'architecture reprennent la main. En associant des plantes et des formes à suffisamment grande échelle pour permettre aux visiteurs de se promener à l'intérieur ou en-dessous, Eliasson démontre la force de transformation de l'art et sa faculté à remettre en question des hypothèses fondamentales.

L'une des hypothèses de base des constructeurs veut que nature et architecture diffèrent fondamentalement l'une de l'autre et ne puissent réellement être harmonisées. Certains architectes récusent cependant cette idée, comme en témoigne l'un des projets publiés ici, du nom de Stacking Green (Hô Chi Minh-Ville, Viêtnam, 2011, page 392), par Vo Trong Nghia. Les façades avant et arrière de la petite maison sont entièrement composées de jardinières en béton empilées. Avec en plus un jardin sur le toit, elle procure un refuge à l'abri du bruit, de la chaleur et de la pollution de la ville. L'architecte, qui fait référence aux maisons traditionnelles des cours vietnamiennes dans sa description, ne prétend pas avoir créé une œuvre d'art, mais avoir utilisé la « nature » – ou la végétation en pots – pour lutter contre les maux de la vie citadine. Avec sa ventilation naturelle ou le principe « bioclimatique », Stacking Green peut incontestablement être considérée comme « plus durable » qu'une maison dont toute nature est absente, mais pose la question des limites entre vert et non vert.

LES VOIES DU PROGRÈS

Parmi les architectes manifestement sensibles à l'art figure le lauréat du prix Pritkzer, le Suisse Peter Zumthor. Pour un projet des plus inédits, le mémorial Steilneset (Vardø, Finnmark, Norvège, 2006–11, page 16), il a imaginé une structure longue de 125 mètres à base essentiellement de bois et de toile à voile en hommage aux victimes des procès en sorcellerie qui se sont déroulés dans le Finnmark au

23

XVIIe siècle. Flanqué d'un cube en verre noir qui contient l'œuvre *Les Damnées, les possédées, les aimées* de Louise Bourgeois, aujourd'hui décédée, le principal bâtiment du mémorial est situé sur la côte septentrionale rocheuse de la Norvège, chacune de ses 91 fenêtres est garnie d'une lampe suspendue en mémoire des victimes de traitements barbares. Le projet dans son ensemble est le résultat d'une collaboration entre Zumthor et Bourgeois et s'inscrit dans l'effort en cours pour marquer par des œuvres d'art et d'architecture majeures les sites qui bordent les routes touristiques nationales de Norvège. «Et c'est exactement ce que nous ressentons ici à Steilneset, loin au nord et dans la partie la plus orientale de la Norvège – un art spectaculaire dans un cadre naturel superbe et sauvage», a déclaré la reine Sonja de Norvège lors de l'inauguration du mémorial le 23 juin 2011, avant de poursuivre: «Steilneset symbolise l'intolérance d'une autre époque, mais peut aussi nous rappeler les préjugés, les injustices et les persécutions qui existent encore aujourd'hui[10].» Inspiré en partie par les casiers de bois diagonal utilisés pour sécher le poisson dans la région, le mémorial Steilneset pourrait évoquer un style d'architecture qui n'a jamais posé le moindre problème de pollution ou de «durabilité». C'est une architecture porteuse d'un message, mais aussi une construction qui, pour le mémorial principal, est tout près d'apporter la réponse à la question de ce qui rend réellement un bâtiment écologiquement «durable». Il a été créé dans le respect – respect de l'architecte pour l'endroit, l'histoire et sa collaboration avec l'une des grandes artistes du moment. Ce respect rend presque vains les mécanismes complexes des notations LEED. «Et les arts de la vie furent tous changés en arts de la mort à Albion», écrit Blake. À Vardø, les arts de la mort sont conjurés, écartés et bannis par un geste de respect. La signification de ce geste va bien au-delà de la «durabilité» au sens purement architectural du terme, elle se rapproche peut-être plutôt de la définition de 1987 des Nations unies qui évoque les «voies du progrès social, économique et politique».

UNE FRAGILITÉ INHÉRENTE

Les projets sélectionnés ici l'ont été dans la volonté délibérée d'éviter les définitions purement technologiques de la durabilité – ce qui revient à dire que, si la certification LEED platine est, certes, une excellente chose, une certaine luminosité par exemple peut aussi rendre un bâtiment plus proche de la durabilité que la suite de façades aveugles, polluantes et polluées qui se succèdent le long de la plupart de nos rues. Le Fragile Lab (Anvers, Belgique, 2005–07, page 194) d'Import-Export Architecture abrite le magasin et le domicile (400 mètres carrés) des propriétaires d'une marque de mode. Les étais tubulaires d'acier inclinés inspirés par le bambou, un mur végétal à l'intérieur et, en fin de compte, sa transparence et sa fragilité évidentes semblent en faire un candidat pour notre sélection. Mais plutôt que de se demander ce qui rend un bâtiment «vert» ou durable, on pourrait, à l'inverse, se demander ce qui rend l'architecture non durable et agressivement contre-productive? La réponse la plus simple tient en un mot, l'«arrogance»: celle des architectes et constructeurs, mais aussi sans aucun doute celle des clients qui ne s'intéressent qu'au projet qu'ils ont en tête. On pense immédiatement à la définition de 1993 du Congrès mondial des architectes: «Le développement durable implique de répondre à nos besoins aujourd'hui sans compromettre la capacité des générations futures à répondre aux leurs.» Il existe de très nombreux moyens de répondre à cette injonction et les organisations comme l'USGBC ont tenté de les codifier le plus possible: ne pas se procurer ses matériaux à l'autre bout du monde, opter pour des ressources renouvelables, protéger les bâtiments du soleil et trouver des moyens d'en réduire la consommation. S'il s'agissait uniquement de se sentir en accord avec soi-

24
Patrick Eriksson, MenTouGou
Eco Valley, Beijing, China, 2009–10

même, il est malheureusement évident que bon nombre de clients, architectes et constructeurs choisiraient d'en « avoir le plus possible pour leur argent » – la construction la plus somptueuse, irresponsable et emblématique que l'argent peut acheter. Mais la reconnaissance d'une fragilité fondamentale, ou l'acceptation de la modestie ne devraient-elles pas être les clés d'une véritable durabilité en architecture ?

ÉCOUTER SON PORTE-MONNAIE

Et que se passerait-il si d'un seul coup l'énergie commençait à devenir de plus en plus chère et si des incidents comme celui de la centrale nucléaire de Fukushima entraient enfin dans la conscience collective, dénonçant l'illusion d'une énergie illimitée bon marché pour ce qu'elle est – une imposture ? La motivation de « sauver la planète » pourrait-elle suffire à rendre l'architecture rigoureusement durable ou, là encore, l'économie de marché fonctionne-t-elle mieux qu'on ne le craindrait ? À partir de maintenant, les prix de l'énergie vont continuer d'augmenter et la nécessité d'arrêter de la gaspiller inutilement va s'imposer d'elle-même. Ainsi, peut-être qu'après tout, les forces du marché rappellent l'architecture à l'ordre, obligeant tous ceux qui ne se soucient pas du réchauffement de la planète à cesser de gaspiller les matériaux et l'énergie parce que cela commence vraiment à coûter trop cher. Ce que vos poumons et vos yeux ne vous disent pas, votre porte-monnaie le fera.

[1] http://blog.archpaper.com/wordpress/archives/29467, consulté le 12 janvier 2012.

[2] « Face au boom des panneaux solaires, Londres coupe de moitié les subventions », *Le Monde*, 27 décembre 2011.

[3] « George Osborne's false economy is the death of greenest government ever », www.guardian.co.uk/environment/damian-carrington-blog/2011/nov/29/green-autumn-statement-osborne-economy-environment, consulté le 12 janvier 2012.

[4] « The Problem with Biofuels », *The Washington Post*, éditorial, 27 février 2008, http://www.washingtonpost.com/wp-dyn/content/article/2008/02/26/AR2008022602827.html, consulté le 16 janvier 2012.

[5] Nate Berg, « Why the Shenzhen and Hong Kong Biennale Rejected Sustainability as a Theme », http://www.theatlanticcities.com/arts-and-lifestyle/2011/12/why-hong-kong-shenzhen-bi-city-biennale-rejected-sustainability-theme/790/, consulté le 12 janvier 2012.

[6] http://www.comarchitect.org/WebHelp/9_sustainable_development_definition.htm, consulté le 12 janvier 2012.

[7] http://www.holcimfoundation.org/T700/HolcimFoundationorigins.htm, consulté le 16 janvier 2012.

[8] http://www.gccds.org/buildings/patty/patty.html, consulté le 16 janvier 2012.

[9] http://www.olafureliasson.net/studio.html, consulté le 17 janvier 2012.

[10] http://www.kongehuset.no/c27262/nyhet/vis.html?tid=92483, consulté le 16 janvier 2012.

ATELIERS 115

Ateliers 115 Architectes
115 Avenue Jean-Baptiste Clément
92100 Boulogne
France

Tel: +33 1 41 10 00 00
Fax: +33 1 49 09 01 48
E-mail: contact@ateliers115.fr
Web: www.ateliers115.fr

ION ENESCU, the architect of the Green Office (published here), was born in Bucharest, Romania, in 1951. He received his diploma from the Ion Mincu Superior School of Architecture and Urbanism (Bucharest, 1976). He worked in Romania from 1976 to 1988, and then as an architect with Atelier 2M (Paris, 1988–97), which had been created in 1967 by Daniel Montaut. Enescu remained as an Associated Architect and Manager with Atelier 2M, which changed its name to Ateliers 115 in 2010. The firm presently has about 40 employees and is directed by Daniel Montaut, Ion Enescu, Jean-Baptiste Montaut, and their Associates Jean-Claude Martinez and Hervé Outters. Recent and current work of the office includes the AFNOR Headquarters (Saint-Denis, 2002; extension, 2010); EADS Research Center (Suresnes, 2005); Le Crystalys (Vélizy-Villacoublay, 2007); NVH Building (Neuilly-sur-Seine, 2007); the Green Office (Meudon, 2009–11, published here); and the Cœur d'Orly Building B2 (Orly, 2012), all in France.

ION ENESCU, Architekt des Green Office (hier vorgestellt), wurde 1951 in Bukarest, Rumänien, geboren. Sein Diplom absolvierte er an der Ion-Mincu-Hochschule für Architektur und Stadtplanung (Bukarest, 1976). Von 1976 bis 1988 arbeitete er in Rumänien, später als Architekt bei Atelier 2M (Paris, 1988–97), einem 1967 von Daniel Montaut gegründeten Büro. Enescu blieb als assoziierter Architekt und Manager bei Atelier 2M. Seit 2010 firmiert das Büro unter dem Namen Ateliers 115. Derzeit beschäftigt es 40 Mitarbeiter unter Leitung von Daniel Montaut, Ion Enescu, Jean-Baptiste Montaut und den assoziierten Architekten Jean-Claude Martinez und Hervé Outters. Jüngere und aktuelle Projekte des Büros sind unter anderem: Hauptniederlassung AFNOR (Saint-Denis, 2002, Erweiterung 2010), EADS Forschungszentrum (Suresnes, 2005), Le Crystalys (Vélizy-Villacoublay, 2007), NVH-Gebäude (Neuilly-sur-Seine, 2007), Green Office (Meudon, 2009–11, hier vorgestellt) sowie das Cœur-d'Orly-Gebäude B2 (Orly, 2012), alle in Frankreich.

ION ENESCU, l'architecte du Green Office (publié ici), est né à Bucarest en 1951. Il est diplômé de l'Université d'architecture et d'urbanisme Ion Mincu (Bucarest, 1976). Il a d'abord travaillé en Roumanie de 1976 à 1988, puis avec Atelier 2M (Paris, 1988–97), créé en 1967 par Daniel Montaut. Il est resté l'un des architectes associés et gérants de l'agence, rebaptisée Ateliers 115 en 2010. La société compte aujourd'hui près de 40 employés et est dirigée par Daniel Montaut, Ion Enescu, Jean-Baptiste Montaut et leurs associés Jean-Claude Martinez et Hervé Outters. Leurs réalisations récentes et en cours comprennent le siège de l'AFNOR (Saint-Denis, 2002 ; extension en 2010) ; le Centre de recherches EADS (Suresnes, 2005) ; l'immeuble de bureaux Le Crystalys (Vélizy-Villacoublay, 2007) ; l'immeuble NVH (Neuilly-sur-Seine, 2007) ; le Green Office (Meudon, 2009–11, publié ici) et le bâtiment B2 de l'ensemble le Cœur d'Orly (Orly, 2012), toutes en France.

GREEN OFFICE

Meudon, France, 2009–11

*Address: 11 Avenue du Maréchal Juin, Meudon 92190, near Paris, France
Area: 21 700 m². Client: Bouygues Immoblier for STERIA
Cost: not disclosed Collaboration: Florian Texier, Franck Françoise,
Nicolas Vignau (all with Ateliers 115)*

The outstanding feature of this office building is its capacity to generate more energy than it consumes: 62 kWh/m² consumed versus 64 kWh/m² generated per year with photovoltaic panels and a cogeneration (CHP) system. A north–south orientation optimizes natural light and avoids excessive heat gain. The basic 13.5-meter width of the building allows users to benefit from available daylight. There are no spaces in the building without windows. Air conditioning is not used in the structure, but façade glazing and density were carefully calculated to limit solar gain. Reinforced-concrete construction with 20 centimeters of insulation, double-pane glazing that is operable where required, suspended fans to encourage air circulation, and a green wall on the west side, are some of the features designed to control energy consumption and induce user comfort. The materials used in the building, including wood, were selected for their environmental sustainability.

Schlüsselmerkmal des Bürogebäudes ist seine positive Energiebilanz: Einem Jahresverbrauch von 62 kWh/m² stehen 64 kWh/m² Energiegewinn aus einer Photovoltaikanlage und Kraft-Wärme-Kopplung (KWK) gegenüber. Die Nord-Süd-Ausrichtung sorgt für optimale Tageslichtnutzung und vermeidet übermäßigen Solargewinn. Dank einer Grundbreite von 13,5 m der Baukörper profitieren die Nutzer vom verfügbaren Tageslicht; im gesamten Gebäude gibt es keine fensterlosen Zonen. Auf Klimatisierung des Baus wurde verzichtet, doch Verglasung und Fassadenstärke wurden sorgsam auf eine Minimierung des Solargewinns zugeschnitten. Energiesparende und raumklimaverbessernde Maßnahmen sind unter anderem die Stahlbetonkonstruktion mit 20 cm starker Dämmung, Isolierverglasung mit teilweise zu öffnenden Fenstern, Deckenventilatoren zur Verbesserung der Durchlüftung sowie eine begrünte Wand an der Westseite des Baus. Die Materialien für den Innenausbau, darunter Holz, wurden nach Nachhaltigkeit gewählt.

La caractéristique la plus remarquable de cet immeuble de bureaux est sa capacité à produire plus d'énergie qu'il n'en consomme : 64 kW/h/m² contre 62 kW/h/m² par an grâce à des panneaux photovoltaïques et un système de cogénération (PCCE). L'orientation nord-sud permet d'optimiser l'éclairage naturel et d'éviter tout gain excessif de chaleur. La largeur de base de 13,5 m du bâtiment permet à ses occupants de profiter de la lumière du jour. On n'y trouve aucun espace dénué de fenêtres. Il n'y a pas d'air conditionné, mais le vitrage des façades et la densité ont été calculés soigneusement pour limiter l'apport solaire. La construction en béton renforcé avec une couche isolante de 20 cm, le double-vitrage qui peut être ouvert au besoin, les ventilateurs au plafond pour favoriser la circulation de l'air et un mur végétal du côté ouest ne sont que quelques-uns des moyens trouvés pour réguler la consommation d'énergie et créer du confort pour les utilisateurs. Les matériaux utilisés, dont le bois, ont été choisis pour leur durabilité environnementale.

The main qualities of this structure lie in its efficiency. Its clean, rectilinear design does not break new ground, but holds its own.

Die große Stärke dieses Gebäudes liegt in seiner Effizienz. Der schlichte, geradlinige Entwurf ist nicht bahnbrechend, weiß sich jedoch zu behaupten.

La principale qualité de la construction est son efficacité. Les lignes pures et rectilignes du design n'ont rien de réellement innovant, mais l'ensemble est honorable.

An aerial photo of the building and a plan show the main volume and courtyards of the structure. The roofs are covered with photovoltaic panels.

Eine Luftaufnahme und ein Grundriss zeigen den zentralen Baukörper mit seinen Innenhöfen. Die Dachflächen werden für Photovoltaikanlagen genutzt.

La photo aérienne du bâtiment et le plan montrent le volume principal et les cours de la structure. Les toits sont recouverts de panneaux photo-voltaïques.

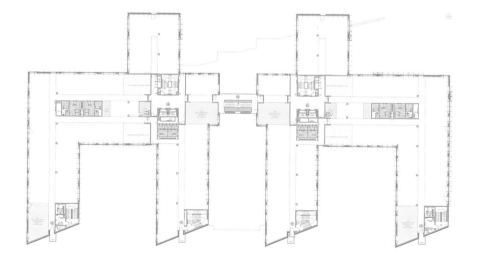

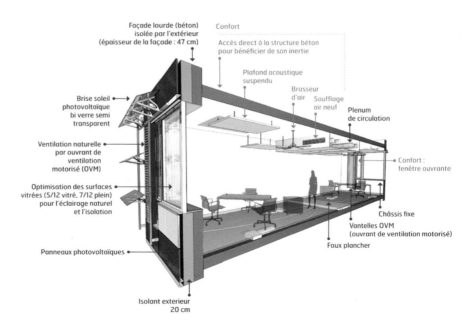

Façade lourde (béton)
isolée par l'extérieur
(épaisseur de la façade : 47 cm)

Confort

Accès direct à la structure béton
pour bénéficier de son inertie

Plafond acoustique
suspendu

Brasseur
d'air

Souffalge
air neuf

Plenum
de circulation

Brise soleil
photovoltaïque
bi verre semi
transparent

Ventilation naturelle
par ouvrant de
ventilation
motorisé (OVM)

Optimisation des surfaces
vitrées (5/12 vitré, 7/12 plein)
pour l'éclairage naturel
et l'isolation

Confort :
fenêtre ouvrante

Châssis fixe

Vantelles OVM
(ouvrant de ventilation motorisé)

Panneaux photovoltaïques

Faux plancher

Isolant exterieur
20 cm

A drawing (right) explains the strategy of the architects to protect the interiors from excessive heat or cold, reducing energy consumption. Below, a terrace with a large overhanging canopy.

Die Zeichnung rechts illustriert planerische Maßnahmen zum Schutz vor übermäßigem Aufheizen oder Auskühlen der Räume und damit zur Senkung des Energieverbrauchs. Unten eine überdachte Terrasse.

Le schéma (à droite) montre la stratégie adoptée par les architectes pour protéger l'intérieur des bâtiments de la chaleur et du froid en réduisant la consommation d'énergie. Ci-dessous, une terrasse sous un vaste toit en surplomb.

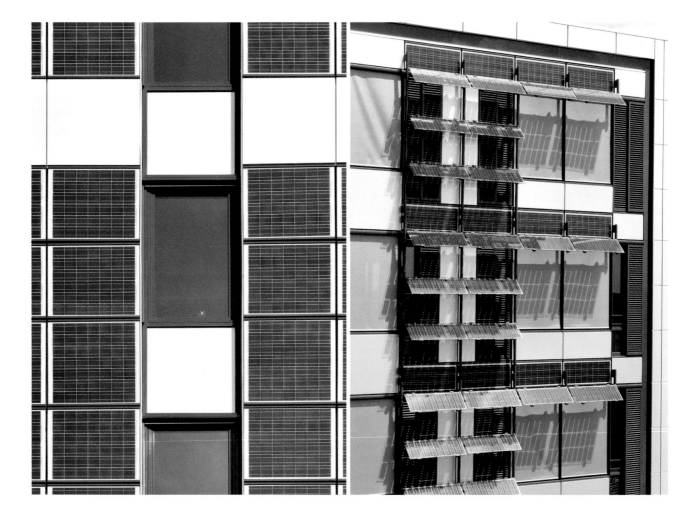

Images and drawings show the use of photovoltaic panels on the façades of the buildings. Right, vertical gardens also insulate the building at some point, and add to its aesthetic appeal.

Aufnahmen und Zeichnungen veranschaulichen die Nutzung der Fassaden des Gebäudes für Photovoltaikmodule. Rechts im Bild vertikale Gärten, die auch zur Dämmung sowie zum ästhetischen Reiz des Baus beitragen.

Photos et schémas montrent l'utilisation des panneaux photovoltaïques sur les façades. À droite, le jardin vertical contribue dans une certaine mesure à l'isolation du bâtiment et ajoute à son intérêt esthétique.

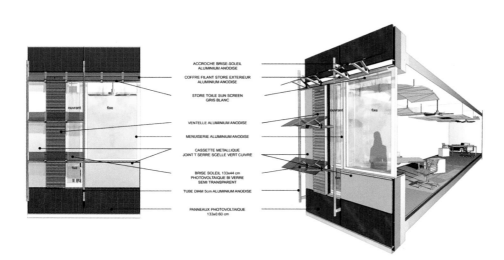

ACCROCHE BRISE-SOLEIL
ALUMINIUM ANODISE

COFFRE FILANT STORE EXTERIEUR
ALUMINIUM ANODISE

STORE TOILE SUN SCREEN
GRIS BLANC

VENTELLE ALUMINIUM ANODISE

MENUISERIE ALUMINIUM ANODISE

CASSETTE METALLIQUE
JOINT T SERRE SCELLE VERT CUIVRE

BRISE SOLEIL 133x44 cm
PHOTOVOLTAIQUE BI VERRE
SEMI TRANSPARENT

TUBE DIAM 5cm ALUMINIUM ANODISE

PANNEAUX PHOTOVOLTAIQUE
133x0.60 cm

ouvrant   fixe

HAGY BELZBERG

Belzberg Architects
2919 ½ Main Street
Santa Monica, CA 90405
USA

Tel: +1 310 453 9611
Fax: +1 310 453 9166
E-mail: hb@belzbergarchitects.com
Web: www.belzbergarchitects.com

HAGY BELZBERG received his M.Arch degree from the Harvard GSD and began his professional career with explorations of non-standardized construction methodology involving digital manufacturing. In 2000, he was awarded the contract to design the interior space of Frank Gehry's Walt Disney Concert Hall, where he utilized digital machining and prefabrication to work within the complex existing structure. In 2008, he was selected as an "Emerging Voice" by the Architectural League of New York. His work includes the Los Angeles Museum of the Holocaust (Los Angeles, California, 2003–10, published here); 20th Street Offices (Santa Monica, California, 2009); Kona Residence (Kona, Hawaii, 2010); 9800 Wilshire Boulevard Offices (Beverly Hills, California, 2012); City of Hope Cancer Research Museum (Duarte, California, 2013); and the Occidental College Center for Global Affairs (Los Angeles, California, 2013), all in the USA.

HAGY BELZBERG schloss sein Studium mit einem M.Arch am Harvard GSD ab und begann seine Laufbahn mit Forschungen zu Konstruktionsmethoden mit nicht-standardisierten Bauteilen und digitaler Fertigung. 2000 gewann er die Ausschreibung für den Innenausbau der Walt Disney Concert Hall von Frank Gehry, wo er mit digitalen Fertigungsmethoden und digitaler Vorfertigung arbeitete, um dem komplexen Bau gerecht zu werden. 2008 wurde er vom Architektenverband New York als „Neues Talent" ausgezeichnet. Zu seinen Projekten zählen das Holocaust-Museum in Los Angeles (Los Angeles, Kalifornien, 2003–10, hier vorgestellt), Büros an der 20th Street (Santa Monica, Kalifornien, 2009), die Villa Kona (Kona, Hawaii, 2010), Büros am 9800 Wilshire Boulevard (Beverly Hills, Kalifornien, 2012), das City of Hope Museum für Krebsforschung (Duarte, Kalifornien, 2013) und das Occidental College am Center for Global Affairs (Los Angeles, Kalifornien, 2013), alle in den USA.

HAGY BELZBERG a obtenu son M.Arch à la Harvard GSD et a débuté sa carrière en explorant les méthodologies de construction non standardisées faisant intervenir la fabrication numérique. En 2000, il reçoit commande de l'intérieur de la salle de concerts Walt Disney conçue par Frank Gehry et il a recours à l'usinage numérique et à la préfabrication pour son travail dans la structure existante complexe. En 2008, il fait partie des « voix émergeantes » sélectionnées par la Ligue architecturale de New York. Ses réalisations comprennent le musée de l'Holocauste de Los Angeles (2003–10, publié ici) ; les bureaux de la 20th Street (Santa Monica, Californie, 2009) ; la résidence Kona (Kona, Hawaii, 2010) ; les bureaux du 9800 Wilshire Boulevard (Beverly Hills, Californie, 2012) ; le musée de la recherche sur le Cancer City of Hope (Duarte, Californie, 2013) et le Center for Global Affairs du Occidental College (Los Angeles, 2013), toutes aux États-Unis.

LOS ANGELES
MUSEUM OF THE HOLOCAUST

Los Angeles, California, USA, 2003–10

*Address: 100 S. The Grove Drive, Los Angeles, CA 90036, USA, tel: +1 323 651 3704, www.lamoth.org
Area: 1394 m². Client: E. Randol Schoenberg. Cost: $14.8 million*

The site area of the museum, including its green roof, is just under 3000 square meters. Seen from above, the structure appears essentially as a series of paths and low walls.

Die bebaute Fläche des Museums einschließlich des begrünten Dachs beläuft sich auf knapp 3000 m². Von oben erscheint der Bau als Netzwerk aus Wegen und niedrigen Mauern.

La surface du musée avec son toit végétalisé, atteint presque 3000 m². Vue du haut, la structure semble essentiellement composée de sentiers et de murs bas.

An entrance appears as hardly more than a slit in the earth reached by a sloped concrete and glass-lined walkway.

Der Eingang ist optisch kaum mehr als ein Einschnitt im Gelände, der über einen abschüssigen Betonplattenweg mit beidseitigen Fensterbändern erschlossen wird.

L'entrée semble juste une fente dans la terre où l'on pénètre par une chaussée en pente de béton doublé de verre.

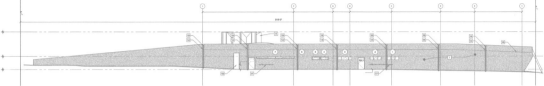

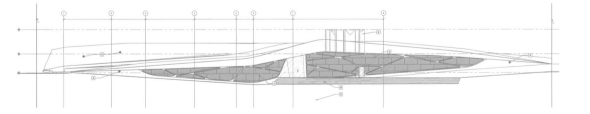

Completed in November of 2010, the new building for the **LOS ANGELES MUSEUM OF THE HOLOCAUST** is located within a public park adjacent to the existing Los Angeles Holocaust Memorial in Los Angeles. The museum is dedicated to commemoration and education, providing free education to the entire community with special consideration to underserved and underfunded schools, as well as to the Greater Los Angeles school system. The museum has one of the largest green roofs in Southern California and was certified LEED Gold by the US Green Building Council. The structure is embedded into the park landscape, allowing the green roof to occupy a maximum amount of area and providing thermal insulation. The green roof is entirely watered using an underground source. Exterior lighting comes from off-the-grid LED solar light poles that save as much as 75% in energy consumption. Products with recycled content account for 20% of the material costs. Embedded rebars include 80% recycled content for example. Over 75% of the building benefits from natural daylight and views to the outdoors. The land, owned by the city of Los Angeles, was donated solely because of the subterranean design scheme. The architect concludes: "The choice to use sustainability as a fundamental conceptual element rather than a supplemental one allowed the site, building, and community to work in tandem and, ultimately, made the project more effective in its mission as an educational and cultural institution."

Das **HOLOCAUST-MUSEUM IN LOS ANGELES**, fertiggestellt im November 2010, liegt in einem Park in unmittelbarer Nachbarschaft zum Holocaust Memorial in Los Angeles. Das Museum versteht sich als Gedächtnisstätte und bietet Bildungsprogramme an, darunter kostenfreie Veranstaltungen für kommunale Einrichtungen, insbesondere für Schulen mit geringem kulturellen Angebot und Schulen aus dem Großraum Los Angeles. Das Museum mit einer der größten begrünten Dachanlagen Südkaliforniens wurde mit einem LEED-Zertifikat in Gold ausgezeichnet. Das Dach des in den Park gebetteten Gebäudes nimmt einen Großteil der bebauten Fläche ein und sorgt zugleich für Wärmedämmung. Das begrünte Dach wird ausschließlich mit Grundwasser bewässert. Vom Stromnetz unabhängige LED-Solar-Lichtsäulen sorgen für Licht im Außenraum, wodurch der Energieverbrauch um bis zu 75% gesenkt werden konnte. 20% des Budgets entfiel auf recycelte Baumaterialien. So bestehen die integrierten Bewehrungsstäbe aus 80% Recyclingmaterial. Über 75% des Gebäudes werden mit Tageslicht versorgt und bieten Ausblick in die Umgebung. Das städtische Baugelände wurde nur wegen der unterirdischen Planung der Anlage freigegeben. Der Architekt schreibt: „Die Entscheidung für Nachhaltigkeit war zentrales Element unseres Konzepts statt ein nachträglicher Gedanke. Sie ermöglichte das Zusammenspiel von Gelände, Gebäude und Kommune. Letztendlich sorgt sie dafür, dass das Projekt effektiver als Bildungs- und Kulturstätte arbeiten kann."

Achevé en novembre 2010, le nouveau bâtiment du **MUSÉE DE L'HOLOCAUSTE DE LOS ANGELES** est situé dans un jardin public adjacent au mémorial de l'Holocauste. Il est consacré à la commémoration et à l'éducation et propose des cours gratuits à l'ensemble de la communauté, en prenant spécialement en considération les écoles défavorisées et sous-financées, ainsi que le système scolaire du grand Los Angeles. Le musée possède l'un des plus vastes toits végétalisés du Sud de la Californie et a été certifié LEED or par l'US Green Building Council. La structure a été enterrée afin que le toit occupe l'espace maximal, tout en assurant l'isolation thermique. Sa végétation est entièrement irriguée par une source souterraine. L'éclairage extérieur est assuré par des lampadaires solaires à LED non raccordés au réseau qui permettent d'économiser jusqu'à 75 % d'énergie. Les produits recyclables représentent 20 % des frais de matériel. Les barres d'armature enterrées sont recyclables à 80 %. Plus de 75 % du bâtiment reçoit la lumière du jour et a vue sur l'extérieur. Le terrain, propriété de la ville de Los Angeles, a uniquement été donné pour le concept souterrain. L'architecte conclut : « Le choix de la durabilité comme élément conceptuel fondamental, plutôt que simplement en complément, a permis de travailler en tandem au site, à la construction et à la communauté pour rendre finalement le projet plus efficace dans sa mission d'institution culturelle et éducative. »

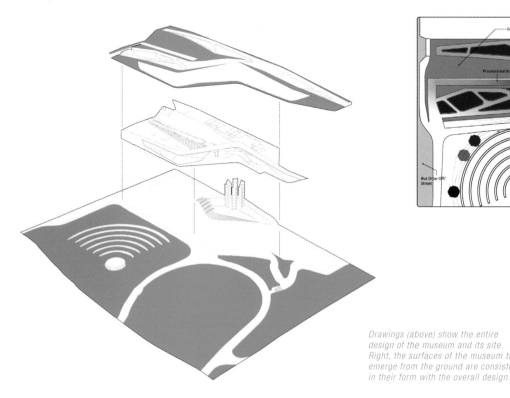

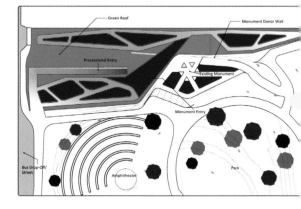

Die Gestaltung von Museumsbau und Gelände ist an den Zeichnungen oben ablesbar. Die aus dem Boden aufsteigenden Fassaden des Baus fügen sich optisch schlüssig in den Gesamtentwurf.

Drawings (above) show the entire design of the museum and its site. Right, the surfaces of the museum that emerge from the ground are consistent in their form with the overall design.

Les plans (ci-dessus) montrent l'ensemble du musée et du site. À droite, les formes des surfaces qui émergent du sol correspondent au design global.

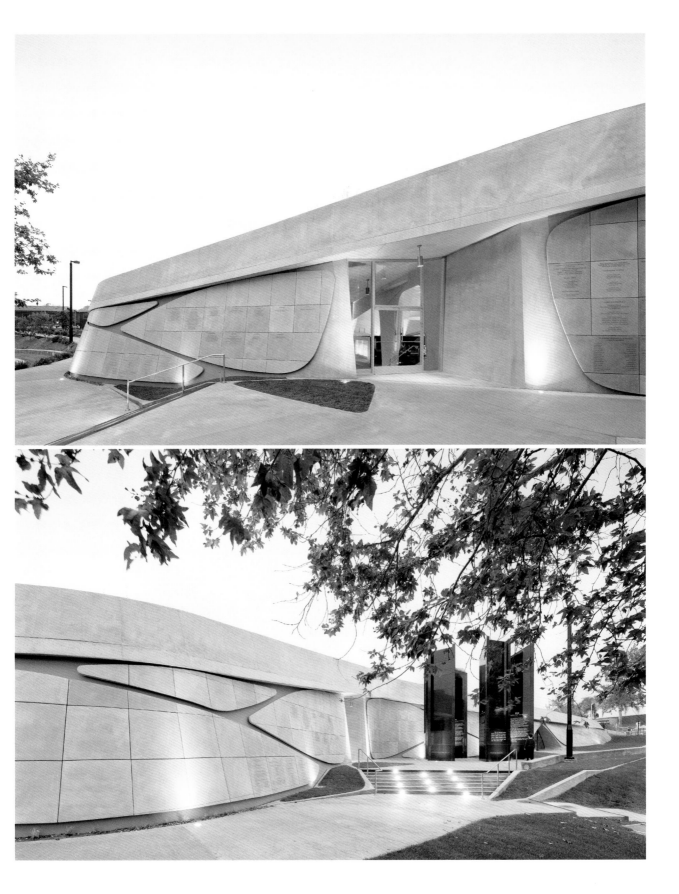

Interior views show an elegant use of concrete and glass, with an intentional, subterranean appearance in keeping with the subject of the institution.

Der elegante Einsatz von Beton und Glas wird an diesen Innenansichten deutlich. Die spürbare Absenkung des Baus unter die Erde korrespondiert atmosphärisch mit der thematischen Ausrichtung des Museums.

Ces vues de l'intérieur témoignent d'un emploi plein d'élégance du béton et du verre, l'aspect délibérément souterrain correspondant à l'objet de l'institution.

Displays are integrated into the volumes of the structure: here, an entrance ramp is visible on the left of the image.

Präsentationsflächen wurden zum Teil als Einbauten in den Baukörper integriert. Links im Bild eine Zugangsrampe.

Des écrans sont intégrés aux volumes de la structure : on voit ici une rampe d'entrée à gauche de la photo.

The continuous concrete walls have openings that allow natural light into the gallery or lobby spaces, as seen in these images.

Die als Kontinuum gestalteten Beton-wände sind mit Öffnungen durchsetzt, durch die Tageslicht in Galerien und Foyers fällt, wie hier zu sehen.

Les murs ininterrompus de béton sont percés d'ouvertures qui font entrer la lumière du jour dans le musée ou forment des espaces publics comme on le voit ici.

BEN WOOD STUDIO SHANGHAI

Ben Wood Studio Shanghai
Unit 302, Building 28, Xintiandi
119 Ma Dang Road
Shanghai 200021
China

Tel: +86 21 6336 5183
Fax: +86 21 6336 5182
E-mail: jwei@studioshanghai.co
Web: www.studioshanghai.co

Benjamin Wood received his M.Arch from MIT in 1984. His first commission in China was Xintiandi, a cultural entertainment district in Shanghai. The project received a 2003 Award of Excellence from the Urban Land Institute. His most significant contribution to a major project outside of China was as the Chief Architect of the 64 000-seat New Soldier Field in Chicago, co-designed with his former partner Carlos Zapata. Following the completion of the stadium, he set up a full-time design studio in Shanghai. His Associate **DELPHINE YIP-HORSFIELD**, born in 1973 in Hong Kong, became his Partner in the firm in 2005. Yip received her M.Arch degree from the Harvard GSD (1999), and worked at Tsao & McKown (New York, 1998), and then at Wood & Zapata in Boston (1999–2000), before joining Wood & Zapata, Shanghai, in 2000. She is the chief master planner and architect for Naked Home Village and Naked Stables Private Reserve (Moganshan, Zhejiang, 2010–11, published here). Their work includes Chongqing Tiandi (LEED Gold certified, Chongqing, 2008); Expo Housing Cultural Project (Shanghai, 2011); and Foshan Lingnan Tiandi (Foshan, 2012), all in China.

Benjamin Wood absolvierte seinen M.Arch 1984 am MIT. Sein erster Auftrag in China war die Planung des Kultur- und Einkaufsviertels Xintiandi in Shanghai (2003 mit dem Exzellenzpreis des Urban Land Institute ausgezeichnet). Woods wichtigste Beteiligung an einem Projekt außerhalb Chinas war die Planungsleitung des New Soldier Field in Chicago, einem Stadion mit 64 000 Plätzen (Entwurf mit Woods ehemaligem Partner Carlos Zapata). Nach Fertigstellung des Stadions gründete Wood sein Büro in Shanghai, das er in Vollzeit führt. **DELPHINE YIP-HORSFIELD**, geboren 1973 in Hongkong und zunächst assoziierte Architektin bei Wood, wurde 2005 Partnerin. Yip absolvierte ihren M.Arch am Harvard GSD (1999) und arbeitete für Tsao & McKown (New York, 1998) sowie für Wood & Zapata in Boston (1999–2000), ehe sie 2000 zu Wood & Zapata, Shanghai, wechselte. Sie ist leitende Architektin und Planerin für das Naked Home Village und die Naked Stables Private Reserve (Moganshan, Zhejiang, 2010–11, hier vorgestellt). Zu den Projekten des Büros zählen das Chongqing Tiandi (LEED-Zertifikat in Gold, Chongqing, 2008), ein Wohn- und Kulturprojekt für die Expo in Shanghai (Shanghai, 2011) sowie Foshan Lingnan Tiandi (Foshan, 2012), alle in China.

Benjamin Wood a obtenu son M.Arch au MIT en 1984. Sa première commande en Chine a été le district Xintiandi, un quartier de loisirs et de culture à Shanghai. Le projet a reçu en 2003 un prix d'excellence de l'Urban Land Institute. Sa principale contribution à un projet d'envergure hors de Chine a été la direction architecturale du stade de 64 000 places New Soldier Field à Chicago, conçu en coopération avec son partenaire d'alors Carlos Zapata. Après le stade, il a ouvert une agence de design à Shanghai. Son associée **DELPHINE YIP-HORSFIELD**, née en 1973 à Hong Kong, est sa partenaire depuis 2005. Elle a obtenu son M.Arch à la Harvard GSD (1999) et a travaillé chez Tsao & McKown (New York, 1998), puis chez Wood & Zapata à Boston (1999–2000) avant de rejoindre Wood & Zapata à Shanghai en 2000. Elle est la responsable en chef de la planification et l'architecte du complexe hôtelier Naked Home Village et Naked Stables Private Reserve (Moganshan, Zhejiang, 2010–11, publié ici). Leurs réalisations comprennent l'ensemble Chongqing Tiandi (certifié LEED or, Chongqing, 2008); un projet culturel d'habitat pour l'Expo (Shanghai, 2011) et le complexe Foshan Lingnan Tiandi (Foshan, 2012), toutes en Chine.

NAKED STABLES PRIVATE RESERVE

Moganshan, Zhejiang Province, China, 2010–11

*Address: No. 37, Shangxiazhuang Village, Paitou Town, Deqing County, Zhejiang
Province, China, www.nakedretreats.cn/naked-stables-private-reserve/. Area: 14 120 m²
Client: Naked Retreats. Cost: not disclosed*

This luxury nature retreat located in a forested valley about two and a half hours' drive from Shanghai was designed with an "uncompromising focus on authentic sustainability and green building design." The aim was to become the first resort of its size in Asia to achieve LEED Platinum certification. The 24-hectare domain of the **NAKED STABLES PRIVATE RESERVE** includes 121 rooms situated in 30 Tree Top Villas and 40 Earth Huts, three restaurants, and a conference center. There are also a spa and wellness center, three swimming pools, a fully equipped equestrian center, a pottery studio, bamboo gallery, teahouse, project museum, and an amphitheater hosting concerts and cultural performances. Prefabricated structural insulated panels (SIP) were used for the Tree Top Villas because of their well-documented environmental efficiency. The Earth Huts were built with rammed-earth walls employing local soil, rebars, cement, and insulation. Both the villas and the huts have their own energy meters so that guests can monitor their own consumption. Electric vehicles are used to transport guests around the domain. The resort is dedicated to the preservation of flora and fauna in its forested region.

Das naturnahe Luxushotel liegt in einem bewaldeten Tal zweieinhalb Autostunden von Shanghai und wurde mit „entschiedenem Augenmerk auf echte Nachhaltigkeit und grüne Bauplanung" konzipiert. Ziel war es, als erste Hotelanlage Asiens dieser Größenordnung ein LEED-Zertifikat in Platin zu erreichen. Das 24 ha große Anwesen des **NAKED STABLES PRIVATE RESERVE** umfasst 30 Tree Top Villas und 40 Earth Huts mit insgesamt 121 Zimmern, drei Restaurants und einem Konferenzzentrum. Zum Komplex gehören außerdem ein Spa und Wellnesscenter, drei Swimmingpools, eine voll ausgestattete Reithalle, eine Töpferwerkstatt, eine Bambusgalerie, ein Teehaus, ein Projektmuseum und ein Amphitheater für Konzerte und Kulturveranstaltungen. Bei den Tree Top Villas wurden SIP-Paneele wegen ihrer hervorragenden Umwelteigenschaften verbaut. Die Earth Huts wurden in Stampflehmbauweise aus lokalem Lehm in Kombination mit Bewehrungsstäben, Zement und Dämmmaterialien errichtet. Villas und Hütten sind mit individuellen Energiezählern ausgestattet, sodass die Gäste ihren eigenen Verbrauch verfolgen können. Auf dem Gelände steht den Gästen ein Transportservice mit Elektrofahrzeugen zur Verfügung. Die Anlage hat sich bewusst dem Schutz von Flora und Fauna auf dem bewaldeten Anwesen verschrieben.

Cette luxueuse retraite en pleine nature, nichée au cœur d'une vallée boisée à environ deux heures et demi de Shanghai a été conçue « sans compromis sur la durabilité authentique et la conception verte ». L'objectif était de construire le premier complexe de cette taille certifié LEED platine en Asie. Le domaine **NAKED STABLES PRIVATE RESERVE** de 24 hectares se compose de 121 chambres dans 30 « villas » au sommet d'arbres et 40 « cabanes » de terre, 3 restaurants et un centre de conférences. Il comprend également un spa et un centre de bien-être, trois piscines, un centre équestre parfaitement équipé, un atelier de poterie, une galerie de bambou, une maison de thé, un musée en projet et un amphithéâtre qui accueille des concerts et événements culturels. Des panneaux structurels isolants (SIP) préfabriqués ont été utilisés pour les villas dans les arbres en raison de leur efficacité environnementale bien documentée. Les cabanes de terre se composent de murs en pisé construits avec de la terre locale, de barres d'armature, de ciment et de matériaux isolants. Villas et cabanes ont toutes leur propre compteur afin que les hôtes puissent réguler leur consommation d'énergie. Les clients sont transportés sur le domaine dans des véhicules électriques. Le complexe tout entier est voué à la sauvegarde de la faune et de la flore dans la région forestière.

As can be seen in the drawing below, and in the photos, this resort complex is inserted into a hilly, wooded site, with a number of residences cantilevered out over the slopes.

Wie die Zeichnung (unten) und Aufnahmen zeigen, liegt die Hotelanlage in einer bewaldeten Berglandschaft. Einige der Bauten kragen über den Abhang aus.

Comme on le voit sur le schéma ci-dessous et les photos, le complexe est niché parmi des collines boisées et bon nombre des logements sont construits en porte-à-faux par rapport aux pentes.

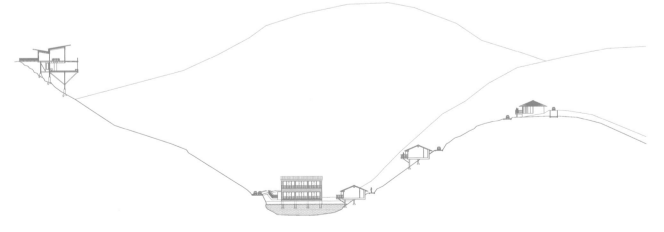

Interiors of a Tree Top Villa offer all the conveniences and comfort found in an urban hotel, but the residences are perched above the forest, as can be seen in the image on the right of a terrace at the Naked Leaf Spa.

Die Ausstattung der Tree Top Villas bietet den Komfort eines urbanen Hotels, obwohl die Hotelanlage über der Waldlandschaft schwebt, wie rechts der Blick auf eine Terrasse im Naked Leaf Spa belegt.

Les villas dans les arbres offrent à l'intérieur toutes les commodités et tout le confort d'un hôtel en ville, sauf qu'elles sont perchées en hauteur dans la forêt, comme on le voit sur la photo de droite d'une terrasse du spa Naked Leaf.

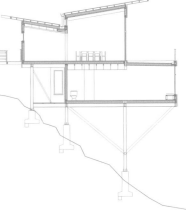

This page, a section drawing of a Tree Top Villa. Right page, plans show the basic, rectangular forms of the buildings.

Oben rechts der Querschnitt einer Tree Top Villa. Grundrisse (rechte Seite) zeigen die schlichte recht-eckige Grundform der Bauten.

Sur cette page, vue en coupe d'une villa dans un arbre. Page de droite, les plans montrent les formes rectan-gulaires de base des bâtiments.

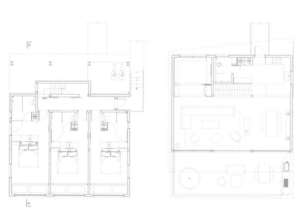
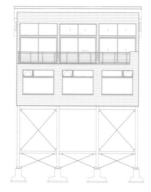
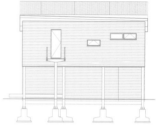

Right, a first-floor plan of the pavilion. Below, a Tree Top Villa terrace.

Rechts der Etagengrundriss eines
Pavillons auf Höhe des ersten Stocks.
Unten die Terrasse einer Treetop Villa.

À droite, plan du premier étage du
pavillon. Ci-dessous, terrasse d'une
villa dans un arbre.

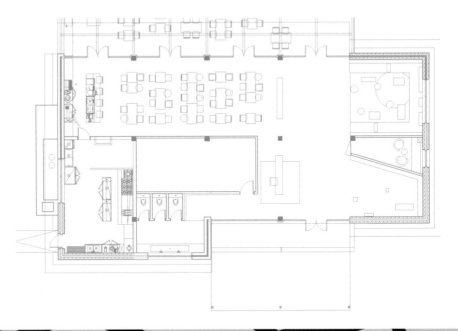

Above, the tea gallery. Right, a water-color plan of the entire complex.

Oben die sogenannte Tee-Galerie. Rechts eine aquarellierte Zeichnung der Gesamtanlage.

Ci-dessus, la galerie de thé. À droite, plan peint à l'aquarelle de l'ensemble du complexe.

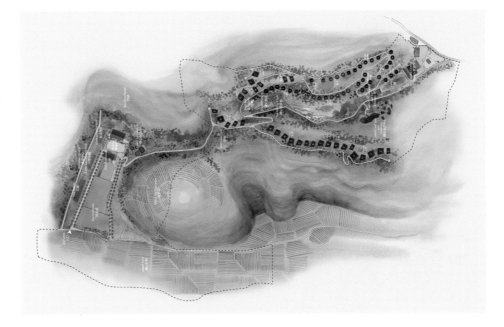

BIG

BIG
Bjarke Ingels Group
Nørrebrogade 66d, 2nd floor
2200 Copenhagen N
Denmark

Tel: +45 72 21 72 27 / Fax: +45 35 12 72 27
E-mail: big@big.dk / Web: www.big.dk

BJARKE INGELS was born in 1974 in Copenhagen. He graduated from the Royal Academy of Arts School of Architecture (Copenhagen, 1999) and attended the ETSAB School of Architecture (Barcelona). He created his own office in 2005 under the name Bjarke Ingels Group (BIG), after having cofounded PLOT Architects in 2001 and collaborated with Rem Koolhaas at OMA (Rotterdam). In 2004 he was awarded the Golden Lion at the Venice Biennale for the Stavanger Concert House. One of his latest completed projects, the Mountain (Copenhagen, Denmark, 2006–08), has received numerous awards including the World Architecture Festival Housing Award, Forum Aid Award, and the MIPIM Residential Development Award. **DAVID ZAHLE** is a Partner at BIG. His collaboration with Bjarke Ingels began in 2002 and he is overseeing the Amager Bakke Waste-to-Energy Plant published here. BIG is now led by eight Partners and has also opened an office in New York. The firm designed the Danish Expo Pavilion (Shanghai, China, 2010); the Superkilen Master Plan (Copenhagen, Denmark, 2011); Shenzhen International Energy Mansion (Shenzhen, China, 2013); the Danish Maritime Museum (Elsinore, Denmark, 2013); the Faroe Islands Education Center (Thorshavn, Faroe Islands, Denmark, 2014); the Amager Bakke Waste-to-Energy Plant (Copenhagen, Denmark, 2009–, published here); Tallinn Town Hall (Estonia); and the National Library of Astana (Kazakhstan).

BJARKE INGELS wurde 1974 in Kopenhagen geboren. Er schloss sein Studium an der Architekturfakultät der Königlichen Akademie der Künste ab (Kopenhagen, 1999) und besuchte die Architekturfakultät der ETSAB in Barcelona. 2005 gründete er sein eigenes Büro Bjarke Ingels Group (BIG), nachdem er 2001 PLOT Architects mitbegründet und Projekte mit Rem Koolhaas/OMA (Rotterdam) realisiert hatte. Für seinen Entwurf des Konzerthauses in Stavanger erhielt er 2004 auf der Biennale in Venedig den Goldenen Löwen. Eines seiner aktuellsten Projekte, Mountain (Kopenhagen, Dänemark, 2006–08) wurde mit zahlreichen Preisen ausgezeichnet, darunter dem World Architecture Festival Housing Award, dem Forum Aid Award und dem MIPIM Residential Development Award. **DAVID ZAHLE** ist Partner bei BIG. Er arbeitet seit 2002 mit Bjarke Ingels zusammen und leitet die Planung des hier vorgestellten Müllheizkraftwerks in Amager Bakke. BIG hat inzwischen acht Partner und unterhält ein Büro in New York. Das Team entwarf den Dänischen Pavillon für die Expo 2010 (Shanghai, China), den Masterplan für die Freifläche Superkilen (Kopenhagen, Dänemark, 2011), das Internationale Energiezentrum in Shenzhen (Shenzhen, China, 2013), das Dänische Schifffahrtsmuseum (Helsingør, Dänemark, 2013), das Bildungszentrum der Färöer-Inseln (Thorshavn, Färöer-Inseln, Dänemark, 2014), das Müllheizkraftwerk Amager Bakke (Kopenhagen, Dänemark, 2009–, hier vorgestellt), das Rathaus in Tallinn (Estland) sowie die Nationalbibliothek in Astana (Kasachstan).

BJARKE INGELS est né en 1974 à Copenhague. Il est diplômé de l'École d'architecture de l'Académie royale des beaux-arts (Copenhague, 1999) et a également suivi les cours de l'École d'architecture ETSAB (Barcelone). Il a ouvert son cabinet en 2005 sous le nom Bjarke Ingels Group (BIG), après avoir participé à la fondation de PLOT Architects en 2001 et collaboré avec Rem Koolhaas à OMA (Rotterdam). Il a reçu le Lion d'or 2004 à la Biennale de Venise pour la salle de concerts de Stavanger. L'un de ses derniers projets, les Mountain Dwellings (Copenhague, 2006–08), a reçu plusieurs récompenses dont le prix logement du World Architecture Festival, le prix Forum Aid et le prix MIPIM développement résidentiel. **DAVID ZAHLE** est l'un des partenaires de BIG. Il a rejoint l'agence en 2002 et supervise le Centre de transformation des déchets en énergie publié ici. BIG est actuellement dirigé par huit partenaires et a ouvert un bureau à New York. L'agence a conçu le Pavillon danois pour l'Exposition universelle de Shanghai (Shanghai, 2010) ; le plan directeur du site Superkilen (Copenhague, 2011) ; la Shenzhen International Energy Mansion (Shenzhen, Chine, 2013) ; le Musée maritime danois (Elseneur, Danemark, 2013) ; le Centre éducatif des îles Féroé (Thorshavn, îles Féroé, Danemark, 2014) ; le Centre de transformation des déchets en énergie d'Amager Bakke (Copenhague, 2009–, publié ici) ; l'hôtel de Ville de Tallinn (Estonie) et la bibliothèque nationale d'Astana (Kazakhstan).

AMAGER BAKKE
WASTE-TO-ENERGY PLANT

Copenhagen, Denmark, 2009

Address: Amagerforbrænding Kraftværksvej 31, 2300 Copenhagen, Denmark, tel: +45 32 68 93 00, www.amfor.dk
Area: 95 000 m² (building); 90 000 m² (landscape); 32 000 m² (roof + ski slope); 6500 m² (visitor center)
Client: Amagerforbraending. Cost: €460 million
Collaboration: realities:united (Interactive Façade), AKT (Façade and Structural Engineering),
Topotek/Man Made Land (Landscape), Glessner Group

This waste-to-energy plant, to be located on the outskirts of Copenhagen, is envisaged as a center for new recreational activities. The architects state: "Most of the recently built power plants are merely functional boxes, wrapped in an expensive gift paper. The main 'function' of the façade is to hide the fact that factories are having a serious image/branding problem. We want to do more than just create a beautiful skin around the factory. We want to add functionality! We propose a new breed of waste-to-energy plant, one that is economically, environmentally, and socially profitable." The design lifts one end of the structure to integrate the smokestack "into the overall architecture of the plant," and lowers another end to accommodate public access. A 6500-square-meter administrative and visitor center is integrated into the envelope of the structure. BIG suggests that the 32 000-square-meter roof of the plant should become an artificial ski slope, which would be "ecological and usable all year round."

Das am Stadtrand von Kopenhagen geplante Müllheizkraftwerk ist als Naherholungsgebiet konzipiert. Die Architekten erklären: „Die meisten kürzlich gebauten Kraftwerke sind rein funktionale ‚Boxen', verpackt in teures Geschenkpapier. Die zentrale ‚Funktion' dieser Fassaden liegt darin, zu kaschieren, dass diese Fabriken ein echtes Image-/Brandingproblem haben. Wir wollen mehr, als der Fabrik nur eine ästhetische Fassade zu geben. Wir wollen einen Zugewinn an Funktionalität! Unser Konzept für eine neue Generation von Müllheizkraftwerken ist in wirtschaftlicher, ökologischer und soziologischer Hinsicht profitabel." Der Entwurf integriert den Schornstein in die seitlich entsprechend hochgezogene „Gesamtarchitektur des Kraftwerks" und zieht eine andere Seite des Baus bis auf den Boden hinab. Dort ist die öffentliche Erschließung geplant. Unter der Hülle des Komplexes verbirgt sich außerdem ein 6500 m² großes Verwaltungs- und Besucherzentrum. BIG plant, das 32 000 m² große Dach des Kraftwerks als künstliche Skiabfahrt zu realisieren, die „ökologisch und das ganze Jahr über nutzbar" sein soll.

Le Centre de transformation des déchets en énergie, qui sera construit dans la banlieue de Copenhague, est aussi conçu comme un centre de nouvelles activités de loisirs. Pour les architectes : « Parmi les centrales électriques construites récemment, la plupart sont uniquement des « boîtes » fonctionnelles emballées dans un papier cadeau de grand prix. La principale "fonction" de la façade est de cacher que les usines ont un grave problème d'image de marque. Nous voulons faire plus que simplement imaginer une belle enveloppe autour de l'usine, nous voulons y ajouter une fonctionnalité nouvelle ! Nous nous proposons de créer une usine de retraitement de déchets d'un genre nouveau, à la fois économiquement, écologiquement et socialement rentable. » L'une des extrémités de la structure a été relevée pour intégrer la cheminée « à l'architecture globale de l'usine », tandis que l'autre a été abaissée pour loger l'accès au public. Un centre administratif et un espace ouvert au public de 6500 m² est inséré dans l'enveloppe de l'ensemble. BIG propose de transformer le toit de 32 000 m² en piste de ski artificielle, « écologique et utilisable toute l'année ».

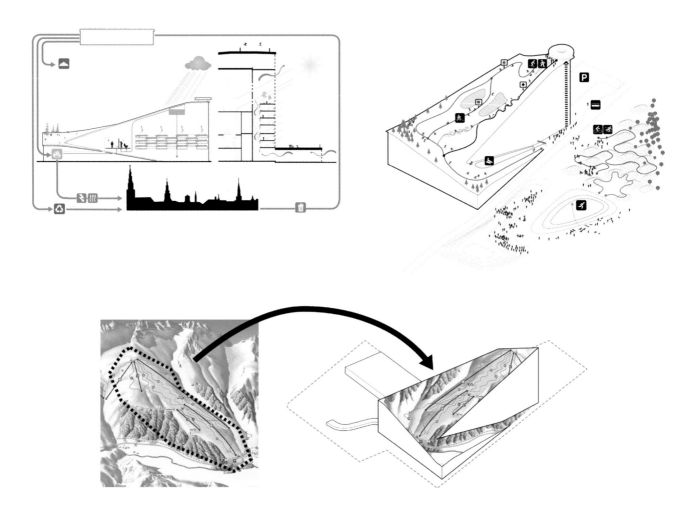

The waste-to-energy plant makes use of a considerable area that usually goes to waste—the roof—where here, skiers are depicted in winter. The energy process and ecological implication of the complex are seen in the drawings to the left.

Das Müllheizkraftwerk nutzt eine maßgebliche, üblicherweise unge-nutzte Fläche – das Dach. Dort sind auf dieser Simulation Skifahrer in einer Schneelandschaft zu sehen. Energieprozesse und ökologische Aspekte des Komplexes sind den Zeichnungen links zu entnehmen.

Le Centre de transformation des déchets en énergie exploite une surface considérable qui est généralement perdue : le toit, où des skieurs sont ici représentés en hiver. Le processus énergétique et les conséquences éco-logiques du complexe sont expliqués par les schémas à gauche.

The plant interiors make way for natural light, plants and, above all, public activity, quite the contrary of most waste-treatment plants.

Innen zeichnet sich das Kraftwerk durch einfallendes Tageslicht, Begrünung und öffentliche Zugänglichkeit aus – zweifellos ein Gegenentwurf zu den meisten herkömmlichen Müllverwertungsanlagen.

L'intérieur de l'usine est ouvert à la lumière naturelle, la végétation et, surtout, l'activité publique – contrairement à la plupart des usines de traitement des déchets.

Public spaces inside are imagined as being quite generous (above). Below, elevation drawings show the relation of the ski slope to the entire complex.

Öffentliche Bereiche im Innern sind großzügig geplant (oben). Aufrisse (unten) veranschaulichen das räumliche Verhältnis der Skiabfahrt zum Gesamtkomplex.

Les espaces publics de l'intérieur ont été conçus avec une grande générosité (ci-dessus). Ci-dessous, les plans en élévation montrent la piste de ski par rapport au complexe dans son ensemble.

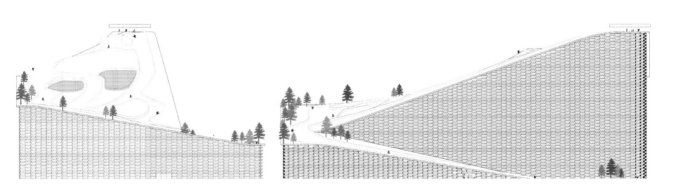

BNIM

BNIM
106 West 14th Street, Suite 200
Kansas City, MO 64105
USA

Tel: +1 816 783 1500 / Fax: +1 816 783 1501
Web: www.bnim.com

BNIM was founded in 1970 in Kansas City, and currently has offices there as well as in Houston, Des Moines, Los Angeles, and San Diego, with about 100 employees. The firm has established its presence in the area of sustainable design, community redevelopment, urban planning, campus master planning, and residential and corporate buildings. BNIM was granted the prestigious 2011 AIA Architecture Firm Award. **LAURA LESNIEWSKI** received her M.Arch degree from UC Berkeley. She was the project manager for the Omega Center for Sustainable Living (Rhinebeck, New York, 2007–09, published here), while McDowell led the design team. **STEVE MCDOWELL** received a Bachelor of Environmental Design degree from the University of Kansas, and is presently Director of Design at BNIM. He also was closely involved with the Omega Center. Aside from the Omega Center, BNIM's work includes the LEED Gold–certified JE Dunn Construction World Headquarters (Kansas City, 2009; with 360 Architecture); Kiowa County K-12 Schools (Greensburg, 2010); the Iowa Utilities Board Office of the Consumer Advocate (pending certification, Des Moines, 2011); the Todd Bolender Center for Dance and Creativity (Kansas City, 2011); and the Kauffmann Center for the Performing Arts (Kansas City, 2011; designed by Moshe Safdie and Associates, in collaboration with acoustician Yasuhisa Toyota, and BNIM as joint architect of record), all in the USA.

BNIM wurde 1970 in Kansas City gegründet, wo das Büro – neben Houston, Des Moines, Los Angeles und San Diego – Niederlassungen mit rund 100 Mitarbeitern betreibt. Profilieren konnte sich das Büro insbesondere in den Bereichen Nachhaltige Architektur, Sanierung von Stadtvierteln, Stadtplanung, der Masterplanung universitärer Campusanlagen sowie mit Wohn- und Bürobauten. 2011 wurde BNIM vom AIA mit dem renommierten Architecture Firm Award ausgezeichnet. **LAURA LES-NIEWSKI** absolvierte ihren M.Arch an der UC Berkeley. Sie war Projektleiterin des Omega Center for Sustainable Living (Rhinebeck, New York, 2007–09, hier vorgestellt), während McDowell das Entwurfsteam leitete. **STEVE MCDOWELL** absolvierte einen Bachelor in Umweltplanung an der University of Kansas und ist derzeit Entwurfsleiter bei BNIM. Auch er war maßgeblich bei der Planung des Omega Center beteiligt. Neben dem Omega Center realisierte BNIM unter anderem die Internationale Firmenzentrale des Bauunternehmens JE Dunn, LEED-Zertifikat in Gold (Kansas City, 2009, mit 360 Architecture), die Kiowa County K-12-Schulen (Greensburg, 2010), das Büro der Verbraucherzentrale Iowa, Abteilung Energieversorgung (Zertifizierungsprozess läuft, Des Moines, 2011), das Todd Bolender Center für Tanz und Kreativität (Kansas City, 2011) sowie das Kauffmann Center für Darstellende Künste (Kansas City, 2011, Entwurf von Moshe Safdie and Associates, in Zusammenarbeit mit Yasuhisa Toyota (Akustiker) und BNIM als offizieller Planungspartner), alle in den USA.

BNIM a été fondée en 1970 à Kansas City où l'agence a encore un bureau, ainsi qu'à Houston, Des Moines, Los Angeles et San Diego. Elle compte une centaine d'employés. Elle s'est imposée dans les secteurs du design durable, du redéveloppement communautaire, de l'urbanisme, de la planification générale de campus et des constructions résidentielles et commerciales. BNIM a reçu le prestigieux prix Architecture Firm Award de l'AIA en 2011. **LAURA LESNIEWSKI** a obtenu son M.Arch à l'université de Californie Berkeley. Elle a été chef de projet du Centre Omega pour l'intégration durable (Rhinebeck, New York, 2007–09, publié ici), tandis que McDowell dirigeait l'équipe design. **STEVE MCDOWELL** est titulaire d'un bachelor de design environnemental de l'université du Kansas ; il est actuellement directeur du design à BNIM. Il a également beaucoup participé au Centre Omega. Outre le Centre Omega, les réalisations de BNIM comprennent le siège mondial, certifié LEED or, de JE Dunn Construction (Kansas City, 2009 ; en collaboration avec 360 Architecture) ; le centre scolaire du comté de Kiowa (Greensburg, Kansas, 2010) ; l'immeuble de bureaux des services de défense des consommateurs (certification en cours, Des Moines, Iowa, 2011) ; le Centre Todd Bolender de la danse et de la créativité (Kansas City, 2011) et le Centre Kauffmann des arts du spectacle (Kansas City, 2011 ; design par Moshe Safdie and Associates, en collaboration avec l'acousticien Yasuhisa Toyota et BNIM en tant qu'architecte associé responsable), toutes aux États-Unis.

OMEGA CENTER
FOR SUSTAINABLE LIVING
Rhinebeck, New York, USA, 2007–09

Address: 150 Lake Drive, Rhinebeck, New York 12572, USA, tel: +1 845 266 4301, http://eomega.org/
Area: 581 m². Client: Omega Institute. Cost: $2.8 million

The Omega Institute was founded in 1977 with the ambitious goal: "To look everywhere for the most effective strategies and inspiring traditions that might help people bring more meaning and vitality into their lives." In 2006 they decided to develop a sustainable wastewater filtration facility using alternative treatment methods for their 79-hectare campus. The building designed by BNIM includes not only primary treatment facilities, but also a classroom and laboratory. Treated water is used for garden irrigation. The Omega Center was one of the winners of the AIA COTE Top Ten Green Projects Awards for 2010. Its sustainable features include its massing and solar orientation, natural ventilation, a geothermal heat pump, 100% of campus energy requirements from an off-site wind power source, 100% of the building's net annual energy produced by photovoltaic arrays at the facility, rainwater collection and reuse for toilet flushing, the on-site ecological wastewater treatment system that handles waste from more than 70 buildings on the campus, bioswales and native planting in the parking lot for on-site storm-water management, and the elimination of PVC, mercury, CFCs, HCFCs, neoprene, and other toxic building materials. Finally, salvaged or highly recycled materials were used to the greatest extent possible.

Das Omega Institute wurde 1977 mit dem ambitionierten Ziel gegründet, „nach den wirkungsvollsten Strategien und inspirierendsten traditionellen Lebensformen Ausschau zu halten, die sinn- und vitalitätsstiftend wirken können". 2006 beschloss das Institut, eine nachhaltige Abwasserfiltrationsanlage für ihren 79 ha großen Campus zu bauen, die nach ökologischen Prinzipien arbeitet. Im Neubau von BNIM sind nicht nur die Aufbereitungsanlagen untergebracht, sondern auch ein Seminarraum und ein Labor. Das aufbereitete Wasser wird zur Bewässerung der Grünanlagen genutzt. 2010 war das Omega Center unter den Preisträgern der „Top Ten Green Projects Awards" des Umweltkomitees (COTE) des AIA. Nachhaltige Aspekte des Projekts sind unter anderem: Masse und Ausrichtung des Baus, natürliche Durchlüftung, Erdwärmepumpe, Versorgung des Campus' zu 100% aus Windkraftanlagen an getrenntem Standort, Netto-Energiebedarf des Gebäudes zu 100% gedeckt mit einer angeschlossenen Solaranlage, Regenwassernutzung für Toilettenspülung, ökologische Abwasseraufbereitung vor Ort für über 70 Campusgebäude, biologische Drängräben, Begrünung des Parkplatzes mit einheimischen Pflanzen zur Verbesserung der Regenwasserversickerung sowie Verzicht auf beziehungsweise Entfernung von PVC, Quecksilber, FCKWs, Neopren und anderen giftigen Baumaterialien. Es wurden weitestgehend recycelte Baustoffe eingesetzt.

L'Institut Omega a été fondé en 1977 avec l'objectif ambitieux de « chercher en tous lieux les stratégies les plus efficaces et les traditions édifiantes susceptibles d'aider les gens à introduire plus de sens et de vitalité dans leurs vies ». En 2006, l'Institut décide de développer une installation durable de filtration des eaux usées qui utilise des méthodes de traitement alternatives pour son campus de 79 hectares. Le bâtiment créé par BNIM comporte une usine d'épuration primaire, mais aussi une salle de classe et un laboratoire. L'eau traitée est utilisée pour le jardin. Le Centre Omega a remporté l'un des prix du Top Ten Green Projects Awards du Comité pour l'environnement de l'AIA en 2010. Il doit notamment son caractère durable à sa concentration et son orientation en fonction du soleil, sa ventilation naturelle, une pompe à chaleur géothermique, une centrale électrique éolienne annexe qui couvre 100 % des besoins en énergie du campus, les panneaux solaires qui produisent 100 % de l'énergie annuelle nette du bâtiment, la récupération de l'eau de pluie et sa réutilisation pour les toilettes, le système de traitement écologique des eaux usées sur site qui gère les déchets de plus de 70 bâtiments du campus, des fossés végétalisés biologiques, des plantations locales sur le parking pour la gestion sur place des eaux pluviales et le refus du PVC, du mercure, des CFC, des HCFC, du néoprène ou de tout autre matériau de construction toxique. Les matériaux de récupération ou hautement recyclés ont été utilisés dans la plus grande mesure possible.

Despite its ambitious sustainability agenda and the use of reclaimed lumber for façades (above), the Omega Center projects the image of a modern facility, underlined by the building section perspective seen just above.

Trotz ambitionierter ökologischer Agenda und einer Fassadenverkleidung aus Altholz (oben) präsentiert sich das Omega Center als moderne Einrichtung, was der perspektivische Querschnitt bestätigt.

Malgré ses hautes ambitions de durabilité et l'emploi de bois de récupération pour les façades (ci-dessus), le Centre Omega donne une image de modernité encore soulignée par la perspective en coupe du bâtiment juste au-dessus.

The main building with its tilted roof is seen above in a photo and below in drawings: the west elevation is above the fully glazed south elevation.

Das Hauptgebäude mit seinem Pultdach auf einem Foto (oben) und auf Zeichnungen (unten): oben der westliche Aufriss, darunter der voll verglaste Südaufriss.

On voit ici, sur la photo ci-dessus et les schémas ci-dessous, le bâtiment principal et son toit de tuiles : l'élévation ouest se trouve au-dessus de l'élévation sud entièrement vitrée.

Arrays of solar panels contribute to the energy sustainability of the Omega Center. Below, an overall site plan of the complex.

Eine Solaranlage unterstützt die energetische Nachhaltigkeit des Omega Center. Unten ein Überblicksplan des Komplexes.

Des ensembles de panneaux solaires contribuent à la durabilité énergétique du Centre Omega. Ci-dessous, un plan global du site sur lequel est construit le complexe.

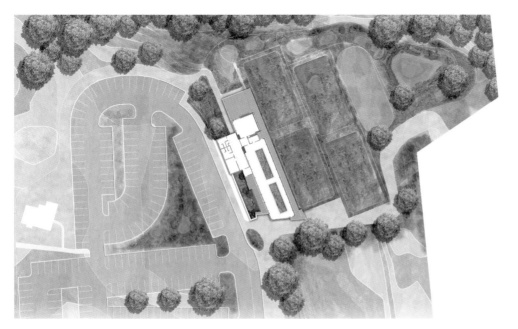

BROOKS + SCARPA

Brooks + Scarpa
4611 West Slauson Avenue
Los Angeles, CA 90043
USA

Tel: +1 323 596 4700
Fax: +1 310 453 9606
E-mail: info@brooksscarpa.com
Web: brooksscarpa.com

LAWRENCE SCARPA was educated at the University of Florida (M.Arch, 1987) and worked in the offices of Paul Rudolph in New York (1982–84) and Holt Hinshaw Pfau Jones in San Francisco (1987–88), before founding Pugh + Scarpa with Gwynne Pugh in 1988. He created Brooks + Scarpa with Angela Brooks in 2010. Scarpa has won four AIA COTE "Top Ten Green Building" Awards. **ANGELA BROOKS** received her M.Arch degree at the SCI-Arc in 1991. She worked at Pugh + Scarpa beginning in 1991, having previously spent time at Skidmore, Owings & Merrill (San Francisco, 1988–89) amongst other positions. The work of the firm includes a house for Make-it-Right (New Orleans, Louisiana, 2007–11); the CAM Museum (Raleigh, North Carolina, 2011); Yin-Yang House (Venice, California, 2011, published here); Green Dot Charter High School (Lennox, California, 2007–12); Siqueiros Interpretive Cultural Museum (Los Angeles, California, 2008–12); Vasquez Rocks Museum (Aqua Dolce, California, 2007–13); Aronson Fine Arts Center at Laumeier Sculpture Park (Saint Louis, Missouri, 2008–13); an automotive research facility (Monterrey, Mexico, 2011–13); and Plummer Park (West Hollywood, California, 2008–14), all in the USA unless stated otherwise.

LAWRENCE SCARPA studierte an der University of Florida (M.Arch, 1987) und war für Paul Rudolph in New York (1982–84) und Holt Hinshaw Pfau Jones in San Francisco (1987–88) tätig, bevor er 1988, mit Gwynne Pugh, das Büro Pugh + Scarpa gründete. 2010 gründete er mit Angela Brooks das Büro Brooks + Scarpa. Scarpa wurde mit vier „Top Ten Green Projects Awards" des Umweltkomitees (COTE) des AIA ausgezeichnet. **ANGELA BROOKS** absolvierte ihren M.Arch 1991 am SCI-Arc. Seit 1991 war sie für Pugh + Scarpa tätig, nachdem sie zuvor unter anderem für Skidmore, Owings & Merrill (San Francisco, 1988–89) gearbeitet hatte. Zu den Projekten des Büros zählen ein Haus für die Initiative Make-it-Right (New Orleans, Louisiana, 2007–11), das CAM Museum (Raleigh, North Carolina, 2011), das Yin-Yang House (Venice, Kalifornien, 2011, hier vorgestellt), die Green Dot Charter High School (Lennox, Kalifornien, 2007–12), das Siqueiros Interpretive Cultural Museum (Los Angeles, Kalifornien, 2008–12), das Vasquez Rocks Museum (Aqua Dolce, Kalifornien, 2007–13), das Aronson Fine Arts Center im Laumeier Sculpture Park (Saint Louis, Missouri, 2008–13), eine Forschungseinrichtung für die Automobilindustrie (Monterrey, Mexiko, 2011–13) sowie der Plummer Park (West Hollywood, Kalifornien, 2008–14), alle in den USA, sofern nicht anders angegeben.

LAWRENCE SCARPA a fait ses études à l'université de Floride (M.Arch, 1987) et a travaillé dans les agences de Paul Rudolph à New York (1982–84) et Holt Hinshaw Pfau Jones à San Francisco (1987–88) avant d'ouvrir Pugh + Scarpa avec Gwynne Pugh en 1988. Il a fondé Brooks + Scarpa avec Angela Brooks en 2010. Il a déjà remporté quatre prix du Top Ten Green Building Awards du Comité pour l'environnement de l'AIA. **ANGELA BROOKS** a obtenu son M.Arch à l'École SCI-Arc en 1991. Elle a travaillé à Pugh + Scarpa à partir de 1991, après, notamment, Skidmore, Owings & Merrill (San Francisco, 1988–89). Leurs réalisations comprennent une maison pour la fondation Make-it-Right (La Nouvelle-Orléans, 2007–11) ; le Musée d'art contemporain de Raleigh (Caroline-du-Nord, 2011) ; la Yin-Yang House (Venice, Californie, 2011, publiée ici) ; le lycée privé Green Dot (Lennox, Californie, 2007–12) ; le Musée interprétatif et culturel Siqueiros (Los Angeles, 2008–12) ; le musée de Vasquez Rocks (Aqua Dolce, Californie, 2007–13) ; le Centre artistique Aronson du parc des sculptures Laumeier (Saint Louis, Missouri, 2008–13) ; le Centre de recherches automobiles (Monterrey, Mexique, 2011–13) et le parc Plummer (West Hollywood, Californie, 2008–14), toutes aux États-Unis sauf si précisé.

YIN-YANG HOUSE

Venice, California, USA, 2011

Address: n/a. Area: 437 m²
Client: not disclosed. Cost: $1.7 million

The **YIN-YANG HOUSE** is a home for a family with several children organized around a series of courtyards and other outdoor spaces that integrate with the interior of the house. The bedrooms were intentionally designed to be small and simple, allowing for larger public spaces and "emphasizing the family over individual domains." Materials used, such as the bamboo interior, composite stone and tile countertops, and bathroom finishes, are recycled, while the house also has a green roof. Other environmental features include blown-in cellulose insulation, radiant heating, and a 12 kW solar photovoltaic panel system, the largest available on the commercial market, which is also used to provide shade from the sun for the residence. The architects proudly note: "The owners have been in the home for over nine months and have yet to receive a power bill."

Das **YIN-YANG HOUSE**, Domizil einer Familie mit mehreren Kindern, ist um eine Reihe von Innenhöfen und Außenbereichen organisiert, die mit dem Innenraum verschränkt wurden. Schlafzimmer wurden bewusst klein und schlicht gehalten, zugunsten größerer Gemeinschaftsräume und „Familienbereiche" statt „individueller Bereiche". Baustoffe wie Bambus für den Innenausbau, Verbundstein- oder geflieste Arbeitsflächen und Badausstattung sind recycelt. Das Dach des Hauses ist begrünt. Weitere ökologische Merkmale sind die Zellulose-Einblasdämmung, eine Fußbodenheizung sowie eine 12-kW-Solaranlage (die größte derzeit auf dem Verbrauchermarkt verfügbare), die zugleich Schatten spendet. Die Architekten merken an: „Obwohl die Eigentümer inzwischen über neun Monate in ihrem Haus wohnen, haben sie noch keine Stromrechnung bekommen."

La **YIN-YANG HOUSE** est une maison pour une famille de plusieurs enfants conçue autour de plusieurs cours et autres espaces extérieurs intégrés à l'intérieur de la maison. Les chambres ont été volontairement créées petites et simples afin d'ouvrir de plus grands espaces communs et de « favoriser la famille par rapport à des aspects plus individuels de la vie ». Les matériaux sont recyclés, comme le bambou de l'intérieur, les bars de pierre composite carrelés ou les finitions de la salle de bains, tandis que le toit est végétalisé. Parmi les autres caractéristiques écologiques, on peut noter l'isolation en cellulose soufflée, le chauffage à rayonnement et un ensemble de panneaux solaires photovoltaïques de 12 kW, le plus important disponible sur le marché, qui fournit aussi de l'ombre à la maison. Les architectes notent avec fierté que « les propriétaires habitent la maison depuis neuf mois et attendent encore leur première facture d'électricité ».

The house seen on the west side (left page) and on the east (above). Below, the west and east elevations of the house.

Das Haus in einer Westansicht (linke Seite) und von Osten (oben). Unten West- und Ostaufriss des Baus.

La maison côté ouest (page de gauche) et côté est (ci-dessus). Ci-dessous, élévations ouest et est de la maison.

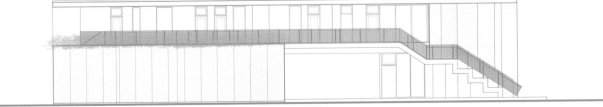

The interiors are brightly light, with full-height glazing in the living spaces seen below. The composition of the interiors is strictly rectilinear.

Die Innenräume sind hell, die Wohnbereiche (unten) geschosshoch verglast. Die Innenräume sind konsequent geradlinig in ihrer Anlage.

Les intérieurs sont extrêmement clairs du fait des vitrages sur toute la hauteur des murs dans les pièces de séjour ci-dessous. L'aménagement des pièces est strictement rectiligne.

Above, upper-floor terrace and green roof. Below, the ground-floor plan with a garage on the upper left, and a play yard on the lower right.

Oben ein Balkon im ersten Stock und ein begrüntes Dach. Unten der Grundriss des Erdgeschosses mit der Garage oben links und einem Garten zum Spielen unten rechts.

Ci-dessus, terrasse et toit végétalisé. Ci-dessous, plan du rez-de-chaussée avec un garage en haut à gauche et une cour en bas à droite.

CENTERBROOK

Centerbrook Architects and Planners, LLC
67 Main Street
PO Box 955
Centerbrook, CT 06409
USA

Tel: +1 860 767 0175 / Fax: +1 860 767 8719
E-mail: holahan@centerbrook.com
Web: www.centerbrook.com

MARK SIMON, born in 1946 in New York, graduated in 1968 from Brandeis University with a B.A. in Sculpture. He received his M.Arch from Yale University in 1972. He worked in the office of Warren Platner after graduation and then in the office of Charles Moore, beginning in 1974. He became a Partner in Moore Grover Harper, and then helped found Centerbrook in 1975, together with Bill Grover, Jeff Riley, and Chad Floyd, working initially on his own residential green projects. In 2008 Bill Grover became Partner Emeritus. Jim Childress was made a Partner in 1996, and Charles Mueller and Jon Lavy were made Principals of Centerbrook in 2002 and 2010 respectively. Today, Mark Simon is one of four Partners at Centerbrook Architects and Planners in Centerbrook, Connecticut. In addition to Lakewood House (northeast USA, 2004–08, published here), recent and current work of Centerbrook designed by Simon includes the Choate Residence Hall (Wallingford, Connecticut, 2008); Yale University Athletic Campus (New Haven, Connecticut, 2011); the Master Plan for the Yale Peabody Museum (New Haven, Connecticut, 2012); the Math and Science Building for the Berkshire School (Sheffield, Massachusetts, 2012); the Campus Master Plan and Library Addition for Lancaster Historical Society (Lancaster, Pennsylvania, 2012); the Academic and Science Wing for the University School (Hunting Valley, Ohio, 2012); and the Campus Master Plan for University Liggett School (Grosse Pointe Woods, Michigan, 2012), all in the USA.

MARK SIMON, 1946 in New York geboren, schloss sein Studium 1968 an der Brandeis University mit einem B.A. in Bildhauerei ab. 1972 absolvierte er einen M.Arch an der Yale University. Nach dem Studienabschluss arbeitete er bei Warren Platner, ab 1974 im Büro von Charles Moore. Er wurde Partner bei Moore Grover Harper und gründete 1975 mit Bill Grover, Jeff Riley und Chad Floyd das Büro Centerbrook. Dort arbeitete er zunächst an eigenen grünen Wohnbauprojekten. Seit 2008 ist Bill Grover Partner Emeritus. 1996 wurde Jim Childress Partner, 2002 und 2010 wurden Charles Mueller und Jon Lavy leitende Architekten des Büros. Heute ist Mark Simon einer von vier Partnern bei Centerbrook Architects and Planners in Centerbrook, Connecticut. Neben dem Lakewood House (Nordosten der USA, 2004–08, hier vorgestellt), sind weitere aktuelle Projekte von Mark Simon das Wohnheim Choate (Wallingford, Connecticut, 2008), der Sportcampus der Yale University (New Haven, Connecticut, 2011), der Masterplan für das Yale Peabody Museum (New Haven, Connecticut, 2012), das Gebäude für Mathematik und Naturwissenschaften an der Berkshire School (Sheffield, Massachusetts, 2012), der Masterplan für den Campus und die Bibliothekserweiterung der Lancaster Historical Society (Lancaster, Pennsylvania, 2012), ein akademischer und naturwissenschaftlicher Flügel für die University School (Hunting Valley, Ohio, 2012) sowie der Masterplan für den Campus der University Liggett School (Grosse Pointe Woods, Michigan, 2012), alle in den USA.

MARK SIMON, né en 1946 à New York, a obtenu un B.A. en sculpture à l'université Brandeis en 1968. Il est également titulaire d'un M.Arch obtenu à Yale en 1972. Après ses études, il a travaillé dans les agences de Warren Platner, puis de Charles Moore à partir de 1974. Il est devenu l'un des partenaires de Moore Grover Harper avant de fonder Centerbrook avec Bill Grover, Jeff Riley et Chad Floyd en 1975, pour travailler tout d'abord à ses propres projets résidentiels écologiques. Bill Grover est devenu partenaire émérite en 2008. Jim Childress a rejoint les autres partenaires en 1996, tandis que Charles Mueller et Jon Lavy sont devenus les principaux responsables de Centerbrook en 2002 et 2010. Aujourd'hui, Mark Simon est l'un des quatre partenaires de l'agence Centerbrook Architects and Planners de Centerbrook, Connecticut. En plus de la maison Lakewood (Nord-Est des États-Unis, 2004–08, publiée ici), les réalisations récentes et en cours de Centerbrook conçues par Simon comprennent la résidence du collège Choate (Wallingford, Connecticut, 2008) ; le complexe sportif de l'université Yale (New Haven, Connecticut, 2011) ; le plan directeur du musée Peabody de Yale (New Haven, 2012) ; le bâtiment des mathématiques et des sciences de l'École Berkshire (Sheffield, Massachusetts, 2012) ; le plan directeur du campus et l'extension de la bibliothèque de la Société historique de Lancaster (Lancaster, Pennsylvanie, 2012) ; l'aile scolaire et scientifique du collège University School (Hunting Valley, Ohio, 2012) et le plan directeur du campus de la University Liggett School (Grosse Pointe Woods, Michigan, 2012), toutes aux États-Unis.

LAKEWOOD HOUSE

Northeast USA, 2004–08

Address: n/a. Area: 521 m² (main house)
Client: not disclosed. Cost: not disclosed

Located in a pine forest by a lake, the "rustic" aspect of this house is emphasized by the large tree trunks set horizontally on the southern porch walls to filter daylight. The complex includes the main house, a guesthouse, workshop, boathouse, and smaller outbuildings. Sustainable geothermal heating and cooling, abundant insulation, natural and local materials, and passive solar design are all part of the scheme. **LAKEWOOD HOUSE** uses biofuel in a high-efficiency Buderus boiler, allowing electricity consumption for heating and cooling to be half of what it would be in a typical structure built to code. A computerized energy management control system also minimizes energy use. Icynene spray foam insulation up to 30 centimeters thick was used for the ceiling and in a thickness of 25 centimeters for tall walls. Cabinets, floors, and ceilings were made from cherry wood harvested from the property.

Das in einem Kiefernwald an einem See gelegene Haus wirkt besonders „rustikal" durch große Baumstämme, die quer vor Südfassade und -Terrasse gesetzt wurden und das einfallende Licht filtern. Der Komplex umfasst ein Haupthaus, ein Gästehaus, eine Werkstatt, ein Bootshaus sowie kleinere Nebenbauten. Nachhaltige Aspekte des Entwurfs sind eine Erdwärmeheizung- und Kühlung, umfassende Dämmung, der Einsatz natürlicher, lokaler Materialien sowie die passive Nutzung von Sonnenenergie. Im **LAKEWOOD HOUSE** wird Biobrennstoff in einem Hochleistungskessel von Buderus verfeuert; der Stromverbrauch für Heizung und Klimaanlage konnte, im Vergleich zu Bauten nach konventionellen Vorgaben, um die Hälfte reduziert werden. Auch ein elektronisch gesteuertes Energiesparsystem trägt zur Minimierung des Verbrauchs bei. Die Decken erhielten eine bis zu 30 cm starke Schaumdämmung aus Icynene, hohe Wände eine bis zu 25 cm starke Dämmung. Schränke, Böden und Decken wurden aus Kirschholz gefertigt, das auf dem Grundstück geschlagen wurde.

L'apparence « rustique » de cette maison située dans un bois de pins au bord d'un lac est encore soulignée par les immenses troncs d'arbres posés horizontalement entre les murs du porche sud pour filtrer la lumière du jour. Le complexe comprend une résidence principale, une maison d'hôtes, un atelier, un hangar à bateaux et des dépendances plus petites. Le projet comprend le chauffage et la climatisation géothermiques durables, l'isolation renforcée, l'utilisation de matériaux naturels et régionaux ou encore le système solaire passif. La **MAISON LAKEWOOD** est dotée d'une chaudière Buderus haute efficacité à biocarburant, ce qui réduit de moitié la consommation d'électricité pour le chauffage et la climatisation par rapport aux structures conventionnelles. Un système informatisé de contrôle et de gestion de l'énergie permet également de minimiser la consommation. La mousse expansée icynène a été utilisée pour l'isolation du plafond (30 cm d'épaisseur) et des grands murs (25 cm). Les placards, les sols et les plafonds sont en bois de cerisier récolté sur la propriété.

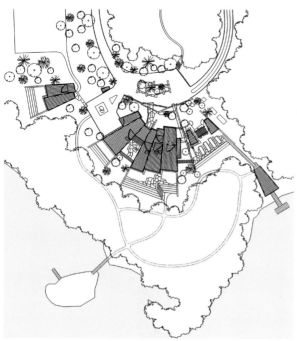

The site plan to the left and the image on the left page show the radiating pavilion-like design of the house. Above, horizontal tree trunks mark the façade of part of the house.

Der Grundstücksplan links und die Aufnahme auf der linken Seite lassen die fächerartig angeordneten Pavillonelemente des Entwurfs erkennen. Die Fassade zeichnet sich zum Teil durch horizontal vorgehängte Baumstämme aus.

Le plan du site ci-contre et la photo page de gauche montrent la conception rayonnante de type pavillon de la maison. Ci-dessus, des troncs d'arbres posés horizontalement marquent en partie la façade.

Plans show the ground floor (left) and
the first floor (right), confirming the
radiating form seen in overall images
and the site plan.

Grundrisse von Erdgeschoss (links)
und erstem Stock (rechts) bestätigen
die Fächerform, die sich auf Gesamtansicht und Grundstücksplan andeutet.

Plans du rez-de-chaussée (à gauche)
et du premier étage (à droite) avec, là
encore, la forme rayonnante qu'on voit
déjà sur les photos et le plan du site.

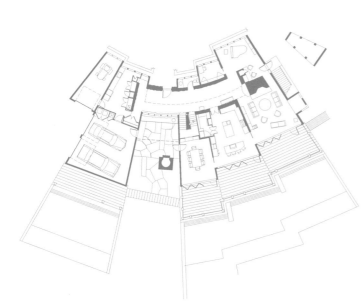
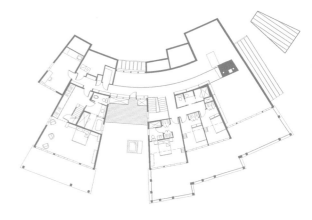

Below and right page, living room and
stairway pictures with the emphasis
on wood or natural stone relate the
residence to its forested environment.

Ansichten von Wohnbereich und
Treppe (unten und rechte Seite), die
durch den auffälligen Einsatz von Holz
und Naturstein den Bezug zwischen
Haus und Waldlandschaft schaffen.

Ci-dessous et page de droite, salon
et cage d'escalier : l'accent mis sur
le bois et la pierre naturels créent un
lien entre la maison et la forêt environnante.

Unexpected windows and vertical openings enliven the play of spaces inside the house. Right, the double-height glazing of the master bedroom lights the sloping roof and stepped volumes above the bed.

Überraschende Fenster und vertikale Lichtbänder sorgen für ein lebendiges Zusammenspiel der einzelnen Bereiche im Haus. Rechts die geschosshohe Verglasung des Hauptschlafzimmers, durch das Licht auf Dachschräge und die Abtreppung über dem Bett fällt.

Des fenêtres à des endroits inattendus et des ouvertures verticales égayent les espaces intérieurs. À droite, le vitrage double hauteur de la chambre principale éclaire le plafond incliné et les volumes en escalier au-dessus du lit.

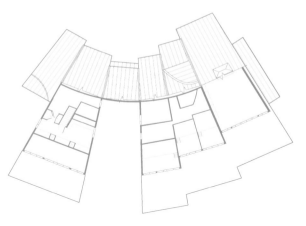

The loft level is seen in the plan above. The double height of the living area is articulated with sloping surfaces.

Der Grundriss oben zeigt das loftartige Hauptgeschoss. Die doppelte Geschosshöhe des Wohnbereichs wird durch Schrägen zusätzlich artikuliert.

On voit l'étage loft sur le plan ci-dessus. La double hauteur du salon est articulée par des plans inclinés.

DÉCALAAGE

SARL DécaLaage
130 Rue Vallot
74400 Chamonix
France

Tel: +33 4 50 53 81 65
E-mail: contact@decalaage.com
Web: www.decalaage.com

DécaLaage (a play on the word *décalage* or "shift" in English) was formed by Emmanuelle Guérard and Christophe de Laage in Chamonix in 2007. Emmanuelle Guérard graduated from the École d'architecture Paris la Seine in 2000. She worked in the office of Patrice Robaglia (Paris, 2001), moved to Chamonix the following year and concentrated on a number of refurbishment and small construction projects there prior to the creation of DécaLaage. **CHRISTOPHE DE LAAGE** obtained his diploma from the same school in 1999 and moved to Chamonix, where he worked on refurbishment and private house design. Their work includes the renovation and extension of the Hotel du Globe (Argentière, 2007–08); the refurbishment of the Hotel des Lanchers (Les Praz de Chamonix, 2010); the Refuge du Goûter (Saint-Gervais-les-Bains, 2010–12, published here); and a group of 19 houses (Thones, ongoing), all in France.

DécaLaage (Wortspiel mit frz. *décalage*, dt. Diskrepanz oder Verschiebung) wurde 2007 von Emmanuelle Guérard und Christophe de Laage in Chamonix gegründet. Emmanuelle Guérard schloss ihr Studium 2000 an der Ecole d'architecture Paris la Seine ab. Sie arbeitete im Büro von Patrice Robaglia (Paris, 2001), zog im darauffolgenden Jahr nach Chamonix und konzentrierte sich vor der Gründung von DécaLaage auf verschiedene Sanierungen und kleinere Bauprojekte. **CHRISTOPHE DE LAAGE** absolvierte sein Diplom 1999 an derselben Hochschule und zog ebenfalls nach Chamonix, wo er zunächst an Sanierungen und privaten Wohnbauten arbeitete. Zu den Projekten des Teams zählen die Sanierung und Erweiterung des Hôtel du Globe (Argentière, 2007–08), die Sanierung des Hôtel des Lanchers (Les Praz de Chamonix, 2010), die Bergstation Refuge du Goûter (Saint-Gervais-les-Bains, 2010–12, hier vorgestellt) und eine Siedlung mit 19 Häusern (Thones, in Arbeit), alle in Frankreich.

DécaLaage a été ouvert par Emmanuelle Guérard et Christophe de Laage à Chamonix en 2007. Elle est diplômée de l'École d'architecture Paris la Seine (2000) et a travaillé dans l'agence de Patrice Robaglia (Paris, 2001), avant de déménager à Chamonix l'année suivante où elle a surtout travaillé à de nombreux projets de réaménagement et de petites constructions et où elle a créé DécaLaage. **CHRISTOPHE DE LAAGE** a obtenu son diplôme dans la même école en 1999 et a ensuite rejoint lui aussi Chamonix où il s'est consacré à des projets de réaménagement et des maisons particulières. Leurs réalisations comprennent la rénovation et l'extension de l'hôtel du Globe (Argentière, 2007–08); le réaménagement de l'hôtel des Lanchers (Les Praz de Chamonix, 2010); le refuge du Goûter (Saint-Gervais-les-Bains, 2010–12, publié ici) et un complexe de 19 maisons (Thones, en cours), toutes en France.

REFUGE DU GOÛTER

Saint-Gervais-les-Bains, France, 2010–12

Address: alt. 3835 m; Les Glaciers, Saint-Gervais-les-Bains 74170, France,
tel: +33 4 50 54 40 93/6 01 48 62 37, www.refugedugouter.fr
Area: 700 m². Client: FFCAM. Cost: €6.5 million. Collaboration: Groupe H

The spectacular setting of the Refuge du Goûter and its somewhat "alien" appearance are less in contradiction than they might appear since all possible care has been taken to make the structure sustainable.

Der spektakuläre Standort des Refuge du Goûter und seine eher „fremde" Erscheinung sind ein geringerer Widerspruch, als man meinen könnte: Es wurde größtmöglicher Aufwand betrieben, um den Bau nachhaltig zu gestalten.

Le décor spectaculaire autour du refuge du Goûter et son apparence quelque peu « extraterrestre » sont moins contradictoires qu'on ne pourrait le penser car le plus grand soin a été apporté pour en faire une structure la plus durable possible.

Located at an altitude of 3835 meters above sea level, which is to say quite high even by the standards of mountain refuges, this wood and stainless-steel structure is a stopping point for those wishing to climb the Mont Blanc. Originally built in 1960 with 75 beds, the **REFUGE DU GOÛTER** was extended in 1990 to add 40 more beds. Coal and propane gas were used for the energy requirements of the building. The first studies for this new building were undertaken by the previous firm of Christophe de Laage, which was Parizet, Avanzini, and De Laage, which then evolved to form a new team including DécaLaage, Groupe H, and Charpente Concept. The construction permit was granted in 2008 for a new, four-level, 120-bed facility, and the demolition of the main part of the earlier structure was also authorized. The design assumes an elliptical form, not unlike an egg, and is oriented toward oncoming winds of 238 kilometers per hour. It is anchored on pilotis, and the use of just 10 cubic meters of concrete minimizes the impact on the site. The entire structure was designed in pieces that could be lifted by standard helicopters. Sophisticated glulam techniques allow the locally grown pine used to be up to 30% lighter than normal materials. Recycled wood fiber insulation, 54 square meters of photovoltaic panels, and a cogeneration system using colza oil further insure optimum sustainability.

In einer Höhe von 3835 m ü. NN, einer sogar für Hütten ungewöhnlich hohen Lage, dient dieser Bau aus Holz und Edelstahl als Station auf dem Aufstieg zum Mont Blanc. Der **REFUGE DU GOÛTER**, ursprünglich 1960 mit 75 Betten erbaut, wurde 1990 um 40 Betten erweitert. Für die Energieversorgung wurden Kohle und Propangas verwendet. Erste Studien für den Neubau erfolgten noch unter Federführung des früheren Büros von Christophe de Laage (Parizet, Avanzini, De Laage), aus dem sich ein neues Team aus DécaLaage, Groupe H und Charpente Concept formierte. 2008 wurde die Baugenehmigung für einen Neubau mit 120 Betten erteilt, auch der Abriss des Vorgängerbaus wurde genehmigt. Die Orientierung des elliptischen Entwurfs, einem Ei nicht unähnlich, ergab sich aus Berücksichtigung der Windgeschwindigkeiten von bis zu 238 km/h. Der auf Pilotis verankerte Bau kommt mit nur 10 m³ Beton aus, was den Eingriff in das Gelände minimiert. Der gesamte Bau wurde in Einzelteilen geplant, die mit regulären Helikoptern vor Ort geflogen werden konnten. Dank ausgereifter Schichtholztechniken konnte das einheimische Kiefernholz zu rund 30% leichter verbaut werden. Eine Dämmung aus recycelten Holzfasern, eine 54 m² große Solaranlage sowie eine rapsölbetriebene Kraft-Wärme-Kopplungs-Anlage sorgen für optimale Nachhaltigkeit.

Situé à 3835 m au-dessus du niveau de la mer, ce qui est plutôt haut, même pour un refuge de montagne, cette structure de bois et d'acier inoxydable constitue un arrêt pour les alpinistes qui partent à l'assaut du mont Blanc. Construit initialement en 1960 avec 75 lits, le **REFUGE DU GOÛTER** a été agrandi en 1990 pour accueillir 40 lits supplémentaires. Les besoins en énergie sont couverts par du charbon et du propane. Les premières études pour le nouveau bâtiment ont été réalisées par l'agence précédente de Christophe de Laage – Parizet, Avanzini et De Laage – qui a ensuite évolué pour former une nouvelle équipe avec DécaLaage, Groupe H et Charpente concept. Le permis de construire a été accordé en 2008 pour un nouvel établissement de 120 lits sur quatre niveaux, la démolition de la majeure partie de l'ancienne structure ayant également été autorisée. L'ensemble, qui présente une forme elliptique rappelant un œuf, est orienté en fonction du vent, qui peut souffler à 238 km/h. Il est construit sur pilotis et le béton utilisé a été limité à 10 m³ afin de minimiser l'impact sur le site naturel. Le bâtiment est entièrement composé d'éléments qui peuvent être portés par des hélicoptères standard. Des techniques de lamellé-collé très élaborées ont rendu le pin cultivé localement jusqu'à 30 % plus léger que des matériaux traditionnels. L'isolation en fibre de bois recyclé, 54 m² de panneaux photovoltaïques et un système de cogénération à l'huile de colza sont également les garants d'une durabilité optimale.

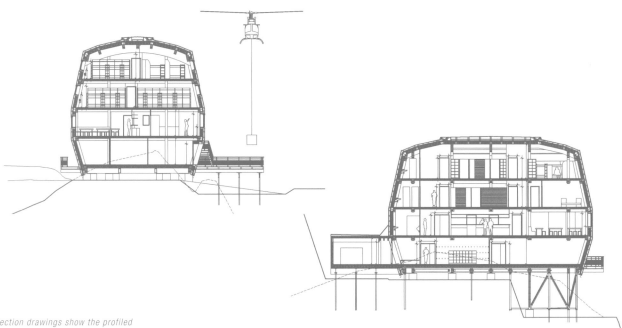

Section drawings show the profiled form of the refuge and its metal shell, calculated to withstand strong winds in this exposed location.

Querschnitte lassen das Profil der metallverkleideten Berghütte erkennen, die auf die hohen Windlasten in der exponierten Lage angelegt wurde.

On voit sur les plans en coupe la forme profilée du refuge et sa coque métallique, calculés pour résister aux vents violents sur ce site très exposé.

The sketch to the right shows the point of entry, the curved form of the structure, and the rotation of the axis of the elliptical plan. Below, the structure in its forbidding mountain site.

Die Skizze rechts illustriert den in den Boden eingelassenen Auflagebereich, die geschwungene Form der Konstruktion und die Rotationsachse des elliptischen Grundrisses. Unten der Bau in seinem unwirtlichen Umfeld.

Le croquis à droite montre le point d'entrée, la forme arrondie de la structure et la rotation de l'axe du plan elliptique. Ci-dessous, le refuge dans son site montagneux inhospitalier.

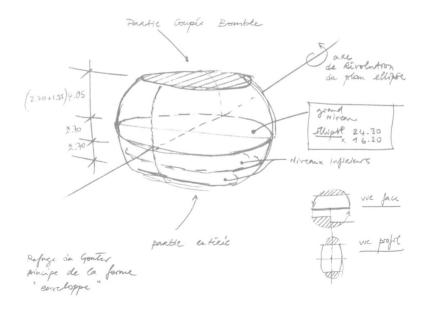

The interiors are in wood, in contrast to the gray metallic exterior. Below, plans show the elliptical shape of the building and its internal spatial divisions.

Die Holzeinbauten kontrastieren mit der grauen Metallhülle des Außenbaus. Grundrisse (unten) lassen die elliptische Grundform des Gebäudes und dessen Raumaufteilung erkennen.

L'intérieur en bois contraste avec l'extérieur gris métallique. Ci-dessous, on voit sur les plans la forme elliptique du bâtiment et ses divisions internes.

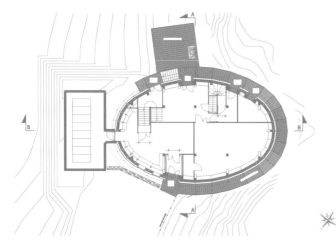

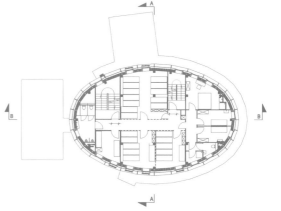

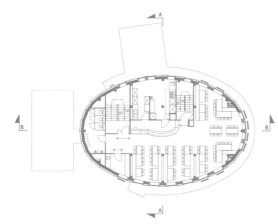

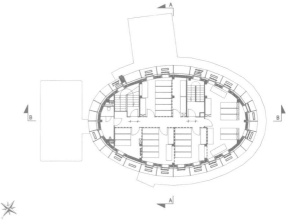

The dining area is seen above, and the bunk-bed style dormitories are visible in the image on the right.

Oben eine Aufnahme des Speiseraums, rechts einer der Schlafsäle mit Etagenbetten.

Ci-dessus le réfectoire, à droite les dortoirs à lits superposés.

Clifftop Ho

DEKLEVA GREGORIČ

dekleva gregorič arhitekti
Dalmatinova 11
1000 Ljubljana
Slovenia

Tel: +386 1 430 52 70
Fax: +386 1 430 52 71
E-mail: arh@dekleva-gregoric.com
Web: www.dekleva-gregoric.com

ALJOŠA DEKLEVA was born in 1972, in Postojna, Slovenia, and **TINA GREGORIČ** was born in 1974 in Kranj, Slovenia. They created their firm in 2003 in Ljubljana. They both graduated from the Faculty of Architecture of the University of Ljubljana and went on to study at the Architectural Association in London (AA), where they received Master's degrees in Architecture in 2002. At the AA they cofounded an international architectural network called RAMTV. They seek to focus on social, material, and historic contexts in their architectural projects. Their work includes the XXS House (Ljubljana, 2004); a metal recycling plant (Pivka, 2005–07); Pertot Showroom (Trieste, Italy, 2006–08); Housing L (Sežana, 2004–09); the Clifftop House (Maui, Hawaii, USA, 2004–11, published here); and Razgledi Perovo Housing (Kamnik, 2008–11, also published here), all in Slovenia unless stated otherwise.

ALJOŠA DEKLEVA wurde 1972 in Postojna, Slowenien, **TINA GREGORIČ** 1974 in Kranj, Slowenien, geboren. Ihr erstes Büro gründeten sie 2003 in Ljubljana. Beide studierten nach ihrem Abschluss an der Architekturfakultät der Universität Ljubljana an der Architectural Association in London (AA), wo sie 2002 ihren M.Arch absolvierten. An der AA waren sie Mitbegründer des Netzwerks RAMTV. Bei ihren Projekten gilt ihr besonderes Augenmerk sozialen, materiellen und historischen Kontexten. Zu ihren Arbeiten zählen das XXS House (Ljubljana, 2004), eine Metallrecyclinganlage (Pivka, 2005–07), ein Showroom für Pertot (Triest, Italien, 2006–08), Housing L (Sežana, 2004–09), das Clifftop House (Maui, Hawaii, USA, 2004–11, hier vorgestellt), und die Wohnsiedlung Razgledi Perovo (Kamnik, 2008–11, ebenfalls hier vorgestellt), alle in Slowenien, sofern nicht anders angegeben.

ALJOŠA DEKLEVA est né en 1972, à Postojna, en Slovénie, et **TINA GREGORIČ** en 1974 à Kranj, également en Slovénie. Ils ont ouvert leur agence en 2003 à Ljubljana. Ils sont tous les deux diplômés de la faculté d'architecture de l'université de Ljubljana et ont poursuivi leurs études à l'Architectural Association (AA) de Londres où ils ont obtenu un master en architecture en 2002. C'est là également qu'ils ont fondé un réseau international d'architectes appelé RAMTV. Dans leurs projets architec-turaux, ils essaient de se concentrer sur les aspects sociaux, matériels et historiques. Leurs réalisations comprennent la maison XXS (Ljubljana, 2004) ; une usine de recyclage de métal (Pivka, 2005–07) ; l'espace d'exposition Pertot (Trieste, Italie, 2006–08) ; le logement L (Sežana, 2004–09) ; la maison Clifftop (Maui, Hawaii, États-Unis, 2004–11, publiée ici) et le lotissement Razgledi Perovo (Kamnik, 2008 –11, publié ici), toutes en Slovénie sauf si précisé.

CLIFFTOP HOUSE

Maui, Hawaii, USA, 2004–11

Address: n/a
Area: 250 m² (500 m² of covered space)
Client: Robert & Dražena stroj
Cost: not disclosed. Collaboration: Flavio Coddou, Lea Kovič

This house was designed with a particular emphasis on the site and its perfect ocean view. The architects, admittedly not familiar with such a spectacular natural site, decided to create several "houses" under a common roof that "also serves as a folded wooden deck and integrates the house with the landscape." Because of the very large roof and the nature of the site, cross ventilation eliminates the need for air conditioning. Local wood was used for the floor, terrace, ceilings, and roof, although concrete blocks were used for construction. The owner, an industrial designer, supervised the construction with the architects. The owner writes: "We really wanted to finish construction using natural materials… there are absolutely no paints used anywhere in the house, all walls are covered by custom-made stucco mixed from white concrete, coral sand, dune sand, and lime, all wood is just oiled with pure tang oil, and there is no lacquer or polyurethane used anywhere. All walls are solid concrete (blocks filled with concrete); the timber used on the roof, ceiling, floor, outside deck, glass fascia framing, sliding doors and windows (all fabricated on site), etc. is all Ironwood aka Ipe (chosen for its hardness, natural color, and being able to withstand elements without the use of protective finishes). All vertical panels used to build the kitchen, interior doors, closets, and cabinets are solid bamboo plywood (chosen for its hardness, stability despite changing humidity, as well as its natural grain and color when oiled, contrasting well with the Ironwood)."

Besonderes Augenmerk beim Entwurf dieses Hauses galt dem Grundstück und dem dramatischen Seepanorama. Die Architekten, erklärtermaßen nicht an so spektakuläre Naturgrundstücke gewöhnt, entschieden sich, „mehrere Häuser" unter einem Dach zu konzipieren, „das zugleich als gefaltete Holzterrasse dient und das Haus in die Landschaft integriert". Dank des ungewöhnlich großen Dachs und seiner Lage ist der Bau so gut durchlüftet, dass sich eine Klimaanlage erübrigt. Für Böden, Terrasse, Decken und Dach wurde lokales Holz verbaut, gemauert wurde mit Formsteinen aus Beton. Der Eigentümer, ein Industriedesigner, unterstützte die Architekten bei der Bauleitung. Er schreibt: „Wir wollten den Bau unbedingt mit natürlichen Materialien realisieren … im ganzen Haus wurde konsequent auf den Einsatz von Farben verzichtet, alle Wände wurden mit speziell gefertigtem Putz aus weißem Beton, Korallensand und Kalk verputzt, alle Holzflächen mit reinem Tungöl geölt, auch sonst wurden keinerlei Lacke oder Polyurethane verarbeitet. Die Wände sind aus Beton (ausgegossener Mauerstein), Dach, Decken, Böden, Terrasse, Traufbretter, Schiebetüren und Fenster aus Ipé-Hartholz (unsere Wahl aufgrund von Materialhärte, natürlicher Färbung und seiner Witterungsbeständigkeit ohne weitere Versiegelung). Für Kücheneinbauten, Türen im Innenbereich, Wandschränke und Schränke wurde mit massivem Bambussperrholz gearbeitet (dank seiner Härte und Formstabilität bei variierender Luftfeuchtigkeit sowie der natürlichen Maserung und Farbgebung nach Ölbehandlung ein idealer Kontrast zum Ipé-Hartholz)."

La maison a été conçue en tenant tout particulièrement compte du site et de sa vue imprenable sur l'océan. Les architectes, peu familiers d'un site naturel aussi spectaculaire, ont choisi de créer plusieurs « maisons » sous un même toit qui « forme également une plate-forme plissée en bois et intègre la maison au paysage ». Avec cet immense toit et étant donné la nature du site, la ventilation transversale rend l'air conditionné superflu. Le sol, la terrasse, les plafonds et le toit sont en bois local mais des blocs de béton ont été utilisés pour la construction. Le propriétaire, un designer industriel, a supervisé les travaux avec les architectes. Il écrit : « Nous voulions absolument des matériaux naturels pour les finitions … aucune peinture n'a été utilisée dans toute la maison, les murs sont recouverts d'un stuc fait sur mesure à partir de béton blanc, de sable corallien, de sable de dune et de chaux, le bois est simplement passé à l'huile de tung sans aucun vernis ni polyuréthane. Les murs sont en béton plein (blocs pleins de béton), le bois du toit, des plafonds, du sol, de la terrasse, des encadrements de fenêtres, des portes et baies coulissantes (toutes construites sur place) est de l'ipé ou ironwood (choisi pour sa dureté, sa coloration naturelle et sa résistance aux intempéries qui ne nécessite aucun enduit de protection). Tous les panneaux verticaux qui forment la cuisine, les portes intérieures, les placards et les meubles de rangement sont en contreplaqué de bambou massif (choisi pour sa dureté, sa stabilité aux changements d'humidité, sa veinure naturelle et sa teinte, une fois huilé, qui contraste joliment avec l'ipé). »

The profile of the house, seen in the section drawings to the left and in the images above, makes it seem to emerge in an organic way from its spectacular natural setting on the island of Maui.

Das Profil des Hauses (Querschnitte links und Aufnahmen oben) weckt den Eindruck, der Bau wachse geradezu organisch aus der spektakulären Landschaft der Insel Maui empor.

Le profil de la maison, qu'on voit sur les schémas en coupe ci-contre et les photos ci-dessus, donne l'impression de la faire émerger presque organiquement du spectaculaire décor naturel sur l'île de Maui.

Pictures showing the angled wooden roof of the house and its apparently closed exterior. The plan on this page shows the ocean views and the parking area.

Les photos montrent le toit anguleux en bois et son aspect extérieur fermé. Le plan présente les vues sur l'océan et le parking.

Aufnahmen der Dachschrägen des Hauses und des scheinbar geschlossenen Außenbaus. Der Grundriss illustriert den Panoramablick aufs Meer und die Autostellplätze.

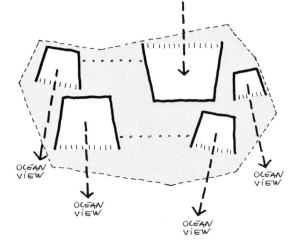

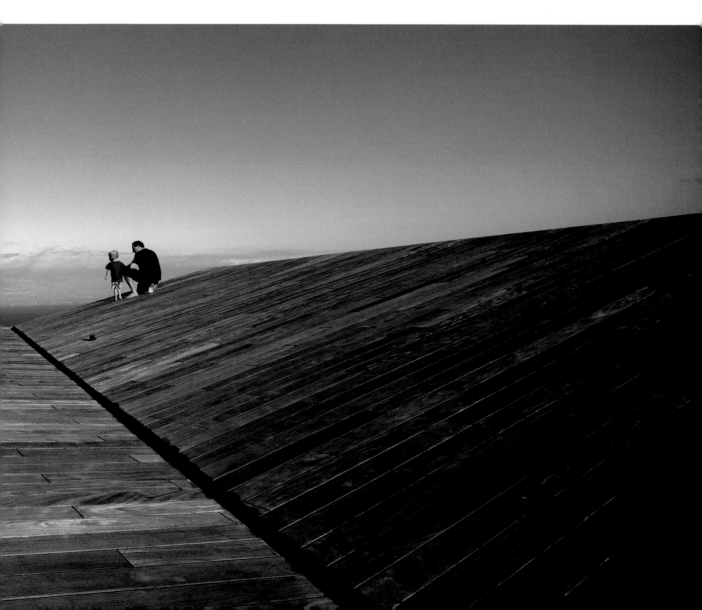

A sheltered wooden terrace offers uninhibited view of the coastline. Below, a sketch showing the natural ventilation scheme used that avoids air conditioning.

Von der geschützten Holzterrasse bietet sich unverstellter Ausblick auf die Küste. Die Skizze unten veranschaulicht die Prinzipien natürlicher Durchlüftung, die künstliche Klimatisierung verzichtbar macht.

Une terrasse en bois abritée offre une vue illimitée sur le littoral. Ci-dessous, le croquis montre le principe de ventilation naturelle qui permet d'éviter le recours à l'air conditionné.

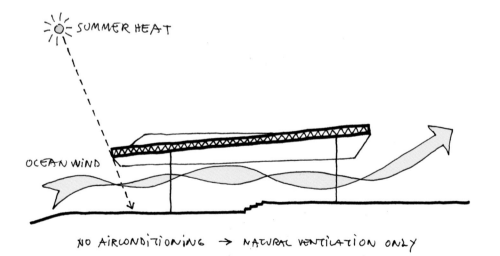

SUMMER HEAT

OCEAN WIND

NO AIRCONDITIONING → NATURAL VENTILATION ONLY

The drawings above show the progressive assembly of the house, including its built-in furniture and enveloping roof deck.

Die Zeichnungen oben visualisieren die verschiedenen Bauphasen des Hauses bis hin zu den Einbauten und dem Terrassendach, das den Bau umschließt.

Les schémas présentent l'assemblage progressif de la maison, y compris ses meubles encastrés et son toit en terrasse enveloppant.

Wooden ceilings and floors continue the extensive presence of this material, that gives a rather dark appearance to the interiors, in contrast to the bright views of the shore.

In den Holzdecken und -böden setzt sich das dominante Materialthema fort, das das Interieur eher dunkel und als Kontrast zum hellen Küstenpanorama erscheinen lässt.

Les plafonds et sols en bois rendent encore plus prépondérante la présence de ce matériau qui confère un aspect plutôt sombre à l'intérieur de la maison et contraste avec la clarté des vues sur la côte.

RAZGLEDI PEROVO HOUSING
Kamnik, Slovenia, 2008–11

Address: Perovo, Kamnik, Slovenia, tel: +386 1 430 41 50, www.razgledi-perovo.si
Area: 3142 m² (6 semi-detached houses + 6 individual houses)
Client: Sava IP, d.o.o. Cost: not disclosed
Collaboration: Martina Marčan, Daniel Schwartz, Tea Smrke

The exposed site of these low-energy houses offers a view of the Kamniško-Savinjske Alps about 30 minutes' drive from Ljubljana. The architects imagined high structures with the ground floor acting as a "pedestal" supporting two smaller volumes. Garden terraces are oriented so that residents do not disturb each other. The architects emphasize that "flexibility is an important property of the houses and an integral part of the structural concept. All of the load-bearing walls are located on the perimeter, which enables custom layouts of the rooms inside, both on the ground floor and on the second floor." Along the same line of concern for the inhabitants, the architects convinced the promoters to create a number of individual houses as opposed to the originally envisaged strict alignments of semi-detached residences within the already strict urban planning.

Dank ihres unverbauten Umfelds haben diese Niedrigenergiehäuser freien Blick auf die Kamniško-Savinjske Alpen rund 30 Autominuten von Ljubljana. Die Architekten entwarfen vergleichsweise hohe Bauten, deren Erdgeschoss als „Sockel" fungiert, auf dem zwei kleinere Volumina ruhen. Die Ausrichtung der Gärten sorgt für geringstmögliche Störung unter den Nachbarn. Die Architekten betonen: „Flexibilität ist ein entscheidendes Merkmal dieser Häuser und integraler Bestandteil des Strukturkonzepts. Da ausschließlich die Außenwände als tragende Wände geplant wurden, ist ein persönlicher Zuschnitt der Innenräume möglich, im Erdgeschoss ebenso wie in der oberen Etage." Ähnlich auf die Belange der Bewohner bedacht, überzeugten die Architekten den Bauträger, auch Einzelhäuser zu realisieren, statt der ursprünglich geplanten ausschließlichen Gliederung in Doppelhäuser in einem ohnehin rigiden Bebauungsplan.

L'emplacement exposé de ces maisons à faibles besoins énergétiques donne sur les Alpes de Kamniško-Savinjske, à 30 min de voiture environ de Ljubljana. Les architectes ont imaginé des constructions en hauteur où le rez-de-chaussée forme un « piédestal » soutenant deux volumes plus petits. Les terrasses jardins sont orientées de manière à ce que les habitants ne se gênent pas les uns les autres. Les architectes soulignent que « la flexibilité est l'une des caractéristiques principales des maisons et fait partie intégrante du concept de construction. Tous les murs porteurs sont en périmètre, ce qui permet un découpage sur mesure des pièces à l'intérieur, au rez-de-chaussée comme à l'étage ». Dans ce même souci des habitants, les architectes ont convaincu les promoteurs de construire des maisons individuelles plutôt que les alignements sévères de maisons jumelées prévus au départ par la planification urbaine rigoureuse.

Steeply angled roofs alternate in the
complex in a pattern that gives the
impression under certain angles of a
purely geometric composition.

Die gegenläufige Anordnung der
steilen Pultdächer fügt sich zu einem
Muster, das den Komplex aus manchen
Blickwinkeln wie eine streng geometri-
sche Komposition erscheinen lässt.

Les toits anguleux en pente raide du
complexe alternent pour former un
motif qui donne l'impression d'une
composition purement géométrique
vue sous certains angles.

The positioning of the houses allows for the creation of protected court-yard spaces, and greenery surrounds much of the complex.

Durch die Anordnung der Häuser ent-stehen geschützte Hof- und Garten-bereiche. Ein Großteil der Anlage ist von Grünzonen umgeben.

La disposition des maisons ouvre des cours protégées, tandis que l'ensemble est en grande partie entouré de verdure.

Set up on their gray bases, the triangular forms of the houses create a kind of musical pattern. Parking spaces (above) and courtyard gardens are part of each residence.

Die Dreiecksform der Häuser auf ihren grauen Sockelgeschossen wirkt fast wie eine musikalische Komposition. Alle Häuser verfügen über Autostellplätze (oben) und Hofgärten.

Sur leurs bases grises, les formes triangulaires des maisons se succèdent comme sur un air de musique. Elles comprennent chacune un espace parking (ci-dessus) et une cour avec jardin.

An internal wooden stairway eschews handrails in favor of black netting that adds an aesthetic touch while assuring the safety, even of children.

Im Treppenhaus wurde auf Geländer verzichtet, stattdessen wurden schwarze Netze installiert, die einerseits ästhetische Akzente setzen, andererseits für Sicherheit sorgen, auch im Hinblick auf Kinder.

À l'intérieur, la cage d'escalier en bois troque ses rampes contre un filet noir qui ajoute à son esthétique en assurant la sécurité, notamment des enfants.

DJURIC+TARDIO

Djuric+Tardio Architectes
17 Rue Ramponeau
75020 Paris
France

Tel: +33 1 40 33 06 41
Fax: +33 1 40 33 93 87
E-mail: contact@djuric-tardio.com
Web: www.djuric-tardio.com

MIRCO TARDIO was born in 1970 in Italy and studied at the Polytechnic Institute of Milan and the Ecole Paris-Belleville. He has lived in France since 1996. Between 2000 and 2009 he worked in the offices of Chaix & Morel and the Ateliers Jean Nouvel. **CAROLINE DJURIC** was born in France in 1974 and studied at the Ecole Paris-Belleville before working in the same offices as Tardio. Winners of the Europan 7 contest in 2004, they created their office in Paris the same year. Their recent work includes a 174-apartment complex in Arcueil (2009–); 44 apartments in Le Mans (2008–11); and "Eco-Neighborhoods" in Le Havre (2010–) and Langoiran-Bordeaux (2010–). They have designed several single-family residences, including the Eco-Sustainable House published here (Antony, 2010–11), all in France. Djuric+Tardio are also working on a number of projects in tandem with Chaix & Morel and Jean Nouvel. Much of their production has been related to research into durable wooden structures.

MIRCO TARDIO, geboren 1970 in Italien, studierte am Polytechnikum Mailand und der Ecole Paris-Belleville und lebt seit 1996 in Frankreich. Zwischen 2000 und 2009 war er für Chaix & Morel und Ateliers Jean Nouvel tätig. **CAROLINE DJURIC**, geboren 1974 in Frankreich, studierte an der Ecole Paris-Belleville und arbeitete im Anschluss für dieselben Büros. Nachdem das Team 2004 den Europan-7-Wettbewerb für sich entscheiden konnte, erfolgte im selben Jahr die Bürogründung in Paris. Zu ihren jüngeren Projekten zählen ein Komplex mit 174 Wohnungen in Arcueil (2009–), 44 Wohnungen in Le Mans (2008–11) sowie die „Eco-Siedlungen" in Le Havre (2010–) und Langoiran-Bordeaux (2010–). Das Team plante zahlreiche Einfamilienhäuser, darunter die hier vorgestellte Maison Eco-Durable (Antony, 2010–11), alle in Frankreich. Djuric+Tardio arbeiten darüber hinaus an verschiedenen Projekten mit Chaix & Morel und Jean Nouvel. Ein Großteil ihrer Projekte entwickelte sich aus der intensiven Auseinandersetzung mit nachhaltigen Holzbauweisen.

MIRCO TARDIO est né en 1970 en Italie et a fait ses études à l'Institut polytechnique de Milan et à l'École Paris-Belleville. Il vit en France depuis 1996. Entre 2000 et 2009, il a travaillé dans les agences Chaix & Morel et aux Ateliers Jean Nouvel. **CAROLINE DJURIC** est née en France en 1974 et a fait ses études à l'École Paris-Belleville avant de travailler dans les mêmes agences que Tardio. Vainqueurs du concours Europan 7 en 2004, c'est cette année qu'ils ont ouvert leur agence à Paris. Leurs dernières réalisations comprennent un complexe de 174 appartements à Arcueil (2009–) ; 44 appartements au Mans (2008–11) et des « éco-quartiers » au Havre (2010–) et à Langoiran prés de Bordeaux (2010–). Ils ont également conçu plusieurs maisons individuelles, parmi lesquelles la Maison éco-durable publiée ici (Antony, 2010–11), toutes en France. Enfin, Djuric + Tardio travaillent aussi à plusieurs projets en tandem avec Chaix & Morel et Jean Nouvel. Leurs productions sont pour la plupart liées à la recherche de structures durables en bois.

ECO-SUSTAINABLE HOUSE

Antony, France, 2010–11

Address: n/a. Area: 246 m². Client: not disclosed. Cost: not disclosed
Collaboration: Amandine Albertini, Iris Menage, Thomas Panconi

This house was built in just 10 months, including its special concrete foundations. The wooden structure cost €278 000 to build. Low-temperature gas-fired heating is used under the floors, and double-paned argon-filled windows insure appropriate insulation. A "clean" work site, natural ventilation, and the use of rainwater for the garden are some of the other environmental features of the house. The house is intended to "propose a design process and construction system allowing for prefabrication and modular design." Rather than the traditional roof implied by local construction regulations, the architects preferred to open the top of the house with a planted terrace. Kiwis, squash, and grapes are all grown on this terrace. The interior design allows for the easy transformation of volumes according to family needs through such devices as large sliding walls. The house was completely prefabricated with Finnish wood panels that include wood fiber insulation in a workshop and were assembled on site in just two weeks.

Das Haus konnte, inklusive seines speziellen Betonfundaments, in nur zehn Monaten erbaut werden. Die Baukosten des Holzbaus beliefen sich auf 278 000 Euro. Eingebaut wurden ein Gasniedertemperaturkessel mit Fußbodenheizung sowie dämmende Isolierglasfenster mit Argonfüllung. Weitere umweltfreundliche Aspekte des Hauses sind eine „saubere" Baustelle, natürliche Durchlüftung und Regenwassernutzung für den Garten. Das Haus dient zugleich als Modellentwurf für „einen Planungsprozess und ein Bausystem, das Vorfertigung und modulare Entwurfsformen erlaubt". Statt eines traditionellen Giebeldachs (nach örtlichen Bauvorgaben vorgesehen) entschieden sich die Architekten für einen offenen Giebel mit begrünter Dachterrasse, auf der Kiwis, Kürbis und Wein wachsen. Im Innern des Baus erlauben großflächige Schiebeelemente das problemlose Umkonfigurieren der Räume je nach den Bedürfnissen der Familie. Das Haus wurde im Werk vollständig aus finnischen Holzfaserdämmplatten vorgefertigt und vor Ort in nur zwei Wochen erbaut.

La maison a été construite en seulement 10 mois, y compris les fondations en béton spécial. La structure en bois a coûté 278 000 €. Le chauffage au sol à basse température est alimenté au gaz et les fenêtres en double-vitrage à l'argon assurent une isolation adaptée. Un chantier « propre », la ventilation naturelle et l'utilisation de l'eau de pluie pour le jardin ne sont que quelques-uns des autres aspects écologiques de la maison. L'objectif était de « proposer un processus de création et un système de construction permettant la préfabrication et une conception modulaire ». Plutôt que le toit traditionnel préconisé par les règlements locaux en matière de construction, les architectes ont préféré l'ouvrir pour en faire une terrasse où sont cultivés des kiwis, des courges et du raisin. Le découpage intérieur permet la transformation facile des volumes en fonction des besoins de la famille au moyen de dispositifs tels que de grandes cloisons coulissantes. La maison a été entièrement préfabriquée en atelier en panneaux de bois finlandais avec isolant en fibre de bois, et assemblée sur le site en seulement deux semaines.

Surrounded by much more
ordinary suburban houses, the
Eco-Sustainable House stands out
because of its open wood frame
and terraces. Right, a site plan.

Die von ungleich konventionelleren
Bauten gerahmte Maison Eco-Durable
fällt auch durch seine offene Holzkonstruktion und die Holzterrassen auf.
Rechts ein Grundstücksplan.

Entourée de maisons de banlieue plus
ordinaires, la Maison éco-durable
s'en distingue par sa charpente
ouverte et ses terrasses. À droite,
un plan de l'ensemble.

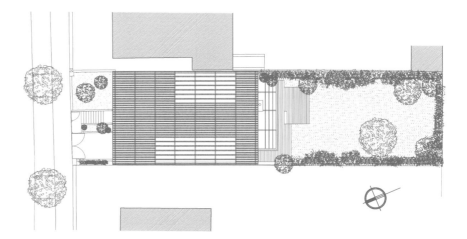

The pitched roof is actually no more than an open wooden frame. Symbolizing the form of the ordinary house, it offers an upper-story wooden terrace.

Das Giebeldach ist im Grunde nichts anderes als eine offene Holzrahmenkonstruktion. Es symbolisiert traditionellere Hausformen und dient zugleich als Dachterrasse in Holz.

Le toit en pente n'est rien d'autre qu'une charpente ouverte en bois. Elle reproduit la forme d'une maison classique et ouvre une terrasse en bois au dernier étage de la maison.

The terrace to the left shares with the rooftop a sense of protected openness engendered by the light wooden frame.

Die Terrasse links ist ebenso geschützt und zugleich offen wie das Dach, ein Effekt, der sich der leichten Holzrahmenkonstruktion verdankt.

La terrasse de gauche partage avec celle du toit un sentiment d'ouverture protégée engendré par la charpente légère en bois.

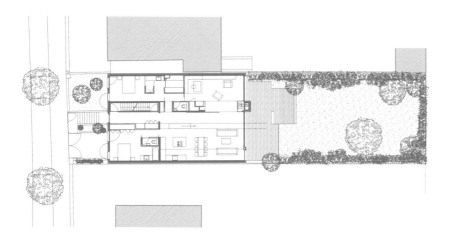
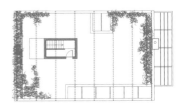

A floor plan and the image below show the rectilinear clarity of the design, which is filled with natural light—and here, very few visible sources of artificial light.

Etagengrundrisse wie die Aufnahme unten belegen die geradlinige Klarheit des Entwurfs, der von Tageslicht durchflutet wird – tatsächlich sind hier nur wenige künstliche Lichtquellen erkennbar.

Le plan de niveau et la photo ci-dessous mettent en évidence la clarté rectiligne du design, baigné de lumière naturelle – avec ici de rares sources de lumière artificielle visibles.

Bright interiors are assured by the floor and ceiling color scheme but also by large sliding windows that open into the garden or a terrace (right).

Die hellen Innenräume profitieren von der Farbwahl bei Böden und Wänden ebenso wie von den großflächigen Schiebefenstern, die sich zu Garten und Terrasse (rechts im Bild) öffnen.

La gamme de couleurs choisie pour le sol et le plafond garantit une grande luminosité à l'intérieur, mais aussi les grandes fenêtres coulissantes qui ouvrent sur le jardin ou une terrasse (à droite).

ECOSISTEMA URBANO

Ecosistema Urbano Arquitectos Ltd.
Estanislao Figueras 6
28008 Madrid
Spain

Tel/Fax: +34 91 559 16 01
E-mail: info@ecosistemaurbano.com
Web: www.ecosistemaurbano.com

Ecosistema Urbano was created in 2000 by **BELINDA TATO**, born in Madrid in 1971, who studied at the ETSA of Madrid (1999) and the Bartlett School of Architecture, London (1996), and **JOSE LUIS VALLEJO**, born in Bilbao in 1971, who also studied at the ETSAM (1999) and Bartlett School (1996). Currently the team is involved in research projects concerning the future of city design that they call "eco-techno-logical cities," financed by the Spanish Ministry of Industry. They are working on several urban proposals for different Spanish municipalities (in the spirit of the Ecoboulevard of Vallecas in Madrid, Spain, 2006), and one of their projects—Air Tree, Madrid Pavilion Public Space—represented Madrid at Shanghai Expo 2010 in China. They have also worked on an Internet network (ecosistemaurbano.org, 2007–10); Ecópolis Plaza, Rivas Vaciamadrid (Madrid, Spain, 2009–10, published here); and are currently developing Stortorget, the main public square of Hamar in Norway ("DreamHamar," 2011–).

Gegründet wurde Ecosistema Urbano 2000 von **BELINDA TATO**, geboren 1971 in Madrid, Studium an der ETSA Madrid (1999) und der Bartlett School of Architecture, London (1996), sowie **JOSE LUIS VALLEJO**, geboren 1971 in Bilbao, Studium ebenfalls an der ETSAM (1999) und der Bartlett School (1996). Derzeit ist das Team beteiligt an Forschungsprojekten zur Zukunft der Stadtplanung – sogenannter „öko-techno-logischer Städte" –, gefördert vom spanischen Ministerium für Industrie. Das Büro arbeitet an einer Reihe von Stadtplanungsentwürfen für verschiedene spanische Gemeinden (wie den Ecoboulevard in Vallecas, Madrid, Spanien, 2006). Ein Projekt des Büros – Air Tree, Pavillon der Stadt Madrid – vertrat Madrid auf der Expo 2010 in Shanghai. Das Team entwickelte außerdem ein Internet-Netzwerk (<ecosistemaurbano.org>, 2007–10), entwarf die Ecópolis Plaza, Rivas Vaciamadrid (Madrid, Spanien, 2009–10, hier vorgestellt) und arbeitet aktuell an einem Entwurf für den Stortorget, den alten Marktplatz in Hamar, Norwegen („DreamHamar", 2011–).

Ecosistema Urbano a été fondé en 2000 par **BELINDA TATO**, née à Madrid en 1971 où elle a étudié à l'ETSA (1999), après l'École d'architecture Bartlett de Londres (1996), et **JOSE LUIS VALLEJO**, né à Bilbao en 1971, qui a également étudié à l'ETSAM (1999) et à l'École Bartlett (1996). L'équipe participe actuellement à des projets de recherche sur l'avenir du design urbain baptisés « eco-techno-logical cities » et financés par le ministère espagnol de l'Industrie. Ils travaillent à plusieurs projets urbains pour différentes municipalités en Espagne (dans l'esprit de l'Écoboulevard de Vallecas à Madrid, 2006), l'un d'entre eux – Árbol de Aire, l'Arbre d'air, Madrid, pavillon de l'Espace public – a représenté Madrid à l'Expo de Shanghai 2010. Ils ont également collaboré à un réseau Internet (<ecosistemaurbano.org>, 2007–) ; à Ecópolis Plaza, Rivas Vaciamadrid (Madrid, 2009–10, publié ici) et sont en train de développer Stortorget, la principale place de Hamar, en Norvège (« DreamHamar », 2011–).

ECÓPOLIS PLAZA

Rivas Vaciamadrid, Madrid, Spain, 2009–10

Address: Plaza Ecópolis 1, Rivas Vaciamadrid 28529, Madrid, Spain
Area: 3000 m², 7500 m² of public space. Client: City Council of Rivas Vaciamadrid
Cost: €2.7 million

This project includes a public space, a kindergarten, and a children's play center. The goal of the architects, as they explain it, is to engage in the "transformation of a faceless site in Madrid's urban sprawl, surrounded by industry and heavy traffic transportation infrastructure, into a public space for social interaction providing a building for childcare." They seek, too, to integrate the concept of sustainability "into daily life." The project aims to reduce energy consumption but also to make users aware of their own energy use. A bioclimatic design is coupled with an energy simulation developed by the Thermodynamics Research Group of the Industrial Engineering School in Seville. Half of the building is buried, though a 700-square-meter glass façade faces south. A bioclimatic textile layer was superimposed over a light steel structure. The textile cladding is partially movable and is connected to sensors that detect the position of the sun. The sewage system ends in a lagoon in front of the building where wastewater from the building is naturally purified by macrophyte aquatic plants. The **ECOPÓLIS PLAZA** project received the highest "eco-label" (A grade) granted under Spanish law, and was built at a cost 35% lower than a conventional building, according to the architects.

Der Komplex umfasst einen öffentlichen Platz, einen Kindergarten und einen Spielplatz. Erklärtes Ziel der Architekten war es, „ein gesichtsloses Grundstück in der zersiedelten urbanen Landschaft von Madrid, inmitten von Industrie und stark befahrenen Verkehrswegen, durch den Bau einer Kindertagesstätte in einen öffentlichen Raum zu verwandeln, an dem soziale Interaktion möglich wird". Nicht zuletzt ging es ihnen auch darum, Nachhaltigkeit „in den Alltag" zu integrieren. Das Projekt will den Energieverbrauch des Baus senken und gleichzeitig bei den Nutzern ein Bewusstsein für ihren Verbrauch wecken. Unterstützt wurde die bioklimatische Planung durch ein Programm für Energiesimulation, entwickelt von der Thermodynamischen Forschungsgruppe an der Hochschule für Wirtschaftsingenieurwesen in Sevilla. Während das Gebäude zur Hälfte im Boden versenkt ist, öffnet sich eine 700 m² große Glasfassade nach Süden. Über der Stahlleichtbaukonstruktion wurde eine bioklimatische Textilmembran installiert. Die zum Teil beweglichen Textilbahnen werden über Sonnensensoren gesteuert. Abwässer werden in eine Sickergrube vor dem Gebäudekomplex geleitet, wo sie mithilfe von aquatischen Makrophyten natürlich geklärt werden. Die **ECOPÓLIS PLAZA** wurde mit dem höchsten spanischen Umweltzertifikat (Stufe A) ausgezeichnet und konnte den Architekten zufolge mit einer Kostenersparnis von 35 % gegenüber konventioneller Bauten realisiert werden.

Le projet comprend un espace public, un jardin d'enfants et un espace de jeux pour enfants. L'objectif des architectes, expliquent-ils, est d'engager la « transformation d'un site anonyme de l'extension urbaine de Madrid, entouré d'industries et d'infrastructures de transport au trafic dense, en un espace public dédié à l'interaction sociale avec un bâtiment pour accueillir des enfants ». Ils cherchent aussi à intégrer le concept de durabilité « à la vie quotidienne ». Le projet vise à réduire la consommation énergétique, mais aussi à faire prendre conscience aux usagers de leur propre consommation. Pour cela, un schéma bioclimatique est couplé à un système de simulation énergétique mis au point par le groupe de recherches en thermodynamique de l'École de génie industriel de Séville. La moitié du bâtiment est enterrée mais une façade vitrée de 700 m² fait face au sud. Une épaisseur textile bioclimatique a été tendue sur une structure légère d'acier, elle est en partie mobile et reliée à des capteurs qui détectent la position du soleil. Le système d'évacuation aboutit à un lagon devant le bâtiment où les eaux usées sont purifiées naturellement par des plantes aquatiques macrophytes. Le projet **ECOPÓLIS PLAZA** a reçu l'« écolabel » le plus élevé (niveau A) de la législation espagnole et, selon les architectes, sa construction a coûté 35 % moins cher qu'un bâtiment traditionnel.

The yellow covering of the building is partially made of textiles that can be withdrawn according to the position of the sun.

Die gelbe Gebäudehülle wurde partiell als Textilmembranen realisiert, die je nach Sonnenstand ein- und ausfahrbar sind.

La couverture jaune du bâtiment est en partie faite de textiles qui peuvent être retirés selon la position du soleil.

As the section drawing below shows, the structure is partially underground, with angled forms that echo those of the site.

Wie auf der untenstehenden Zeichnung zu sehen, ist der Bau teilweise im Boden versenkt. Die winklige Linienführung greift die Linien des Terrains auf.

Comme le montre le schéma en coupe ci-dessous, la structure est partiellement enterrée et ses formes anguleuses font écho à celles du site.

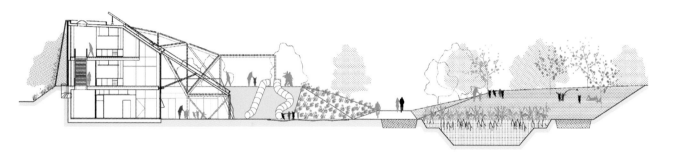

The bright, cheerful structure has large covered areas that are useful in the heat of Madrid. Aside from its yellow color the building has a somewhat industrial appearance.

Der leuchtend-bunte, freundliche Bau hat großflächige überdachte Bereiche: sinnvoll in der Hitze von Madrid. Abgesehen von seiner gelben Hülle mutet das Gebäude recht industriell an.

La structure claire et gaie est dotée de vastes surfaces couvertes appréciables sous la chaleur madrilène. À part sa couleur jaune, le bâtiment présente une apparence presque industrielle.

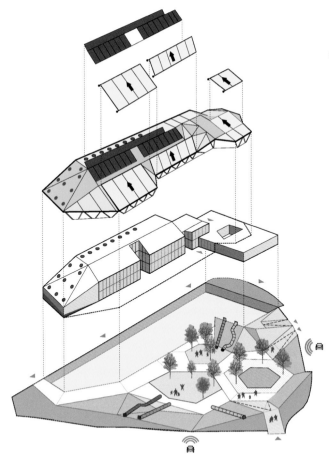

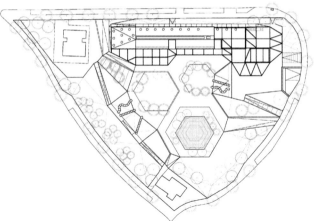

Zeichnungen veranschaulichen das Gelände und die verschiedenen Schichtungen der Architektur. Spiel-plätze (unten) und Spielzonen im Freien, die sich überdachen lassen (rechts), bieten Kindern ein abwechs-lungsreiches Umfeld.

On voit sur les schémas le site et les différents niveaux de construction. Les terrains de jeux (ci-dessous) et les espaces de jeu extérieurs qui peuvent être couverts (à droite) créent un environnement très varié pour les enfants.

Drawings show the site and the different layers of the architecture. Play areas (below) and external play zones that can be covered (right) make for a varied environment for children.

Interior spaces are as bright and cheerful as the exterior. Substantial ceiling height, natural light, and yellow detailing assure the continuity between inside and out.

Das Interieur ist ebenso leuchtend-bunt und freundlich wie die Außenanlagen. Für Kontinuität sorgen besonders hohe Decken, Tageslicht und gelbe Farbakzente.

Les espaces intérieurs sont aussi lumineux et gais que l'extérieur. Une grande hauteur de plafond, la lumière naturelle et les finitions en jaune forment une continuité entre l'intérieur et l'extérieur.

Concrete, steel, and glass form the volumes, leaving a great flexibility for the actual use of the high, open interior.

Beton, Stahl und Glas definieren den Bau und bieten erhebliche Flexibilität bei der praktischen Nutzung der hohen offenen Räume.

Les volumes sont créés à partir de béton, d'acier et de verre, ce qui laisse une grande souplesse pour l'exploitation des hauts espaces intérieurs ouverts.

Circular openings admit daylight
while the yellow color scheme is in
harmony with the basic tone chosen
for the whole structure. The angled
building is complemented in these
images by an angled ramp.

*Tageslicht fällt durch kreisrunde
Fensteröffnungen; die gelben
Akzente greifen das Farbschema des
Komplexes auf. Die schräge Rampe
auf diesen Aufnahmen korrespondiert
mit der winkligen Formensprache des
Baus.*

*Des ouvertures circulaires laissent
entrer la lumière du jour, tandis que
la couleur jaune s'accorde à celle
choisie pour l'ensemble de la structure. Une rampe à angles aigus complète ici la construction anguleuse.*

OLAFUR ELIASSON

Studio Olafur Eliasson
Christinenstr. 18/19, Haus 2
10119 Berlin / Germany
E-mail: studio@olafureliasson.net / Web: www.olafureliasson.net

OLAFUR ELIASSON was born in 1967 in Copenhagen, Denmark, of Icelandic parents. He attended the Royal Academy of Fine Arts in Copenhagen (1989–95). Early in his career he moved to Germany, establishing Studio Olafur Eliasson as an experimental laboratory in Berlin, and he now lives and works in Copenhagen and Berlin. He is a Professor at the Berlin University of the Arts, where he founded the Institute for Spatial Experiments in 2009. He has had solo exhibitions at the Musée d'Art Moderne de la Ville de Paris, and the ZKM in Karlsruhe, and represented Denmark in the 2003 Venice Biennale. More recent solo exhibitions include "Take your time: Olafur Eliasson," which was organized by the San Francisco Museum of Modern Art (San Francisco, California, USA) and traveled to the Museum of Modern Art and PS1 Contemporary Art Center in New York (2007–08); "Your chance encounter" at the 21st Century Museum of Contemporary Art (Kanazawa, Japan, 2009); "Innen Stadt Aussen" (Inner City Out) at Martin Gropius Bau (Berlin, Germany, 2010); and "Seu corpo da obra" (Your body of work) (São Paulo, Brazil, 2011). His installations feature elements appropriated from nature—billowing steam evoking a water geyser, rainbows, or fog-filled rooms. By introducing "natural" phenomena, such as water, mist, or light, into an artificial setting, be it a city street or an art gallery, the artist encourages viewers to reflect on their perception of the physical world. Two works published here are Dufttunnel (Wolfsburg, Germany, 2004); and the Flower Archway, Botanical Garden (Culiacán, Sinaloa, Mexico, 2005–08); while "Your Rainbow Panorama," a 150-meter circular walkway with colored glass panes situated on top of ARoS Museum in Aarhus, Denmark, opened in May 2011; and Harpa Reykjavik Concert Hall and Conference Center, for which Eliasson created the façade in collaboration with Henning Larsen Architects, was inaugurated in August 2011.

OLAFUR ELIASSON wurde 1967 als Sohn isländischer Eltern in Kopenhagen geboren, wo er an der Königlich Dänischen Akademie der Künste studierte (1989–95). Bereits zu Beginn seiner Laufbahn zog er nach Deutschland und gründete das Studio Olafur Eliasson als experimentelles Labor in Berlin. Heute lebt und arbeitet er in Kopenhagen und Berlin. Er ist Professor an der Universität der Künste Berlin, wo er 2009 das Institut für Raumexperimente gründete. Eliasson hatte Einzelausstellungen am Musée d'Art Moderne de la Ville de Paris sowie dem ZKM in Karlsruhe und vertrat Dänemark auf der Biennale 2003 in Venedig. Jüngere Einzelausstellungen sind unter anderem „Take Your Time: Olafur Eliasson", initiiert vom San Francisco Museum of Modern Art (San Francisco, Kalifornien), danach am Museum of Modern Art and PS1 Contemporary Art Center in New York (2007–08), „Your chance encounter" am 21st Century Museum of Contemporary Art (Kanazawa, Japan, 2009), „Innen Stadt Außen" im Martin Gropius Bau (Berlin, Deutschland, 2010) und „Seu corpo da obra" (Your body of work) (São Paulo, Brasilien, 2011). Für seine Installationen eignet sich Eliasson Naturerscheinungen an – waberndern Wasserdampf, der an Geysire erinnert, Regenbögen oder Räume voller Nebel. Durch das Versetzen „natürlicher" Phänomene – wie Wasser, Nebel oder Licht – in künstliche Umgebungen, ob Straße oder Galerie, regt der Künstler dazu an, über die Wahrnehmung physikalischer Phänomene nachzudenken. Zwei hier vorgestellte Arbeiten sind der Dufttunnel (Wolfsburg, Deutschland, 2004) und der Flower Archway (dt. Blumenbogen, Botanischer Garten, Culiacán, Sinaloa, Mexiko, 2005–08). „Your Rainbow Panorama", ein 150 m langer, farbig verglaster Rundgang auf dem Dach des ARoS Museum in Århus, Dänemark, wurde im Mai 2011 eröffnet. Das Harpa-Konzerthaus und Konferenzzentrum in Reykjavík, für das Eliasson in Kollaboration mit Henning Larsen Architects die Fassade gestaltet, wurde im August 2011 eingeweiht.

OLAFUR ELIASSON est né en 1967 à Copenhague de parents islandais. Il a suivi les cours de l'Académie royale des beaux-arts de Copenhague (1989–95) et est venu s'installer en Allemagne dès le début de sa carrière, faisant du Studio Olafur Eliasson un laboratoire expérimental à Berlin. Il vit et travaille aujourd'hui à Copenhague et Berlin. Il est professeur à l'Université des arts de Berlin et y a fondé l'Institut d'expérimentation spatiale en 2009. Il a déjà présenté des expositions personnelles au Musée d'art moderne de la ville de Paris et au ZKM de Karlsruhe et a représenté le Danemark à la Biennale de Venise 2003. Parmi ses expositions plus récentes, on peut citer : « Take your time: Olafur Eliasson », organisée par le Musée d'art moderne de San Francisco (Californie), qui a également été présentée au MoMA et au Centre d'art contemporain PS1 à New York (2007–08) ; « Your chance encounter » au Musée d'art contemporain du XXIᵉ siècle (Kanazawa, Japon, 2009) ; « Innen Stadt Aussen » au Martin Gropius Bau (Berlin, 2010) et « Seu corpo da obra » (Votre corps de travail) (São Paulo, 2011). Ses installations mettent en avant des éléments réappropriés de la nature – bouillonnements de vapeur qui évoquent l'eau d'un geyser, arcs-en-ciel ou pièces emplies de brume. En introduisant ainsi des phénomènes « naturels » tels que l'eau, le brouillard ou la lumière dans un cadre artificiel, rue ou galerie d'art, l'artiste invite les spectateurs à réfléchir à leur perception du monde physique. Deux œuvres sont publiées ici, le *Dufttunnel* (Wolfsburg, Allemagne, 2004) et le *Flower Archway* (Jardin botanique, Culiacán, Sinaloa, Mexique, 2005–08) ; tandis que *Your Rainbow Panorama*, un sentier circulaire de 150 m orné de vitres colorées sur le toit du musée ARoS d'Århus, au Danemark, a ouvert en mai 2011 et que la salle de concerts et centre de conférences Harpa de Reykjavík, dont Eliasson a créé la façade en collaboration avec Henning Larsen Architects, a été inaugurée en août 2011.

DUFTTUNNEL

Wolfsburg, Germany, 2004

Address: StadtBrücke, 38440 Wolfsburg, Germany
www.wolfsburg-citytour.de/wolfsburg-tourist/Dufttunnel/dufttunnel.html
Area: 23.7 m (length), 4.05 m (diameter). Client: Autostadt GmbH
Cost: not disclosed

This site-specific work, located in the city where Volkswagen is based, is made up of 2160 plants in ceramic pots arranged in three stainless-steel tubular sections that revolve at different speeds. Visitors walk through the tunnel on a steel grating while the plants turn slowly around them. Depending on the season, one of six types of plants is used: yellow wallflower (*Cheiranthus cheiri*), horned violet (*Viola cornuta*), heliotrope (*Heliotropium arborescens*), lesser calamint (*Calamintha nepeta*), lavender (*Lavandula angustifolia*), and sage (*Salvia officinalis*). If the idea of rows of potted plants is a familiar one, the fact that they actually surround viewers and move is surprising. It is difficult to classify this work as one of pure architecture, but its concept surely qualifies it as a "green" work.

Die ortspezifische Installation in der VW-Autostadt besteht aus 2160 Pflanzen in Keramiktöpfen in einem röhrenförmigen Gestell aus drei Edelstahlringen, die in unterschiedlichem Tempo langsam rotieren. Besucher laufen über Stahlrosten durch den Tunnel, während sich die Pflanzen langsam um sie drehen. Je nach Jahreszeit werden die Töpfe mit unterschiedlichen Pflanzen bepflanzt: Goldlack (*Cheiranthus cheiri*), Hornveilchen (*Viola cornuta*), Vanilleblume (*Heliotropium arborescens*), Bergminze (*Calamintha nepeta*), Lavendel (*Lavandula angustifolia*) und Salbei (*Salvia officinalis*). Während Topfpflanzen in Reih und Glied ein vertrautes Alltagsphänomen sein mögen, überraschen sie doch, wenn sie den Betrachter umfangen und in Bewegung sind. Die Installation lässt sich schwerlich als rein architektonisch kategorisieren, doch konzeptuell ist sie ohne Frage als „grünes" Projekt einzuordnen.

Cette œuvre *in situ*, installée dans la ville où siège Volkswagen, est composée de 2160 plantes dans des pots de céramique disposés sur trois sections tubulaires en acier inoxydable qui tournent à différentes vitesses. Les visiteurs traversent le tunnel sur une grille en acier tandis que les pots tournent lentement autour d'eux. Selon la saison, six variétés sont plantées : la giroflée ravenelle (*Cheiranthus cheiri*), la violette cornue (*Viola cornuta*), l'héliotrope (*Heliotropium arborescens*), le calament (*Calamintha nepeta*), la lavande (*Lavandula angustifolia*) et la sauge (*Salvia officinalis*). Si l'idée de rangées de pots de fleurs n'est pas originale, il est surprenant de les voir entourer les spectateurs et bouger. Cette œuvre peut difficilement être classée comme purement architecturale, mais le concept en fait sans aucun doute une œuvre « verte ».

Though it assumes the form of a "tunnel" this work is actually more of a bridge, with rotating elements and the curious spectacle offered to walkers of being surrounded by potted plants.

Die Installation mag scheinen wie ein Tunnel – ist aber tatsächlich eine Brücke mit rotierenden Ringelementen und bietet den Besuchern das ungewöhnliche Vergnügen, von Topfpflanzen umringt zu sein.

Malgré sa forme de « tunnel », l'œuvre tient en fait plus d'un pont, avec ses éléments rotatifs et le curieux spectacle que forment les pots de fleurs qui les entourent pour les visiteurs qui la traversent.

THE FLOWER ARCHWAY
Botanical Garden, Culiacán, Sinaloa, Mexico, 2005–08

Botanical Garden, Culiacán, Sinaloa, Mexico, 2005–08
Area: 4.1 m (height), 11.5 m (diameter). Client: Isabel and Agustin Coppel Collection
Cost: not disclosed

The Botanical Garden of Culiacán was founded in 1986. The Mexican curator Patrick Charpenel was chosen to elaborate a contemporary art project that brings together 35 international artists, including Dan Graham, Herzog & de Meuron, James Turrell, Tacita Dean, and Olafur Eliasson. Made with stainless steel and plants (*Parthenocissus quinquefolia, Bignonia ignea, Thunbergia grandiflora, Petrea volubilis, Congea tomentosa*), Eliasson's installation is a five-segment archway over a two-meter-wide central opening. The expanding latticework designs consist of over 50 overlapping spines. From certain points of view, the shape appears unsymmetrical although the five arches are identical. The symmetry of the structure can be experienced by walking under and through it, between the arch feet. In this instance, an architectural form is subsumed in the plants that cover it, making the distinction between the "built" form and nature very difficult to distinguish.

Der Botanische Garten von Culiacán wurde 1986 gegründet. Der mexikanische Kurator Patrick Charpenel wurde betraut, ein zeitgenössisches Kunstprojekt zu entwickeln und brachte 35 internationale Künstler zusammen, darunter Dan Graham, Herzog & de Meuron, James Turrell, Tacita Dean und Olafur Eliasson. Eliassons Installation aus Edelstahl und Pflanzen (*Parthenocissus quinquefolia, Bignonia ignea, Thunbergia grandiflora, Petrea volubilis, Congea tomentosa*) besteht aus einem fünfteiligen Blumenbogen, der sich um eine zentrale, 2 m große runde Öffnung orientiert. Das strahlenförmige Gitterwerk entfaltet sich aus über 50 einander kreuzenden Speichen. Aus bestimmten Blickwinkeln wirkt die Konstruktion asymmetrisch, obwohl die fünf Bögen identisch sind. Die Symmetrie wird augenfällig, sobald man sich unter und durch die Installation begibt und zwischen den Bögen hindurchläuft. Hier wird eine architektonische Konstruktion gänzlich von Pflanzen vereinnahmt: Es fällt zunehmend schwer, zwischen „gebautem" und natürlichem Umfeld zu unterscheiden.

Le Jardin botanique de Culiacán a été fondé en 1986. Le conservateur mexicain Patrick Charpenel a été sélectionné pour concevoir un projet d'art contemporain qui réunit 35 artistes du monde entier, parmi lesquels Dan Graham, Herzog & de Meuron, James Turrell, Tacita Dean et Olafur Eliasson. Faite d'acier inoxydable et de plantes (*Parthenocissus quiquefolia, Bignonia ignea, Thunbergia grandiflora, Petrea volubilis, Congea tomentosa*), l'installation d'Eliasson forme une arche en cinq segments qui entourent une ouverture centrale large de deux mètres. Le vaste treillis est composé de plus de 50 lattes qui se chevauchent. Sa forme apparaît asymétrique sous certains points de vue, alors même que les cinq arceaux sont identiques. La symétrie de la structure peut être ressentie en marchant dessous et en la traversant, entre les pieds de l'arche. Dans cet exemple, une forme architecturale est subsumée sous les végétaux qui la recouvrent, ce qui rend la forme « construite » et la nature très difficiles à distinguer.

Though the structure has some similarity to garden trellises, growing vegetation makes it appear almost as though it is an organic part of the garden itself.

Die an ein Spalier erinnernde Konstruktion verschwindet fast unter den rankenden Pflanzen und wird so zum organischen Bestandteil der Parkanlage.

Bien qu'elle présente une certaine similitude avec un treillage de jardin, le développement de la végétation donne à la structure l'apparence d'une partie organique du jardin en soi.

The pattern of the trellis has an
organic basis, but it is its lightness
and specific form that make it seem
to partially disappear into the wooded
setting in this image.

Das Muster des Gerüsts basiert auf
organischen Formen; dank seiner
Leichtigkeit und höchst eigenwilligen
Form scheint es hier fast mit der
baumbestandenen Kulisse zu verschmelzen.

Le motif treillagé a une base organique, mais c'est sa légèreté et
sa forme spécifique qui le font
ici presque disparaître dans le
décor boisé.

DICK VAN GAMEREN

Dick van Gameren architecten B.V.
Willem Fenengastraat 4B
1096 BN Amsterdam
The Netherlands

Tel: +31 20 462 78 00
Fax: +31 20 462 78 19
E-mail: info@vangameren.com
Web: www.dickvangameren.com

DICK VAN GAMEREN was born in 1962 in Amersfoort, the Netherlands. He studied at Delft University of Technology in the Faculty of Architecture (1981–88). From 1988 to 1991 he worked in the office of Mecanoo Architecten, and from 1991 to 1993 was a Partner in Van Gameren Mastenbroek Architecten. He was subsequently part of De Architectengroep (1993–2004), before creating his present firm in 2005. He has been the Chairman of the Department of Architecture, Delft University of Technology, Faculty of Architecture since 2008. He won a 2007 Aga Khan Award for the Dutch Embassy (Addis Ababa, Ethiopia, 2005). He completed the Laakhaven office and apartment complex (The Hague, 2004); and a residential care center (Berkenstede, Diemen, 2006). More recently he created the Villa 4.0 ('t Gooi, 2010–11, published here); the exhibition design for "I Promise to Love You" (Kunsthal, Rotterdam, 2011); and completed the refurbishment of the Drents Museum (Assen, 2011), all in the Netherlands.

DICK VAN GAMEREN wurde 1962 in Amersfoort, Niederlande, geboren und studierte an der Architekturfakultät der TU Delft (1981–88). Von 1988 bis 1991 arbeitete er für Mecanoo Architecten, von 1991 bis 1993 als Partner bei Van Gameren Mastenbroek Architecten. Im Anschluss war er zunächst für De Architectengroep (1993–2004) tätig, bevor er 2005 sein heutiges Büro gründete. Seit 2008 ist er Dekan der Architekturfakultät der TU Delft. 2007 wurde er für die Niederländische Botschaft in Addis Abeba (Äthiopien, 2005) mit dem Aga Khan Award ausgezeichnet. Van Gameren realisierte den Büro- und Apartmentkomplex Laakhaven (Den Haag, 2004) und ein Zentrum für betreutes Wohnen (Berkenstede, Diemen, 2006). In jüngerer Zeit konnten die Villa 4.0 ('t Gooi, 2010–11, hier vorgestellt), die Ausstellungsarchitektur für „I Promise to Love You" (Kunsthalle Rotterdam, 2011) und der Umbau des Drents Museum (Assen, 2011) fertiggestellt werden, alle in den Niederlanden.

DICK VAN GAMEREN est né en 1962 à Amerfoort, aux Pays-Bas. Il a fait ses études à la faculté d'architecture de l'Université de technologie de Delft (1981–88). De 1988 à 1991, il a travaillé dans l'agence Mecanoo Architecten, puis de 1991 à 1993 en tant que partenaire de Van Gameren Mastenbroek Architecten. Il a ensuite participé à De Architectengroep (1993–2004) avant de créer sa société actuelle en 2005. Il dirige le département d'architecture de la faculté d'architecture à l'Université technologique de Delft depuis 2008. En 2007, il a gagné un prix Aga Khan pour l'ambassade des Pays-Bas (Addis-Abeba, Éthiopie, 2005). Il a réalisé notamment le complexe de bureaux et de logements Laakhaven (La Haye, 2004) et un centre de soins résidentiel (Berkenstede, Diemen, 2006) ainsi que, plus récemment, la Villa 4.0 ('t Gooi, 2010–11, publiée ici) ; la conception de l'exposition « I Promise to Love You » (Kunsthal, Rotterdam, 2011) et le réaménagement du musée Drents (Assen, 2011), toujours aux Pays-Bas.

VILLA 4.0
't Gooi, The Netherlands, 2010–11

Address: n/a. Area: 540 m²
Client: not disclosed. Cost: not disclosed
Collaboration: IDing Interior Design; Michael van Gessel Landscape Design

This design began with an existing house, built in 1967, and then enlarged in 1972 and 2001, with a conscious scheme to make the best use of materials already on the site. Roofs, façades, and floors were reinsulated, while the old wood-frame windows were replaced with aluminum units with insulated glass. The interior design firm IDing was given the responsibility of creating a "timeless" design for the inside of the renovated house. A low-temperature floor-heating system was installed. A solar boiler is used for hot water, but the house does not benefit from a great deal of direct sunlight. Natural ventilation was privileged, through such devices as a sliding glass roof over the kitchen and a roof hatch in the living room. A rooftop pump draws water from a nearby brook and sprays it onto the roof, from where it runs back to the brook. A high-efficiency wood-burning stove was installed in the kitchen, and all artificial lighting is LED-based. Gray water is placed in a tank that purifies it using an organic technique. It is then discharged into the brook. Brook water is also used for all watering. The garden, created by landscape architect Michael van Gessel, is tended without herbicides or fertilizers.

Ausgangspunkt des Entwurfs war ein Altbau von 1967 mit Erweiterungen von 1972 und 2001 und die bewusste Entscheidung, die gegebene Situation bestmöglich zu nutzen. Dach, Fassade und Böden wurden neu gedämmt, die alten Holzfenster durch Isolierglasfenster mit Alurahmen ersetzt. Das Innenarchitekturbüro IDing erhielt den Auftrag, ein „zeitloses" Interieur für den renovierten Bau zu gestalten. Eine Niedertemperatur-Fußbodenheizung wurde installiert. Warmwasser wird mit einem Solarboiler erzeugt, wobei das Haus nicht übermäßig von direktem Sonnenlicht profitiert. Natürliche Durchlüftung wird unterstützt durch Elemente wie ein Glasschiebedach über der Küche und eine Dachluke im Wohnzimmer. Eine auf dem Dach installierte Pumpe pumpt Wasser von einem nahe gelegenen Bach auf das Dach, wo es versprüht wird und über einen Ablauf wieder in den Bach gelangt. In der Küche wurde ein Hochleistungs-Holzofen installiert, die gesamte künstliche Beleuchtung ist LED-basiert. Grauwasser wird in einem Tank gesammelt, biologisch geklärt und in den Bach geleitet. Das Bachwasser wird darüber hinaus zur Bewässerung des Gartens genutzt. Dieser wurde vom Landschaftsarchitekten Michael van Gessel gestaltet und wird ohne Einsatz von Herbiziden oder Dünger gepflegt.

La réflexion a commencé à partir d'une maison existante, construite en 1967, puis agrandie en 1972 et 2001, avec la volonté délibérée de tirer le meilleur profit possible des matériaux déjà présents. L'isolation des toits, façades et sols a été refaite, tandis que les anciens encadrements de fenêtres en bois ont été remplacés par de nouveaux en aluminium et verre isolé. Le cabinet d'architecture intérieure IDing a été chargé de créer un design « intemporel » pour l'intérieur de la maison rénovée. Un chauffage au sol à basse température a été installé. L'eau chaude est fournie par une chaudière solaire mais l'ensoleillement direct n'est pas très important. La ventilation naturelle a été privilégiée au moyen de dispositifs tels qu'un toit vitré coulissant au-dessus de la cuisine et une lucarne dans le salon. Une pompe sur le toit aspire l'eau d'un ruisseau voisin et la vaporise sur le toit d'où elle s'écoule et rejoint le ruisseau. Un poêle à bois haute efficacité a été installé dans la cuisine et tout l'éclairage artificiel est à base de LED. Les eaux ménagères sont recueillies dans une citerne où elles sont purifiées écologiquement. Elles sont ensuite déversées dans le ruisseau dont l'eau sert également à l'arrosage. Le jardin, créé par l'architecte paysagiste Michael Van Gessel, est entretenu sans herbicides ni engrais.

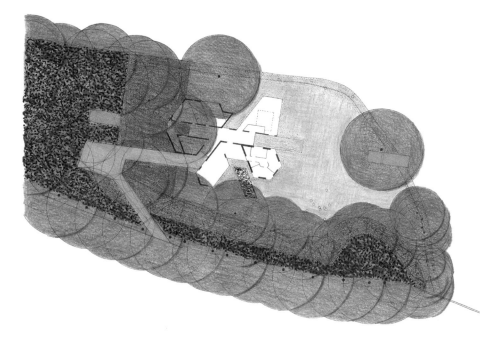

Seen in a site plan (left) or in these photos, the house seems to be well integrated into its natural setting, but the architecture does not consciously or visibly put forward its "sustainable" credentials.

Wie auf dem Grundstücksplan (links) und den Aufnahmen zu sehen, fügt sich das Haus in die landschaftliche Umgebung, auch wenn seine Architektur ihre „Nachhaltigkeit" nicht sichtbar nach außen trägt.

Sur le plan du site (à gauche) ou les photos, la maison semble bien intégrée à son cadre naturel, même si l'architecture ne met pas consciemment ou visiblement en avant son caractère « durable ».

The somewhat "fractured" plan of the single-story house is seen left. The image below shows how the volumes are opened to their setting, with floor-to-ceiling glazing alternating with opaque walls.

Links der fast fragmentiert wirkende Grundriss des Bungalows. Unten im Bild die zu ihrem Umfeld geöffneten Volumina des Baus. Geschosshohe Verglasung und geschlossene Oberflächen wechseln einander ab.

On voit à gauche le plan « fracturé » de la maison de plain-pied et sur la photo ci-dessous comment les différents volumes ouvrent sur le décor, le vitrage du sol au plafond alternant avec des murs opaques.

Very open glazed walls and floor surfaces near to ground level combine to
make the house permeable to the
exterior and the natural setting.

Dank der sehr offenen verglasten
Wände und Böden auf Niveau des
Baugrunds wird das Haus durchlässig
für Außenraum und landschaftliche
Umgebung.

Des parois vitrées très ouvertes
sont associées à des sols proches
du niveau de la terre pour rendre
la maison perméable à l'extérieur
et au décor naturel.

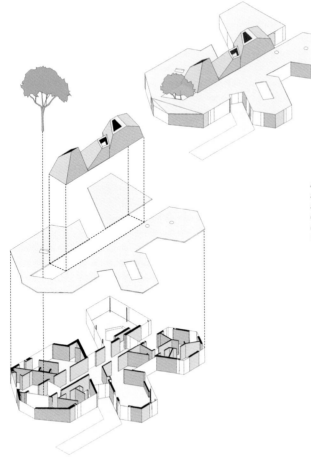

An exploded axonometric drawing shows the plan of the house. Though straight lines dominate, angles and openings enliven the spaces and their exposure to natural light and external views.

Die axonometrische Explosionszeichnung veranschaulicht den Grundriss des Hauses. Hier dominieren gerade Linien, doch auch Schrägen und Wandöffnungen beleben die Räume, lassen Tageslicht einfallen und öffnen Ausblicke.

Le schéma axonométrique éclaté montre le plan de la maison : les lignes droites dominent, mais les angles et les ouvertures animent les différents espaces et leur exposition à la lumière naturelle ou leurs vues sur l'extérieur.

GIGON/GUYER

Annette Gigon/Mike Guyer
Carmenstr. 28
8032 Zurich
Switzerland

Tel: +41 257 11 11
Fax: +41 257 11 10
E-mail: info@gigon-guyer.ch
Web: www.gigon-guyer.ch

Born in 1959, **ANNETTE GIGON** received her diploma from the ETH in Zurich in 1984. She worked in the office of Herzog & de Meuron in Basel (1985–88), before setting up her own practice (1987–89) and creating her present firm with Mike Guyer in 1989. Born in 1958, **MIKE GUYER** also graduated from the ETH in 1984, and worked with Rem Koolhaas (OMA, 1984–87), and then taught with Hans Kollhoff at the ETH (1987–88). Since 2012 they are Professors of Architecture and Technology at the ETH in Zurich. Their built work includes the Kirchner Museum (Davos, 1990–92); the Vinikus Restaurant (Davos, 1990–92); and a renovation of the Oskar Reinhart Collection (Römerholz, Winterthur, 1997–98). Recent and current work includes the Museum for the Albers/Honegger Collection (Mouans-Sartoux, France, 2001–03); the Henze & Ketterer Gallery Kunst-Depot (Wichtrach, 2002–04); a housing development (Brunnenhof, Zurich, 2004–07); the extension of the Swiss Museum of Transport (Lucerne; 2005–09); a housing complex (Zollikerstrasse, Zurich, 2006–11); Prime Tower (Zurich, 2008–11, published here); the Löwenbräu-Areal (Zurich, 2006–12); the C10 Office Building (Zurich); and the Würth Administration Building with Educational and Training Center (Rorschach, 2009–13), all in Switzerland unless otherwise indicated.

ANNETTE GIGON, geboren 1959, absolvierte ihr Diplom 1984 an der ETH Zürich. Sie arbeitete bei Herzog & de Meuron in Basel (1985–88), ehe sie zunächst ihr eigenes Büro (1987–89) und schließlich 1989 ihr heutiges Büro mit Mike Guyer gründete. Auch **MIKE GUYER**, geboren 1958, schloss sein Studium 1984 an der ETH Zürich ab. Anschließend arbeitete er für Rem Koolhaas (OMA, 1984–87) und lehrte mit Hans Kollhoff an der ETH (1987–88). Seit 2012 sind beide Professoren für Architektur und Konstruktion an der ETH Zürich. Zu ihren gebauten Projekten zählen das Kirchner Museum (Davos, 1990–92), das Restaurant Vinikus (Davos, 1990–92) sowie die Renovierung der Sammlung Oskar Reinhart (Römerholz, Winterthur, 1997–98). Jüngere und aktuelle Projekte sind unter anderem ein Museumsbau für die Sammlung Albers/Honegger (Mouans-Sartoux, Frankreich, 2001–03), das Kunst-Depot der Galerie Henze & Ketterer (Wichtrach, 2002–04), die Wohnüberbauung Brunnenhof (Zürich, 2004–07), die Erweiterung des Verkehrshauses der Schweiz (Luzern, 2005–09), Wohnhäuser an der Zollikerstrasse (Zürich, 2006–11), der Prime Tower (Zürich, 2008–11, hier vorgestellt), das Löwenbräu-Areal (Zürich, 2006–12), das Bürogebäude C 10 (Zürich) sowie das Würth Verwaltungsgebäude mit Ausbildungs- und Trainingszentrum (Rorschach, 2009–13), alle in der Schweiz, sofern nicht anders angegeben.

Née en 1959, **ANNETTE GIGON** est diplômée de l'ETH de Zurich (1984). Elle a travaillé dans l'agence Herzog & de Meuron à Bâle (1985–88) avant d'ouvrir son propre cabinet (1987–89), puis de créer la société actuelle avec Mike Guyer en 1989. Né en 1958, **MIKE GUYER** a également obtenu son diplôme à l'ETH en 1984 et a ensuite travaillé avec Rem Koolhaas (OMA, 1984–87) avant d'enseigner avec Hans Kollhoff à l'ETH (1987–88). Ils sont tous les deux professeurs d'architecture et de technologie à l'ETH de Zurich depuis 2012. Leurs réalisations déjà construites comprennent le musée Kirchner (Davos, 1990–92) ; le restaurant Vinikus (Davos, 1990–92) et la rénovation de la collection Oskar Reinhart (Römerholz, Winterthur, 1997–98). Leurs travaux plus récents et en cours comprennent le musée pour la collection Albers/Honegger (Mouans-Sartoux, France, 2001–03) ; le « dépôt d'art » de la galerie Henze & Ketterer (Wichtrach, 2004–07) ; l'extension du Musée suisse des transports (Lucerne, 2005–09) ; un complexe de logements (Zollikerstrasse, Zurich, 2006–11) ; la Prime Tower (Zurich, 2008–11, publiée ici) ; le quartier Löwenbräu (Zurich, 2006–12) ; l'immeuble de bureaux C10 (Zurich) et le bâtiment administratif, centre éducatif et de formation, Würth (Rorschach, 2009–13), tous en Suisse sauf si spécifié.

PRIME TOWER
Zurich, Switzerland, 2008–11

Address: Hardstr. 201, 8005 Zurich, Switzerland, tel: +41 58 800 49 00, http://primetower.ch/en
Area: 49 121 m² (Prime Tower); 6206 m² (Cubus); 2759 m² (Diagonal); 11 200 m² (basement levels). Client: Swiss Prime Site AG, Olten
Cost: not disclosed. Collaboration: Stefan Thommen (Team Manager),
Christian Maggioni (Deputy Team Manager), Pieter Rabijns (Project Manager)

Because Zurich has few towers, this building stands out from most locations in the city: its sophisticated form has transformed an area otherwise notable for its rail lines and road flyovers.

In Zürich, das kaum Hochhäuser hat, ist der Bau fast überall weithin zu sehen: Seine elegante Formgebung gibt dem vor allem von Bahntrassen und Hochstraßen geprägten Stadtviertel ein neues Gesicht.

Zurich ne possède que peu de tours, de sorte que le bâtiment est repérable depuis presque partout dans la ville : sa forme complexe a métamorphosé une zone sinon connue pour ses voies ferrées et ponts autoroutiers.

Gigon/Guyer won the commission to build this project, located in the Maag-Areal district of the Swiss city, in a 2004 competition. The LEED Gold–certified tower uses a ground-water heat-exchange pump, waste-heat recovery from the building and refrigeration devices, coupled heating/cooling with heat and ice storage, and partially operable windows. The complex includes the main 126-meter-high, 36-story office tower, together with Cubus, an office and shop space, and Diagonal, which is a listed industrial building now containing a restaurant, art galleries, and offices. Located at the periphery of Zurich's downtown area, the site was formerly a nearly inaccessible industrial zone. The irregular octagonal plan of the green glass tower and its articulation and cantilevered protrusions imply that it takes on different appearances according to the angle under which it is viewed. The architects were also responsible for the interiors of the entrance hall, conference area, public restaurant, and bar (34th and 35th floors), and the tenant fit-outs for the law firm Homburger, Transammonia AG (16th and 17th floors) and Deutsche Bank (13th to 16th and 33rd floors).

2004 gewannen Gigon/Guyer den Wettbewerb für dieses Projekt im Maag-Areal von Zürich. Besondere Merkmale des mit einem LEED-Zertifikat in Gold ausgezeichneten Turms sind die Grundwassernutzung mittels Wärmepumpe sowie die Abwärmenutzung von Gebäude und Kältemaschinen. Hinzu kommt der Einsatz von Wärme-Kälte-Kopplung mit Wärme- und Eisspeichern und eine natürliche Belüftung durch Fensterschlitze. Der Komplex umfasst einen 36-stöckigen, 126 m hohen Hauptturm sowie die Annexbauten Cubus mit Büro- und Gewerbeflächen sowie Diagonal, ein denkmalgeschützter Industriebau, in dem heute ein Restaurant, Galerien und Büros untergebracht sind. Das am Rande der Zürcher Innenstadt gelegene Areal war früher ein weitgehend unzugängliches Industriegebiet. Der asymmetrische achteckige Grundriss des grünen Glashochhauses, seine Fassadengestaltung und –Auskragungen geben dem Gebäude je nach Blickwinkel ein unterschiedliches Gesicht. Die Architekten gestalteten darüber hinaus das Foyer, den Konferenzbereich, das öffentliche Restaurant mit Bar (34. und 35. Etage) sowie den Mieterausbau für die Anwaltskanzlei Homburger, Transammonia AG (16. und 17. Etage) und die Deutsche Bank (13. bis 16. und 33. Etage).

Gigon/Guyer a gagné un concours en 2004 pour la commande de ce projet, situé dans le district Maag-Areal de Zurich. La tour, labellisée LEED or, est dotée d'une pompe à échangeur de chaleur qui utilise l'eau de la nappe phréatique, de dispositifs de récupération de la chaleur du bâtiment et de refroidissement, d'un système couplé chauffage/climatisation avec stockage de chaleur et de glace et de fenêtres qui s'ouvrent partiellement. Le complexe comprend la tour principale de bureaux, haute de 126 m pour 36 étages, ainsi que Cubus, un espace de bureaux et commerces, et Diagonal, un bâtiment industriel classé qui abrite aujourd'hui un restaurant, des galeries d'art et des bureaux. Le site, en périphérie du centre-ville de Zurich, était auparavant une zone industrielle quasi inaccessible. Le plan octogonal irrégulier de la tour verte en verre, son articulation et ses saillies en encorbellement lui font prendre une apparence différente selon l'angle sous lequel elle est observée. Les architectes ont également été chargés de créer l'intérieur du hall d'entrée, l'espace de conférences, le restaurant public et le bar (34e et 35e étages), tandis que le locataire a aménagé les bureaux de la société juridique Homburger, de Transammonia AG (16e et 17e étages) et de la Deutsche Bank (13e au 16e et 33e étages).

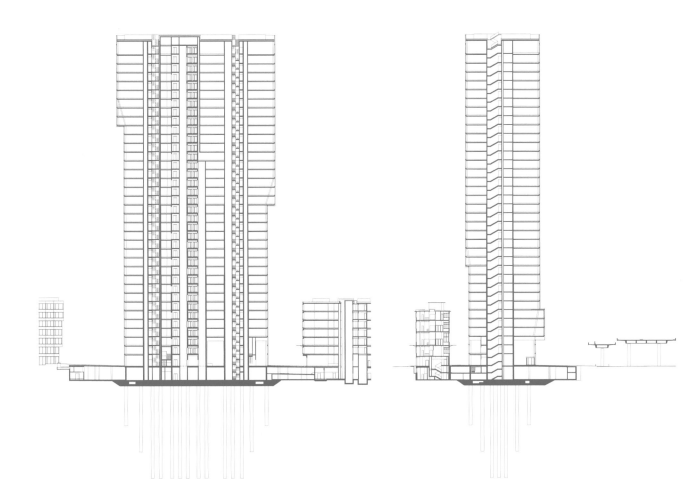

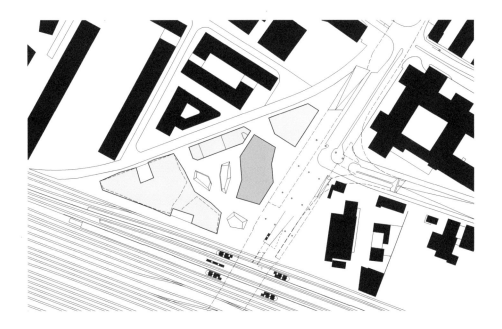

Section drawings show the basic,
efficient forms of the design, which is
part of a complex, enclosed in a
dense road and rail triangle (left). The
blue-green skin of the building is
scaled, giving it relief and variety.

Auf Querschnitten wird die schlichte,
effiziente Formgebung des Entwurfs
deutlich, der in einen Komplex eingebettet und von dichter Straßenbebau-
ung und einem Bahndreieck (links)
umgeben ist. Die blaugraue Außen-
haut des Baus ist geschuppt, was für
Struktur und Abwechslung sorgt.

La vue en coupe montre les formes
de base très efficaces de la structure,
qui fait partie d'un complexe enclos
dans un triangle de routes et voies
ferrées denses (à gauche). L'enveloppe bleu-vert du bâtiment forme
des échelons qui lui confèrent relief
et diversité.

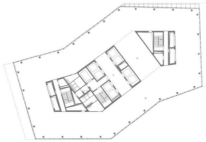

The ground floor lobby of the building (left) was designed by the architects, as were some of the office spaces, such as those of the legal firm Homburger. Floor plans show how the shape of the tower allows for varied office formats.

Die Lobby im Erdgeschoss des Gebäudes (links) ist ein Entwurf der Architekten, ebenso wie ausgewählte Büroflächen, etwa die Räume der Anwaltskanzlei Homburger. Etagengrundrisse belegen die variablen Nutzungsmöglichkeiten für Büroflächen im Turm.

Le hall du rez-de-chaussée (à gauche) a été créé par les architectes, ainsi que certains des espaces de bureaux, tels ceux de la société juridique Homburger. Les plans des étages illustrent la manière dont la forme de la tour influe sur les différents formats de bureaux.

GULF COAST COMMUNITY DESIGN STUDIO

Gulf Coast Community Design Studio
425 Division Street / Biloxi, MS 39530 / USA
Tel: +1 228 436 4661 / Fax: +1 228 435 7181
E-mail: info@gccds.msstate.edu
Web: www.gccds.org

DAVID PERKES was born in 1957 in Utah. He was educated at the University of Utah Graduate School of Architecture (M.Arch, 1985), the Yale School of Architecture (Master of Environmental Design, 1993), and at the Harvard GSD (Loeb Fellow, 2003–04). He is the Founding Director of the Gulf Coast Community Design Studio that works at Mississippi State University with 15 full-time architects, architectural interns, planners, and landscape architects with grant and contract funded annual operating income of about $800 000. Research grant sources include Housing and Urban Development, Department of Energy, Department of Homeland Security, Small Business Administration, and the National Endowment for the Arts. Contracts include the Gulf Coast Renaissance Corporation, Habitat for Humanity, Back Bay Mission, Biloxi Housing Authority, and East Biloxi Coordination Relief and Redevelopment Agency. The work of the studio includes East Biloxi Coordination Center Building (Biloxi, Mississippi, 2007); Broussard House (Biloxi, Mississippi, 2008, published here); John Henry Beck Park Improvements (Biloxi, Mississippi, 2009); Eagle's Nest Play Structure (Pascagoula, Mississippi, 2010); Bayou Auguste Restoration (Biloxi, Mississippi, 2011); Flood-Proof Construction Research (Biloxi, Mississippi, 2011); Katrina Replacement Houses (Gulf Coast, Mississippi, 2006–12); and current work that concerns Temporary Disaster Housing Prototype Design, all in the USA.

DAVID PERKES wurde 1957 in Utah geboren. Sein Studium absolvierte er an der University of Utah, Aufbaustudiengang Architektur (M.Arch, 1985), an der Architekturfakultät der Yale University (Master of Environmental Design, 1993) sowie der Harvard GSD (Loeb Fellow, 2003–04). Er ist Gründungsdirektor des Gulf Coast Community Design Studio an der Mississippi State University, das mit 15 Vollzeit-Architekten, Praktikanten, Planern und Landschaftsarchitekten arbeitet. Der jährliche Umsatz setzt sich aus Fördergeldern und regulären Aufträgen zusammen und beträgt rund 800 000 Dollar. Fördergelder werden unter anderem von folgenden Behörden bereitgestellt: Behörde für Wohnbau und Stadtentwicklung, Energiebehörde, Heimatschutzbehörde, Behörde für Kleinunternehmerförderung und dem National Endowment for the Arts. Auftraggeber sind unter anderem die Gulf Coast Renaissance Corporation, Habitat for Humanity, Back Bay Mission, die Behörde für sozialen Wohnungsbau in Biloxi und die Behörde für Hilfsleistungen und Wiederaufbau in East Biloxi. Zu den Projekten des Studios zählen Gebäude für das Koordinationscenter in East Biloxi (Biloxi, Mississippi, 2007), das Broussard House (Biloxi, Mississippi, 2008, hier vorgestellt), die Modernisierung des John Henry Beck Park (Biloxi, Mississippi, 2009), der Spielplatz Eagle's Nest (Pascagoula, Mississippi, 2010), die Flusssanierung des Bayou Auguste (Biloxi, Mississippi, 2011), ein Forschungsprojekt Hochwasserschutz (Biloxi, Mississippi, 2011), Projekte der Katrina-Neubebauung (Gulf Coast, Mississippi, 2006–12). Aktuell arbeitet das Studio an einem Prototyp für Katastrophen-Notunterkünfte, alle in den USA.

DAVID PERKES est né en 1957 dans l'Utah. Il a fait ses études à la Graduate School of Architecture de l'université de l'Utah (M.Arch 1985), à l'École d'architecture de Yale (master en design environnemental, 1993) et à la Harvard GSD (Loeb Fellow, 2003–04). Il est le directeur fondateur du studio de design communautaire Gulf Coast Community Design Studio qui travaille à l'université du Mississippi avec 15 architectes à plein temps, des étudiants en architecture, des concepteurs et des architectes paysagistes pour un bénéfice d'exploitation annuel financé par des subventions et sur contrat d'environ 800 000 $. Les allocations de recherche accordées viennent notamment des services américains de l'habitat et du développement urbain, du ministère de l'Énergie, du ministère de la Sécurité intérieure, de l'Agence américaine pour les petites entreprises et du Fonds national pour les arts. Les contrats font intervenir les ONG Gulf Coast Renaissance Corporation, Habitat for Humanity, Back Bay Mission, l'Agence pour le logement de Biloxi et l'Agence d'East Biloxi de coordination, secours et réaménagement. Le studio a réalisé ou collabore à plusieurs projets, parmi lesquels le bâtiment du centre de coordination d'East Biloxi (Biloxi, Mississippi, 2007) ; la Broussard House (Biloxi, 2008, publiée ici) ; l'aménagement du parc John Henry Beck (Biloxi, 2009) ; le terrain de jeu Eagle's Nest (Pascagoula, Mississippi, 2010) ; le réaménagement du Bayou Auguste (Biloxi, 2011) ; un projet de recherches en matière de construction résistant aux inondations (Biloxi, 2011) ; des reconstructions de maisons détruites par Katrina (région côtière, Mississippi, 2006–12) et des travaux en cours pour la conception de prototypes de logement temporaire en cas de catastrophe, tous aux États-Unis.

BROUSSARD HOUSE

Biloxi, Mississippi, USA, 2008

Address: n/a. Area: 78 m²
Client: Patty Broussard. Cost: $99 000
Collaboration: Jason Pressgrove, Bryan Bell, Brad Guy, Sergio Palleroni

The **BROUSSARD HOUSE** is a design-build collaboration between the Gulf Coast Community Design Studio, Basic Initiative with Sergio Palleroni, and Design Corps with Bryan Bell. A group of summer students from around the US organized by Brad Guy at Penn State also participated. The area of the house was devastated by Hurricane Katrina, and revised flood maps required any new house to be roughly four meters above grade. David Perkes writes: "The aim of the design is to mitigate the dominant form of an elevated house. The placement of the stair is the genesis of the house design. The stair is located in the center of the house as a space, instead of being attached to the front of the house as an object." The house has two main rooms, separated by an outdoor stair space. LEED certified, the structure is well suited to the local climate. The architect concludes: "The house form and structure respond to surrounding trees, so it is fitting that neighbors and friends of Patty refer to it as 'the tree house.'"

Entwurf und Bau des **BROUSSARD HOUSE** wurde als Kooperation zwischen dem Gulf Coast Community Design Studio, der Basic Initiative mit Sergio Palleroni und dem Design Corps mit Bryan Bell realisiert. Auch eine Gruppe von Sommerkursteilnehmern aus den ganzen USA unter Leitung von Brad Guy, Pennsylvania State University, beteiligte sich am Projekt. Das Haus liegt in einer vom Hurrikan Katrina verwüsteten Gegend und musste aufgrund neuer Hochwasserkarten rund vier Meter über dem Boden aufgeständert werden. David Perkes schreibt: „Der Entwurf war vor allem darauf zugeschnitten, das Haus nicht allzu prominent als Pfahlbau wirken zu lassen. Der gesamte Entwurf entwickelt sich aus der Positionierung der Treppe. Sie ist im Herzen des Baus als eigenständiger Raum platziert, statt als Objekt vor den Bau geschaltet zu sein." Das Haus hat zwei Haupträume, die durch einen Terrassendurchgang mit Treppenzugang voneinander getrennt sind. Der LEED-zertifizierte Bau wurde auf das regionale Klima abgestimmt. Die Architekten resümieren: „Form und Konstruktion des Hauses korrespondieren mit den umstehenden Bäumen, und so ist es treffend, dass Pattys Nachbarn und Freunde vom ‚Baumhaus' sprechen."

La **BROUSSARD HOUSE** est le fruit d'une collaboration de design-construction entre le Gulf Coast Community Design Studio, la Basic Initiative de Sergio Palleroni et Design Corps avec Bryan Bell. Un groupe d'étudiants de tout le pays rassemblé par Brad Guy de Penn State a également participé au projet pendant l'été. L'emplacement de la maison fait partie des zones dévastées par l'ouragan Katrina et les nouvelles cartes des risques d'inondation exigent de chaque nouvelle maison qu'elle soit surélevée à quatre mètres au-dessus du sol. David Perkes la décrit comme suit : « Le design a cherché à alléger la domination de la forme surélevée. L'emplacement de l'escalier est la base de l'ensemble : il est situé au centre de la maison et forme un espace en soi, au lieu d'être fixé à l'avant comme un objet. » La maison se compose de deux pièces principales séparées par un espace ouvert avec l'escalier. Elle est certifiée LEED et bien adaptée au climat local. L'architecte conclut : « La forme et la structure de la maison répondent aux arbres qui l'entourent, c'est pourquoi les voisins et amis de Patty l'appellent "la maison dans les arbres". »

Sitting on its pilings, the house seems like a more ordinary residence that has been lifted off the ground for the obvious reason of potential local flooding, but the central stairway gives it an even more unexpected appearance.

Der Pfahlbau präsentiert sich als gewöhnliches Wohnhaus, das in der hochwassergefährdeten Region als Schutzmaßnahme aufgeständert wurde. Noch ungewöhnlicher ist der zentral positionierte Treppenaufgang.

Sur ses pilotis, la maison ressemble à une maison ordinaire qui aurait été surélevée dans le but évident de la protéger des éventuelles inondations, mais la cage d'escalier centrale lui donne une apparence plus originale.

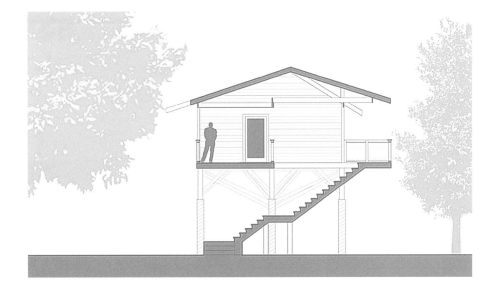

The stairway arrives at the level of
the house in an open terrace area
that ventilates the house and provides
a protected outdoor space.

Auf der Wohnebene führt die Treppe
zunächst zu einer offenen Terrassen-
zone, die zur Durchlüftung des Hauses beiträgt und zugleich als
geschützter Außenbereich dient.

Au niveau de la maison, l'escalier
aboutit à une terrasse ouverte qui
ventile l'ensemble et offre un espace
extérieur protégé.

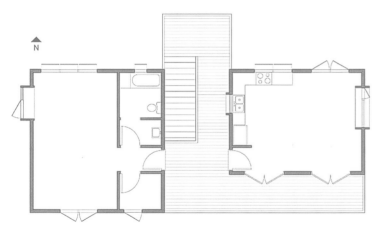

With its simple, high wooden interior and plan that divides the basic volumes in two (left), Broussard House offers more architectural surprises than its upper-story profile announces from the exterior.

Mit seinem schlichten Interieur aus Holz und einem Grundriss, der zwei separate Baukörper zeigt (links), ist das Broussard House überraschender, als das obere Geschoss mit seinem Profil von außen ahnen lässt.

Avec son intérieur de bois simple et haut et son plan divisant le volume en deux (à gauche), la Broussard House réserve plus de surprises architecturales que le profil de l'étage supérieur ne le laisse présager de l'extérieur.

HMC ARCHITECTS

HMC Architects
633 West 5th Street, Third Floor
Los Angeles, CA 90071
USA

Tel: +1 213 542 8300
E-mail: kelly.olson@hmcarchitects.com
Web: www.hmcarchitects.com

HMC was founded in 1940 and specializes in education and healthcare facilities located in the western United States. The architects involved in the Frontier Project (Rancho Cucamonga, California, 2008–09, published here) were **LAURIE CONNELL** (Principal in Charge), **RAYMOND PAN** (Design Principal), and **PASQUAL GUTIERREZ** (Project Manager). Laurie Connell was born in Glendale, California, in 1960 and received her B.Arch degree from California State Polytechnic University in Pomona. Raymond Pan was born in 1971 in Taiwan and received his M.Arch degree at MIT. Pasqual Gutierrez was born in 1948 in Los Angeles and was educated at East Los Angeles College. The recent and current work of HMC includes the McAfee World Headquarters Executive Briefing Center (Santa Clara, California, 2011); Sonia Sotomayor Learning Academies, Los Angeles Unified School District (Los Angeles, California, 2011); J. Paul Leonard Library and Sutro Library, San Francisco State University (San Francisco, California, 2008–12); the First People's Hospital (Foshan, China, 2013); and the Torrance Memorial Medical Center (Torrance, California, 2014), all in the USA unless stated otherwise.

HMC, gegründet 1940, hat sich auf Bauten für Bildungsträger und Krankenhäuser im Westen der Vereinigten Staaten spezialisiert. Am hier vorgestellten Frontier Project (Rancho Cucamonga, Kalifornien, 2008–09) arbeiteten **LAURIE CONNELL** (leitende Architektin), **RAYMOND PAN** (Entwurfsleitung) und **PASQUAL GUTIERREZ** (Projektleitung). Laurie Connell, geboren 1960 in Glendale, Kalifornien, absolvierte ihren B.Arch an der California State Polytechnic University in Pomona. Raymond Pan, geboren 1971 in Taiwan, absolvierte seinen M.Arch am MIT. Pasqual Gutierrez wurde 1948 in Los Angeles geboren und studierte am East Los Angeles College. Jüngere und aktuelle Projekte von HMC sind unter anderem das Executive Briefing Center der Hauptniederlassung von McAfee (Santa Clara, Kalifornien, 2011), das Sonia-Sotomayor-Lernzentrum für die öffentliche Schulbehörde von Los Angeles (Kalifornien, 2011), die J.-Paul-Leonard-Bibliothek und Sutro-Bibliothek der San Francisco State University (San Francisco, Kalifornien, 2008–12), das Erste Volkskrankenhaus (Foshan, China, 2013) und das Torrance-Memorial-Krankenhaus (Torrance, Kalifornien, 2014), alle in den USA, sofern nicht anders vermerkt.

HMC a été fondé en 1940 et s'est spécialisé dans les établissements éducatifs et médicaux dans l'Ouest des États-Unis. Les architectes qui ont participé au projet Frontier (Rancho Cucamonga, Californie, 2008–09, publié ici) sont **LAURIE CONNELL** (responsable), **RAYMOND PAN** (responsable du design) et **PASQUAL GUTIERREZ** (chef de projet). Laurie Connell est née à Glendale, en Californie, en 1960 et a obtenu son B.Arch à l'université polytechnique de Californie, à Pomona. Raymond Pan est né en 1971 à Taiwan et a obtenu son M.Arch au MIT. Pasqual Gutierrez est né en 1948 à Los Angeles et a été formé au East Los Angeles College. Les travaux récents et en cours de HMC comprennent le centre de la direction du siège mondial de McAfee (Santa Clara, Californie, 2011) ; les académies Sonia Sotomayor du secteur scolaire unifié de Los Angeles (Los Angeles, 2011) ; la bibliothèque J. Paul Leonard et la bibliothèque Sutro de l'université de San Francisco (San Francisco, 2008–12) ; le premier hôpital populaire (Foshan, Chine, 2013) et le centre médical Torrance Memorial (Torrance, Californie, 2014), tous aux États-Unis sauf si spécifié.

FRONTIER PROJECT

Rancho Cucamonga, California, USA, 2008–09

Address: 10435 Ashford Street, Rancho Cucamonga, CA 91730–2800, USA,
tel: +1 909 944 6025, www.frontierproject.com
Area: 1366 m². Client: Cucamonga Valley Water District. Cost: $14.5 million

The **FRONTIER PROJECT**, intended to educate the community in sustainable living practices, was HMC's first project to achieve a LEED Platinum certification. Basing the design on "concentric layering of wall shells and spaces," with the outer shell forming a thermal mass made of insulated concrete forms, a second shell in cast-in-place concrete providing structural solidity, and a third shell formed by a north-facing curtain wall that maximizes daylight inside, the building has an inner shell made of redwood planks salvaged from wine vats from a local winery. A garden at the center of the site acts as a bioswale with cistern to collect all storm water within the site. A passive evaporative cooling system is used during the hot and dry seasons, while two solar chimneys and a central cooling tower aid in ventilation. Large glazed surfaces enable visitors to see the surrounding environment.

Das **FRONTIER PROJECT**, eine Bildungseinrichtung, die sich für die Vermittlung nachhaltiger Lebensweisen engagiert, wurde als erstes Projekt des Büros mit einem LEED-Zertifikat in Platin ausgezeichnet. Der Entwurf basiert auf „konzentrisch ineinandergreifenden Gebäudehüllen und Räumen". Die äußere Gebäudehülle aus gedämmten Betonsegmenten fungiert zugleich als thermische Masse, eine zweite Haut aus Ortbeton gibt konstruktive Stabilität, eine dritte, bestehend aus einer Curtain-wall mit Nordausrichtung, sorgt für maximale Versorgung mit Tageslicht. Die innerste Gebäudehülle schließlich, ein Gitter aus Riesenmammutbaum, wurde aus alten Weinfässern eines Weinguts in der Gegend recycelt. Eine Grünanlage im Innenhof dient zugleich als biologischer Drängraben; in einer Zisterne wird der gesamte Nieder-schlag des Grundstücks gesammelt. In heißen, trockenen Jahreszeiten wird passive Verdunstungskühlung genutzt, auch zwei Solarkamine und ein zentraler Windturm tragen zur Belüftung bei. Die großflächige Verglasung ermöglicht den Besuchern Ausblick in die Umgebung.

Le **PROJET FRONTIER**, dont le but est d'éduquer la population aux pratiques de la durabilité, est le premier projet de HMC à avoir reçu une certification LEED platine. Le design est basé sur « des couches concentriques de coques et d'espaces », l'enveloppe extérieure formant une masse thermique en formes de béton isolées, une seconde coque en béton coulé sur place assurant la solidité structurale et une troisième constituée d'un mur rideau face au nord optimisant la lumière du jour à l'intérieur. Le bâtiment présente également une enveloppe intérieure en planches de séquoia récupérées des cuves de vinification d'une cave locale. Au centre, un jardin forme un fossé écologique avec une citerne pour récupérer toutes les eaux pluviales du site. Un système de refroidissement passif par évaporation d'eau fonctionne pendant les saisons chaudes et sèches, tandis que deux cheminées solaires et une tour de refroidissement centrale contribuent à la ventilation. De vastes surfaces vitrées permettent aux visiteurs d'admirer le paysage environnant.

The site plan of the building and
these exterior views show its partially
spiral form materialized by a sloped,
curved entrance path.

*Grundstücksplan und Außenansichten
des Gebäudes zeigen den teilweise
spiralförmig angelegten Entwurf in
Form einer geschwungenen, schrägen
Zugangsrampe.*

*Le plan du site et ces vues exté-
rieures du bâtiment en montrent
la forme de spirale partielle matériali-
sée par une rampe d'accès courbe
et en pente.*

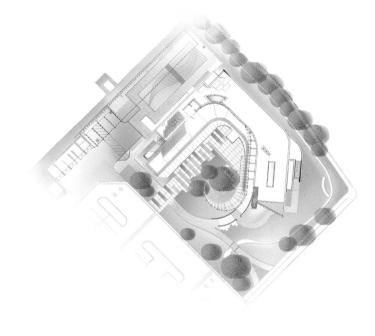

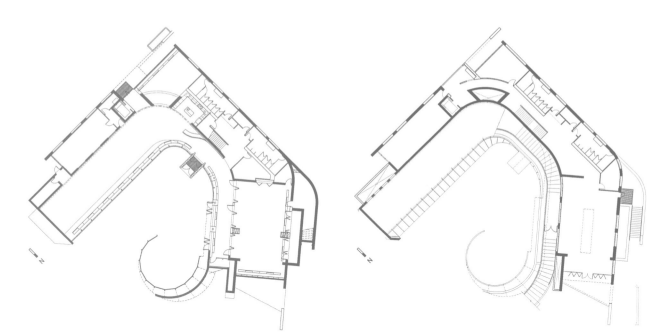

Above, the full-height, angled glazing creates a broad visual connection between the interior and an exterior courtyard, while allowing ample natural light in.

Die geschosshohe, geneigte Glasfront schafft eine großflächige Verbindung zwischen Innenraum und Hof und lässt zugleich großzügig Tageslicht in den Bau einfallen.

Ci-dessus, la paroi vitrée pleine hauteur anguleuse crée une large transition visuelle entre l'intérieur et la cour extérieure, tout en laissant amplement pénétrer la lumière naturelle.

Left page, plans show the spiral entry ramp and the protected inner courtyard, seen from the interior in the image on the lower left.

Grundrisse (linke Seite) zeigen die spiralförmige Zugangsrampe und den geschützten Innenhof, auf der Aufnahme links unten von innen gesehen.

Page de gauche, les plans représentent la rampe d'accès en spirale et la cour intérieure protégée, vue de l'intérieur sur la photo.

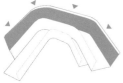

THERMAL MASS

STRUCTURE

EDUCATION

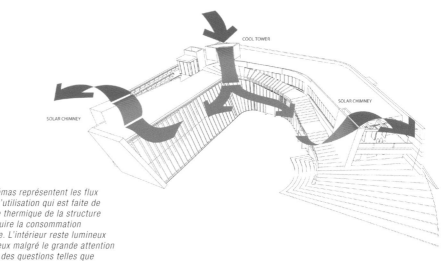

Drawings show airflow and the use of the thermal mass of the structure to reduce energy consumption. Interiors remain bright and spacious despite careful attention to issues such as solar gain.

Zeichnungen visualisieren den Luftwechsel und die Nutzung der thermischen Masse des Gebäudes zur Reduzierung des Energiebedarfs. Trotz sorgfältiger Berücksichtigung solcher Aspekte wie des Solargewinns konnten die Räume hell und großzügig gestaltet werden.

Les schémas représentent les flux d'air et l'utilisation qui est faite de la masse thermique de la structure pour réduire la consommation d'énergie. L'intérieur reste lumineux et spacieux malgré le grande attention portée à des questions telles que l'apport solaire.

HOPKINS ARCHITECTS

Hopkins Architects Partnership
27 Broadley Terrace
London NW1 6LG
UK

Tel: +44 20 77 24 17 51 / Fax: +44 20 77 23 09 32
E-mail: mail@hopkins.co.uk / Web: www.hopkins.co.uk

MICHAEL HOPKINS was born in 1935, in Poole, Dorset (UK), and studied architecture at the Architecture Association in London graduating with a diploma in 1964. He worked subsequently with Leonard Manasseh on the design of new halls of residence at Leicester University. In 1968 he worked with Norman and Wendy Foster on a plan to build an industrial estate at Goole in Yorkshire. Their partnership lasted eight years. In 1976, he founded his own firm. Some of his significant buildings include the Schlumberger Research Center (Cambridge, 1979–81); the Mound Stand at Lord's Cricket Ground (London, 1985–87); Inland Revenue Headquarters (Nottingham, 1993); Glyndebourne Opera House (1994); and the Parliamentary Office, Portcullis House (London, 2001), all in the UK. He won RIBA's Royal Gold Medal in 1994, together with his wife, who is also an architect. **MIKE TAYLOR**, born in 1961, studied at Bristol University and at the Mackintosh School of Architecture in Glasgow and is currently a Senior Partner of Hopkins. He led the design team for Kroon Hall, School of Forestry and Environmental Studies, Yale University (New Haven, Connecticut, USA, 2007–09, published here). The practice's more recent commissions include the Frick Chemistry Laboratory, Princeton University (New Jersey, USA, 2010); Newton and Arkwright Buildings, Nottingham Trent University (Nottingham, UK, 2011); London 2012 Velodrome (London, UK, 2011); UCH Macmillan Cancer Center (London, UK, 2012); WWF-UK Headquarters, Living Planet Center (Woking, UK, 2013); and the Nuovo Ospedale della Spezia (La Spezia, Italy, 2014).

MICHAEL HOPKINS, geboren 1935 in Poole, Dorset (GB), studierte Architektur an der Architecture Association in London, wo er sein Diplom 1964 absolvierte. Im Anschluss arbeitete er mit Leonard Manasseh am neuen Wohnheim der University of Leicester. 1968 entwickelte er mit Norman und Wendy Foster einen Bebauungsplan für ein Industriegebiet in Goole, Yorkshire. Die Architekten waren acht Jahre als Partner tätig. 1976 gründete Hopkins sein eigenes Büro. Zu seinen bedeutendsten Bauten zählen das Schlumberger Research Center (Cambridge, 1979–81), die Mound-Tribüne im Cricketstadion Lord's (London, 1985–87), die Zentrale der Inland Revenue (britische Finanzbehörde; Nottingham, 1993), die Oper in Glyndebourne (1994) sowie die Abgeordnetenbüros im Portcullis House (London, 2001), alle in Großbritannien. 1994 erhielt er gemeinsam mit seiner Frau, die ebenfalls als Architektin praktiziert, die RIBA-Goldmedaille. **MIKE TAYLOR**, Jahrgang 1961, studierte an der University of Bristol und der Mackintosh School of Architecture in Glasgow und ist derzeit Seniorpartner bei Hopkins. Er leitete das Entwurfsteam für die Kroon Hall, Fakultät für Forstwirtschaft und Umweltstudien an der Yale University (New Haven, Connecticut, USA, 2007–09, hier vorgestellt). Jüngere Aufträge des Büros sind unter anderem das Frick-Chemielabor, Princeton University (New Jersey, USA, 2010), das Newton und das Arkwright Building, Nottingham Trent University (Nottingham, GB, 2011), das Velodrom für die Olympiade 2012 in London (London, GB, 2011), das UCH Macmillan-Krebsforschungszentrum (London, GB, 2012), das Living Planet Center, die Zentrale des WWF Großbritannien (Woking, GB, 2013) und das Nuovo Ospedale della Spezia (La Spezia, Italien, 2014).

MICHAEL HOPKINS est né en 1935 à Poole, dans le Dorset (GB) et a fait ses études à l'Architecture Association de Londres dont il a obtenu le diplôme en 1964. Il a ensuite travaillé avec Leonard Manasseh à la conception de nouvelles cités universitaires pour l'université de Leicester. En 1968, il a collaboré avec Norman et Wendy Foster au plan d'une zone industrielle à Goole, dans le Yorkshire. Le partenariat a duré huit ans. En 1976, il a créé sa propre agence. Parmi ses constructions les plus significatives, on peut citer le Centre de recherche Schlumberger (Cambridge, 1979–81) ; la tribune d'honneur du stade de cricket Lord's (Londres, 1985–87) ; le trésor public (Nottingham, 1993) ; l'Opéra de Glyndebourne (1994) et l'immeuble de bureaux de parlementaires Portcullis House (Londres, 2001), toutes au Royaume-Uni. Il a gagné la médaille d'or du RIBA en 1994 avec son épouse, qui est également architecte. **MIKE TAYLOR**, né en 1961, a fait ses études à l'université de Bristol et à l'École d'architecture Mackintosh de Glasgow, il est actuellement l'associé principal de Hopkins. Il a dirigé l'équipe chargée du design pour le Kroon Hall de l'École de sylviculture et d'études environnementales de l'université Yale (New Haven, Connecticut, États-Unis, 2007–09, publiée ici). Les commandes plus récentes du cabinet comprennent notamment le laboratoire de chimie Frick de l'université de Princeton (New Jersey, États-Unis, 2010) ; les bâtiments Newton et Arkwright, université de Nottingham Trent (Nottingham, Grande-Bretagne, 2011) ; le vélodrome pour les JO de Londres 2012 (Londres, 2011) ; le centre de cancérologie et CHU Macmillan (Londres, 2012) ; le siège du WWF Grande-Bretagne, le Living Planet Center (Woking, GB, 2013) et le nouvel hôpital de La Spezia (La Spezia, Italie, 2014).

KROON HALL

School of Forestry and Environmental Studies, Yale University,
New Haven, Connecticut, USA, 2007–09

Address: 195 Prospect Street, New Haven, CT 06511, USA,
tel: +1 203 432 5100, www.environment.yale.edu/. Area: 4958 m². Client: Yale University
Cost: not disclosed. Collaboration: Centerbrook Architects (Executive Architect)

This building, located near the Ingalls Rink designed by Eero Saarinen, was conceived to use 60% less energy and 80% less water than other campus structures. It received a LEED Platinum rating on completion. The architects explain: "Combining modernist design with vernacular references, the building is rectangular in form and is constructed of glass, stone, concrete, and steel. It is located between two historic Neo-Gothic science buildings and, together with these, creates two new courtyards, one of which is actually a green roof that disguises a new service node for the entire district." Horizontal wooden louvers protect the eastern and western façades, while the roof has integrated photovoltaic arrays and skylights. The building features solar hot-water collectors, ground-source heat pumps, a displacement air system, high thermal retention, daylight harvesting, energy-recovering ventilation, a rainwater harvesting and cleansing pond, the green roof already mentioned, and recycled, local, and sustainable building materials. Paperless communication among the architects and consultants in London, New York, and Connecticut "saved more than an estimated $100 000 in paper, time, and delivery costs." The building was chosen as the 2010 "Building of the Year" by *The Architects' Journal* and as one of the 10 greenest buildings in the world by the American Institute of Architects' Committee on the Environment (COTE).

Der Neubau, nicht weit gelegen vom Ingalls Rink, Eero Saarinens Eishockeyhalle, wurde so konzipiert, dass sein Energieverbrauch im Vergleich zu anderen Campusbauten um 60%, der Wasserverbrauch um 80% reduziert werden konnte. Der realisierte Bau wurde mit einem LEED-Zertifikat in Platin ausgezeichnet. Die Architekten erklären: „Das Gebäude, formal ein Rechteck, ist eine Konstruktion aus Glas, Stein, Beton und Stahl, eine Kombination moderner und traditioneller Einflüsse. Es liegt zwischen zwei historischen neogotischen naturwissenschaftlichen Bauten und bildet mit ihnen zwei neue Innenhöfe. Einer der beiden ist zugleich ein begrüntes Dach, unter dem sich eine neue Versorgungszentrale für den gesamten Campusbezirk verbirgt." Horizontale Holzblenden schützen Ost- und Westfassade, in das Dach wurden Oberlichter und Solarmodule integriert. Zur technischen Ausstattung des Baus zählen eine thermische Solaranlage, Erdwärmepumpen, ein Luftaustauschsystem, hohe Wärmedämmung, optimierte Tageslichtnutzung, Wärmerückgewinnung, Regenwassernutzung und eine Pflanzenkläranlage, das bereits erwähnte begrünte Dach sowie der Einsatz recycelter, lokaler und nachhaltiger Baustoffe. Dank papierloser Kommunikation zwischen Architekten und Beratern in London, New York und Connecticut konnten „schätzungsweise über 100 000 Dollar an Kostenaufwand in Form von Papier, Zeit und Porto gespart werden". 2010 wurde die Kroon Hall vom *The Architects' Journal* als „Bau des Jahres" sowie vom Umweltkomitee des AIA (COTE) als eines der zehn grünsten Bauten weltweit ausgezeichnet.

Situé à proximité de la patinoire Ingalls créée par Eero Saarinen, ce bâtiment a été conçu pour consommer 60 % moins d'énergie et 80 % moins d'eau que les autres structures sur le campus. Il a obtenu une certification LEED platine à son achèvement. Les architectes expliquent que « le bâtiment, qui associe un design moderniste et des références locales, présente une forme rectangulaire et est fait de verre, pierre, béton et acier. Il est intercalé entre deux bâtiments scientifiques néogothiques avec lesquels il crée deux nouvelles cours dont l'une est en fait un toit végétalisé qui dissimule un nouveau nœud de services pour tout le quartier ». Des persiennes horizontales en bois protègent les façades est et ouest, tandis que le toit est doté de panneaux photovoltaïques intégrés et de lucarnes. Le bâtiment possède en outre des capteurs solaires à circulation d'eau chaude, des pompes à chaleur géothermiques, un système de déplacement d'air, une rétention thermique élevée, un système d'exploitation de la lumière naturelle, une ventilation à récupération d'énergie, une installation de récupération de l'eau de pluie avec étang d'assainissement, le toit végétalisé déjà mentionné et des matériaux de construction recyclés, régionaux et durables. La communication informatisée – sans papier – entre les architectes et consultants à Londres, New York et dans le Connecticut « a permis des économies de papier, temps et délais de livraison estimées à 100 000 $ ». Le bâtiment a été élu « Bâtiment de l'année » 2010 par *The Architects' Journal* et l'une des constructions les plus vertes du monde par le Comité pour l'environnement (COTE) de l'Institut américain des architectes.

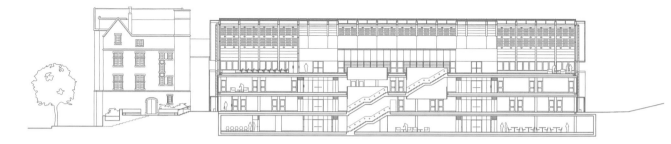

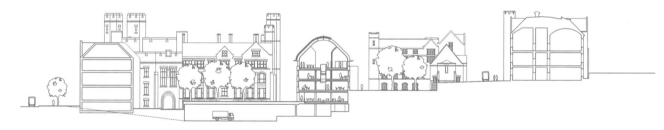

Section drawings (left) show the
forms of the building and its curved
roof. Above, an evening image reveals
the wood interior and the shedlike
form of the building.

Querschnitte (links) zeigen Form des
Baus und seines gerundeten Dachs.
Oben eine abendliche Ansicht, auf der
der Innenausbau in Holz und das an
eine Scheune erinnernde Profil des
Gebäudes zu sehen sind.

Les schémas en coupe (à gauche)
présentent la forme du bâtiment et
son toit arrondi. Ci-dessus, une photo
prise le soir révèle l'intérieur en bois
et la forme de hangar du bâtiment.

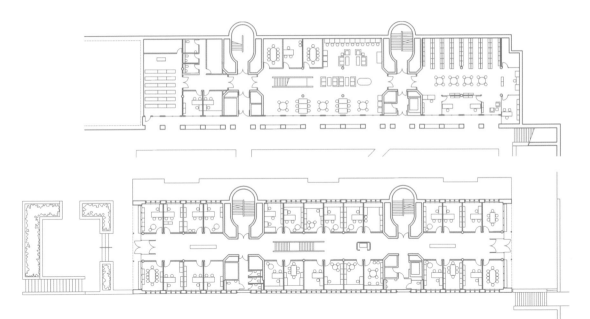

Left, the arch at the top of the building has a nearly continuous skylight, with its curved, wooden structure visible. Above, floor plans, and below a general view of the building in its campus setting.

Links der geschwungene Giebel des Gebäudes mit einem fast durchgängigen Oberlicht: Deutlich wird hier die geschwungene Holzkonstruktion. Oben Etagengrundrisse sowie unten eine Gesamtansicht des Baus im Campuskontext.

À gauche, l'arche qui surmonte la construction avec sa structure apparente en bois courbe est percée d'une lucarne sur presque toute sa longueur. Ci-dessus, plans des étages et ci-dessous, vue générale du bâtiment sur le campus.

IMPORT-EXPORT ARCHITECTURE

Import-Export Architecture
Provinciestraat 30
2018 Antwerp
Belgium

Tel: +32 32 26 76 41
Fax: +32 32 26 76 45
E-mail: iea@iea.be
Web: www.iea.be

JORIS VAN REUSEL was born in Wilrijk, Belgium, in 1969. He studied architecture at the Higher Architecture Institute Sint-Lucas in Ghent (1993), and opened his own office the same year. He created Import-Export Architecture with Oscar Rommens in 1999. **OSCAR ROMMENS** was born in Wilrijk in 1968. He also graduated from the Higher Architecture Institute Sint-Lucas in Ghent (1994). He worked from 1997 to 1999 in the office of Oosterhuis Associates (Rotterdam), before the founding of Import-Export Architecture. Their work includes the Fragile Lab (Antwerp, 2005–07, published here); Ter Pitte (Antwerp, 2005–08, also published here); Woodpecker, a loft and patio house in Antwerp (2009–12); and D.D.D.D., a weekend house for a jewelry designer (Auby, 2010–12). Current work includes The Moon, a children's theater complex (Mechelen, 2010–13); and P-X, a school complex in Hoboken (in collaboration with Plus Office, 2011–14), all in Belgium.

JORIS VAN REUSEL wurde 1969 in Wilrijk, Belgien, geboren. Er studierte Architektur an der Architekturhochschule Sint-Lucas in Gent (1993) und gründete noch im selben Jahr sein eigenes Büro. Sein Büro Import-Export Architecture gründete er 1999 gemeinsam mit Oscar Rommens. **OSCAR ROMMENS** wurde 1968 in Wilrijk geboren. Auch er schloss sein Studium an der Architekturhochschule Sint-Lucas in Gent ab (1994). Vor der Gründung von Import-Export Architecture arbeitete er von 1997 bis 1999 für Oosterhuis Associates (Rotterdam). Zu ihren Projekten zählen Fragile Lab (Antwerpen, 2005–07, hier vorgestellt), Ter Pitte (Antwerpen, 2005–08, ebenfalls hier vorgestellt), Woodpecker, ein Loft und Hofhaus in Antwerpen (2009–12) sowie D.D.D.D., ein Wochenendhaus für einen Schmuckdesigner (Auby, 2010–12). Aktuelle Projekte sind unter anderem The Moon, ein Kindertheater (Mechelen, 2010–13) und P-X, ein Schulkomplex in Hoboken (mit Plus Office, 2011–14), alle in Belgien.

JORIS VAN REUSEL est né à Wilrijk, en Belgique, en 1969. Il a fait des études d'architecture à l'Institut supérieur d'architecture Saint-Luc de Gand (1993) et a créé son agence la même année. Il a ouvert Import-Export Architecture avec **OSCAR ROMMENS** en 1999. Ce dernier est né à Wilrijk en 1968. Il est également diplômé de l'Institut supérieur d'architecture Saint-Luc de Gand (1994) et a travaillé de 1997 à 1999 dans l'agence d'Oosterhuis Associates (Rotterdam) avant la fondation d'Import-Export Architecture. Leurs réalisations comptent le Fragile Lab (Anvers, 2005–07, publié ici) ; le complexe Ter Pitte (Anvers, 2005–08, également publié ici) ; Woodpecker, un loft et patio à Anvers (2009–12) et D.D.D.D., une maison de vacances pour un créateur de bijoux (Auby, 2010–12). Les travaux en cours comprennent La Lune, un complexe théâtral pour enfants (Malines, 2010–13) et P-X, un complexe scolaire à Hoboken (en collaboration avec Plus Office, 2011–14), tous en Belgique.

FRAGILE LAB

Antwerp, Belgium, 2005–07

Address: Kammenstraat 84, Antwerp 2000, Belgium, tel: +32 3 202 50 73, www.fragile.be
Area: 400 m². Client: Natale BVBA. Cost: not disclosed

Right page, the fine glass and steel structure is inserted between older masonry blocks that accentuate the "fragility" that the architects refer to. Floor plates are particularly thin.

Die filigrane Glas-Stahl-Konstruktion wurde zwischen zwei gemauerte Alt-bauten gesetzt, was die von den Architekten intendierte „Fragilität" betont. Die Bodenplatten sind außergewöhnlich dünn.

Page de droite, la délicate structure de verre et d'acier est insérée entre des maçonneries plus anciennes qui accentuent encore la « fragilité » voulue par les architectes. Les plaques de sol sont particulièrement fines.

Above, angled supports and glazing that continues upward to form a balustrade give the impression that the building has no visible means of support.

Die schrägen Stützen und die Verglasung, die in der Verlängerung nach oben eine Balustrade bilden, erzeugen den Eindruck eines geradezu stützenfreien Baus.

Ci-dessus, les étais anguleux et le vitrage qui se poursuit pour former une balustrade en haut du bâtiment donnent l'impression qu'il ne repose sur aucun soutien visible.

This narrow new building was created for the maternity fashion label Fragile on a 100-square-meter site on Kammenstraat in Antwerp. The founders of the firm and owners of this flagship store, Nathalie Vleeschouwer and Jan Bevernage, live in the upper part of the building. The brief thus called for office space, storage areas, and a duplex living zone, as well as the shop. The architects opted for transparency and a feeling of fragility implied by the "steel bamboo" angled tubular supports on the street side and floors just 18 centimeters thick. A luxuriant green wall inside the building runs up a rough black interior façade. In this instance, the natural presence is in tune with the light transparency of the architecture. The architects do not emphasize the "sustainable" qualifications of the building, but they do bring nature within its walls.

Der schmale Neubau auf einem 100 m² großen Grundstück an der Kammenstraat in Antwerpen wurde für Fragile, ein Label für Umstandsmode, realisiert. Nathalie Vleeschouwer und Jan Bevernage, Gründer des Modelabels und Inhaber des Flagshipstores, wohnen im Obergeschoss des Gebäudes. Das Programm sah ein Büro, Lagerräume, eine Maisonettewohnung sowie Ladenflächen vor. Mit schiefen, an Bambus erinnernden Stahlrohrstützen an der Straßenseite und nur 18 cm starken Bodenplatten setzten die Architekten auf Transparenz und Fragilität. An einer schwarz gestrichenen Brandmauer im Innern des Baus rankt sich ein üppig begrünter vertikaler Garten empor. Dieser natürliche Akzent harmoniert mit der lichten Transparenz der Architektur. Zwar steht „Nachhaltigkeit" für die Architekten hier nicht im Vordergrund, dennoch wird bewusst Grün in den Bau integriert.

Le bâtiment étroit a été créé pour la marque de vêtements de grossesse Fragile sur un emplacement de 100 m² dans la Kammenstraat, à Anvers. Les fondateurs de la société et propriétaires de son magasin-phare, Nathalie Vleeschouwer et Jan Bevernage, habitent la partie supérieure du bâtiment. Le cahier des charges prévoyait un espace de bureaux, des zones de stockage et un logement en duplex, en plus de la boutique. Les architectes ont fait le choix de la transparence et d'un sentiment de fragilité conféré par les étais tubulaires anguleux de « bambou en acier » côté rue et des sols épais de seulement 18 cm. Un mur de végétation luxuriante à l'intérieur du bâtiment recouvre une paroi noire brute. La présence de la nature s'accorde ici parfaitement avec la transparence légère de l'architecture. Les architectes n'ont pas mis en avant les caractéristiques « durables » du bâtiment, mais ils ont réussi à faire entrer la nature dans ses murs.

A vertical garden and bright open spaces contribute to the voluntarily ephemeral appearance of the design.

Der bewusst ephemere Eindruck der Architektur wird durch einen vertikalen Garten und helle offene Räume verstärkt.

Un jardin vertical et des espaces clairs et ouverts contribuent à l'aspect volontairement éphémère de l'ensemble.

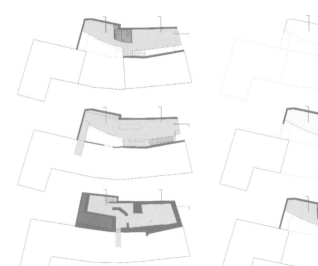

The slightly angled floor plans (top)
contribute to the variety of spaces
seen in these images.

Die leicht winkligen Etagengrundrisse
(oben) tragen zur Vielgestaltigkeit der
hier zu sehenden Räume bei.

Les plans des différents niveaux (en
haut) légèrement anguleux offrent la
grande variété d'espaces qu'on voit ici.

The vertical garden and openness of the building contribute to the impression of a certain closeness to nature that is definitely unusual in a city environment.

Der vertikale Garten und die Offenheit des Baus lassen den Eindruck von Naturnähe entstehen, was in seinem urbanen Umfeld zweifellos ungewöhnlich ist.

Le jardin vertical et le caractère ouvert du bâtiment donnent l'impression d'une certaine proximité avec la nature, résolument inédite dans un environnement urbain.

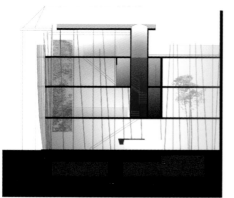

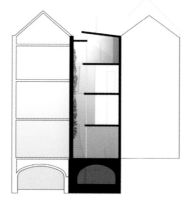

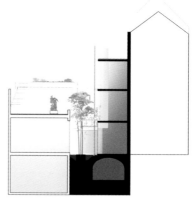

TER PITTE

Antwerp, Belgium, 2005–08

Address: Lange Van Bloerstraat, Antwerp, Belgium
Area: 1500 m². Client: AG Vespa
Cost: not disclosed

Drawings and images demonstrate the ways in which the architects have given variety to the forms and provided for green rooftop gardens.

Zeichnungen und Ansichten belegen die abwechslungsreiche formale Gestaltung des Komplexes und die Konzeption der Dachgärten.

Schémas et photos montrent comment les architectes ont apporté plus de diversité aux formes afin de créer des jardins en végétalisant le toit.

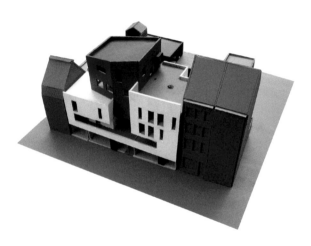

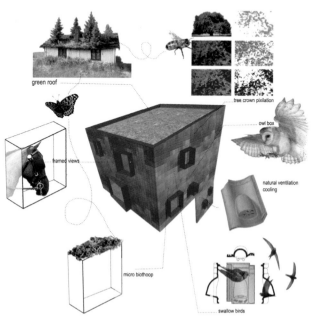

green roof

tree crown pixilation

owl box

framed views

natural ventilation cooling

micro biothoop

swallow birds

The six residences in this grouped complex range in size from 100 to 250 square meters, and also from ground-floor patio dwellings to a triplex penthouse. Working with a limited budget, the architects occupied a central street block formerly occupied by workshops of the Thierry elevator company. Three of the residences are accessible from ground level. A garden in the rear and patios bring both daylight and a sense of the presence of nature into the block. The upper residences also have outdoor terraces. Import-Export imagined a tree crowning the complex rendered visible by a carefully "pixelated" selection of green roof tiles. The tiled volume has a green roof and care has been taken to allow for bird nesting, as seen in the architects' drawings. The architects state: "Despite the limited budget, IEA succeeded in creating an unusual building, one that even addresses the problem of inner-city living in a new way. The 'green' penthouse exists as a peaceful tree crown amidst the still dense street façade."

Die Bandbreite der sechs Wohneinheiten in diesem Komplex reicht von 100 bis 250 m² und von Erdgeschosswohnungen mit Innenhöfen bis hin zu einem dreigeschossigen Penthouse. Die Architekten realisierten ihr Projekt in einem Häuserblock auf dem ehemaligen Gelände des Aufzugsherstellers Thierry. Drei der Wohneinheiten werden auf Straßenniveau erschlossen. Ein rückwärtiger Garten sowie die Innenhöfe bringen Tageslicht und Natur in den Komplex. Auch die oberen Wohneinheiten verfügen über Terrassen. Für den oberen Abschluss des Komplexes entwarf Import-Export eine Pixel-Haut aus Dachziegeln in verschiedenen Grüntönen als Baum-Metapher. Der so verblendete Kubus hat ein begrüntes Flachdach, auf dem auch Vögel nisten können, wie eine Zeichnung der Architekten illustriert. Die Architekten erklären: „Trotz knappen Budgets konnte IEA ein ungewöhnliches Bauprojekt realisieren, das sich der Problematik des Wohnens im Innenstadtbereich auf neue Weise stellt. Das ‚grüne' Penthouse schwebt wie eine friedliche Baumkrone über der kompakten Straßenfassade."

Les six résidences groupées dans ce complexe ont des superficies de 100 à 250 m² et vont du logement à patio au rez-de-chaussée à l'appartement de standing en triplex. Les architectes, qui ne disposaient que d'un budget limité, ont occupé un îlot central qui abritait auparavant les ateliers de la société d'ascenseurs Thierry. Trois des résidences sont accessibles au niveau du sol. Un jardin à l'arrière et les patios font entrer la lumière du jour et une impression de nature à l'intérieur. Les appartements des étages supérieurs disposent également de terrasses. Import-Export a imaginé un arbre couronnant l'ensemble et visualisé par une sélection soigneusement « pixélisée » de tuiles vertes. Le volume sous tuiles a un toit végétalisé et les architectes ont veillé à ce que les oiseaux puissent y nicher, comme le montrent leurs plans. Ils déclarent : « Malgré un budget réduit, IEA a réussi à créer un bâtiment original qui apporte une réponse inédite au problème de l'habitat en centre-ville. L'appartement de standing "vert" prend la forme d'une paisible cime d'arbre qui se dresse parmi les façades denses de la rue. »

The use of green roof tiles on one of the volumes and the variety in surface treatment elsewhere give a "natural" or organic appearance to the complex.

Durch den Einsatz grün lasierter Dachziegel an einem der Baukörper und die facettenreiche Oberflächengestaltung im übrigen Komplex gewinnt die Anlage „natürliche", organische Anmutung.

L'utilisation de tuiles vertes sur l'un des volumes et la diversité des traitements des autres surfaces donnent une apparence « naturelle » ou organique au complexe.

Though manifestly modern, the structures seem in harmony with an older urban environment where progressive construction has made forms that collide and interact.

Trotz der dezidiert modernen Formensprache fügen sich die Bauten harmonisch in den älteren urbanen Baubestand, wo durch wachsende Bautätigkeit verschiedenste architektonische Formen aufeinandertreffen und interagieren.

Bien qu'incontestablement modernes, les nouvelles structures forment une harmonie avec leur environnement urbain plus ancien où la construction a progressivement donné naissance à des formes qui se heurtent et dialoguent.

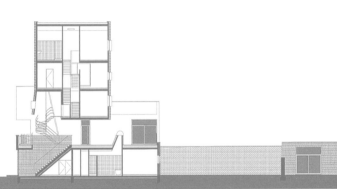

Interiors are simple and efficient, alternating opaque surfaces with rectangular openings.

Die Innenräume sind schlicht und effizient gehalten; opake Wandflächen und geradlinige Fensteröffnungen wechseln einander ab.

Les intérieurs sont simples et rationnels, faisant alterner les surfaces opaques et les ouvertures rectangulaires.

Floor plans show the slightly angled main façade of the complex (right). An interior view shows a long corridor and a full-height glazed opening toward an inner courtyard.

An den Etagengrundrissen ist die leicht schräge Hauptfassade des Komplexes ablesbar (rechts). Eine Innenansicht mit Blick in einen langen Flur und geschosshoher Verglasung zu einem Innenhof.

Les plans des étages montrent la façade principale légèrement anguleuse du complexe (à droite). Une vue intérieure montre un long couloir et une ouverture vitrée sur toute sa hauteur qui donne sur une cour intérieure.

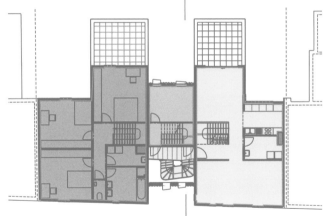

INGENHOVEN ARCHITECTS

ingenhoven architects
Plange Mühle 1
40221 Düsseldorf
Germany

Tel: +49 211 301 01 01
Fax: +49 211 301 01 31
E-mail: info@ingenhovenarchitects.com
Web: www.ingenhovenarchitects.com

CHRISTOPH INGENHOVEN studied architecture at the RWTH (Aachen, 1978–84) and at the Academy of Arts in Düsseldorf under Professor Hans Hollein (1980–81). He founded ingenhoven architects in Düsseldorf in 1985, and the firm acquired a reputation for the design of ecological high-rise buildings. These include the Lufthansa Aviation Center at Frankfurt Airport (Frankfurt, 1999–2006); the European Investment Bank (Luxembourg, Luxembourg, 2004–08, published here); Breezé Tower (Osaka, Japan, 2005–08); the Daniel Swarovski Corporation (Zurich-Männedorf, Switzerland, 2008–10); and 1 Bligh (Sydney, Australia, 2009–11). Ongoing work includes a high-rise complex in Singapore; and the Main Station in Stuttgart (2009–19), all in Germany unless stated otherwise.

CHRISTOPH INGENHOVEN studierte an der RWTH (Aachen, 1978–84) und der Kunstakademie Düsseldorf bei Professor Hans Hollein (1980–81). 1985 erfolgte die Gründung von ingenhoven architects in Düsseldorf; das Büro machte sich einen Ruf mit der Planung umweltfreundlicher Hochhausbauten, darunter dem Lufthansa Aviation Center am Frankfurter Flughafen (Frankfurt am Main, 1999–2006), der Europäischen Investitionsbank (Luxemburg, Luxemburg, 2004–08, hier vorgestellt), dem Breezé Tower (Osaka, Japan, 2005–08), der Daniel Swarovski Corporation (Zürich-Männedorf, Schweiz, 2008–10) und 1 Bligh (Sydney, Australien, 2009–11). Zu den laufenden Projekten des Büros zählen ein Hochhauskomplex in Singapur und der Stuttgarter Hauptbahnhof (2009–19), alle in Deutschland, sofern nicht anders vermerkt.

CHRISTOPH INGENHOVEN a étudié l'architecture à l'Université technique de Rhénanie-Westphalie (RWTH) (Aix-la-Chapelle, 1978–84) et à l'Académie des arts de Düsseldorf auprès du professeur Hans Hollein (1980–81). Il a fondé ingenhoven architects à Düsseldorf en 1985 et l'agence s'est fait une réputation pour ses grands immeubles écologiques. Ils comprennent notamment le Centre d'aviation de Lufthansa à l'aéroport de Francfort (Francfort, 1999–2006) ; la Banque européenne d'investissement (Luxembourg, 2004–08, publiée ici) ; la tour Breezé (Osaka, Japon, 2005–08) ; la tour de la Corporation Daniel Swarovski (Zurich-Männedorf, 2008–10) et 1 Bligh (Sydney, Australie, 2009–11). Les réalisations en cours de l'agence comprennent un complexe d'immeubles à Singapour et la gare de Stuttgart (2009–19), toutes en Allemagne sauf si spécifié.

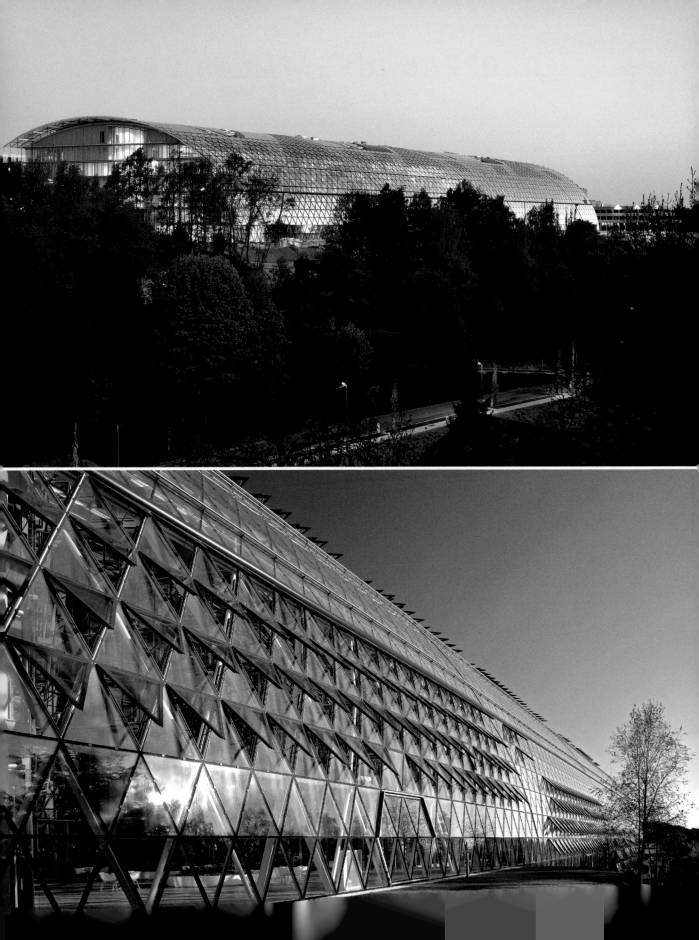

EUROPEAN INVESTMENT BANK

Luxembourg, Luxembourg, 2004–08

*Address: 98–100 Boulevard Konrad Adenauer, 2950 Luxembourg, Luxembourg,
tel: +352 43 79 1, www.eib.org. Area: 65 500 m²
Client: European Investment Bank, Luxembourg. Cost: not disclosed*

The design of ingenhoven architects for the 10-story **EUROPEAN INVESTMENT BANK** won first prize in a 2002 international competition. The building won the 2010 Emilio Ambasz Award for Green Architecture–International Prize. Located on the Kirchberg Plateau like many official buildings, the structure is an extension of a 1980 building by Sir Denys Lasdun. The site of the 170-meter-long tubular glass building is urban on one side and landscaped on the other. The curving glass roof runs over the V-shaped office wings that are connected with atria and winter gardens that serve as a thermal buffer. Operable windows allow for natural ventilation. The building has been noted for its energy efficiency as well as a design that succeeds in promoting communication between the 750 employees who work there. The EIB received a "Very Good" rating under the UK Building Research Establishment Environmental Assessment Method (BREEAM).

Der von ingenhoven architects vorgelegte Entwurf für die **EUROPÄISCHE INVESTITIONSBANK** wurde 2002 in einem internationalen Wettbewerb mit dem ersten Preis ausgezeichnet. 2010 gewann der Bau in der internationalen Kategorie des Emilio Ambasz Award for Green Architecture. Das Projekt, wie viele Verwaltungsgebäude auf dem Kirchbergplateau gelegen, ist die Erweiterung eines von Denys Lasdun entworfenen Baus von 1980. Das Grundstück des 170 m langen, röhrenförmigen Glasbaus ist auf einer Seite urban, auf der anderen landschaftlich geprägt. Die geschwungene Glashülle überspannt die V-förmigen Büroflügel, die durch Atrien und Gärten miteinander verbunden sind, welche zugleich als Klimapuffer wirken. Zu öffnende Fenster ermöglichen eine natürliche Belüftung. Ausgezeichnet wurde der Bau für seine Energieeffizienz ebenso wie für den Entwurf, der bewusst die Kommunikation zwischen den 750 Mitarbeitern fördert. Die EIB erhielt ein „Sehr gut" nach dem britischen BREEAM-Standard.

Le design imaginé par ingenhoven architects pour les dix étages de la **BANQUE EUROPÉENNE D'INVESTISSEMENT** a gagné le premier prix d'un concours international en 2002. L'ensemble a également remporté le prix international Emilio Ambasz pour l'architecture verte en 2010. Situé sur le plateau de Kirchberg, comme de nombreux autres bâtiments officiels, c'est une extension de la structure construite en 1980 par Sir Denys Lasdun. L'emplacement qu'occupe le bâtiment tubulaire en verre long de 170 m présente une face urbanisée et une face paysagère. La toiture vitrée incurvée recouvre les ailes de bureaux en forme de V reliées par des atriums et des vérandas qui tiennent lieu de tampons thermiques. Les fenêtres s'ouvrent et permettent une ventilation naturelle. Le bâtiment a été remarqué pour son efficacité énergétique et comme une conception qui favorise la communication entre les 750 employés qui y travaillent. La BEI a reçu la note « très bien » par la méthode d'évaluation de la performance écologique développée par le Building Research Establishment britannique (BREEAM).

An aerial view shows the long, tubular glass form of the building, with a forested area to the rear and a road in front of it.

Das Luftbild zeigt die lange, röhrenförmige Glashülle des Baus, hinter dem ein Waldgrundstück liegt. Vor dem Bau verläuft eine Straße.

La vue aérienne montre la forme longue et tubulaire du bâtiment en verre, la zone forestière à l'arrière et la route par devant.

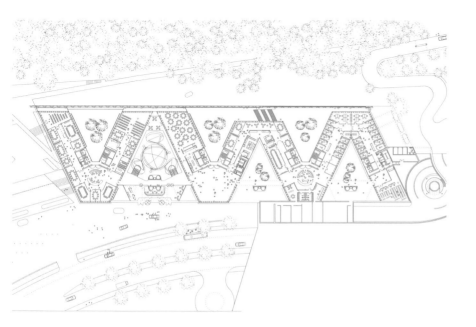

This interior view, looking up to the glazed roof, shows the light structure employed, allowing ample daylight into the main volume of the building.

Die Innenansicht, ein Blick ins gläserne Dach, lässt die Leichtigkeit der Konstruktion deutlich werden, dank derer reichlich Tageslicht in den zentralen des Bereich des Baus fällt.

Cette vue intérieure du toit vitré montre la légèreté de la structure utilisée qui permet à la lumière du jour de pénétrer largement dans le volume principal de construction.

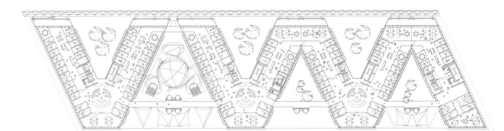

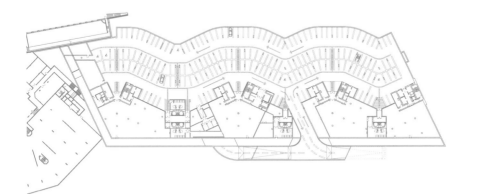

Left, a plan of the parking level of the complex. Above, level 07, an office floor. Below, the dramatically glazed entrance, and right the interior court-yard space with elevators on the left.

Links ein Grundriss der Tiefgarage. Oben Ebene 07, eine Büroetage. Unten der dramatisch verglaste Eingangsbereich und rechts der zentrale Innenhof mit den Aufzügen links im Bild.

À gauche, un plan de l'étage du parking du complexe. Ci-dessus, le niveau 07, un étage de bureaux. Ci-dessous, la spectaculaire entrée vitrée et à droite, la cour intérieure avec les ascenseurs sur la gauche.

Open stairways and passages contribute to the overall impression of clarity imbued in the structure by the architects.

Offene Treppenaufgänge und Flure tragen zur Transparenz bei, die die Architekten dem Bau gaben.

Les cages d'escalier et passages ouverts contribuent à l'impression générale de clarté que les architectes ont imprimé à la structure.

Above, a plan of level 03 with the cafeteria. Below, a lounge area where artificial and natural light are mixed above the wood floor.

Oben ein Etagengrundriss von Ebene 03, auf der die Cafeteria liegt. Unten ein Aufenthaltsbereich mit Holzboden, in dem Tageslicht mit künstlicher Beleuchtung kombiniert wird.

Ci-dessus, un plan du niveau 03 avec la cafétéria. Ci-dessous, un salon où lumière artificielle et naturelle se mêlent sur le plancher de bois.

JENSEN & SKODVIN ARCHITECTS

Jensen & Skodvin Arkitektkontor AS
Sinsenveien 4D
0572 Oslo
Norway

Tel: +47 22 99 48 99
Fax: +47 22 99 48 88
E-mail: office@jsa.no
Web: www.jsa.no

Jensen & Skodvin was established in 1995 by Olav Jensen and Børre Skodvin. The firm currently has nine architects. Born in 1959, **OLAV JENSEN** received his degree from the Oslo School of Architecture in 1985. He has been a Professor at the Oslo School of Design and Architecture since 2004. He was the Kenzo Tange Visiting Critic at Harvard University (1998), and won a 1998 Aga Khan Award for Architecture for the Lepers Hospital, in Chopda Taluka, India. **BØRRE SKODVIN** was born in 1960 and received his degree from the Oslo School of Architecture in 1988. He has been a teacher at the Oslo School of Design and Architecture since 1998. Their built work includes the Storo Metro Station (Oslo, 2003); headquarters and exhibition space for the Norwegian Design Council (Oslo, 2004); Sinsen Metro Station (Oslo, 2005); a Multipurpose City Block (Trondheim, 2005; collaboration with Team Tre); the plan and designs for a new town in south Oslo (2005; not built); the Tautra Maria Convent (Tautra Island, 2004–06); and a thermal bath, therapy center, and hotel (Bad Gleichenberg, Austria, 2005–08, published here). They have worked recently on the Gudbrandsjuvet Tourist project, viewing platforms and bridges (Gudbrandsjuvet, 2008); the Juvet Landscape Hotel (Gudbrandsjuvet, 2007–09); and Giørtz Summer House (Valldal, 2012), all in Norway unless stated otherwise.

Jensen & Skodvin wurde 1995 von Olav Jensen und Børre Skodvin gegründet. Derzeit beschäftigt das Büro neun Architekten. **OLAV JENSEN**, geboren 1959, schloss sein Studium 1985 an der Architektur- und Designhochschule Oslo ab, wo er seit 2004 als Professor tätig ist. Er war Kenzo-Tange-Gastkritiker in Harvard (1998) und wurde 1998 für das Leprakrankenhaus in Chopda Taluka, Indien, mit dem Aga Khan Award for Architecture ausgezeichnet. **BØRRE SKODVIN** wurde 1960 geboren und schloss sein Studium 1988 an der Architektur- und Designhochschule Oslo ab, wo er seit 1998 lehrt. Zu ihren Projekten zählen die Metrostation Storo (Oslo, 2003), die Zentrale und ein Ausstellungsraum für den Norwegischen Designverband (Oslo, 2004), die Metrostation Sinsen (Oslo, 2005), ein Gebäude mit gemischter Nutzung (Trondheim, 2005, mit Team Tre), Planung und Entwurf für ein neues Stadtzentrum in Süd-Oslo (2005, nicht realisiert), das Mariakloster Tautra (Insel Tautra, 2004–06) sowie Therme, Kurhaus und Hotel Bad Gleichenberg (Österreich, 2005–08, hier vorgestellt). In letzter Zeit arbeitete das Büro an Aussichtsplattformen und Brücken für das Gudbrandsjuvet-Tourismusprojekt (Gudbrandsjuvet, 2008), dem Juvet Landscape Hotel (Gudbrandsjuvet, 2007–09) und dem Giørtz-Sommerhaus (Valldal, 2012), alle in Norwegen, sofern nicht anders vermerkt.

Jensen & Skodvin a été fondée en 1995 par Olav Jensen et Børre Skodvin. L'agence se compose aujourd'hui de neuf architectes. Né en 1959, **OLAV JENSEN** a obtenu son diplôme à l'École d'architecture d'Oslo en 1985. Il enseigne à l'École de design et architecture d'Oslo depuis 2004. Il a été le critique invité par Kenzo Tange à l'université de Harvard (1998) et a gagné un prix Aga Khan d'architecture en 1998 pour l'hôpital Lepers de Chopda Taluka, en Inde. **BØRRE SKODVIN** est né en 1960 et a obtenu son diplôme à l'École d'architecture d'Oslo en 1988. Il enseigne à l'École de design et architecture d'Oslo depuis 1998. Leurs réalisations comprennent la station de métro Storo (Oslo, 2003) ; le siège et espace d'exposition du Conseil norvégien du design (Oslo, 2004) ; la station de métro Sinsen (Oslo, 2005) ; un complexe urbain polyvalent (Trondheim, 2005, en collaboration avec Team Tre) ; le plan et la conception d'une ville nouvelle dans le Sud d'Oslo (2005, pas construite) ; le couvent Notre-Dame de Tautra (île de Tautra, 2004–06) et une piscine thermale, centre thérapeutique et hôtel (Bad Gleichenberg, Autriche, 2005–08, publié ici). Récemment, ils ont travaillé au projet touristique, plates-formes d'observation et ponts, de Gudbrandsjuvet (Gudbrandsjuvet, 2008) ; à l'hôtel paysager Juvet (Gudbrandsjuvet, 2007–09) et à la résidence estivale Giørtz (Valldal, 2012), tous en Norvège sauf si spécifié.

THERMAL BATH

Therapy Center, and Hotel, Bad Gleichenberg, Austria, 2005–08

Address: Das Kurhaus, Untere Brunnenstr. 40, 8344 Bad Gleichenberg, Austria,
tel: +43 31 59 22 94 / 40 01, www.lifemedicineresort.com. Area: 17 000 m². Client: HCC/Kappa
Cost: €60 million. Collaboration: Domenig Wallner (Local Architect)

Located in a quiet park, this project includes approximately 50 rooms for medical treatment, a four-star hotel with restaurants and cafés, and a public **THERMAL BATH** for patients and other guests. Waiting areas in the treatment rooms center are arrayed around courtyards allowing in daylight and views of the trees, giving the patients "the impression of waiting in the park itself." One of the main aims of the project, according to the architects, "has been to de-institutionalize the architecture, making it resemble a hospital in as few ways as possible." An advertising firm designed the interior of the complex. The extensive use of wood cladding, together with the green roof, participates in the sustainable aspects of this design, along with the broad use of natural light.

Der in einem ruhigen Kurpark gelegene Komplex umfasst ein Therapiezentrum mit 50 Behandlungsräumen, ein Vier-Sterne-Hotel mit Restaurants und Cafés sowie ein öffentliches **THERMALBAD** für Patienten und externe Gäste. Die Wartebereiche vor den Behandlungsräumen orientieren sich um Innenhöfe. So fällt Tageslicht in den Bau, der Blick in die Bäume vermittelt den Kurenden „das Gefühl, ihre Wartezeit im Park zu verbringen". Eines der Hauptanliegen des Entwurfs war den Architekten zufolge, „der Architektur ihren institutionellen Charakter zu nehmen und ihr so wenig wie möglich das Gesicht einer Klinik zu geben". Eine Agentur gestaltete die Innenräume des Komplexes. Aspekte, die zur Nachhaltigkeit des Entwurfs beitragen, sind der umfassende Einsatz von Holz ebenso wie das begrünte Dach und die ausgeprägte Tageslichtnutzung.

Situé dans un parc tranquille, le complexe se compose d'une cinquantaine de pièces destinées à des traitements médicaux, d'un hôtel quatre étoiles avec restaurants et cafés et d'une **PISCINE THERMALE** publique ouverte aux patients et aux autres visiteurs. Les salles d'attente du centre médical sont disposées autour de cours qui laissent entrer la lumière du jour avec vue sur des arbres afin de donner aux patients « l'impression d'attendre dans le parc même ». L'un des buts principaux pour les architectes « était de désinstitutionnaliser l'architecture, afin qu'elle ressemble le moins possible à un hôpital ». Une société publicitaire a conçu l'intérieur. L'usage extensif du bois en lambris compte, avec le toit végétalisé, parmi les caractéristiques durables du bâtiment, de même que l'exploitation intense de la lumière naturelle.

Wood cladding and the green roof of the complex are visible here. Below a first-floor plan of the complex with its network of courtyard spaces.

Hier im Bild die Holzverschalung sowie die begrünten Dächer des Komplexes. Unten ein Etagengrundriss des Erdgeschosses mit einem Netzwerk von Innenhöfen.

On voit ici le lambris et le toit végétalisé du complexe. Ci-dessous, un plan du premier étage avec son réseau de cours.

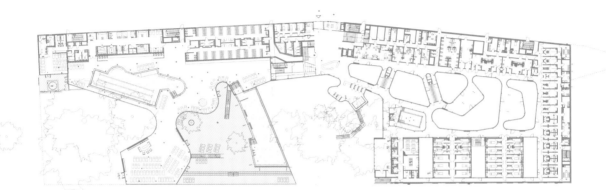

Plans show the relative complexity
of the structure. Below, full-height
glazing and curving walls offer ample
natural life and views through the
complex.

Grundrisse illustrieren die Komplexität der Anlage. Geschosshohe
Verglasung und geschwungene Wände
lassen reichlich Tageslicht in den
Bau einfallen und bieten Durchblicke
durch den gesamten Komplex.

Les plans montrent la relative complexité de l'ensemble. Ci-dessous, le
vitrage pleine hauteur et les courbes
des murs donnent une impression de
grand naturel et permettent de voir à
travers tout le complexe.

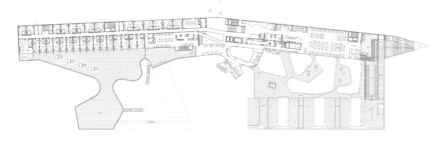

Wood screens are a theme of
the building, offering partial
views through the space and
giving a natural aspect to the
whole—confirmed by the
wood flooring on the terraces
seen here.

*Sichtschutzwände aus Holz
sind ein Leitmotiv. Durch sie
ergeben sich Sichtachsen im
Bau, darüber hinaus sorgen
sie für natürliche Akzente –
unterstrichen wird dieser
Eindruck durch die Holzterrassen hier im Bild.*

*Les panneaux de bois sont
repris dans tout le bâtiment,
ils permettent des vues par-
tielles de l'espace et confèrent à l'ensemble un effet
naturel – souligné par les
sols en bois des terrasses
que l'on voit ici.*

JOHNSEN SCHMALING ARCHITECTS

Johnsen Schmaling Architects
1699 North Astor Street
Milwaukee, WI 53202
USA

Tel: +1 414 287 9000 / Fax: +1 414 287 9025
E-mail: info@johnsenschmaling.com
Web: www.johnsenschmaling.com

BRIAN JOHNSEN received his M.Arch degree from the University of Wisconsin in Milwaukee in 1997. He was a cofounder of Johnsen Schmaling Architects in 2003. **SEBASTIAN SCHMALING** received his M.Arch from the Harvard GSD in 2002. Schmaling, originally from Berlin, had previously attended the University of Wisconsin, where he received another M.Arch degree (1996), and the Technische Universität Berlin, Germany (Vordiplom, Diplom-Ingenieur 1994). He was a cofounder of the firm in 2003 with Brian Johnsen. Their work includes the Storewall corporate headquarters (Milwaukee, 2005); the Camouflage House (Green Lake, 2006); the Blatz Milwaukee, transformation of a former downtown brewery (2006); Celeste 1218, an "urban loft" (Milwaukee, 2007); the Downtown Bar (Milwaukee, 2007–08); and the Ferrous House, a bar and lounge (Spring Prairie, 2007–08, published here). More recently they have worked on the Blur Loft (Milwaukee, 2009); OS House, a sustainable residence (Racine, 2009–10, also published here); Studio for a Composer (Spring Prairie, 2011); Stacked Cabin (Muscoda, 2011); Topo House (Blue Mounds, 2012), all in Wisconsin; and the Mountain Retreat (Big Sky, Montana, 2013), all in the USA.

BRIAN JOHNSEN absolvierte seinen M.Arch 1997 an der University of Wisconsin in Milwaukee. 2003 war er Mitbergünder von Johnsen Schmaling Architects. **SEBASTIAN SCHMALING** absolvierte seinen M.Arch 2002 an der Harvard GSD. Schmaling, ursprünglich aus Berlin, hatte zunächst an der University of Wisconsin studiert, wo er ebenfalls mit einem M.Arch abschloss (1996), sowie an der Technischen Universität Berlin (Vordiplom, Diplom-Ingenieur 1994). 2003 gründete er mit Brian Johnsen das gemeinsame Büro. Zu ihren Projekten zählen die Firmenzentrale von Storewall (Milwaukee, 2005), das Camouflage House (Green Lake, 2006), Blatz Milwaukee, Umbau einer ehemaligen Brauerei (2006), Celeste 1218, ein „urbanes Loft" (Milwaukee, 2007), die Downtown Bar (Milwaukee, 2007–08) und das Ferrous House, Bar und Lounge (Spring Prairie, 2007–08, hier vorgestellt). In jüngerer Zeit arbeitete das Büro am Blur Loft (Milwaukee, 2009), dem OS House, einem nachhaltigen Einfamilienhaus (Racine, 2009–10, ebenfalls hier vorgestellt), dem Studio für einen Komponisten (Spring Prairie, 2011), der Stacked Cabin (Muscoda, 2011), dem Topo House (Blue Mounds, 2012), alle in Wisconsin, sowie dem Mountain Retreat (Big Sky, Montana, 2013), alle in den USA.

BRIAN JOHNSEN a obtenu son M.Arch à l'université du Wisconsin de Milwaukee en 1997. Il a été l'un des cofondateurs de Johnsen Schmaling Architects en 2003 avec **SEBASTIAN SCHMALING.** Ce dernier a obtenu son M.Arch à la Harvard GSD en 2002. Originaire de Berlin, il avait auparavant suivi les cours de l'université du Wisconsin où il a obtenu un autre M.Arch (1996) et de l'Université technique de Berlin (examen intermédiaire, diplôme d'ingénieur en 1994). Leurs réalisations comprennent le Storewall, siège de société (Milwaukee, 2005) ; la Camouflage House (Green Lake, 2006) ; le Blatz, la transformation d'une ancienne brasserie du centre-ville de Milwaukee (2006) ; Celeste 1218, un « loft urbain » (Milwaukee, 2007) ; le bar Downtown (Milwaukee, 2007–08) et la Ferrous House, un bar et lounge (Spring Prairie, 2007–08, publiée ici). Plus récemment, ils ont travaillé au Blur Loft (Milwaukee, 2009) ; à la OS House, une résidence durable (Racine, 2009–10, également publiée ici) ; à un studio pour compositeur (Spring Prairie, 2011) ; à la petite maison Stacked Cabin (Muscoda, 2011) ; à la Topo House (Blue Mounds, 2012), projets tous situés dans le Wisconsin, et à la Mountain Retreat (Big Sky, Montana, 2013), tous aux États-Unis.

OS HOUSE

Racine, Wisconsin, USA, 2009–10

Address: n/a. Area: 180 m². Client: Robert Osborne and Vera Scekic
Cost: not disclosed

This small, sustainable residence for a young family is located in an old downtown neighborhood with lake views. It was one of the first LEED Platinum–certified homes in the Upper Midwest. Sunlight and shading, as well as storm-water management and vegetation, were all carefully studied by the architects during the design process. A ventilated rain screen with soy-based closed-cell foam insulation provides protection from the elements, while the compact form of the house facilitates natural ventilation and reduces the need for artificial light. The architects explain: "The house is designed to operate off the grid throughout most of the year. Power is generated by photovoltaic laminates adhered directly to the roofing membrane, and by an additional, freestanding PV array; excess energy is fed back into the power grid. A deep-well geothermal system provides heating and cooling and supplements the output of the solar water heater. A re-circulating hot-water system and low-flow fixtures reduce water consumption to a minimum."

Das kleine, nach nachhaltigen Prinzipien geplante Haus für eine junge Familie liegt zentral in einem alten Stadtbezirk mit Seeblick. Als eines der ersten Wohnhäuser im nördlichen Mittleren Westen der USA erhielt es ein LEED-Zertifikat in Platin. Bei der Planung setzten sich die Architekten intensiv mit Sonnenstand, Regenwassernutzung und Begrünung auseinander. Eine vorgehängte hinterlüftete Fassade aus geschlossenzelligem, sojabasiertem Schaumstoffmaterial dämmt und schützt vor den Elementen; die kompakte Form des Hauses unterstützt die natürliche Belüftung und reduziert den Bedarf an künstlicher Beleuchtung. Die Architekten erklären: „Das Haus kann den Großteil des Jahres unabhängig vom Stromnetz operieren. Die Stromerzeugung erfolgt mithilfe von Photovoltaik-Verbundfolien, die direkt auf die Dachmembran aufgebracht sind; ein zusätzliches freistehendes Solarmodul ermöglicht die Einspeisung von Energie in das Stromnetz. Eine Erdwärmepumpe versorgt Heiz- und Kühlsysteme und unterstützt zusätzlich die Warmwasserversorgung über eine thermische Solaranlage. Eine Warmwasserzirkulationspumpe und Wasserspararmaturen reduzieren den Wasserverbrauch auf ein Minimum."

Ce petit logement durable destiné à une jeune famille est situé dans un ancien quartier du centre-ville avec vue sur le lac. C'est l'une des premières maisons du haut Midwest à avoir reçu la certification LEED platine. L'ensoleillement et l'ombrage, ainsi que la gestion des eaux pluviales et la végétation, ont fait l'objet d'analyses approfondies par les architectes au cours du processus de conception. Un écran pare-pluie ventilé et son isolation en mousse à cellules fermées à base de soja protège des intempéries, tandis que la forme compacte de la maison favorise la ventilation naturelle et réduit les besoins en lumière artificielle. Les architectes expliquent aussi que « la maison est conçue pour fonctionner presque toute l'année sans être raccordée au réseau électrique. L'électricité est produite par le stratifié photovoltaïque collé directement sur la membrane du toit et par un panneau PV autonome supplémentaire ; le surplus est réinjecté dans le réseau. Un système géothermique profond fournit chauffage et climatisation, tout en complétant l'activité du chauffe-eau solaire. Une installation d'eau chaude à recirculation et des appareils à faible débit permettent de réduire la consommation d'eau au minimum ».

The house stands out from its suburban setting, with the partial overhang of the upper level and the numerous vertical and horizontal openings.

Mit seinem teilweise auskragenden Obergeschoss und den zahlreichen vertikalen und horizontalen Öffnungen sticht das Haus aus der Vorstadtbebauung hervor.

La maison se démarque de son décor de banlieue par le surplomb partiel du dernier étage et ses nombreuses ouvertures verticales et horizontales.

Diagrams show the flow of air through the house, whose lower level is below grade.

Diagramme illustrieren den Luftwechsel im Haus, dessen Parterre zum Teil unter Straßenniveau liegt.

Les schémas représentent le flux d'air qui traverse la maison, dont le niveau inférieur est souterrain.

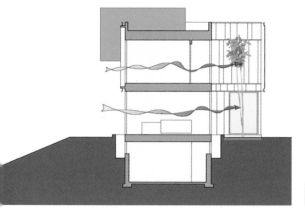

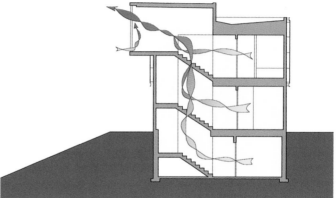

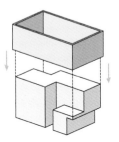
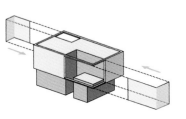

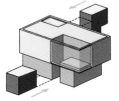

Diagrams show the assembly of the design where simple blocks constitute a rather more complex whole. Below, full-height glazing and wooden floors nearly at ground level contribute to a feeling of openness.

Diagramme veranschaulichen die Bauphasen des Entwurfs, der nicht als komplexe Einheit, sondern aus einfachen Modulen komponiert wurde. Die geschosshohe Verglasung und die Holzböden im Hochparterre sorgen für offenes Raumgefühl.

Schémas de l'assemblage du projet, de simples blocs formant finalement un ensemble plutôt complexe. Ci-dessous, le vitrage sur toute la hauteur et les planchers de bois presque au niveau du sol donnent une impression d'ouverture.

An upper-level wooden terrace offers views to the lake. Below, a plan of the site with the house on the left.

Eine Holzterrasse im Obergeschoss bietet Ausblick auf den See. Unten ein Geländeplan mit dem Haus links im Bild.

Au dernier étage, une terrasse a vue sur le lac. Ci-dessous, un plan du site avec la maison sur la gauche.

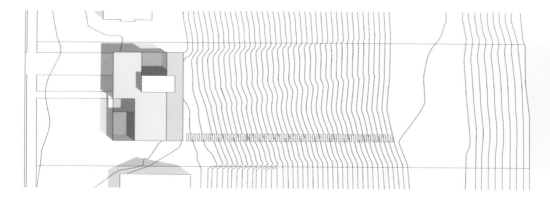

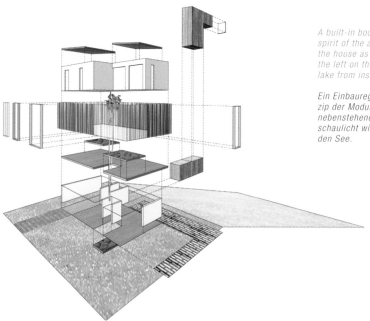

A built-in bookshelf at left is in the spirit of the assembly of the blocks of the house as seen in the drawing to the left on this page. A view of the lake from inside the house (above).

Ein Einbauregal (links) folgt dem Prinzip der Modulbauweise, das auf der nebenstehenden Zeichnung veranschaulicht wird. Oben ein Blick auf den See.

L'étagère encastrée à gauche est parfaitement dans l'esprit d'assemblage des blocs de la maison expliqué sur le schéma à gauche. Vue du lac depuis l'intérieur de la maison (ci-dessus).

FERROUS HOUSE

Spring Prairie, Wisconsin, USA, 2007–08

Address: n/a. Area: 121 m²
Client: Eric and J. J. Edstrom. Cost: not disclosed

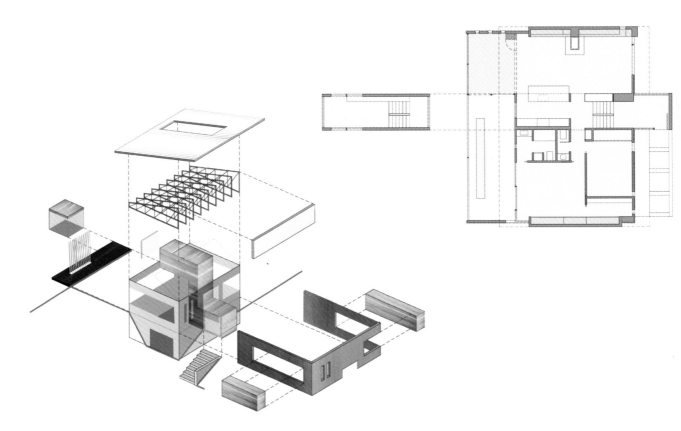

The **FERROUS HOUSE** project involved the "reinvention of a prototypically ill-conceived suburban-production home at the end of its life cycle." Rather than tearing down the old house and rebuilding a new one, the architects took on the task of redesigning it within a limited budget. Foundations, main perimeter walls, and plumbing stacks were reused. The interior was gutted and reorganized to create open, interconnected spaces. Throughout the building, sustainable systems and materials were used, "including low-VOC paints and stains, recycled steel, high-efficiency mechanical systems, Energy Star–rated windows, and locally sourced woods. A high-endurance VaproShield wall membrane and high-efficiency closed-cell expanding foam insulation, sourced from agricultural byproducts to avoid the use of petrochemicals, complement the ventilated perimeter rain screen façade system." Rainwater from the roof is used for natural irrigation of bamboo trees planted near a patio.

Beim **FERROUS HOUSE** ging es darum, „ein geradezu prototypisch schlecht geplantes Vorstadthaus neu zu erfinden, das das Ende seiner Lebensdauer erreicht hatte". Statt den Altbau abzureißen und durch einen Neubau zu ersetzen, stellten sich die Architekten der Herausforderung, das Gebäude in einem knapp gesteckten Budgetrahmen neu zu gestalten. Fundament, Außenwände und Sanitärleitungen wurden beibehalten. Der Bau wurde entkernt und mit ineinandergreifenden Räumen neu organisiert. Im gesamten Haus wurde mit nachhaltigen Systemen und Baustoffen gearbeitet, darunter „schadstoffarmen Farben und Beizen, recyceltem Stahl, Hochleistungshaustechnik, Energiesparfenstern und Holz aus lokaler Forstwirtschaft. Eine hochbeständige Wandmembran (VaproShield) sowie eine hocheffiziente Dämmung aus geschlossenzelligem Dämmschaum aus landwirtschaftlichen Abfallprodukten (um auf petrochemische Produkte verzichten zu können) vervollständigen die vorgehängte hinterlüftete Regenschutzfassade." Regenwasser vom Dach wird zur Bewässerung der Bambuspflanzen an der Terrasse genutzt.

Le projet **FERROUS HOUSE** consistait à « réinventer une maison en fin de vie, produit de banlieue typiquement mal conçu ». Plutôt que de démolir l'ancien bâtiment pour en reconstruire un nouveau, les architectes se sont donné pour tâche de le recomposer avec un budget limité. Les fondations, les principaux murs d'enceinte et les colonnes de plomberie ont été conservés. L'intérieur en revanche a été vidé et réagencé pour créer des espaces ouverts interconnectés. Dans tout le bâtiment, des installations et matériaux durables ont été utilisés, « y compris des peintures et colorants bois à faible teneur en COV, de l'acier recyclé, des systèmes mécaniques haute efficacité, des fenêtres label Energy Star et du bois d'origine locale. Une membrane murale VaproShield très résistante et l'isolation en mousse expansée à cellules fermées haute efficacité, issues de sous-produits agricoles afin d'éviter les produits pétrochimiques, complètent le système périmétrique d'écran pare-pluie ventilé de la façade ». L'eau de pluie qui s'écoule du toit est récupérée pour l'irrigation naturelle de bambous plantés près d'un patio.

Below, before and after views of the house show that the original is quite different from the result. Left page, floor plan and an exploded axonometric drawing show the make-up of the house.

Vorher-/Nachherbilder (unten) belegen, wie stark sich der Vorgängerbau vom Neubau unterscheidet. Grundriss und axonometrische Explosionszeichnung auf der linken Seite veranschaulichen die Anlage des Hauses.

Ci-dessous, vues de la maison avant et après où l'on voit bien que l'original est très différent du résultat. Page de gauche, plan de l'étage et schéma axonométrique éclaté qui montrent l'assemblage de la maison.

Wood on ceilings, some wall surfaces and floors gives a feeling of continuity to the interior, while large windows establish a connection with the exterior.

Der Einsatz von Holz für Decken, einzelne Wandflächen und Böden sorgt für Kontinuität. Die großflächigen Fenster schaffen Verbindungen nach außen.

Le bois des plafonds, de certaines surfaces des murs et des sols donne un sentiment de continuité à l'intérieur, tandis que les grandes fenêtres établissent un lien avec l'extérieur.

K-STUDIO

K-Studio
10 Kalimnou
Kato Chalandri
Athens 15231
Greece

Tel: +30 69 70 70 12 26
Fax: +30 21 06 77 81 88
E-mail: joanna@k-studio.gr
Web: www.k-studio.gr

DIMITRIS KARAMPATAKIS was born in 1979 in Athens, Greece. He studied architecture and received his diploma at the Bartlett, University College London (1997–2004). He worked for Alsop Architects (London, 2001–02), before setting up K-Studio with Konstantinos Karampatakis in 2004. **KONSTANTINOS KARAMPATAKIS** was born in Athens in 1982. He also received his degree from the Bartlett (2002–06) and worked with Alsop in London (2003–04). Recent and completed work of this small firm that employs three other architects and two administrative staff members includes Plane House (Skiathos, Sporades Islands, 2010); Alemagou restaurant and bar (Mykonos, Cycladic Islands, 2010); Hama restaurant and bar (Glyfada, Athens, 2010); Bar Que, restaurant and bar (Nea Erythraia, Athens, 2011); Capanna, a pizzeria trattoria (Kolonaki, Athens, 2011); Bar Bouni (Pilos, Costa Navarino, 2011, published here); and Pix_L House (Serifos, Cycladic Islands, under construction), all in Greece.

DIMITRIS KARAMPATAKIS wurde 1979 in Athen, Griechenland, geboren. Sein Architekturstudium und -Diplom absolvierte er an der Bartlett, University College London (1997–2004). Er arbeitete zunächst für Alsop Architects (London, 2001–02) und gründete 2004 mit Konstantinos Karampatakis das gemeinsame Büro K-Studio. **KONSTANTINOS KARAMPATAKIS** wurde 1982 in Athen geboren. Auch er absolvierte seinen Abschluss an der Bartlett (2002–06) und arbeitete für Alsop in London (2003–04). Jüngere und realisierte Projekte des kleinen Büros, das drei weitere Architekten und zwei Büroangestellte beschäftigt, sind unter anderem das Plane House (Skiathos, Nördliche Sporaden, 2010), Bar und Restaurant Alemagou (Mykonos, Kykladen, 2010), Bar und Restaurant Hama (Glyfada, Athen, 2010), Restaurant und Bar Que (Nea Erythraia, Athen, 2011), Pizzeria Trattoria Capanna (Kolonaki, Athen, 2011), Bar Bouni (Pilos, Costa Navarino, 2011, hier vorgestellt) und das Pix_L House (Serifos, Klykladen, im Bau), alle in Griechenland.

DIMITRIS KARAMPATAKIS est né en 1979 à Athènes. Il a fait des études d'architecture et a obtenu son diplôme à l'École Bartlett de l'University College de Londres (1997–2004), puis a travaillé pour Alsop Architects (Londres, 2001–02) avant d'ouvrir K-Studio avec **KONSTANTINOS KARAMPATAKIS** en 2004. Ce dernier est né à Athènes en 1982. Il a également obtenu son diplôme à la Bartlett (2002–06) et travaille avec Alsop à Londres (2003–04). Les réalisations récentes et achevées de la petite agence, qui compte trois autres architectes et deux employés administratifs, comprennent la Plane House (Skiathos, Sporades, 2010) ; le bar restaurant Alemagou (Mykonos, Cyclades, 2010) ; le restaurant et bar Hama (Glyfada, Athènes, 2010) ; le bar restaurant Bar Que (Nea Erythraia, Athènes, 2011) ; la pizzeria trattoria Capanna (Kolonaki, Athènes, 2011) ; le bar Bouni (Pilos, Costa Navarino, 2011, publié ici) et la Pix_L House (Serifos, Cyclades, en construction), toutes en Grèce.

BAR BOUNI

Pilos, Costa Navarino, Greece, 2011

Address: n/a. Area: 300 m²
Client: Costa Navarino Dunes. Cost: not disclosed

BAR BOUNI is a beach restaurant set on a wooden platform on the beach, allowing waves to break beneath it. The structure of the building is formed by a grid of natural wood columns with an L-shaped wooden volume housing the kitchen, restrooms, and storage space. An inverted field of hanging fabric sheets forms a canopy over the seating area that allows air to circulate and the space to stay cool. An "animated ceiling resembles the waves on the beach and offers a rhythm to the restaurant, just like breathing," according to the architects. They conclude: "The combination of purpose-designed and naturally occurring elements creates a multi-sensory architecture that sits in harmony with the environment, provides a natural, comfortable refuge from the elements, and creates an exciting, sociable atmosphere."

Die **BAR BOUNI** ist ein Strandrestaurant, aufgeständert auf einer hölzernen Plattform am Strand, unter der sich die Wellen brechen können. Strukturell basiert der Bau auf einem Raster aus naturbelassenen Holzstützen; in einem L-förmigen Baukörper sind Küche, Toiletten und Lager untergebracht. Eine „Landschaft aus hängenden Tüchern" bildet das Dach über dem Gastbereich, in dem die Luft frei und kühlend zirkulieren kann. Die „lebendig-bewegte Deckeninstallation spiegelt die Wellen am Strand und gibt dem Restaurant einen atmenden Rhythmus", so die Architekten. Sie fassen zusammen: „Aus einer Kombination gebauter und natürlicher Elemente entsteht eine Architektur für alle Sinne, die sich harmonisch in ihr Umfeld fügt, ein natürlicher und zugleich komfortabler Rückzugsort vor den Elementen, eine reizvolle Atmosphäre zum geselligen Beisammensein."

Le **BAR BOUNI** est un restaurant de plage placé sur une plate-forme en bois sous laquelle les vagues viennent se briser. L'ensemble est formé par un réseau de colonnes en bois naturel et un volume en bois en forme de L qui abrite la cuisine, les toilettes et un espace de rangement. Un champ de pans de tissu suspendus forme un dais au-dessus des tables qui permet la circulation de l'air pour garder à l'espace sa fraîcheur. Ce « plafond animé rappelle les vagues sur la plage et donne au restaurant un certain rythme, comme s'il respirait », expliquent les architectes qui concluent : « La combinaison d'éléments spécialement conçus et d'autres naturellement présents donne naissance à une architecture multisensorielle en harmonie avec son environnement qui procure un abri naturel et agréable contre les éléments, tout en créant une atmosphère conviviale et pleine d'attraits. »

Costa Navarino in the Peloponnese area of southern Greece is known for its luxury tourist resorts. The roof and side of the Bar Bouni are visible above.

Die Costa Navarino am Peloponnes im Süden Griechenlands ist bekannt für ihre Luxushotels. Oben im Bild ein Blick auf das Dach und die Rückwand der Bar Bouni.

Costa Navarino, dans la région du Péloponnèse, au Sud de la Grèce, est connu pour ses complexes touristiques de luxe. On aperçoit ici le toit et le côté du bar Bouni.

The plans for the structure are as simple as its appearance: set up off the beach, it combines rough wood columns with a certain sophistication.

Der Grundriss des Baus ist so schlicht, wie er nach außen erscheint: Die am Strand aufgeständerte Bar ist eine Kombination aus groben Holzpfeilern und dennoch einer gewissen Raffinesse.

Les plans de la structure sont aussi simples qu'elle semble l'être : posée sur la plage, elle allie des colonnes de bois brut à un certain raffinement.

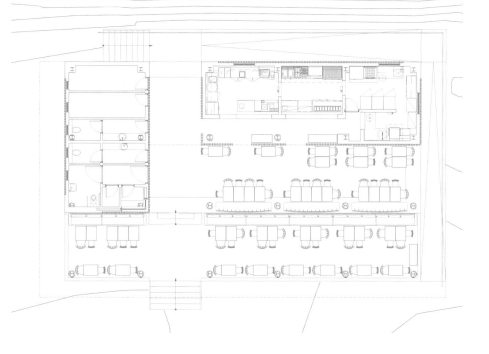

The interior of the restaurant bar is partially shaded by hanging cloths. Wood is the main material for a structure that remains entirely open on three sides.

Im Innern der Bar mit Restaurantbereich hängen Textilsegmente von der Decke. Zentrales Material des an drei Seiten vollständig offenen Baus ist Holz.

L'intérieur du bar restaurant est en partie ombragé par des tissus suspendus. Le bois est le matériau principal d'une structure entièrement ouverte sur trois côtés.

WOLFGANG KERGASSNER

Architekturbüro Wolfgang Kergassner
Herzog-Carl-Str. 2
Scharnhauser Park
73760 Ostfildern
Germany

Tel: +49 711 54 07 09 / 0
Fax: +49 711 54 07 09 / 50
E-mail: buero@kergassner.com
Web: www.kergassner.com

WOLFGANG KERGASSNER was born in Dürnhof, Bad Neustadt (Germany), in 1958. He studied architecture at the Technischen Hochschule Darmstadt (1983–88) and worked with Kauffmann Theilig (Stuttgart, 1988–94), before opening his own office in Stuttgart in 1996. In describing his method, Wolfgang Kergassner emphasizes the issues of cost and scheduling that must be part of each project from the outset. He states: "The planning and execution process, which includes construction, cost, and project management, as well as the experience and evaluation of built projects, prove that very economical projects can be realized with innovative architecture." His work includes the Seele Headquarters (Gersthofen, 1998); Airbus Aircabin (Laupheim, 2001); Scharnhauser Park (Ostfildern, 2003); Linde Agora (Pullach-Höllriegelskreuth, 2008); SAP House in the Park (St. Ingbert, 2009, published here); and Z-UP (Stuttgart, 2009), all in Germany.

WOLFGANG KERGASSNER wurde 1958 in Dürnhof, Deutschland, geboren. Er studierte Architektur an der Technischen Hochschule Darmstadt (1983–88). Nachdem er für Kauffmann Theilig (Stuttgart, 1988–94) tätig war, eröffnete er 1996 ein eigenes Büro in Stuttgart. Kergassner ist besonders wichtig, Kosten- und Terminaspekte von Beginn an mit in den Planungsprozess einzubeziehen. Er erklärt: „Der kreative Zugriff auf den gesamten Planungs- und Ausführungsprozess, das heißt insbesondere Bauleitung, Kosten- und Projektmanagement, sowie die Erfahrung und Auswertung der gebauten Projekte belegen, dass mit innovativer Architektur sehr wirtschaftliche Projekte zu realisieren sind." Zu seinen Projekten zählen das Bürohaus Seele (Gersthofen, 1998), die Airbus Aircabin (Laupheim, 2001), das Bürohaus Scharnhauser Park (Ostfildern, 2003), die Linde Agora (Pullach-Höllriegelskreuth, 2006–08), das SAP Haus im Park (St. Ingbert, 2008, hier vorgestellt) sowie das Z-UP (Stuttgart, 2009), alle in Deutschland.

WOLFGANG KERGASSNER est né à Dürnhof, Bad Neustadt (Allemagne), en 1958. Il a étudié l'architecture à l'École supérieure technique de Darmstadt (1983–88), travaillé avec Kauffmann Theilig (Stuttgart, 1988–94) et ouvert son agence à Stuttgart en 1996. Lorsqu'il décrit sa méthode de travail, Wolfgang Kergassner insiste sur la question du coût et le calendrier qui doit être intégré à chaque projet dès le début : « Le processus de planification et d'exécution, qui comprend la construction, l'étude des coûts et la gestion du projet, ainsi que l'expérience et l'évaluation des projets déjà construits, prouve que des projets très économiques peuvent être réalisés avec une architecture innovante. » Ses réalisations comprennent : le siège de Seele (Gersthofen, 1998) ; le bâtiment Airbus Aircabin (Laupheim, 2001) ; l'immeuble de bureaux Scharnhauser Park (Ostfildern, 2003) ; l'agora Linde (Pullach-Höllriegelskreuth, 2008) ; la Haus im Park de SAP (Saint-Ingbert, 2009, publiée ici) et l'immeuble Z-UP (Stuttgart, 2009), toutes en Allemagne.

SAP HOUSE IN THE PARK

St. Ingbert, Germany, 2009

Address: Neue Bahnhofstr., 66386 St. Ingbert, Germany
Area: 3600 m². Client: SAP Deutschland AG
Cost: not disclosed. Collaboration: Mike Herud, Alexander zur Brügge

St. Ingbert is located in the Saarland region of Germany—it is an old industrial town that now boasts the software maker SAP as one of its major employers. This **HOUSE IN THE PARK** seeks to establish links between the city and the countryside. It is made up of a total of three blocks forming a two-story Y-shaped compositional whole. It includes an office building, kitchen, and delivery and storage area. A Grade II listed house and other existing buildings influenced the new pavilion-like building. The architect regarded the house as a "classical solid" and developed a "skeletal" design for the new building by way of contrast. The ceiling of the new structure is developed from the contours of the slope on the site, and the park area detracted from the site to make way for the construction is made up for with a green roof. The result, as the architects say, is that "the office building is integrated almost invisibly into the park."

Das saarländische St. Ingbert ist eine alte Industriestadt, in der heute das Softwareunternehmen SAP zu den größten Arbeitgebern zählt. Das **HAUS IM PARK** wurde bewusst als Bindeglied zwischen Stadt und Landschaft konzipiert. Die drei Volumina des Baus bilden ein zweistöckiges Y-förmiges Gesamtensemble: Hier befinden sich Büros, Küche sowie Lieferzone und Lagerbereiche. Eine denkmalgeschützte Villa und weitere Bauten auf dem Gelände nahmen Einfluss auf die Formensprache des pavillonartigen Neubaus. Als Antwort auf den „klassischen Massivbau" der Villa entwickelte der Architekt ein „Skelettsystem" für den Neubau. Die Dachkonturen des Neubaus entwickelten sich aus den Höhenlinien des Hanges, während das begrünte Dach die bebauten Grünflächen kompensiert. Auf diese Weise, so der Architekt, integriert sich „das Bürohaus … nahezu unsichtbar in den Park".

Saint-Ingbert est une ancienne ville industrielle de Sarre, en Allemagne, qui s'enorgueillit aujourd'hui de la présence du fabricant de logiciels SAP, l'un de ses principaux employeurs. La **HAUS IM PARK** vise à établir des liens entre la ville et la campagne. Elle se compose de trois blocs formant une composition d'ensemble en Y à deux étages. Ils comprennent un bâtiment de bureaux, une cuisine et une zone de stockage et livraison. La nouvelle construction pavillonnaire a été influencée par une maison classée en catégorie II et d'autres bâtiments existants : l'architecte a considéré la maison comme « classique et solide » et a développé par contraste une structure « squelettique » pour son nouveau bâtiment. Le plafond du nouvel ensemble est inspiré des courbes et des pentes du site, tandis qu'un toit végétalisé compense la zone de parc perdue pour faire place à la construction. Le résultat, affirment les architectes, est « un bâtiment de bureaux intégré au parc de manière presque invisible ».

A drawing (below) and photos show how the building, shaped like a truncated Y, fits into its setting, descending a slope.

Eine Zeichnung (unten) und Ansichten machen deutlich, wie der Bau, ein angeschnittenes Y, in das abschüssige Grundstück eingebettet wurde.

Le schéma (ci-dessous) et les photos montrent comment le bâtiment, en forme de Y tronqué, est intégré au décor sur une pente descendante.

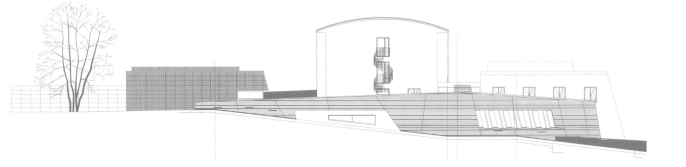

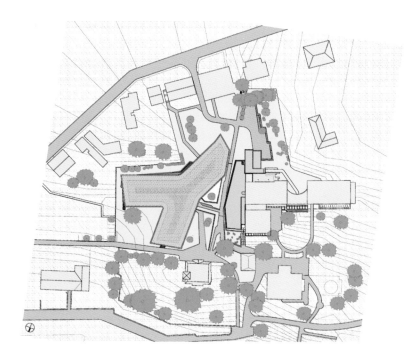

A site drawing shows the building in
light green surrounded in part by
trees. Green also seems to be the
favorite color of the cafeteria
designer.

Ein Grundstücksplan zeigt den Bau in
hellgrün im teilweise baumbestandenen Umfeld. Grün ist offenbar auch
die Lieblingsfarbe des Innenarchitek-
ten der Cafeteria.

Un plan du site représente le bâtiment en vert clair en partie entouré
d'arbres. Le vert semble également
être la couleur préférée du designer
de la cafétéria.

Partially inserted into the land, the building makes ample use of wood cladding and offers generous views of the park.

Das teilweise im Boden versenkte Gebäude wurde großflächig mit Holz verschalt und bietet weite Blicke in den Park.

Partiellement inséré dans le paysage, le bâtiment fait un usage important des revêtements en bois et offre de larges vues du parc.

KJELLGREN KAMINSKY

Kjellgren Kaminsky Architecture AB
Ekmansgatan 3
411 32 Göteborg
Sweden

Tel: +46 31 761 20 01
E-mail: press@kjellgrenkaminsky.se
Web: www.kjellgrenkaminsky.se

Born in 1979 in Göteborg, Sweden, **FREDRIK KJELLGREN** is an architect and interior designer. He studied at Chalmers Architecture (Göteborg, 2000–05) and the School of Design and Crafts (HDK, Göteborg, 2003–06). After his studies he worked in Göteborg in the offices of Wingårdhs Architecture (2005–06), Ten Celsius (2005–06), and Kanozi Architects (2006–07). In 2007 Kjellgren, together with Joakim Kaminsky, won the international architectural competition for Strandbaden Dance Restaurant and they created the firm Kjellgren Kaminsky Architecture. **JOAKIM KAMINSKY** was born in Göteborg in 1978. He studied civil engineering at Chalmers (1997–2000) and architecture at the same institution (2000–04). He worked at UNStudio (Amsterdam, 2004–05) and at Wingårdh Arkitektkontor (2005–06), before the creation of his present office. They have both lectured on the "Supersustainable City" and designed more than 20 energy-passive houses, including the Villa Nyberg (Borlänge, Sweden, 2010, published here).

FREDRIK KJELLGREN, geboren 1979 in Göteborg, Schweden, ist Architekt und Innenarchitekt. Er studierte Architektur an der Technischen Hochschule Chalmers (Göteborg, 2000–05) und der Hochschule für Design und Kunsthandwerk (HDK, Göteborg, 2003–06). Nach dem Studium arbeitete er in Göteborg für Wingårdhs Arkitektkontor (2005–06), Ten Celsius (2005–06) und Kanozi Architects (2006–07). 2007 gewann Kjellgren mit Joakim Kaminsky den internationalen Architekturwettbewerb für das Tanzlokal Strandbaden. Es folgte die Bürogründung von Kjellgren Kaminsky Architecture. **JOAKIM KAMINSKY** wurde 1978 in Göteborg geboren. Er studierte Bauingenieurwesen an der Technischen Hochschule Chalmers (1997–2000) und Architektur an derselben Hochschule (2000–04). Vor der Gründung des eigenen Büros arbeitete er für UNStudio (Amsterdam, 2004–05) und Wingårdh Arkitektkontor (2005–06). Beide lehrten zum Thema „Supersustainable City" (Supernachhaltige Stadt) und entwarfen über 20 Passivhäuser, darunter auch die Villa Nyberg (Borlänge, Schweden, 2010, hier vorgestellt).

Né en 1979 à Göteborg, en Suède, **FREDRIK KJELLGREN** est architecte et décorateur d'intérieur. Il a fait des études d'architecture à Chalmers (Göteborg, 2000–05) et à l'École des métiers du design (HDK, Göteborg, 2003–06), puis a travaillé à Göteborg dans les agences Wingårdh Arkitektkontor (2005–06), Ten Celsius (2005–06) et Kanozi Architects (2006–07). En 2007, il gagne avec Joakim Kaminsky le concours international d'architecture pour le restaurant et salle de danse Strandbaden et ils créent la société Kjellgren Kaminsky Architecture. **JOAKIM KAMINSKY** est né à Göteborg en 1978. Il a fait des études de génie civil (1997–2000) et d'architecture (2000–04) à Chalmers. Il a travaillé à UNStudio (Amsterdam, 2004–05) et Wingårdh Arkitektkontor (2005–06) avant de créer l'agence actuelle. Ils ont donné tous les deux des conférences sur la « cité superdurable » et ont créé plus de 20 maisons passives, dont la villa Nyberg (Borlänge, Suède, 2010, publiée ici).

VILLA NYBERG
Borlänge, Sweden, 2010

Address: n/a. Area: 156 m²
Client: Nyberg family. Cost: €470 000

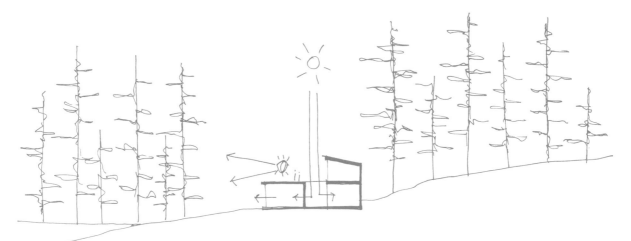

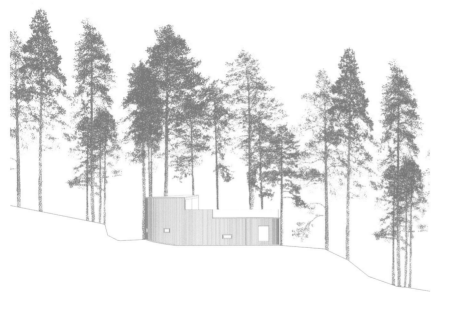

Drawings show the insertion of the house into its natural setting with sun angles indicated on the left page. The house is clad in vertical wood planks.

Zeichnungen veranschaulichen die Einbettung des Hauses in die landschaftliche Umgebung. Sonnenstände sind auf der linken Seite illustriert. Das Haus wurde vertikal mit Holz verschalt.

Les schémas montrent comment la maison s'insère dans son cadre naturel, avec les angles d'ensoleillement sur la page de gauche. La maison est revêtue de planches verticales.

It was in 2009 that Kjellgren and Kaminsky produced a series of passive-energy house designs, and the **VILLA NYBERG** was the first of these to be built. The design strategy relies in part on the energy produced by people in the house, and household equipment. A careful study of the air tightness of the structure is part of their scheme, and they have set a Swedish record in this area. Set on a lake in a pine forest in central Sweden, the house has a living room and kitchen that face the lake, while the private parts of the house face the forest and have much smaller window areas. The round shape avoids thermal or "cold" bridges and reduces the enclosing wall area. Built largely in wood, the house fits into its site and surely brings the concept of the passive-energy house to a new level.

2009 entwarfen Kjellgren und Kaminsky eine Reihe von Passivbauten, von denen die **VILLA NYBERG** als erster Bau realisiert wurde. Das Entwurfskonzept basiert auf der Nutzung von Abwärme, die von den Bewohnern und den elektrischen Geräten im Haus produziert wird. Intensive Studien zur Luftdichtheit des Baus waren Voraussetzung für die Umsetzung des Konzepts: Tatsächlich gelang es, hier einen neuen schwedischen Rekord aufzustellen. Das in einem Kiefernwald an einem See gelegene Haus hat ein Wohnzimmer und eine Küche mit Seeblick, während die Privatbereiche des Baus zum Wald orientiert und mit wesentlich kleineren Fenstern ausgestattet sind. Durch den Rundbau konnten „Wärmebrücken" vermieden und die Wandfläche insgesamt reduziert werden. Das überwiegend als Holzbau realisierte Haus fügt sich in sein Umfeld und setzt zweifellos neue Maßstäbe für den Passivhausbau.

En 2009, Kjellgren et Kaminsky réalisent une série de plans pour des maisons passives, parmi lesquelles la **VILLA NYBERG** – première à avoir été construite – au bord d'un lac dans une forêt de pins du Centre de la Suède. La stratégie de conception repose en partie sur l'énergie produite par les habitants de la maison et les équipements ménagers. Le projet comporte une étude approfondie de l'étanchéité à l'air de la structure, domaine dans lequel elle a battu le record suédois. Le salon et la cuisine donnent sur le lac, tandis que les espaces privés sont face à la forêt et ont des fenêtres beaucoup plus petites. La forme ronde permet d'éviter les ponts thermiques ou « froids » et de réduire la surface de murs. Construite essentiellement en bois, la maison s'intègre bien au site et fait franchir un pas de plus au concept de maison passive.

Sparsely furnished, the house has a wooden floor covering that radiates out to match the rounded forms of the house.

Das sparsam möblierte Haus ist mit Holzboden ausgestattet, der fächerartig den Konturen des Rundbaus folgt.

Meublée avec sobriété, le bois du sol rayonne pour s'adapter aux formes rondes de la maison.

A picture window connects the interior of the house to its natural surroundings. Right, in the living area, large windows punctuate the walls of the house that face the lake.

Ein Panoramafenster schafft Verbindungen zwischen Innenraum und landschaftlicher Umgebung. Große Fensteröffnungen im Wohnbereich (rechts) ziehen sich durch die zum See gewandte Seite des Hauses.

Une baie vitrée relie l'intérieur de la maison à son environnement naturel. À droite, dans le salon, de vastes fenêtres ponctuent les murs qui font face au lac.

MATHIAS KLOTZ

Mathias Klotz
Los Colonos 0411
Providencia, Santiago
Chile

Tel: +56 2 233 6613 / Fax: +56 2 232 2479
E-mail: estudio@mathiasklotz.com
Web: www.mathiasklotz.com

MATHIAS KLOTZ was born in 1965 in Viña del Mar, Chile. He received his architecture degree from the Pontificia Universidad Católica de Chile in 1991. He created his own office in Santiago the same year. He has taught at several Chilean universities and was Director of the School of Architecture of the Universidad Diego Portales in Santiago (2001–03). Recent work includes the Casa Viejo (Santiago, 2001); the Smol Building (Concepción, 2001); the Faculty of Health, Diego Portales University (Santiago, 2004); the remodeling of the Cerra San Luis House (Santiago, 2004); the Ocho al Cubo House (Marbella, Zapallar, 2005); La Roca House (Punta del Este, Uruguay, 2006); the Techos House (Nahuel Huapi Lake, Patagonia, Argentina, 2006–07); the 11 Mujeres House (Cachagua, 2007); 20 one-family houses in La Dehesa (Santiago); and the Buildings Department San Isidro (Buenos Aires, Argentina), all in Chile unless stated otherwise. Mathias Klotz has received numerous awards for sustainable design including Green Good Design awards in 2010 for the La Roca House, and for the Nicanor Parra Library of the Diego Portales University (Santiago, 2010–11, published here), plus a 2011 Holcim Award for the same building.

MATHIAS KLOTZ wurde 1965 in Viña del Mar, Chile, geboren. Er schloss sein Architekturstudium 1991 an der Pontificia Universidad Católica de Chile ab. Sein eigenes Büro gründete er im gleichen Jahr in Santiago. Klotz hat an verschiedenen Universitäten Chiles gelehrt und war Dekan der Architekturfakultät der Universidad Diego Portales in Santiago (2001–03). Zu seinen neueren Projekten zählen unter anderem die Casa Viejo (Santiago, 2001), das Geschäftszentrum Smol (Concepción, 2001), die Fakultät für Gesundheitswissenschaften an der Universidad Diego Portales (Santiago, 2004), der Umbau der Casa Cerra San Luis (Santiago, 2004), die Casa Ocho al Cubo (Marbella, Zapallar, 2005), die Casa La Roca (Punta del Este, Uruguay, 2006), die Casa Techos (Nahuel-Huapi-See, Patagonien, Argentinien, 2006–07), die Casa 11 Mujeres (Cachagua, 2007), 20 Einfamilienhäuser in La Dehesa (Santiago) sowie die Baubehörde in San Isidro (Buenos Aires, Argentinen), alle in Chile, sofern nicht anders vermerkt. Für seine nachhaltige Architektur wurde Mathias Klotz mit zahlreichen Preisen ausgezeichnet, darunter 2010 mit dem Preis für „Green Good Design" für die Casa La Roca und die Bibliothek Nicanor Parra an der Universidad Diego Portales (Santiago, 2010–11, hier vorgestellt) sowie 2011 mit einem Holcim Award für dasselbe Projekt.

MATHIAS KLOTZ est né en 1965 à Viña del Mar, au Chili. Il a obtenu son diplôme d'architecture à l'Université catholique pontificale du Chili en 1991 et a créé son agence à Santiago la même année. Il a enseigné dans plusieurs universités chiliennes et a dirigé l'École d'architecture de l'université Diego Portales de Santiago (2001–03). Ses réalisations récentes comptent la Casa Viejo (Santiago, 2001) ; le bâtiment Smol (Concepción, 2001) ; la faculté des sciences de la santé de l'université Diego Portales (Santiago, 2004) ; le réaménagement de la Casa Cerra San Luis (Santiago, 2004) ; la Casa Ocho al Cubo (Marbella, Zapallar, 2005) : la Casa La Roca (Punta del Este, Uruguay, 2006) ; la Casa Techos (lac Nahuel Huapi, Patagonie, Argentine, 2006–07) ; la Casa 11 Mujeres (Cachagua, 2007) ; 20 maisons individuelles à La Dehesa (Santiago) et le service de la construction de San Isidro (Buenos Aires), toutes au Chili sauf si précisé. Mathias Klotz a reçu de nombreux prix pour ses créations durables, notamment en 2010 le prix de design Green Good pour la Casa La Roca et la bibliothèque Nicanor Parra de l'université Diego Portales (Santiago, 2010–11, publiée ici) et en 2011 un prix Holcim pour le même bâtiment.

NICANOR PARRA LIBRARY

Diego Portales University, Santiago, Chile, 2010–11

*Address: Vergara 324, Santiago, Región Metropolitana, Chile,
www.bibliotecanicanorparra.cl / www.udp.cl/index2.asp. Area: 5000 m². Client: Diego Portales University
Cost: not disclosed. Collaboration: Francisco Reyes, Eduardo Ruiz, Pedro Pedraza*

*The architect used a sculptural
arrangement of concrete blocks to
mark the different levels above this
central atrium.*

*Der Architekt arbeitete mit einem
Arrangement aus skulpturalen Beton-
blöcken, um die verschiedenen
Ebenen über dem zentralen Atrium
zu akzentuieren.*

*Les architectes ont conçu un arran-
gement sculptural de blocs de béton
pour marquer les différents niveaux
au-dessus du hall central.*

A variety of treatments for floors and walls enlivens the space, as does the admission of natural light.

Eine Vielzahl verschiedener Boden- und Wandstrukturen sowie das einfallende Tageslicht beleben den Raum.

Les sols et les murs variés égayent l'espace, tout comme la lumière naturelle.

Diego Portales University is located near the center of Santiago in an area called Sur Poniente. In 2003, with approximately 12 000 students, the university decided to expand its campus, and Mathias Klotz was hired as an advisor, and as a designer of three of the nine new buildings planned. A new central library was added to his responsibilities for the university, and construction began there early in 2010. The library is designed with an emphasis on natural light and ventilation. Passive systems and materials that reflect and filter light were employed. The architect explains: "The new building appears as a green volume, whose vegetation works as a solar filter for the western orientation. It also symbolically represents the responsible attitude of the institution, which, with this building, applied for a LEED Gold certification… becoming the first and only university building in Chile developed under these parameters. In the interior, façades that are exposed to the sun are also protected with vegetation." The plants used were inspired by natural meadows, "a reference to what used to be the Santiago Valley, before the arrival of the conquerors."

Die Universidad Diego Portales liegt unweit des Stadtzentrums von Santiago im Bezirk Sur Poniente. 2003, mit rund 12 000 eingeschriebenen Studierenden, beschloss die Universität den Ausbau ihrer Campusanlagen: Mathias Klotz wurde als Berater hinzugezogen und erhielt den Auftrag, drei der insgesamt neun geplanten Neubauten zu entwerfen. Schließlich betraute man ihn darüber hinaus mit einer neuen Zentralbibliothek für die Universität. Die Bauarbeiten begannen Anfang 2010. Besonderes Augenmerk lag hier auf natürlicher Belichtung und Durchlüftung. Zum Einsatz kamen außerdem Prinzipien der Solararchitektur sowie lichtfilternde und reflektierende Materialien. Der Architekt führt aus: „Der Neubau präsentiert sich als grüner Baukörper, dessen begrünte Westfassade als Sonnenfilter fungiert. Darüber hinaus steht er für die Verantwortlichkeit der Hochschule, die mit diesem Gebäude den Antrag auf ein LEED-Zertifikat in Gold gestellt hat … und damit der erste und einzige Universitätsbau Chiles ist, der nach entsprechenden Kriterien geplant wurde. Auch im Innern des Baus wurden die der Sonne zugewandten Fassaden durch Begrünung geschützt." Die Pflanzenauswahl orientierte sich an der Flora von Wildwiesen, „eine Erinnerung daran, was das Tal von Santiago früher einmal war, vor Ankunft der Eroberer".

L'université Diego Portales est située dans un quartier appelé Sur Poniente proche du Centre de Santiago. Comptant environ 12 000 étudiants en 2003, elle a décidé d'agrandir son campus et Mathias Klotz a été engagé comme conseiller et concepteur de trois des neuf bâtiments prévus. Il s'est vu confier, en plus de ses responsabilités universitaires, la réalisation d'une nouvelle bibliothèque centrale dont la construction a débuté en 2010. La bibliothèque a été conçue en tenant particulièrement compte de la lumière naturelle et de la ventilation. Des systèmes énergétiques passifs et des matériaux qui réfléchissent et filtrent la lumière ont été utilisés. Les architectes expliquent que « le nouveau bâtiment a l'apparence d'un bloc de verdure dont la végétation tient lieu de filtre solaire pour l'orientation vers l'ouest. Il incarne également de manière symbolique l'attitude responsable de l'institution qui a demandé une certification LEED or pour ce bâtiment. […] C'est désormais le premier et le seul bâtiment universitaire au Chili développé selon ces paramètres. À l'intérieur, les façades exposées au soleil sont également protégées par de la végétation. Les plantes choisies ont été inspirées par les prairies naturelles, « une réminiscence de ce qu'était la vallée de Santiago avant l'arrivée des conquérants espagnols ».

Above, a rooftop terrace and garden offers views of the city and the surrounding mountains.

Eine begrünte Dachterrasse (oben) bietet Ausblick auf die Stadt und die Berge des Umlands.

Ci-dessus, une terrasse sur le toit et jardin avec vue sur la ville et les montagnes environnantes.

The irregular concrete block pattern
seen in the atrium is also visible on
the main façade of the building.
Below, full-height glazing at the
entrance.

Das schon im Atrium gesehene
unregelmäßige Muster aus Beton-
blöcken findet sich auch an der
Hauptfassade des Gebäudes wieder.
Unten der geschosshoch verglaste
Eingangsbereich.

Le motif irrégulier de blocs de béton
qui orne le hall se retrouve sur la
façade principale du bâtiment.
Ci-dessous, paroi vitrée sur toute sa
hauteur à l'entrée de la bibliothèque.

The architect skillfully manipulates surface treatments and the use of natural light, whether with the irregular bars seen above, or the openings that create a pattern of light.

Der Architekt spielt gekonnt mit Oberflächen und Tageslicht, ob nun in Form der unregelmäßigen Metallstäbe oben im Bild oder von Lichtbändern, die Musterspiele entstehen lassen.

L'architecte a joué habilement sur les traitements des surfaces et la lumière naturelle, notamment avec les barres irrégulières vues en haut ou les ouvertures qui créent un motif lumineux.

A glass ceiling is an unusual feature of the building, seen on the right page. Here again, opacity and transparency are orchestrated in unexpected ways.

Ein auffälliger Akzent des Baus ist eine Geschossdecke aus Glas (rechte Seite). Auch hier orchestriert der Architekt Opazität und Transparenz auf überraschende Weise.

Le plafond de verre qu'on voit page de droite est l'un des éléments originaux du bâtiment. Là encore, opacité et transparence sont orchestrées pour surprendre.

Darkness and light are also used by Mathias Klotz to enliven space, whether it be near a café area or in a reading space.

Auch das Wechselspiel von Dunkelheit und Licht nutzt Mathias Klotz, um Räume zu beleben, ob nun in einem Cafébereich oder einem Lesesaal.

Mathias Klotz utilise aussi l'obscurité et la lumière pour enjoliver l'espace, à côté d'un café ou dans une salle de lecture.

The patterned floor seems to respond to the somewhat irregular screens on the upper floors—with a nearly blank concrete wall between the two.

Das Bodenmuster wirkt wie eine Antwort auf die unregelmäßigen Wandschirme in den oberen Geschossen – dazwischen eine nahezu schmucklose Sichtbetonwand.

Le motif du sol semble faire écho aux écrans irréguliers des étages supérieurs – séparés par une paroi de béton presque vierge.

KENGO KUMA

Kengo Kuma & Associates
2–24–8 Minami Aoyama
Minato-ku
Tokyo 107–0062
Japan

Tel: +81 3 3401 7721 / Fax: +81 3 3401 7778
E-mail: kuma@ba2.so-net.ne.jp
Web: www.kkaa.co.jp

Born in 1954 in Kanagawa, Japan, **KENGO KUMA** graduated in 1979 from the University of Tokyo with an M.Arch degree. In 1985–86 he received an Asian Cultural Council Fellowship Grant and was a Visiting Scholar at Columbia University. In 1987 he established the Spatial Design Studio, and in 1991 he created Kengo Kuma & Associates. His work includes the Karuizawa Resort Hotel (Karuizawa, 1993); Kiro-san Observatory (Ehime, 1994); Atami Guesthouse, Guesthouse for Bandai Corp (Atami, 1992–95); the Japanese Pavilion for the Venice Biennale (Venice, Italy, 1995); Tomioka Lakewood Golf Club House (Tomioka, 1993–96); and Toyoma Noh-Theater (Miyagi, 1995–96). He has also completed the Great (Bamboo) Wall Guesthouse (Beijing, China, 2002); One Omotesando (Tokyo, 2003); LVMH Osaka (Osaka, 2004); the Nagasaki Prefecture Art Museum (Nagasaki, 2005); and the Zhongtai Box, Z58 building (Shanghai, China, 2003–06). Recent work includes the Steel House (Bunkyo-ku, Tokyo, 2005–07); Sakenohana (London, UK, 2007); Tiffany Ginza (Tokyo, 2008); Nezu Museum (Tokyo, 2007–09); Museum of Kanayama (Ota City, Gunma, 2009); Glass Wood House (New Canaan, Connecticut, USA, 2007–10); Yusuhara Marche (Yusuhara, Kochi, 2009–10); the GC Prostho Museum Research Center, Torii Matsu Machi (Aichi, 2009–10); and the Yusuhara Wooden Bridge Museum (Yusuhara-cho, Takaoka-gun, Kochi, 2010, published here), all in Japan unless stated otherwise.

KENGO KUMA, geboren 1954 in Kanagawa, Japan, schloss sein Studium 1979 an der University of Tokyo mit einem M.Arch ab. 1985–86 erhielt er ein Stipendium des Asian Cultural Council und war Gastdozent an der Columbia University. 1987 gründete er das Büro Spatial Design Studio, 1991 folgte die Gründung von Kengo Kuma & Associates. Zu seinen Projekten zählen die Hotelanlage Karuizawa (Karuizawa, 1993), das Planetarium Kiro-san (Ehime, 1994), ein Gästehaus für Bandai (Atami, 1992–95), der Japanische Pavillon für die Biennale in Venedig (Venedig, Italien, 1995), ein Clubhaus für den Tomioka-Lakewood-Golfclub (Tomioka, 1993–96) und das No-Theater in Toyoma (Miyagi, 1995–96). Darüber hinaus realisierte er das Gästehaus Great (Bamboo) Wall (Peking, China, 2002), One Omotesando (Tokio, 2003), LVMH Osaka (Osaka, 2004), das Kunstmuseum der Präfektur Nagasaki (Nagasaki, 2005) sowie die Zhongtai Box, Z58 (Shanghai, China, 2003–06). Jüngere Projekte sind unter anderem das Steel House (Bunkyo-ku, Tokio, 2005–07), Sakenohana (London, GB, 2007), Tiffany Ginza (Tokio, 2008), das Nezu Museum (Tokio, 2007–09), das Museum der Burgruine von Kanayama (Ota, Gunma, 2009), das Glass Wood House (New Canaan, Connecticut, USA, 2007–10), Yusuhara Marché (Yusuhara, Kochi, 2009–10), das Forschungszentrum am GC Prostho Museum (Torii Matsu Machi, Aichi, 2009–10) sowie das Yusuhara Wooden Bridge Museum (Yusuhara-cho, Takaoka-gun, Kochi, 2010, hier vorgestellt), alle in Japan sofern, nicht anders angegeben.

Né en 1954 à Kanagawa (Japon), **KENGO KUMA** est diplômé d'architecture de l'université de Tokyo (1979). En 1985–86, il bénéficie d'une bourse de l'Asian Cultural Council et devient chercheur invité à l'université Columbia. En 1987, il crée le Spatial Design Studio et, en 1991, Kengo Kuma & Associates. Parmi ses réalisations : l'hôtel de vacances Karuizawa (Karuizawa, 1993) ; l'observatoire Kiro-san (Ehime, 1994) ; la maison d'hôtes d'Atami pour Bandai Corp (Atami, 1992–95) ; le Pavillon japonais pour la Biennale de Venise 1995 ; le club-house du golf du lac de Tomioka (Tomioka, 1993–96) et le théâtre de nô Toyoma (Miyagi, 1995–96). Il a également réalisé la maison d'hôtes de la Grande Muraille (de bambou) (Pékin, 2002) ; l'immeuble One Omotesando (Tokyo, 2003) ; l'immeuble LVMH Osaka (2004) ; le Musée d'art de la préfecture de Nagasaki (Nagasaki, 2005) et l'immeuble Zhongtai Box, Z58 (Shanghai, 2003–06). Plus récemment, il a construit la Steel House (Bunkyo-ku, Tokyo, 2005–07) ; le restaurant Sakenohana (Londres, 2007) ; l'immeuble Tiffany Ginza (Tokyo, 2008) ; le musée Nezu (Tokyo, 2007–09) ; le musée de Kanayama (Ota, Gunma ; 2009) ; la Glass Wood House (New Canaan, Connecticut, 2007–10), le marché de Yusuhara (Yusuhara, Kochi, 2009–10) ; le centre de recherches du musée GC Prostho, Torii Matsu Machi (Aichi, 2009–10) et le musée du Pont de bois de Yusuhara (Yusuhara-cho, Takaoka-gun, Kochi, 2010, publié ici), tous au Japon sauf si spécifié.

YUSUHARA WOODEN BRIDGE MUSEUM

Yusuhara-cho, Takaoka-gun, Kochi, Japan, 2010

Address: 3799–3 Taro-gawa Yusuhara-cho, Takaoka-gun, Kochi Prefecture, Japan
Area: 445 m². Client: Tomio Yano, Mayor of Yusuhara
Cost: not disclosed

Kengo Kuma makes a skillful combination of old Japanese building methods with modern materials, as can be seen in the image below. Right, a site drawing.

Kunstvoll verbindet Kengo Kuma alte japanische Kragtechniken in Holzbauweise mit modernen Materialien, wie unten zu sehen. Rechts ein Grundstücksplan.

Kengo Kuma associe avec habileté les anciennes méthodes de construction japonaises et les matériaux modernes, on le voit ci-dessous. À droite, un plan du site.

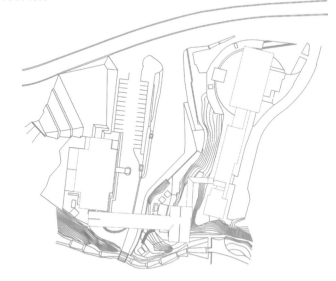

Making an unusual connection between older buildings nearby and its own traditionally inspired wooden structure, the museum is a bridge and vice versa.

Das Museum als Brücke, die Brücke als Museum: ein ungewöhnliches Bindeglied zwischen den älteren Nachbarbauten und der von traditionellen Bauweisen inspirierten Holzarchitektur des Neubaus.

Le musée, qui établit un lien inédit entre les bâtiments voisins plus anciens et sa propre structure en bois d'inspiration traditionnelle, est un pont, tout comme le pont est un musée.

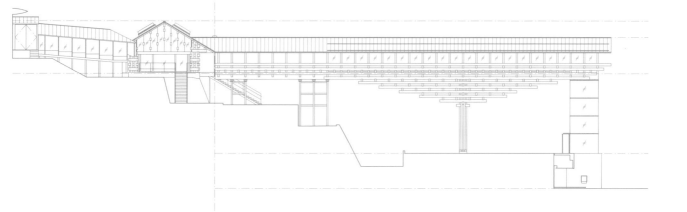

This new structure, extending an existing facility, was built as an exhibition space. The structure, with one level below grade and two above, is in wood with a partly steel frame, and reinforced concrete is also used. The maximum height of the building is 13.8 meters. The reason for the bridge-like design is that the structure connects a hotel and spa operated by the town, formerly separated by a cliff and a road. The facility includes a workshop and space for an artist-in-residence program. Kengo Kuma writes: "In this project, we challenged a structural system which is composed of small parts, referring to the cantilever structure often employed in traditional architecture in Japan and China. It is a great example of sustainable design, as you can achieve a big cantilever even without large-sized materials." Locally grown red cedar was used to create laminated timber with small sections, allowing the structure to better blend into its forest setting.

Der als Erweiterung eines bestehenden Komplexes geplante Neubau wurde als Ausstellungsraum konzipiert. Realisiert wurde das Gebäude mit einem Unter- und zwei Obergeschossen weitgehend in Holzbauweise über einem Stahlrahmen und Stahlbetonelementen. An seiner höchsten Stelle erreicht der Bau 13,8 m. Als Bindeglied zwischen einem von der Kommune betriebenen Hotel und Spa, die ursprünglich durch einen Steilabhang und eine Straße getrennt waren, wurde der Neubau als Brücken-konstruktion gestaltet. Im neuen Gebäude sind auch eine Werkstatt und ein Aufenthaltsprogramm für Künstler untergebracht. Kengo Kuma schreibt: „Dieses Projekt war auch eine Auseinandersetzung mit einer kleinteiligen Tragwerksform, eine Bezugnahme auf Kragtechniken, einer typischen historischen Bauform der chinesischen und japanischen Architektur. Ein großartiges Beispiel für nachhaltige Architektur, das belegt, dass große Ausleger auch ohne großteilige Bauelemente realisierbar sind." Die vergleichsweise kurzen Schichtholzsegmente wurden aus Riesen-Thuja aus nachhaltiger Forstwirtschaft gefertigt und tragen dazu bei, dass sich der Bau in die bewaldete Umgebung fügt.

La nouvelle structure, extension d'une autre existante, est construite comme un espace d'exposition. L'ensemble, composé d'un niveau en dessous du sol et de deux au-dessus, est en bois avec une ossature partiellement en acier et du béton armé. Le bâtiment ne dépasse pas 13,8 m de haut. La construction de type pont s'explique par le fait que le bâtiment relie un hôtel et un spa exploités par la municipalité et auparavant séparés par un escarpement et une route. Il comprend un atelier et l'espace nécessaire à un artiste en résidence. Kengo Kuma écrit : « Dans ce projet, nous remettons en question un système structurel composé de petits éléments, en référence aux structures en porte-à-faux souvent employées par les architectures traditionnelles chinoise et japonaise. C'est un magnifique exemple de conception durable qui montre qu'on peut réaliser un pont cantilever de grandes dimensions sans utiliser de pièces trop massives. » Du cèdre rouge cultivé sur place a été utilisé pour créer un lamellé à fines sections afin que le bâtiment puisse mieux se fondre dans son décor forestier.

The architect uses an inverted wood stacking method that is unique to Asia, and Japan in particular. Below, an axonometric drawing shows the different parts of the project. Left, the entrance area.

Der Architekt arbeitet mit einer Kragtechnik in Holzbauweise, die besonders typisch für Asien und insbesondere für Japan ist. Unten eine Axonometrie, die die verschiedenen Elemente des Entwurfs veranschaulicht. Links der Eingangsbereich.

L'architecte a eu recours à une méthode de superposition inversée du bois spécifique de l'architecture asiatique, et du Japon en particulier. Ci-dessous, le schéma axonométrique montre les différentes parties de l'ensemble. À gauche, l'entrée.

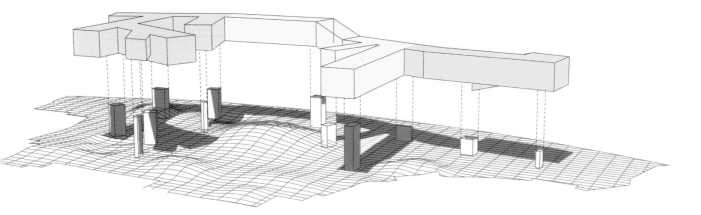

An atmosphere seen in some Japanese temples pervades the interiors and walkways of the museum.

Interieur und Korridore des Museums erinnern atmosphärisch an manche japanische Tempelbauten.

L'intérieur et les allées du musée sont imprégnés d'une atmosphère qu'on retrouve dans certains temples japonais.

Wood is omnipresent in the structure. One of Japan's greatest living architects, Kuma manages the difficult synthesis between his real understanding of the past and the requirements of the present.

Holz ist im gesamten Gebäude omnipräsent. Kuma, einer der größten lebenden japanischen Architekten, gelingt die schwierige Gratwanderung zwischen echtem Geschichtsbewusstsein und den Anforderungen der Gegenwart.

Le bois est omniprésent. Kuma, l'un des plus grands architectes japonais encore en vie, réussit la difficile synthèse entre son interprétation réelle du passé et les exigences du présent.

LAKE | FLATO

Lake I Flato
311 Third Street
San Antonio, TX 78205
USA

Tel: +1 210 227 3335 / Fax: +1 210 224 9515
E-mail: marketing@lakeflato.com
Web: www.lakeflato.com

ROBERT HARRIS was born in 1965 in Springfield, Ohio, and received his degrees in architecture at Texas Tech University (B.Arch, 1988) and at the University of Texas (Austin, M.Arch, 1992). He joined Lake I Flato in 1994 and is a Partner in the firm, which was founded by David Lake and Ted Flato in 1984. Robert Harris has more than 20 years of experience in environmental issues including land preservation advocacy and sustainable urban design. He was the founding Director of the US Green Building Council (USGBC) Balcones Chapter (Central Texas) and is presently serving on the national board of the USGBC. His work includes the Hotel San Jose (Austin, Texas, 2001); Dog Team Too Loft and Studio (San Antonio, Texas, 2004); Government Canyon Visitor Center (Helotes, Texas, 2005); Friends Meetinghouse (San Antonio, Texas, 2006); the Shangri-La Botanical Gardens and Nature Center (Orange, Texas, 2005–07, published here); and the Lance Armstrong Livestrong Foundation (Austin, Texas, 2008–09, also published here). Current work includes the Gulf Coast Research Laboratory Marine Education Center (Ocean Springs, Mississippi, 2012–14); and the Austin Central Library (Austin, Texas, 2010–15), all in the USA.

ROBERT HARRIS, geboren 1965 in Springfield, Ohio, absolvierte seine Abschlüsse in Architektur an der Texas Tech University (B.Arch, 1988) und der University of Texas (Austin, M.Arch, 1992). Seit 1994 ist er für Lake I Flato tätig – 1984 von David Lake und Ted Flato gegründet –, wo er heute Partner ist. Robert Harris blickt auf 20 Jahre Erfahrung im Umweltbereich zurück, als aktiver Förderer des Umweltschutzs ebenso wie in der nachhaltigen Stadtplanung. Er ist Gründungsdirektor der Regionalabteilung des US Green Building Council (USGBC) in Balcones (Central Texas) und derzeit im Bundesvorstand des USGBC. Zu seinen Projekten zählen das Hotel San Jose (Austin, Texas, 2001), ein Loft und Studio für Dog Team Too (San Antonio, Texas, 2004), ein Besucherzentrum im Government Canyon (Helotes, Texas, 2005), das Friends Meetinghouse (San Antonio, Texas, 2006), der Botanische Garten mit Naturzentrum Shangri-La (Orange, Texas, 2005–07, hier vorgestellt) sowie die Lance Armstrong Livestrong Foundation (Austin, Texas, 2008–09, ebenfalls hier vorgestellt). Zu seinen aktuellen Projekten zählen das Forschungslabor am Bildungszentrum für Meereskunde der Gulf-Coast-Region (Ocean Springs, Mississippi, 2012–14) und die Zentralbibliothek von Austin (Austin, Texas, 2010–15), alle in den USA.

ROBERT HARRIS est né en 1965 à Springfield, Ohio, et est diplômé en architecture de l'Université technique du Texas (B.Arch, 1988) et de l'université du Texas (Austin, M.Arch, 1992). Il a rejoint Lake I Flato en 1994 et il est désormais partenaire de l'agence fondée par David Lake et Ted Flato en 1984. Il dispose d'une expérience de plus de 20 ans en matière d'environnement, notamment de campagnes pour la préservation du sol et d'urbanisme durable. Il est le directeur fondateur de l'US Green Building Council (USGBC) Balcones Chapter (Texas central) et est actuellement membre du bureau national de l'USGBC. Ses réalisations comprennent l'hôtel San Jose (Austin, Texas, 2001) ; le loft et studio Dog Team Too (San Antonio, Texas, 2004) ; le Centre d'accueil des visiteurs de Government Canyon (Helotes, Texas, 2005) ; la « Maison des assemblées des amis » (San Antonio, 2006) ; le Jardin botanique et Centre de découverte de la nature Shangri-La (Orange, Texas, 2005–07, publié ici) et la Fondation Livestrong de Lance Armstrong (Austin, 2008–09, également publiée ici). Parmi ses projets en cours, on peut citer le Centre éducatif marin du laboratoire de recherches du golfe du Mexique (Ocean Springs, Mississippi, 2012–14) et la bibliothèque centrale d'Austin (2010–15), tous aux États-Unis.

Jeffery C. Garvey
Board of Directors
Conference Room

UNITY IS STRENGTH.

LIVESTRONG FOUNDATION

Austin, Texas, USA, 2008–09

Address: 2201 East 6th Street, Austin, Texas 78702–3456, USA, tel: +1 512 236 8820, www.livestrong.org
Area: 2787 m². Client: Lance Armstrong Foundation
Cost: not disclosed. Collaboration: Ryan Jones, Brandon Anderson, Matt Wallace

An open canopy and landscaping near the entrance to the foundation, which was launched by the former cycling champion Lance Armstrong.

Ein Vordach und eine Grünzone unweit des Eingangs zur Stiftung, die vom ehemaligen Radsportprofi Lance Armstrong gegründet wurde.

Auvent ouvert et aménagement paysager à l'entrée de la fondation créée par l'ancien champion cycliste Lance Armstrong.

An interior view and a perspective
drawing of the spaces show how a
system of wooden boxes placed in an
irregular pattern provide the required
functional spaces.

Ein Blick ins Innere des Baus
und eine Perspektivzeichnung ver-
deutlichen, wie die geforderten
funktionalen Zonen durch ein System
unregelmäßig platzierter hölzerner
„Boxen" entstehen.

La vue intérieure ci-dessus et le
schéma en perspective des différents
espaces montrent comment un
ensemble de cabines en bois disposées irrégulièrement fournit les
espaces fonctionnels requis.

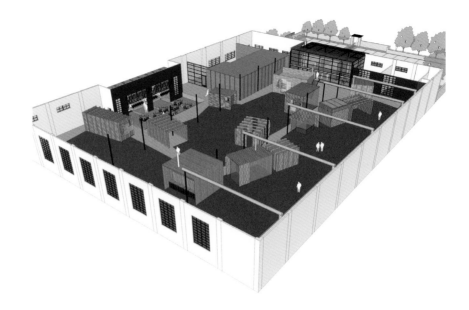

The Lance Armstrong Foundation purchased a run-down warehouse which it asked Lake|Flato to transform to create office space, meeting rooms, dining facilities, an in-house gymnasium, open-air courtyard, and parking for the staff of 62. Of the materials from the original warehouse 88% were recycled and used in the new project. Of the remaining materials 28% were sourced within a radius of 800 kilometers of the site. North-facing clerestory windows were added to bring daylight into the structure. This measure, together with the installation of efficient systems, allows the foundation structure to consume approximately 39% less than a conventional office building of the same size. Materials selected and used in the building avoid toxic chemicals. Fly ash, a by-product of coal-burning power plants, will replace 40% of the cement used in this project, thus reducing the project's carbon footprint. As the former bicycle racing champion Lance Armstrong states: "We kept an eye on the materials and the impact this building would have on the land around." The **LIVESTRONG FOUNDATION** has a LEED Gold certification.

Nachdem die Lance Armstrong Foundation einen alten Speicher gekauft hatte, beauftragte sie Lake|Flato mit dem Umbau zum Stiftungsgebäude mit Büroflächen, Konferenzräumen, einer Kantine, einer Sporthalle, einem offenen Innenhof und einem Parkplatz für ihr Team mit 62 Mitarbeitern. 88% der Baustoffe des Altbaus konnten recycelt und im Neubau wiederverwertet werden. 28% der verbauten Materialien konnten in einem Radius von 800 km um den Standort bezogen werden. Um Tageslicht in den Bau zu lassen, wurden nach Norden orientierte Oberlichter in das Sheddach integriert. Dank dieser Maßnahme und der Installation energieeffizienter Haustechnik kommt die Stiftung mit rund 39% weniger Strom aus als ein konventionelles Gebäude gleicher Größe. Die verwendeten Baustoffe sind bewusst schadstofffrei. Flugasche, ein Abfallprodukt in Kohlefeueranlagen, macht hier als Zusatzstoff 40% des verbauten Zements aus und reduziert damit die CO_2-Bilanz des Gebäudes. Der ehemalige Radsportprofi Lance Armstrong erklärt: „Wir haben besonders auf die Materialien und die Auswirkungen des Baus auf die landschaftliche Umgebung geachtet." Die **LIVESTRONG FOUNDATION** wurde mit einem LEED-Zertifikat in Gold ausgezeichnet.

La fondation de Lance Armstrong a acquis un entrepôt délabré et a demandé à Lake|Flato de le transformer pour y créer un espace de bureaux, des salles de réunion, des possibilités de restauration, une salle de gymnastique, une cour et un parking pour ses 62 employés. Les matériaux du bâtiment d'origine ont été recyclés et utilisés à 88% pour le nouveau projet, tandis que 28% autres ont été produits dans un rayon de 800 km autour du site. Des fenêtres à claire-voie ont été ajoutées côté nord pour faire entrer plus de jour. Avec le choix de systèmes efficaces, elles permettent à la Fondation de consommer environ 39% de moins qu'un immeuble de bureaux classique de même taille. Les matériaux sélectionnés et utilisés ne contiennent pas de produits chimiques toxiques. Les cendres volantes, un sous-produit des centrales électriques au charbon, remplacent ainsi 40% du ciment utilisé afin de réduire l'empreinte carbone du projet. Selon les termes de l'ancien champion cycliste Lance Armstrong : « Nous n'avons jamais perdu de vue les matériaux et l'impact du bâtiment sur le paysage environnant. » La **FONDATION LIVESTRONG** a obtenu une certification LEED or.

Above and left page, the wooden boxes are arranged beneath the high roof which admits natural light, while limiting direct sun.

Oben und linke Seite: Die Boxen aus Holz sind unter einem hohen Dach verteilt, das Tageslicht einfallen lässt, direkte Sonneneinstrahlung jedoch einschränkt.

Ci-dessus et page de gauche, les cabines en bois sont placées sous le toit très haut, qui laisse pénétrer la lumière naturelle mais limite l'ensoleillement direct.

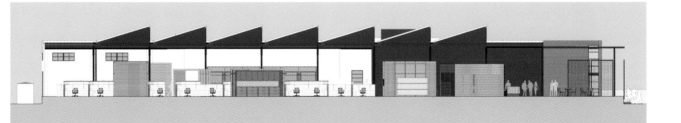

SHANGRI-LA BOTANICAL GARDENS AND NATURE CENTER

Orange, Texas, USA, 2005–07

Address: 2111 West Park Avenue, Orange, Texas 77630, USA,
tel: +1 409 670 9113, www.shangrilagardens.org. Area: 3623 m². Client: Stark Foundation
Cost: $8.7 million. Collaboration: Joseph Benjamin, Jennifer Young

The work of Lake I Flato includes a visitor center, an outdoor education center, classroom pavilions, and bird-viewing blinds.

Der Entwurf von Lake I Flato umfasst einen offenen Lehrbereich, Pavillons für Lehrveranstaltungen sowie Vogel-beobachtungsstationen.

Les réalisations de Lake I Flato comprennent un centre d'accueil des visiteurs, un centre éducatif en plein air, des salles de classe pavillonnaires et des postes d'observation des oiseaux.

The **SHANGRI-LA CENTER** is located on a 102-hectare site and "serves primarily as an interpretive center for the site's native ecosystems—cypress and tupelo swamp, wooded uplands, and prairie lowlands—as well as a facility for study and research." The project team used wood salvaged from trees felled by a hurricane in 2005, although that was not part of the original scheme. New structures minimize "conditioned space," using wide canopies, while the nature discovery lab and pavilion, outdoor classrooms, bird blind, and boathouse were also designed for minimal impact, set above the land on a helical pier foundation and powered by photovoltaic panels. The USGBC profile of the project reads: "The energy performance of the new facilities is as successful as its integration into its site. Effective day lighting, LED lighting, a high efficiency geothermal-based heat pump, sophisticated controls, and photovoltaic panels contribute to a 72% reduction in energy use. The Shangri-La Nature Center earned the first LEED for New Construction Platinum rating in the state of Texas and the Gulf Coast region."

Das **SHANGRI-LA-ZENTRUM** liegt auf einem 102 ha großen Gelände und „informiert vor allem über die einheimischen Ökosysteme – das Sumpfgebiet mit Zypressen und Tupelobäumen, das bewaldete Hochland und die Präriegebiete – und dient als Studien- und Forschungsstätte". Das Planungsteam nutzte unter anderem Bauholz von Bäumen, die 2005 vom Hurrikan entwurzelt worden waren, was ursprünglich nicht geplant war. Bei den Neubauten wurde weitgehend auf „klimatisierte Räume" verzichtet und auf offene Pavillonbauten gesetzt. Auch das Naturentdeckerlabor mit seinem Pavillon, die offenen Lehrbereiche, Vogelbeobachtungsstationen und ein Bootshaus wurden auf minimale Umweltauswirkung angelegt und in Pfahlgründung über dem Boden aufgeständert. Die Stromversorgung erfolgt über Solarmodule. Das USGBC schreibt: „Die Energieeffizienz der Neubauten ist ebenso gelungen wie ihre Einbettung in das landschaftliche Umfeld. Effektive Tageslichtnutzung, LED-Systeme, eine Hochleistungs-Erdwärmepumpe, präzise Steuerungssysteme und Solarmodule sorgen für eine Senkung des Stromverbrauchs um 72 %. Das Shangri-La-Naturzentrum wurde als erster Neubau im Staat Texas und der Gulf-Coast-Region mit einem LEED-Zertifikat in Platin ausgezeichnet."

Le **CENTRE SHANGRI-LA** occupe un site de 102 hectares et « constitue avant tout un centre d'information sur les écosystèmes natifs du site – marais à cyprès et tupélos, hautes terres boisées et basses prairies –, ainsi qu'un établissement de recherches et d'études ». L'équipe chargée du projet a utilisé du bois récupéré sur des arbres abattus par un ouragan en 2005, bien que cela n'ait pas été prévu au départ. Les nouvelles structures réduisent au minimum l'« espace conditionné » au moyen de vastes marquises ou auvents, tandis que le laboratoire et pavillon de découverte de la nature, les salles de classe en plein air, le poste d'observation des oiseaux et le hangar à bateaux ont été conçus pour avoir un impact minimal, posés sur des fondations à piliers hélicoïdaux et alimentés en énergie par des panneaux photovoltaïques. Le profil USGBC du projet explique que « les performances énergétiques des nouvelles structures sont aussi réussies que leur intégration au site naturel. Éclairage naturel efficace, éclairage artificiel par LED, pompe à chaleur géothermique haute efficacité, système de surveillance complexe et panneaux photovoltaïques contribuent à une réduction de 72 % de la consommation d'énergie. Le Centre de découverte de la nature Shangri-La a obtenu la première certification LEED platine pour une nouvelle construction dans le Texas et sur la côte du golfe du Mexique ».

The wooden education center structure is slightly lifted off the ground and has a skylight in the center of the double-pitched roof.

Der Lehrpavillon, ein Holzbau, ist leicht über dem Boden aufgeständert und hat ein Oberlicht im Scheitel des Giebeldachs.

Le centre éducatif en bois est légèrement surélevé et son toit à double pente est percé au centre d'une lucarne.

A drawing of the nature discovery center shows the angles of the sun vis-à-vis the roof. Above an axial view of one of the Lake|Flato buildings showing its fundamental harmony with the natural setting.

Eine Zeichnung der Naturentdecker-station veranschaulicht den Sonnen-stand im Verhältnis zum Dach. Eine axiale Ansicht eines der von Lake|Flato entworfenen Bauten lässt deren harmonische Einbettung in die Landschaft deutlich werden.

Ce schéma du Centre de découverte de la nature montre les angles du soleil par rapport au toit. Ci-dessus, une vue axiale de l'un des bâtiments construits par Lake|Flato met en évidence sa profonde harmonie avec le cadre naturel.

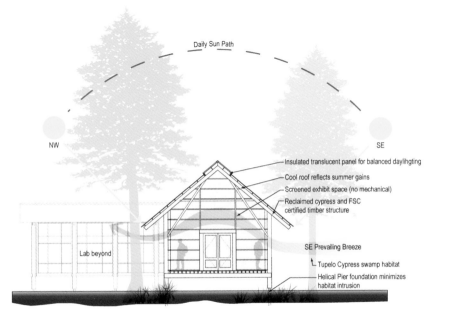

Daily Sun Path

NW

SE

Insulated translucent panel for balanced daylihgting

Cool roof reflects summer gains

Screened exhibit space (no mechanical)

Reclaimed cypress and FSC certified timber structure

SE Prevailing Breeze

Tupelo Cypress swamp habitat

Helical Pier foundation minimizes habitat intrusion

Lab beyond

Lake|Flato's work for Shangri La received the first LEED Platinum certification for new construction on the Gulf Coast. It opened to the public on March 11, 2008.

Lake|Flatos Shangri-La-Entwurf wurde als erstes Neubauprojekt an der Gulf Coast mit einem LEED-Zertifikat in Silber ausgezeichnet. Das Zentrum wurde am 11. März 2008 eröffnet.

Le travail de Lake|Flato au Centre Shangri-La a obtenu la première certification LEED platine pour une nouvelle construction sur la côte du golfe du Mexique. Le Centre a ouvert ses portes au public le 11 mars 2008.

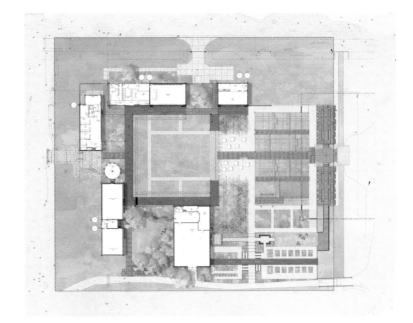

LEAPFACTORY

LEAPfactory
Via Alessandria 51/E
10152 Turin
Italy

Tel: +39 011 230 80 42
Fax: +39 011 230 80 19
E-mail: info@leapfactory.it
Web: www.leapfactory.it

STEFANO TESTA was born in Milan, Italy, in 1966 and graduated in architecture in 1992 from the Milan Polytechnic. He is a Partner in the architecture office Cliostraat in Turin. **LUCA GENTILCORE**, born in San Remo in 1978, studied architecture at Turin Polytechnic, from which he graduated in 2004. In 2008 he founded is own office, Gandolfi Gentilcore Architetti, in Turin. The pair created LEAPfactory (which stands for Living Ecological Alpine Pod) in 2010. This Italian firm seeks to design and produce a new generation of shelters and technological structures. The alpine refuge published here (the Gervasutti Refuge, Mont Blanc, Courmayeur, Italy, 2011) is only one of the LEAPfactory projects. They are working on a number of other modular products for "living at zero impact" in sensitive environments that need protection. The architects are currently studying a modular system to dispose of human waste and other refuse in high-altitude structures. They state: "The temporary nature and the recoverability of the module mean that you can live in an environment and at the same time respect it."

STEFANO TESTA wurde 1966 in Mailand, Italien, geboren und schloss sein Architekturstudium 1992 am Mailänder Polytechnikum ab. Er ist Partner beim Architekturbüro Cliostraat in Turin. **LUCA GENTILCORE**, geboren 1978 in San Remo, studierte Architektur an der Polytechnischen Hochschule Turin, wo er 2004 seinen Abschluss machte. 2008 gründete er sein eigenes Büro Gandolfi Gentilcore Architetti in Turin. 2010 gründeten die beiden Architekten LEAPfactory (kurz für Living Ecological Alpine Pod). Schwerpunkt des italienischen Büros ist die Planung und Realisierung einer neuen Generation von Schutzhütten und Forschungsstationen. Die hier vorgestellte Hütte (Gervasutti-Hütte, Mont Blanc, Courmayeur, Italien, 2011) ist nur eines der von LEAPfactory entworfenen Projekte. Das Team arbeitet an diversen weiteren Modulkonzepten, die geeignet sind, in sensiblen Naturschutzgebieten „ohne Umweltauswirkungen wohnen zu können". Aktuell arbeiten die Architekten an einem Modul zur Entsorgung von Abwasser und anderen Abfällen in Hochgebirgsstationen. Sie erklären: „Die Tatsache, dass unser Modul temporär und rückbaubar ist, bedeutet, dass man in einem Umweltkontext leben und ihn zugleich schützen kann."

STEFANO TESTA est né à Milan en 1966, il est diplômé (1992) de l'École polytechnique de Milan. Il est partenaire de l'agence d'architecture Cliostraat de Turin. **LUCA GENTILCORE**, né à San Remo en 1978, a étudié l'architecture à l'École polytechnique de Turin dont il a obtenu le diplôme en 2004. Il a fondé son agence, Gandolfi Gentilcore Architetti, en 2008 à Turin. Ils ont ouvert tous les deux LEAPfactory (abréviation de Living Ecological Alpine Pod) en 2010. L'agence italienne cherche à créer et réaliser une nouvelle génération de refuges et structures technologiques. Le refuge alpin publié ici (refuge Gervasutti, mont Blanc, Courmayeur, Italie, 2011) n'est que l'un des projets de LEAPfactory. L'équipe travaille aussi à de nombreux autres produits modulaires pour un « habitat à impact zéro » dans des environnements sensibles à protéger. Les architectes étudient notamment en ce moment un système modulaire pour se débarrasser des déchets humains et autres détritus dans les structures de haute altitude. Ils affirment que « le caractère temporaire et récupérable du module permet de vivre dans un environnement tout en le respectant ».

GERVASUTTI REFUGE

Mont Blanc, Courmayeur, Italy, 2011

Address: alt. 2835 m; Courmayeur, Val Ferret, Mont Blanc, Aosta, Italy,
www. sucaiweb.weebly.com/il-bivacco.html
Area: 30 m². Client: Italian Alpine Club, CAI Turin
Cost: €250 000

The new "Bivacco Gervasutti" designed by Luca Gentilcore and Stefano Testa is intended to be a replicable prototype refuge anchored at an altitude of 2835 meters to the side of Mont Blanc. It replaces an existing structure dedicated to the Italian mountaineer Giusto Gervasutti. The hut can accommodate 12 people and was brought up to the site in 600-kilogram composite laminate sandwich modules with a "standard" helicopter. A composite trapezoidal beam was attached to the mountainside at just six points to anchor the structure. Photovoltaic panels are arrayed on the curved roof of the hut. The architects suggest that similar structures could be used in eco-tourism or sports locations, "for temporary facilities (medical assistance, check points, rest stops, press offices…), and in the commercial field (sales offices, ticket offices)." Though the **GERVASUTTI REFUGE** resolutely avoids trying to "blend in" to its surroundings, its reversible nature and its minimal ecological impact do, indeed, make it a model for future high-altitude designs at any rate.

Das neue „Bivacco Gervasutti", entworfen von Luca Gentilcore und Stefano Testa, wurde als reproduzierbarer Prototyp einer Bergstation entwickelt und wurde auf 2835 m Höhe in einem Abhang des Mont Blanc verankert. Es ersetzt eine ältere, dem Bergsteiger Giusto Gervasutti gewidmete Hütte. Die Station bietet Platz für zwölf Personen und wurde in 600 kg schweren Sandwich-Verbundmodulen mit einem „regulären" Helikopter vor Ort gebracht. Zur Verankerung des Baus wurde ein trapezförmiger Verbundträger an nur sechs Punkten am Abhang fixiert. Auf dem geschwungenen Dach der Hütte wurden Solarmodule installiert. Die Architekten schlagen vor, ähnliche Bauten auch in umweltgerechten Feriengebieten und Sportgebieten einzusetzen, „für temporäre Einrichtungen (medizinische Versorgung, Kontrollstellen, Raststationen, Pressestellen…), aber auch für kommerzielle Zwecke (Verkaufsstellen, Kartenkassen)". Auch wenn die **GERVASUTTI-HÜTTE** offensichtlich alles andere will, als mit ihrem Umfeld „zu verschmelzen", ist sie dank ihrer Rückbaubarkeit und ihrer minimalen Umweltauswirkung zweifellos ein Vorreiter für die Hochgebirgsarchitektur der Zukunft.

Le nouveau « Bivacco Gervasutti » conçu par Luca Gentilcore et Stefano Testa se veut un prototype reproductible de refuge, ancré à 2835 m d'altitude sur un versant du mont Blanc. Il remplace une structure existante dédiée à l'alpiniste italien Giusto Gervasutti. L'abri peut loger 12 personnes et a été amené sur le site par un hélicoptère « classique » sous forme de modules sandwich de stratifié composite de 600 kg chacun. Une poutre composite trapézoïdale a été fixée au versant par seulement six points pour ancrer l'ensemble de la structure. Des panneaux photovoltaïques couvrent le toit arrondi de la cabane. Les architectes proposent d'utiliser des structures semblables pour l'écotourisme ou certains sports, « pour des installations temporaires (postes de secours, postes de contrôle, aires de repos, services de presse…) et dans le secteur commercial (bureau de vente, guichets) ». Et si le **REFUGE GERVASUTTI** évite résolument toute tentative de « se fondre » dans le paysage, sa nature réversible et son impact minimal sur l'environnement n'en font pas moins véritablement un modèle pour le design d'altitude du futur.

The structure is seen in place in
these images, and in an elevation
drawing below. Though it may appear
somewhat incongruous in its setting,
the structure is fully respectful of
environmental concerns.

Die Aufnahmen zeigen den Bau an
seinem Standort, unten ein Aufriss.
Obwohl der Bau vergleichsweise
fremd in seinem Umfeld wirkt, ist er
doch umfassend auf ökologische
Belange abgestimmt.

On voit la structure en place sur les
photos et le plan en élévation à
droite. Malgré son aspect incongru
dans le décor, elle est parfaitement
respectueuse de l'environnement.

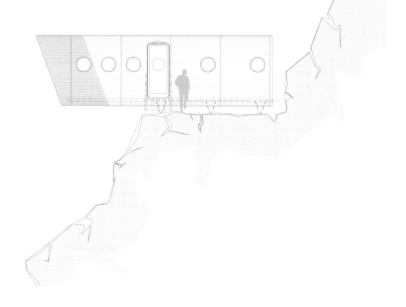

Left page, four images show the
delivery by helicopter of the modular
sections of the refuge, with its photovoltaic panels installed on the roof.

Linke Seite: Vier Bilder illustrieren die
Anlieferung der Module für die Berg-
station per Helikopter. Im Dach sind
Solarmodule integriert.

Page de gauche, quatre photos
montrent la livraison par hélicoptère
des éléments modulaires du refuge
avec ses panneaux photovoltaïques
sur le toit.

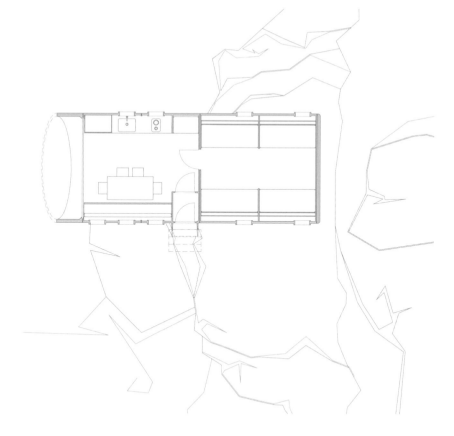

Above, a section drawing of the small
structure; left, a worker securing the
elements of the refuge on the roof.

Oben ein Querschnitt des kleinen
Bauwerks. Links ein Arbeiter bei der
Sicherung baulicher Elemente auf
dem Dach der Station.

Ci-dessus, plan en coupe de la petite
structure ; à gauche, fixation des éléments sur le toit.

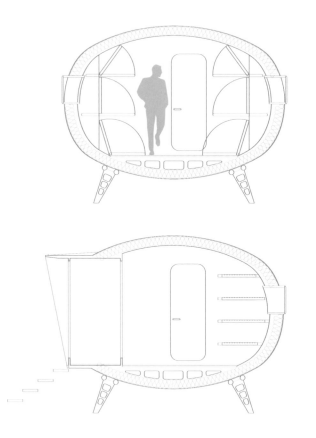

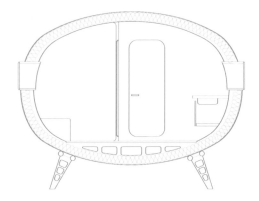

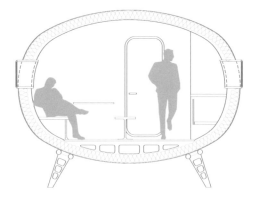

Drawings of the interior of the refuge and photos show its modern, but small space. Similarities to naval or even submarine architecture come to mind.

Zeichnungen und Aufnahmen der Hütte von innen zeigen moderne, wenn auch kleine Räume. Der Vergleich mit Schiffs- oder U-Bootsarchitektur drängt sich auf.

Les schémas et photos de l'intérieur du refuge en montrent l'espace moderne, mais petit. On pense à l'architecture navale, ou même à un sous-marin.

KEN SUNGJIN MIN

SKM Architects
SKM Building
60–15 Samseong-dong, Gangnam-gu
Seoul 135–896
South Korea

Tel: +82 2 543 2027
Fax: +82 2 548 2027
E-mail: skm@skma.com
Web: www.skma.com

KEN SUNGJIN MIN received his B.Arch degree from the University of Southern California, School of Architecture (1989), and his M.Arch in Urban Design (MAUD) from the Harvard GSD (1993). He created SKM Architects in 1996. The recent work of the firm includes the Hilton Namhae Golf and Spa (Nam-myeon, Namhae-gun, 2006); the Kumgang Ananti Golf & Spa Resort (Gangwon-do, North Korea, 2008); Lake Hills Suncheon Country Club (Suncheon, JeollaNam-do, 2008); Asiana Airlines Weihai Point Golf & Resort (Weihai, China, 2009); Asiana Airlines Laolaob Bay Golf & Spa Resort (Saipan, Marianas, USA, 2009); Arumdaun Golf & Spa Resort (Chungcheongnam-do, 2009); Ananti Club Seoul (Gapyeoung-gun, Gyeonggi-do, 2009–10, published here); Cheong Pyeong Village, 70 prestigious single-family houses (Gyeonggi-do, ongoing); and the Anmyeun Island Newtown Master Plan (Chungcheongnam-do, ongoing), all in South Korea unless stated otherwise.

KEN SUNGJIN MIN absolvierte seinen B.Arch an der Architekturfakultät der University of Southern California (1989) und seinen M.Arch in Stadtplanung (MAUD) an der Harvard GSD (1993). 1996 gründete er sein Büro SKM Architects. Jüngere Projekte des Büros sind unter anderem das Hilton Namhae Golf & Spa (Nam-myeon, Namhae-gun, 2006), das Kumgang Ananti Golf & Spa Resort (Gangwon-do, Nordkorea, 2008), der Lake Hills Suncheon Country Club (Suncheon, JeollaNam-do, 2008), das Asiana Air-lines Weihai Point Golf & Resort (Weihai, China, 2009), das Asiana Airlines Laolaob Bay Golf & Spa Resort (Saipan, Marianas, USA, 2009), der Arumdaun Golf & Spa Resort (Chungcheongnam-do, 2009), der Ananti Club Seoul (Gapyeoung-gun, Gyeonggi-do, 2009–10, hier vorgestellt), das Cheong Pyeong Village, 70 Luxus-Einfamilienhäuser (Gyeonggi-do, in Planung) und der Masterplan für eine Neustadt auf der Insel Anmyeon (Chungcheongnam-do, in Planung), alle in Südkorea, sofern nicht anders angegeben.

KEN SUNGJIN MIN a obtenu son B.Arch à l'École d'architecture de l'université de Caroline du Sud (1989) et son M.Arch en urbanisme (MAUD) à la Harvard GSD (1993). Il a créé SKM Architects en 1996. Les réalisations récentes de l'agence comprennent le golf et spa Hilton Namhae (Nam-myeon, Namhae-gun, 2006) ; la station de golf thermale Kumgang Ananti (Gangwon-do, Corée-du-Nord, 2008) ; le club de loisirs Lake Hills Suncheon (Suncheon, JeollaNam-do, 2008) ; la station & golf Asiana Airlines de Weihai Point (Weihai, Chine, 2009) ; la station de golf thermale Asiana Airlines de Laolaob Bay (Saipan, îles Mariannes, États-Unis, 2009) ; la station de golf thermale Arumdaun (Chungcheongnam-do, 2009) ; le club Ananti de Séoul (Gapyeoung-gun, Gyeonggi-do, 2009–10, publié ici) ; le village Cheong Pyeong de 70 maisons individuelles de prestige (Gyeonggi-do, en cours) et le plan directeur d'une ville nouvelle sur l'île d'Anmyeun (Chungcheongnam-do, en cours), toutes en Corée-du-Sud sauf si spécifié.

ANANTI CLUB SEOUL

Gapyeoung-gun, Gyeonggi-do, South Korea, 2009–10

Address: Bangil-ri San 90–2, Seorak-myeon, Gapyeoung-gun, Gyeonggi-do, South Korea, www.ananticlub.com
Area: 1320 m². Client: Emerson Pacific Group .Cost: $19.9 million

This clubhouse is located at the foot of a famous mountain near Seoul, surrounded by a dense forest. In part to avoid damage to the scenery, the essential facilities, with the exception of a canopy and tower building, were built below grade. The architect additionally explains: "In an effort to save energy costs and increase the building's sustainability, 92% of the building area was inserted into the earth." A dark, 9 x 10-meter reception hall leads into the clubhouse proper. The whole structure was conceived in a mode of privacy where spectacular architectural gestures were avoided. The architect continues: "A unique controlled atmosphere harmonized with nature was composed through the juxtaposition of the organic shape of the main entrance space, a linear restaurant, and a tower building. It was planned to allow only selected views of the scenery by calculating window position and height throughout. It was planned to make architecture soak into the site as a part of nature, but also to make nature visible inside the architecture through selected openings."

Das Clubhaus liegt am Fuße eines berühmten Gipfels unweit von Seoul, inmitten einer Waldlandschaft. Unter anderem motiviert durch den Wunsch, die Landschaft nicht zu verstellen, wurden die Haupteinrichtungen des Komplexes, mit Ausnahme eines Vordachs und eines mehrgeschossigen Gebäudes, unter die Erde verlegt. Der Architekt führt ergänzend aus: „Um Energiekosten zu senken und die Nachhaltigkeit des Baus zu fördern, wurden 92% der bebauten Fläche in den Boden versenkt." Ein dunkles, 9 x 10 m großes Foyer bietet Zugang zum Clubhaus. Der gesamte Komplex wurde zurückhaltend gestaltet, auf spektakuläre architektonische Gesten wurde verzichtet. Der Architekt fügt an: „Ein einzigartiger, harmonisch auf die landschaftliche Umgebung abgestimmter Eindruck entstand durch Kontrastierung der organischen Formensprache des Zugangsgebäudes, einem linear gestalteten Restaurant und einem mehrgeschossigen Gebäude. Durch exakte Berechnung der Fensterpositionierung und -höhe im gesamten Bau wurden einzelne Ausblicke gezielt in den Fokus gerückt. Die Architektur sollte sich als organischer Teil der Landschaft in das Gelände fügen, die Landschaft aber zugleich durch ausgewählte Ausblicke hervorgehoben werden."

Le club est situé au pied d'un massif montagneux proche de Séoul, très fréquenté et entouré d'une forêt dense. C'est en partie pour éviter de dégrader le paysage que l'essentiel des installations, à l'exception d'un bâtiment sous auvent et de la tour, a été construit sous le niveau du sol. L'architecte explique aussi que «dans un effort pour économiser des frais d'énergie et accroître la durabilité du bâtiment, 92 % de sa surface a été intégrée sous terre». Un hall de réception sombre de 9 x 10 m mène au club proprement dit. L'ensemble de la structure a été conçu sur un mode intime qui renonce délibérément à toute architecture trop spectaculaire. L'architecte poursuit :«Une atmosphère unique soigneusement contrôlée et en harmonie avec la nature a été composée par la juxtaposition de la forme organique de l'entrée principale, un restaurant linéaire et la tour. Nous avons voulu ne donner accès qu'à certaines vues choisies du décor en calculant la position des fenêtres et la hauteur totale. Nous avons voulu faire plonger l'architecture dans le site comme un élément naturel, mais aussi rendre la nature visible dans l'architecture au moyen d'ouvertures choisies. »

A section drawing shows: 1. tennis court and lounge; 2. drop-off; 3. main lobby; and 4. start house.

Der Querschnitt zeigt: 1. Tennisplätze und Lounge, 2. Zufahrt, 3. Lobby und 4. das sogenannte Start House.

Schéma en coupe : 1. court de tennis et lounge ; 2. dépose ; 3. hall principal et 4. accueil.

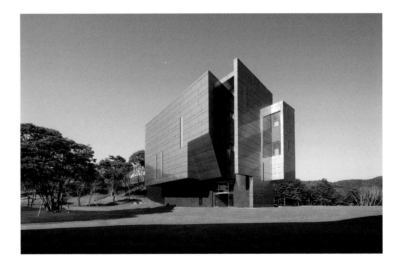

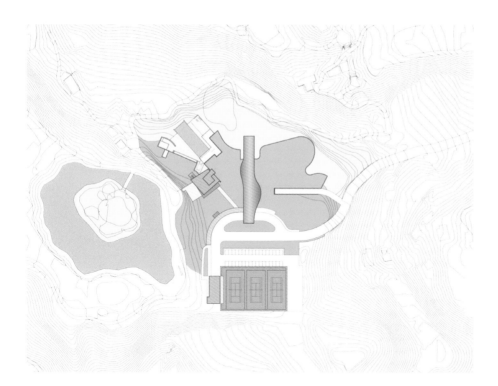

On the site plan, left: 1. clubhouse;
2. tower; 3. drop-off canopy;
4. tennis court; and 5. tennis lounge.

Auf dem Lageplan (links): 1. Clubhaus, 2. Turm, 3. überdachte Zufahrt,
4. Tennisplätze und 5. Tennislounge.

Plan du site à gauche : 1. clubhouse ; 2. tour ; 3. auvent de l'entrée ; 4. court de tennis et 5. lounge
du tennis.

The curving drop-off canopy is one of
the more striking aspects of the
architectural design, which combines
rectilinear elements with freer forms.

Das geschwungene Dach der Zufahrt
ist einer der markantesten Aspekte
des Entwurfs, in dem sich geradlinige
Elemente ebenso wie freiere Formen
finden.

Les courbes de l'auvent à l'entrée
constitue l'un des aspects les plus
frappants de cette architecture qui
associe éléments rectilignes et
formes plus libres.

REALITIES:UNITED

realities:united
Studio for Art and Architecture
Falckensteinstr. 48
10997 Berlin
Germany

Tel: +49 30 20 64 66 30
Fax: +49 30 20 64 66 39
E-mail: info@realu.de
Web: www.realities-united.de

realities:united, a "studio for art and architecture," was founded in 2000 by brothers **JAN AND TIM EDLER** from the artists' collective "Kunst und Technik" (Art and Technology), which has operated one of Berlin's first beach bars at Monbijoupark from 1997 until 2000. This is where the basic idea for the river-swimming-pool project came from in 1998 in collaboration with Denise Dih (DODK). Their work includes BIX, Communicative Display Skin for the Kunsthaus Graz (Graz, Austria, 2003); SPOTS, Light and Media Installation, Potsdamer Platz (Berlin, Germany, 2005); MuseumX, Imaginary Museum for the Museum Abteiberg (Mönchengladbach, Germany, 2006); Crystal Mesh, Façade Installation for the Iluma Urban Entertainment Center (Singapore, 2009); NIX, Spatial Light and Media Installation for the European Central Bank (Frankfurt, Germany, 2007–11); and C4, Façade Integrated Media Installation for the Espacio de Creación Artística Contemporáneae (Córdoba, Spain, 2012). Aside from the Spree River Flussbad scheme (Berlin, Germany, 1998–2020, published here), realities:united also developed the concept for BIG Vortex ("What does a ton of CO_2 look like?"), the winning competition entry, "Smoke Ring Generator Installation" for BIG's Amager Bakke Waste-to-Energy Plant (Copenhagen, Denmark, 2009–, page 74).

realities:united wurde 2000 als „Studio für Kunst und Architektur" von den Brüdern **JAN UND TIM EDLER** vom Künstlerkollektiv „Kunst und Technik" gegründet, das von 1997 bis 2000 eine der ersten Strandbars Berlins am Monbijoupark betrieb. Hier entstand 1998 im Zuge einer Kollaboration mit Denise Dih (DODK) auch die Grundidee zu einem Flussbad. Zu den Projekten des Teams zählen BIX, Medienfassade für das Kunsthaus Graz (Graz, Österreich, 2003), SPOTS, Licht- und Medieninstallation am Potsdamer Platz (Berlin, Deutschland, 2005), MuseumX, imaginärer Museumsbau für das Museum Abteiberg (Mönchengladbach, Deutschland, 2006), Crystal Mesh, Fassadeninstallation für das Iluma Urban Entertainment Center (Singapur, 2009), NIX, Entwurf für eine räumliche Licht- und Medienfassade für die Europäische Zentralbank (Frankfurt am Main, Deutschland, 2007–11) sowie C4, integrierte Medienfassade für den Espacio de Creación Artística Contemporáneae (Córdoba, Spanien, 2012). Neben dem Konzept für ein Flussbad in der Spree (Berlin, Deutschland, 1998–2020, hier vorgestellt) entwickelte realities:united außerdem das Konzept für BIG Vortex („Wie sieht eine Tonne CO_2 aus?"), der Gewinnerbeitrag „Smoke Ring Generator Installation" für das Müllheizkraftwerk Amager Bakke von BIG (Kopenhagen, Dänemark, 2009–, Seite 74).

Le « studio d'art et d'architecture » realities:united a été créé en 2000 par les frères **JAN ET TIM EDLER** du collectif d'artistes « Kunst und Technik » (Art et technologie), qui avait exploité l'un des premiers bars de plage de Berlin au parc Monbijou de 1997 à 2000. C'est là que la première idée du projet de piscine fluviale a vu le jour en 1998 avec la collaboration de Denise Dih (DODK). Leurs réalisations comprennent BIX, la « peau » écran communicante du Kunsthaus de Graz (Autriche, 2003) ; SPOTS, une installation lumineuse et médiatique Potsdamer Platz (Berlin, 2005) ; MuseumX, un musée imaginaire pour celui de l'Abteiberg (Mönchengladbach, Allemagne, 2006) ; Crystal Mesh, une installation en façade pour le Centre de loisirs urbains Iluma (Singapour, 2009) ; NIX, une installation lumineuse et médiatique spatiale pour la Banque centrale européenne (Francfort, 2007–11) et C4, une installation médiatique intégrée à la façade de l'Espacio de Creación Artística Contemporáneae (Cordoue, Espagne, 2012). En plus du projet de piscine dans la Spree (Berlin, 1998–2020, publié ici), realities:united a développé pour BIG le concept de Vortex (« À quoi ressemble une tonne de CO_2 ? »), un « générateur de ronds de fumée » qui a gagné le concours pour le Centre de transformation des déchets en énergie d'Amager Bakke créé par BIG (Copenhague, 2009–, page 74).

FLUSSBAD

Berlin, Germany, 1998–2020

*Address: River Spree, Kupfergraben (between Schlossplatz and the Bode Museum), Berlin, Germany
Area: 745-meter-long natural swimming pool (Segment A); 390-meter-long,
7200-square-meter constructed wetland to purify the running water in a natural way (Segment B);
640-meter inner-city green area on the river (Segment C). Client: Kunst und Technik e.V. Cost: not disclosed*

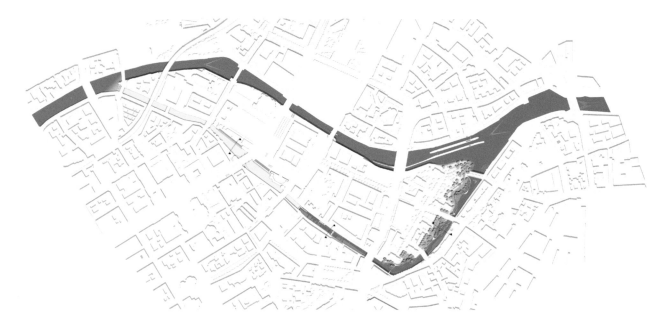

The plan shows Berlin's historic center and Museum Island. The Flussbad project appears in color below the river, with the three segments as indicated in the drawing at the top of the right page.

Der Kartenausschnitt zeigt die historische Mitte Berlins mit der Museumsinsel. Das Flussbad erscheint farbig markiert unterhalb des Hauptflusslaufs. Drei Abschnitte sind auf der Zeichnung oben rechts zu erkennen.

Plan du centre historique de Berlin et de l'île des Musées. Le projet de bain fluvial est marqué en couleur sous la rivière, les trois segments comme indiqué sur le schéma en haut de la page de droite.

This unusual project aims to transform the Spree River near Museum Island in Berlin into a **SWIMMING POOL**. It was the winner of the prestigious 2011 Holcim Gold Award for sustainable construction and infrastructure designs and the 2012 Global Holcim Bronze Award. An upstream 780-meter-long filter basin biotope would be used to purify the water. A stairway would make the 750-meter-length of the Kupfergraben between Schlossplatz and the Bode Museum accessible to swimmers and pedestrians. Emphasizing his hope that the project might increase ecological awareness about the river, realities:united Principal Tim Edler stated: "The planned conversion involves above all a functional resuscitation of the section of the river that, for something more than 100 years, has no longer had any productive function for the city of Berlin. A primary aim of the plan is to return to the traditional practice of understanding and using the river as an active means of urban development. Today's imbalanced use of the river solely as a transport route and wastewater canal no longer offers any prospect of that."

Das außergewöhnliche Konzept sieht vor, einen Abschnitt der Spree an der Museumsinsel in Berlin in ein **FLUSSBAD** umzuwandeln. Der Entwurf wurde 2011 mit dem renommierten Holcim Award für nachhaltiges Bauen und Infrastruktur in Gold ausgezeichnet sowie 2012 mit einem Holcim Award in Bronze. Eine flussaufwärts gelegene Pflanzenkläranlage würde das Wasser auf einer Länge von 780 m biologisch klären. Eine Treppenanlage soll einen 750 m langen Abschnitt des Kupfergrabens zwischen Schlossplatz und Bode-Museum zum Schwimmen und für Spaziergänger zugänglich machen. Tim Edler, leitender Architekt bei realities:united, versteht das Projekt als Beitrag, um ein Bewusstsein für das Flussbiotop zu wecken: „Die geplante Umnutzung bedeutet vor allem eine funktionale Wiederbelebung des Flussabschnitts, der für die Stadt Berlin seit etwas mehr als 100 Jahren keine produktive Funktion mehr hat. Ein Hauptanliegen des Vorhabens besteht in der Rückkehr zur traditionellen Praxis, den Fluss als aktives Mittel für die Stadtentwicklung zu begreifen und einzusetzen. Die einseitige Widmung des Flusses als Verkehrsweg und Abwasserkanal, wie sie heute besteht, bietet dafür keine Perspektive mehr."

Ce projet original vise à transformer la Spree en **PISCINE** près de l'île des Musées. Il a remporté le prestigieux prix Holcim or pour la construction durable et la conception d'infrastructures en 2011 et le prix Global Holcim bronze en 2012. Le biotope d'un bassin filtrant en amont, long de 780 m, servirait à purifier l'eau. Un escalier rendrait les 750 m du Kupfergraben, entre la Schlossplatz et le musée Bode, accessibles aux nageurs et piétons. Faisant valoir son espoir que le projet renforce la prise de conscience écologique de la rivière, le responsable de realities:united Tim Edler explique que « la transformation prévue consiste avant tout à faire revivre de manière fonctionnelle une portion de la rivière qui n'exerce plus aucune fonction productive pour la ville de Berlin depuis un peu plus d'un siècle. L'un des objectifs premiers du projet est de renouer avec la pratique traditionnelle de connaissance et d'exploitation de la rivière comme un moyen actif de développement urbain. Son utilisation actuelle en tant que seule voie de transport et canal d'évacuation des eaux usées est totalement déséquilibrée et n'ouvre plus aucune perspective dans ce sens ».

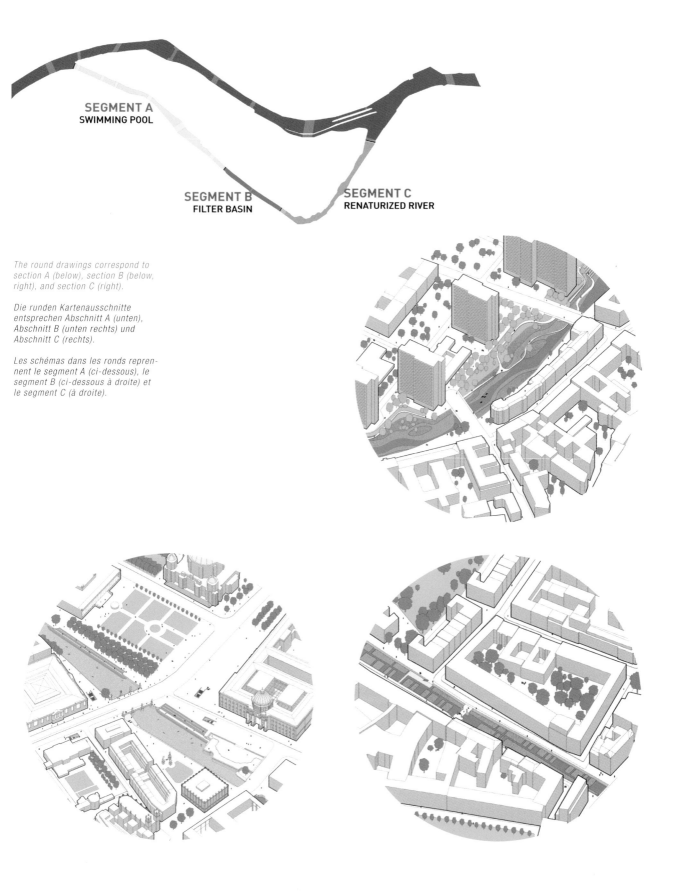

SEGMENT A
SWIMMING POOL

SEGMENT B
FILTER BASIN

SEGMENT C
RENATURIZED RIVER

The round drawings correspond to section A (below), section B (below, right), and section C (right).

Die runden Kartenausschnitte entsprechen Abschnitt A (unten), Abschnitt B (unten rechts) und Abschnitt C (rechts).

Les schémas dans les ronds prennent le segment A (ci-dessous), le segment B (ci-dessous à droite) et le segment C (à droite).

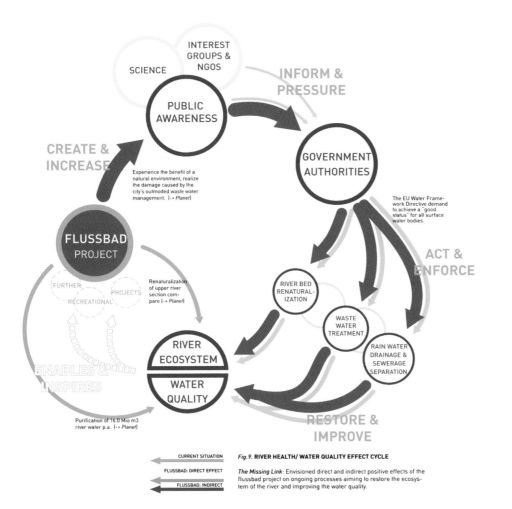

CREATE & INCREASE

INTEREST GROUPS & NGOS

SCIENCE

PUBLIC AWARENESS

INFORM & PRESSURE

Experience the benefit of a natural environment, realize the damage caused by the city's outmoded waste water management. (-> Planer)

GOVERNMENT AUTHORITIES

The EU Water Framework Directive demand to achieve a "good status" for all surface water bodies.

FLUSSBAD PROJECT

ACT & ENFORCE

FURTHER PROJECTS

RECREATIONAL

Renaturalization of upper river section compare (-> Planer)

RIVER BED RENATURAL-IZATION

WASTE WATER TREATMENT

RAIN WATER DRAINAGE & SEWERAGE SEPARATION

ENABLES & INSPIRES

RIVER ECOSYSTEM

WATER QUALITY

Purification of 16.0 Mio m3 river water p.a. (-> Planer)

RESTORE & IMPROVE

CURRENT SITUATION

FLUSSBAD: DIRECT EFFECT

FLUSSBAD: INDIRECT

Fig. 9. **RIVER HEALTH/ WATER QUALITY EFFECT CYCLE**

The Missing Link: Envisioned direct and indirect positive effects of the flussbad project on ongoing processes aiming to restore the ecosystem of the river and improving the water quality.

Right, a functional diagram of a filter basin. Above, the river health/ water-quality effect cycle is self-explanatory.

Rechts eine schematische Darstellung der Pflanzenkläranlage. Das Diagramm des Wirkungskreislaufs von Flussgesundheit und Wasserqualität ist selbsterklärend.

À droite, plan fonctionnel du bassin filtrant. Ci-dessus, le cycle d'action sur la santé de la rivière/la qualité de l'eau se passe d'explications.

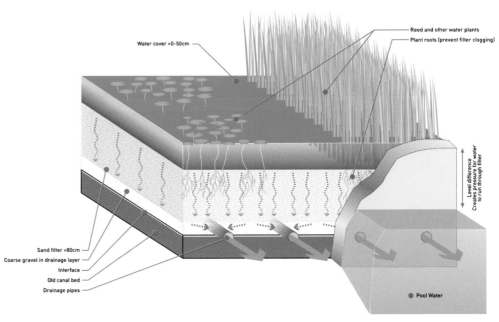

Reed and other water plants
Plant roots (prevent filter clogging)
Water cover >0-50cm
Level difference Creates pressure for water to run through filter
Sand filter >80cm
Coarse gravel in drainage layer
Interface
Old canal bed
Drainage pipes
Pool Water

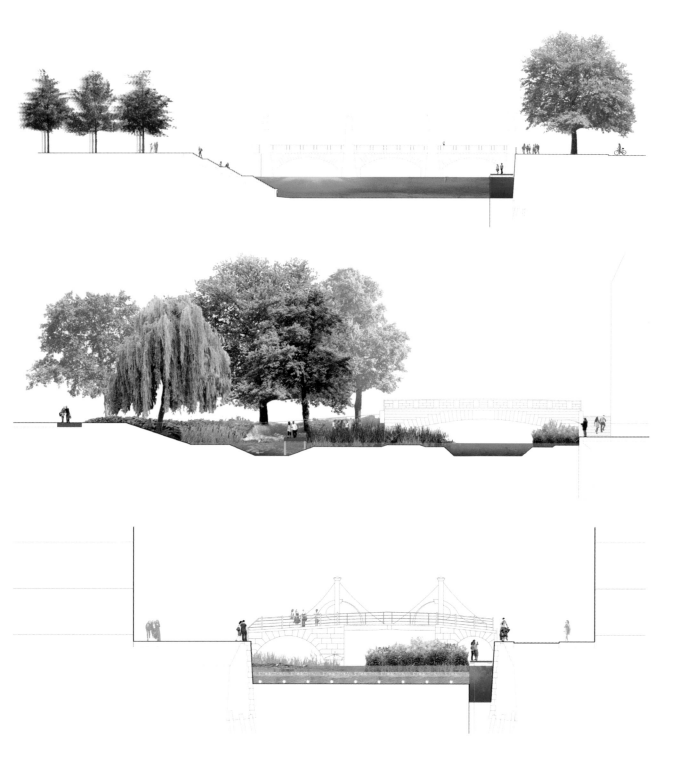

Top, section A, showing the swimming pool; middle, section C, the "renaturized" river; and bottom, section B, the filter basin.

Abschnitt A (oben) zeigt das Flussbad, Abschnitt C (Mitte) den renaturierten Flusslauf, Abschnitt B (unten) die Pflanzenkläranlage.

En haut, segment A, la piscine ; au milieu, segment C, la rivière « renaturalisée » et en bas, segment B, le bassin filtrant.

TODD SAUNDERS

Saunders Arkitektur AS
Vestre Torggaten 22
5015 Bergen
Norway

Tel: +47 975 25 761
E-mail: post@saunders.no
Web: www.saunders.no

TODD SAUNDERS was born in 1969 in Gander, Newfoundland (Canada). He obtained his M.Arch from McGill University (Montreal, Canada, 1993–95) and a Bachelor of Environmental Planning from the Nova Scotia College of Art and Design (1988–92). He has worked in Austria, Germany, Russia, Latvia, and Norway (since 1997). He teaches part-time at the Bergen School of Architecture. His work includes the Aurland Lookout (with Tommie Wilhelmsen, Aurland, 2006); Villa Storingavika (Bergen, 2004–07); Villa G (Hjellestad, Bergen, 2007–09); and Solberg Tower and Park (Sarpsborg, Østfold, 2010), all in Norway. He is currently realizing the Fogo Island Studios, four of which have been completed out of a program of six (Fogo Island, Newfoundland, Canada, 2010–11, published here), and is also completing the Fogo Island Inn (2012) in the same location.

TODD SAUNDERS wurde 1969 in Gander, Neufundland, Kanada, geboren. Er absolvierte seinen M.Arch an der McGill University (Montreal, Kanada, 1993–95) sowie einen Bachelor in Umweltplanung am Nova Scotia College of Art and Design (1988–92). Er war in Österreich, Deutschland, Russland, Lettland und Norwegen (seit 1996) tätig. Er lehrt in Teilzeit an der Bergen School of Architecture. Zu seinen Projekten zählen der Aurland-Aussichtspunkt (mit Tommie Wilhelmsen, Aurland, 2006), die Villa Storingavika (Bergen, 2004–07), die Villa G (Hjellestad, Bergen, 2007–09) und der Solberg-Turm und -Park (Sarpsborg, Østfold, 2010), alle in Norwegen. Aktuell arbeitet er an den Fogo Island Studios, von denen vier der insgesamt sechs Studios bereits fertiggestellt sind (Fogo Island, Neufundland, Kanada, 2010–11, hier vorgestellt). Außerdem beteiligt sich Saunders an einem Wettbewerb für den Fogo Island Inn (2012) am selben Standort.

Né en 1969 à Gander (Terre-Neuve, Canada), **TODD SAUNDERS** a obtenu son M.Arch à l'université McGill (Montréal, 1993–95) et un bachelor en planification environnementale au Collège d'art et de design de la Nouvelle-Écosse (1988–92). Il a travaillé en Autriche, Allemagne, Russie, Lituanie et Norvège (depuis 1996). Il enseigne à temps partiel à l'École d'architecture de Bergen. Parmi ses réalisations, toutes en Norvège : le belvédère d'Aurland (avec Tommie Wilhelmsen, Aurland, 2006) ; la villa Storingavika (Bergen, 2004–07) ; la villa G (Hjellestad, Bergen, 2007–09) et la tour et le parc Solberg (Sarpsborg, Østfold, 2010). Il travaille en ce moment aux ateliers sur l'île de Fogo, dont quatre sont achevés sur six (île de Fogo, Terre-Neuve, Canada, 2010–11, publiés ici) et termine l'hôtel Fogo Island Inn (2012) au même endroit.

SQUISH STUDIO

Fogo Island, Newfoundland, Canada, 2011

Address: n/a. Area: 28 m²
Client: Shorefast Foundation and Fogo Island Arts Corporation
Cost: not disclosed

The **SQUISH STUDIO** is located near the small town of Tilting on the eastern end of Fogo Island. First settled in the mid 18th century, Tilting was recently designated as a National Cultural Landscape District of Canada. The angled, white form of the studio obviously contrasts with local architecture, and sits directly on the rocky shore. The southern end of the studio rises to a height of six meters, while the opposite side does not surpass three meters. The architect explains: "The compact, trapezium-shaped plan of the studio is augmented by the extension of the east and west exterior walls to create a sheltered, triangulated south entry deck and a north terrace that overlooks the ocean. From a distant view, the streamlined form of the Squish Studio becomes apparent with its high back and low (squished) front designed, in part, to deflect the winds from the stormy North Atlantic." Power is supplied by solar panels located on an adjacent hill. The interior and exterior are clad in white-painted spruce planks.

Das **SQUISH STUDIO** liegt unweit der kleinen Stadt Tilting am östlichen Ende von Fogo Island. Tiltin, erstmals Mitte des 18. Jahrhunderts besiedelt, wurde erst kürzlich zum nationalen Landschaftskulturgebiet Kanadas erklärt. Die spitzwinklige weiße Form des Baus kontrastiert unverkennbar mit der lokalen Architektursprache und liegt direkt an der felsigen Küstenlinie. Während das Studio an der Südseite bis zu 6 m hoch ist, misst die gegenüberliegende Seite gerade einmal drei Meter. Der Architekt erklärt: „Der kompakte, trapezförmige Grundriss des Studios gewinnt zusätzlich an Dramatik durch die vorgezogenen Ost- und Westfassaden, wodurch ein geschützter Eingangsbereich nach Süden und eine Nordterrasse mit Blick aufs Meer entsteht." Aus der Ferne wird deutlich, dass die windschnittige Form des Squish Studio mit der hochgezogenen Rückwand und der niedrigen („squished", dt. gestauchten) Front zum Teil auch als Schutz vor den stürmischen Winden des Nordatlantik geplant wurde. Die Energieversorgung erfolgt über eine Solaranlage auf einem nahe gelegenen Hügel. Innen und außen wurde der Bau mit weiß lackierter Fichte verschalt.

Le **SQUISH STUDIO** est situé à proximité de la petite ville de Tilting, à l'extrémité orientale de l'île de Fogo. Colonisée pour la première fois au milieu du XVIIIᵉ siècle, le district canadien de Tilting a été désigné récemment paysage culturel national. La forme anguleuse et la couleur blanche de l'atelier contrastent délibérément avec l'architecture locale, d'autant plus qu'il est placé directement sur la côte rocheuse. L'extrémité sud se dresse à une hauteur de six mètres, tandis que le côté opposé ne dépasse pas trois mètres. L'architecte explique que « le plan compact en forme de trapèze du bâtiment est agrandi par les prolongations des murs extérieurs est et ouest, qui créent un porche d'entrée triangulaire abrité au sud et une terrasse au nord au-dessus de l'océan ». Vue de loin, la forme profilée du Squish Studio apparaît avec sa haute façade arrière et sa façade avant basse (écrasée) conçues notamment pour dévier les vents violents de l'Atlantique Nord. L'électricité est fournie par des panneaux solaires placés sur une colline voisine. L'intérieur et l'extérieur du bâtiment sont recouverts de planches d'épicéa peintes en blanc.

With its curious, angled forms and the way it sits lightly on the site, the Squish Studio seems to hover between two dimensions and three.

Das Squish Studio mit seiner ungewöhnlichen, schiefwinkligen Form tangiert den Baugrund kaum und changiert geradezu zwischen Zwei- und Dreidimensionalität.

Avec ses étranges formes anguleuses et la légèreté avec laquelle il est posé, le Squish Studio semble flotter entre deux et trois dimensions.

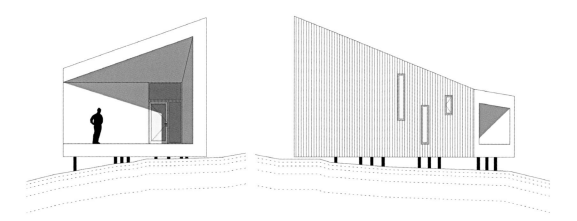

Though there is not a great deal of floor space, ceiling height and the generous glazing give the structure a very open feeling, surely propitious to the creation of works of art.

Trotz begrenzter Nutzfläche gewinnt der Bau durch seine Deckenhöhe und großzügige Verglasung besondere Offenheit, was dem künstlerischen Schaffensprozess sicher zuträglich ist.

Malgré une surface au sol réduite, la hauteur du plafond et le généreux vitrage confèrent à l'ensemble un sentiment de grande ouverture certainement propice à la création d'œuvres d'art.

The interiors are as simple and "clean" as might be expected from the exterior of the structure—the empty space allows artists to create as they will.

Wie schon der Außenbau vermuten lässt, ist das Interieur schlicht und klar gehalten – der leere Raum lässt den Künstlern freie Hand bei seiner Nutzung.

L'intérieur est aussi simple et « pur » que l'extérieur du bâtiment le laisse présager – l'espace vide permet aux artistes de laisser libre cours à leur créativité.

TOWER STUDIO
Fogo Island, Newfoundland, Canada, 2011

Address: n/a. Area: 48 m²
Client: Shorefast Foundation and Fogo Island Arts Corporation
Cost: not disclosed

The **TOWER STUDIO** is located on the rocky coastline of Shoal Bay on Fogo Island. The three-level structure has an overall height of almost 10 meters. The entry has a kitchenette, compost toilet, and wood-burning fireplace. The double-height studio has a generous skylight facing north. A mezzanine juts into this studio space. Todd Saunders explains: "Aside from the geometric complexity of the space, the second feature that adds to a sense of disorientation is the elimination of architectural detail and the fact that all vertical, horizontal, and inclined surfaces, clad in smooth plywood, are painted a brilliant white." A hatch provides access to a rooftop deck. Like the other Fogo Island Studios, the Tower Studio is "100% off the grid with no connection to public services." The studios do not rely on municipal water supply, sewer lines, or the electrical power grid.

Das **TOWER STUDIO** liegt an der Felsküste von Shoal Bay auf Fogo Island. Der dreigeschossige Bau erreicht eine maximale Höhe von 10 m. Im Eingangsbereich befinden sich eine Küchenzeile, eine Komposttoilette und ein Kaminofen. Das eigentliche Studio mit doppelter Geschosshöhe ist mit einem großzügigen Dachfenster nach Norden ausgestattet. Ein Mezzaningeschoss ragt in den Studiobereich hinein. Todd Saunders erklärt: „Abgesehen von der geometrischen Komplexität des Raums trägt zweitens auch der Verzicht auf architektonische Details und die Tatsache, dass sämtliche vertikalen, horizontalen und schrägen Oberflächen mit nahtlosem Sperrholz verkleidet und strahlend weiß lackiert wurden, zur visuellen Desorientierung bei." Durch eine Dachluke ist Zugang zu einer Dachterrasse möglich. Wie bei den übrigen Studiobauten auf Fog Island ist der Turm zu „100% vom öffentlichen Stromnetz unabhängig und hat keinen Anschluss an die öffentliche Infrastruktur". Die Studios sind nicht auf städtische Wasserversorgung, Abwasserentsorgung oder das Stromnetz angewiesen.

Le **TOWER STUDIO** est situé sur le littoral rocheux de la baie Shoal, sur l'île de Fogo. La structure à trois niveaux atteint une hauteur totale de presque 10 m. L'entrée comporte une kitchenette, des toilettes à compost et une cheminée à bois. Le studio, dont la hauteur est double, est doté d'une généreuse lucarne face au nord. Une mezzanine fait saillie dans cet espace. Todd Saunders explique : « En plus de la complexité géométrique de l'espace, le second trait qui ajoute au sens de la désorientation est la suppression de tout détail architectural et le fait que toutes les surfaces verticales, horizontales et inclinées, revêtues de contreplaqué lisse, sont peintes dans un blanc éclatant. » Une trappe donne accès à une terrasse sur le toit. Comme les autres studios de l'île de Fogo, Tower Studio est « 100 % autonome par rapport au réseau électrique, sans aucune connexion aux services publics ». Il ne dépend pas de l'alimentation en eau de la municipalité, ni des canalisations d'égout ou du réseau public d'électricité.

Like the Squish Studio, the Tower Studio seems like a drawing that has come to life, or rather taken three-dimensional form. It stands out from its rugged site, but somehow fits in well nonetheless.

Das Tower Studio wirkt, wie schon das Squish Studio, wie eine ins Dreidimensionale versetzte Zeichnung. Obwohl der Bau aus der Felslandschaft heraussticht, fügt er sich dennoch ein.

Comme le Squish Studio, le Tower Studio ressemble à un dessin qui aurait pris vie, ou plutôt une forme tridimensionnelle. Il se détache sur le site accidenté, mais s'y intègre néanmoins aussi en un certain sens.

One angled surface of the dark tower is used to admit light into the building. The doorway is similarly angled, and cut out.

Durch eine der schiefwinkligen Oberflächen des dunklen Turms fällt Licht in den Bau. Auch der Eingang ist auf ähnliche Weise schiefwinklig aus dem Bau herausgeschnitten.

L'une des surfaces anguleuses de la tour sombre laisse entrer la lumière à l'intérieur du bâtiment. L'embrasure découpée de la porte est tout aussi anguleuse.

The triangular skylight floods the white interior with natural light. The contrast between this architectural space and the rough outdoor landscape could not be more striking.

Durch das dreieckige Atelierfenster flutet Tageslicht in das weiße Interieur. Der Gegensatz zwischen der Architektur und der rauen Landschaft könnte nicht größer sein.

La lucarne triangulaire inonde l'intérieur blanc de lumière naturelle, le contraste entre cet espace architectural et le rude paysage extérieur ne pourrait être plus frappant.

ADRIAN SMITH + GORDON GILL

Adrian Smith + Gordon Gill Architecture LLP
111 West Monroe
Suite 2300
Chicago, IL 60603
USA

Tel: +1 312 920 1888
Fax: +1 312 920 1775
E-mail: info@smithgill.com
Web: www.smithgill.com

ADRIAN SMITH received his B.Arch degree from the University of Illinois (Chicago, 1969). He was a design Partner in the office of Skidmore, Owings & Merrill from 1980 to 2003. He was Chief Executive Officer of the SOM Partnership (1993–95) and Chairman of the SOM Foundation (1990–95). He is well known as the designer of towers such as the Burj Khalifa (Dubai, UAE, 2006–09), currently the tallest building in the world. **GORDON GILL** was an Associate Partner at Skidmore, Owings & Merrill LLP and a Director of Design for VOA Associates, before creating Adrian Smith + Gordon Gill Architecture with Adrian Smith and Robert Forest in 2006. He was the designer of "the world's first net zero-energy skyscraper, the Pearl River Tower." Robert Forest received his B.Arch degree from Carleton University (Ottawa, Canada, 1994). He is the management Partner for the Masdar Headquarters and was also involved in the Head Office of the Federation of Korean Industries tower (Seoul, South Korea, 2010–13, published here). The firm's current work includes the Masdar Headquarters (Abu Dhabi, 2007–); and the Kingdom Tower, slated to surpass the Burj Khalifa as the tallest building in the world by "at least 173 meters" (Jeddah, Saudi Arabia, ongoing).

ADRIAN SMITH absolvierte seinen B.Arch an der University of Illinois in Chicago (1969). Von 1980 bis 2003 war er als Partner bei Skidmore, Owings & Merrill für den Entwurf zuständig. Er war Hauptgeschäftsführer der SOM-Partnerschaft (1993–95) und Vorsitzender der SOM Foundation (1990–95). Bekannt wurde er mit seinen Hochhausbauten wie dem Burj Khalifa (Dubai, VAE, 2006–09), dem derzeit höchsten Gebäude der Welt. **GORDON GILL** war assoziierter Partner bei Skidmore, Owings & Merrill LLP und zuständiger Direktor für den Entwurf bei VOA Associates, bevor er 2006 mit Adrian Smith und Robert Forest das Büro Adrian Smith + Gordon Gill Architecture gründete. Er entwarf den Pearl River Tower, den „ersten Nullenergie-Wolkenkratzer der Welt". Robert Forest absolvierte seinen B.Arch an der Carleton University (Ottawa, Kanada, 1994). Er ist geschäftsführender Partner für die Masdar Headquarters sowie beteiligt an der Planung der Zentrale des Koreanischen Industrieverbands (Seoul, Südkorea, 2010–13, hier vorgestellt). Aktuelle Projekte des Büros sind unter anderem die Masdar Headquarters (Abu Dhabi, 2007–) und der Kingdom Tower, der „mindestens 173 m" höher sein wird als der Burj Khalifa und ihn damit als höchstes Gebäude der Welt ablösen dürfte (Jeddah, Saudi-Arabien, in Planung).

ADRIAN SMITH est titulaire d'un B.Arch de l'université de l'Illinois à Chicago (1969). Il a été partenaire concepteur dans l'agence de Skidmore, Owings & Merrill de 1980 à 2003, directeur général du partenariat SOM (1993–95) et président de la fondation SOM (1990–95). Il est connu pour ses tours comme la Burj Khalifa (Dubaï, EAU, 2006–09), la plus haute du monde. **GORDON GILL** a été partenaire associé de Skidmore, Owings & Merrill LLP et directeur du design de VOA Associates avant de créer Adrian Smith + Gordon Gill Architecture avec Adrian Smith et Robert Forest en 2006. Il est le créateur du « premier gratte-ciel zéro énergie du monde, la tour de la Rivière des perles ». Robert Forest est titulaire d'un B.Arch de l'université Carleton (Ottawa, Canada, 1994). Il est le partenaire de gestion du siège de Masdar et a également participé à la tour du siège de la Fédération des industries coréennes (Séoul, 2010–13, publiée ici). Les projets en cours de l'agence comprennent le siège de Masdar (Abou Dhabi, 2007–) et la Kingdom Tower, conçue pour dépasser la Burj Khalifa d'« au moins 173 m », ce qui en fera le bâtiment le plus haut du monde (Djeddah, Arabie Saoudite, en cours).

HEAD OFFICE OF THE FEDERATION OF KOREAN INDUSTRIES

Seoul, South Korea, 2010–13

Address: Yeoi-Dae-Ro Avenue, Seoul, South Korea, www.fki.or.kr/en
Area: 124 000 m². Client: Federation of Korean Industries
Cost: $340 million

Smith Gill won the international competition to design this 240-meter-high tower in 2009. An outstanding feature of the project is a specially designed skin "conceived to help reduce the internal heating and cooling loads of the tower and collect energy by integrating photovoltaic panels into the spandrel areas of the southwest and northwest façades, which receive a significant amount of direct sunlight per day." A large amount of garden space and natural light are also part of the scheme. Located on the central part of Yeoi-Dae-Ro Avenue, the tower will be a visible landmark in the city. The podium of the structure houses a banquet hall, central restaurant, and conference center. The architects are collaborating with the engineering firms Thornton Tomasetti and Environmental Systems Design, as well as the local firm Chang-Jo Architects, on the project.

Smith Gill gewann den internationalen Wettbewerb für den 240 m hohen Turm 2009. Ein Highlight des Projekts ist die Gebäudehülle, speziell konzipiert, „um die Heiz- und Kühllast des Turms zu reduzieren und mittels Solarmodulen Energie zu erzeugen. Diese sind in die Brüstungsbereiche der Südwest- und Nordwestfassaden integriert, die tagsüber beträchtlicher direkter Sonneneinstrahlung ausgesetzt sind." Zum Entwurf gehören außerdem großzügige Grünflächen und natürliche Belichtung. Das zentral an der Yeoi-Dae-Ro Avenue gelegene Hochhaus wird sich als weithin sichtbares Wahrzeichen der Stadt behaupten. Im niedrigeren Annex sind ein Ballsaal, ein Hauptrestaurant und ein Konferenzzentrum geplant. Die Architekten kooperieren mit den Ingenieurbüros Thornton Tomasetti und Environmental Systems Design sowie mit Chang-Jo Architects als Partner vor Ort.

Smith Gill a remporté le concours international pour construire cette tour de 240 m en 2009. L'une des caractéristiques les plus remarquables du projet est l'enveloppe du bâtiment, spécialement « conçue pour contribuer à réduire le chauffage et la charge de climatisation, tout en récupérant de l'énergie grâce aux panneaux photovoltaïques intégrés aux surfaces de remplissage des façades sud-ouest et nord-ouest, exposées à un ensoleillement direct très important pendant la journée ». L'ensemble présente également un espace généreux occupé par un jardin et une abondance de lumière naturelle. Située sur la portion centrale de l'avenue Yeoi-Dae-Ro, la tour sera un point de repère bien visible dans la ville. Le podium annexe abrite une salle de banquets, un restaurant central et un centre de conférences. Les architectes collaborent à ce projet avec les sociétés d'ingénieurs Thornton Tomasetti et Environmental Systems Design, ainsi qu'avec la société locale Chang-Jo Architects.

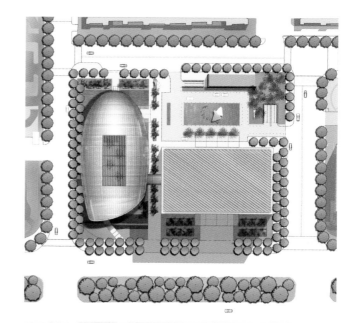

Right, the site plan shows the position of the tower and the landscaped areas that surround it. Above, the sunken plaza of the complex.

Der Grundstücksplan (rechts) veranschaulicht die Position des Turms und der angrenzenden Grünflächen. Oben die abgesenkte Plaza des Komplexes.

À droite, plan du site avec l'emplacement de la tour et les espaces paysagers qui l'entourent. Ci-dessus, la place en contrebas du complexe.

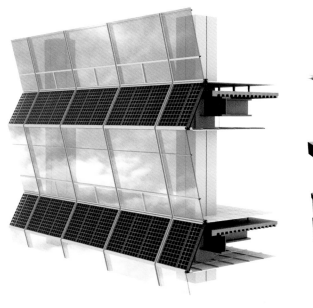

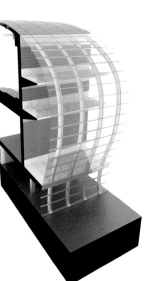

Left, an exterior wall detail drawing
and a podium wall system drawing.
Below, the lobby of the building.

Links eine Zeichnung der Gebäude-
hülle sowie ein Detailausschnitt des
Wandaufbaus des Annexgebäudes.
Unten die Lobby des Turms.

À gauche, détail du mur extérieur et
de la structure du mur du podium.
Ci-dessous, le hall.

Above, a detail of the exterior wall
system and a drawing of the atrium
roof. Right, the podium "nose."

Oben eine Detailansicht der Gebäudehülle und eine Zeichnung des Atriums
unter dem Dach. Rechts die „Nase"
des Annexgebäudes.

Ci-dessus, détail du mur extérieur et
toit de l'atrium. À droite, le « nez » du
podium.

WERNER SOBEK

Werner Sobek Stuttgart GmbH & Co. KG

Albstr. 14

70597 Stuttgart

Germany

Tel: +49 711 767 50 38 / Fax: +49 711 767 50 44

E-mail: stuttgart@wernersobek.com / Web: www.wernersobek.com

WERNER SOBEK was born in 1953 in Aalen, Germany. He studied architecture and civil engineering at the University of Stuttgart (1974–80) and did postgraduate research in "Wide-Span Lightweight Structures" at the University of Stuttgart (1980–86). He received his Ph.D. in Civil Engineering at the same university in 1987. He worked as a structural engineer in the office of Schlaich, Bergermann and Partner (Stuttgart, 1987–91), before creating his own office in 1991. Since 1995 he has been a Professor at the University of Stuttgart, where he succeeded Frei Otto as Director of the Institute for Lightweight Structures and Conceptual Design (ILEK). He is the Mies van der Rohe Professor at the Illinois Institute of Technology. His projects include the Ecole Nationale d'Art Décoratif (Limoges, France, 1991–94); the Dome Service Hall, Deutsche Bank (Hanover, Germany, 1992–95); Art and Media Science Center (Karlsruhe, Germany, 1992–97); Façade Interbank (with Hans Hollein, Lima, Peru, 1996–99); a private residence at Römerstr. 128 (Stuttgart, Germany, 1998–2000); New Bangkok International Airport (with Murphy/Jahn, Thailand, 1995–2004); H16 (Tieringen, Germany, 2005–06); and fair pavilions for Audi and BMW. In 2007, WSGreenTechnologies was cofounded by Klaus Sedlbauer and Werner Sobek in Stuttgart. WSGreenTechnologies "offers integrated planning of buildings taking into consideration all phases of construction, use, and deconstruction." Sobek has been a member of the supervisory board of the German Sustainable Building Council (DGNB) since 2007, and served as its President from 2008 to 2010. Included among recent work are the two projects published here: D10 (Biberbach an der Riss, Germany, 2009–10); and F87 (Berlin, Germany, 2011).

WERNER SOBEK, geboren 1953 in Aalen, Deutschland, studierte Architektur und Bauingenieurwesen an der Universität Stuttgart (1974–80) und arbeitete nach seinem Abschluss an einer Arbeit zum Thema „Flächentragwerke und Leichtbaukonstruktionen" an der Universität Stuttgart (1980–86). 1987 promovierte er an derselben Hochschule. Er arbeitete zunächst als Statiker bei Schlaich, Bergermann und Partner (Stuttgart, 1987–91) und gründete 1991 sein eigenes Büro. Seit 1995 ist er Professor an der Universität Stuttgart, wo er die Nachfolge von Frei Otto antrat und das heutige Institut für Leichtbau Entwerfen und Konstruieren (ILEK) leitet. Er ist Mies-van-der Rohe Professor am Illinois Institute of Technology. Zu seinen Projekten zählen die Ecole Nationale d'Art Décoratif (Limoges, Frankreich, 1991–94), die Kuppel in der Schalterhalle der Deutschen Bank in Hannover (Deutschland, 1992–95), das ZKM in Karlsruhe (Deutschland, 1992–97), die Fassade der Interbank (mit Hans Hollein, Lima, Peru, 1996–99), das Privatwohnhaus R128 (Stuttgart, Deutschland, 1998–2000), der neue Internationale Flughafen Bangkok (mit Murphy/Jahn, Thailand, 1995–2004), das H16 (Tieringen, Deutschland, 2005–06) sowie Messepavillons für Audi und BMW. 2007 gründeten Klaus Sedlbauer und Werner Sobek gemeinschaftlich WSGreenTechnologies. Das Büro „bietet einen integrierten Planungsprozess für alle Arten von Gebäuden. Dieser Planungsprozess berücksichtigt alle Phasen eines Lebenszyklus des Gebäudes." Seit 2007 ist Sobek Mitglied des Präsidiums der Deutschen Gesellschaft für Nachhaltiges Bauen (DGNB), deren Präsident er von 2008 bis 2010 war. Zu seinen jüngeren Entwürfen zählen auch die beiden hier vorgestellten Projekte D10 (Biberbach an der Riss, Deutschland, 2009–10) und F87 (Berlin, Deutschland, 2011).

WERNER SOBEK est né en 1953 à Aalen, en Allemagne. Il a fait des études d'architecture et de génie civil à l'université de Stuttgart (1974–80), puis des recherches de troisième cycle sur « les structures légères de grande envergure » (1980–86). Il a obtenu son Ph.D en génie civil à la même université en 1987. Il a travaillé comme ingénieur constructeur dans l'agence de Schlaich, Bergermann und Partner (Stuttgart, 1987–91) avant de créer sa propre société en 1991. Depuis 1995, il est professeur à l'université de Stuttgart où il a succédé à Frei Otto au poste de directeur de l'Institut des structures légères et de design conceptuel (ILEK). Il est également titulaire de la chaire Mies van der Rohe à l'Illinois Institute of Technology. Ses projets comprennent l'École nationale d'art décoratif (Limoges, 1991–94) ; le hall de services du Dome, Deutsche Bank (Hanovre, Allemagne, 1992–95) ; le Centre scientifique des arts et médias (Karlsruhe, Allemagne, 1992–97) ; la façade de l'Interbank (avec Hans Hollein, Lima, Pérou, 1996–99) ; une résidence privée Römerstr. 128 (Stuttgart, 1998–2000) ; le nouvel aéroport international de Bangkok (avec Murphy/Jahn, 1995–2004) ; H16 (Tieringen, Allemagne, 2005–06) et des pavillons d'exposition pour Audi et BMW. WSGreenTechnologies a été fondé en 2007 par Klaus Sedlbauer et Werner Sobek à Stuttgart. La société « propose la planification intégrée de bâtiments en tenant compte de toutes les phases de construction, exploitation et déconstruction ». Sobek est membre du bureau de surveillance du Conseil allemand pour le bâtiment durable (DGNB) depuis 2007 et en a été le président de 2008 à 2010. Les deux projets publiés ici comptent parmi ses réalisations récentes : D10 (Biberbach an der Ris, Allemagne, 2009–10) et F87 (Berlin, 2011).

D10

Biberbach an der Riss, Germany, 2009–10

Address: n/a. Area: 180 m²
Client: not disclosed. Cost: not disclosed

This is a single-story house with a basement built in a residential area near Ulm. A light slab roof extends beyond the boundaries of the house covering the surrounding patio. Full-height glass walls make this residence somewhat reminiscent of Mies van der Rohe's Farnsworth House (Plano, Illinois, 1945–51), though it has an ethereal lightness that Mies did not achieve just after the war. Then too, **D10** is a thoroughly modern house in terms of its sustainability. The architect states: "The energy concept guarantees that all of the energy required to run the building is gained from regenerative sources. A geothermal energy system and a highly efficient heat pump provide the energy required to produce warm water and meet heating and cooling needs. The entire surface of the roof is fitted with a photovoltaic system that generates more power on an annual average than the building consumes."

Das einstöckige Einfamilienhaus mit Untergeschoss liegt in einem Wohngebiet in der Nähe von Ulm. Ein leichtes auskragendes Flachdach schützt die umlaufende Terrasse. Durch seine geschosshohe Verglasung wirkt der Bau wie eine Hommage an Mies van der Rohes Farnsworth House (Plano, Illinois, 1945–51), wenngleich Sobeks Entwurf von einer schwebenden Leichtigkeit ist, die Mies so kurz nach dem Krieg noch nicht erreichte. Doch **D10** ist auch im Hinblick auf seine Nachhaltigkeit ein durch und durch modernes Haus. Der Architekt führt aus: „Das Energiekonzept garantiert, dass der komplette Energiebedarf des Gebäudes mittels regenerativer Energien gedeckt wird. Die zur Erzeugung von Warmwasser sowie zur Deckung des Heiz- und Kühlbedarfs notwendige Energie wird durch ein Geothermiesystem mit hocheffizienter Wärmepumpe gedeckt. Die komplette Dachfläche ist mit einer Photovoltaikanlage ausgestattet, die im Jahresdurchschnitt mehr als die im Gebäude verbrauchte Energiemenge produziert."

La maison à un seul niveau avec sous-sol a été construite dans une zone résidentielle près d'Ulm. Une dalle légère forme le toit et dépasse de la maison pour couvrir le patio tout autour. Des parois en verre pleine hauteur font de cette résidence une réminiscence de la Farnsworth House de Mies van der Rohe (Plano, Illinois, 1945–51), avec toutefois une légèreté aérienne que Mies n'avait pu obtenir dans l'immédiat après-guerre. **D10** est également une maison parfaitement moderne en terme de durabilité. L'architecte explique que « le concept énergétique garantit que la totalité de l'énergie requise pour faire fonctionner le bâtiment est obtenue à partir de sources renouvelables. Un système géothermique et une pompe à chaleur haute efficacité fournissent l'énergie nécessaire à l'eau chaude et aux besoins de chauffage ou refroidissement. La surface du toit est entièrement couverte d'un ensemble photovoltaïque qui produit annuellement plus d'électricité en moyenne que le bâtiment n'en consomme ».

The extreme simplicity of this architecture might well relate it to the work of Ludwig Mies van der Rohe, albeit in a much more ecologically conscious mode.

Die ausgeprägte Schlichtheit der Architektur zeigt durchaus Verwandt-schaft zu Ludwig Mies van der Rohe, wenn auch mit deutlich umwelt-freundlicherem Akzent.

L'extrême simplicité de l'architecture n'est pas sans rappeler le travail de Ludwig Mies van der Rohe, mais sur un mode bien plus écologique.

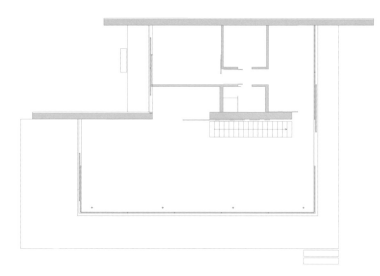

Furniture such as the LC2 armchair
and LC3 couch (original design:
Le Corbusier, Pierre Jeanneret,
Charlotte Perriand, 1928) or an Eileen
Gray end table (original design: 1927)
occupy the otherwise minimalist
space, which is softened somewhat
by the floor-to-ceiling glazing and
views of the garden.

Objekte wie der Sessel LC2 und
die Couch LC3 (Originalentwurf: Le
Corbusier, Pierre Jeanneret, Charlotte
Perriand, 1928) sowie der Beistell-
tisch von Eileen Gray (Originalentwurf
1927) möblieren den ansonsten
minimalistischen Raum, der durch
geschosshohe Verglasung und
Ausblick in den Garten etwas an
Strenge verliert.

Des meubles tels que le fauteuil LC2
et le canapé LC3 (design original :
Le Corbusier, Pierre Jeanneret,
Charlotte Perriand, 1928) ou une
table Eileen Gray (design original :
1927) occupent l'espace sinon
minimaliste, quelque peu adouci
par le vitrage du sol au plafond
et les vues sur le jardin.

The windows are so pure and simple that they almost seem to disappear, making an invisible barrier to the garden that inevitably remains at a distance.

Die schlichten Klarglasfenster verschwinden geradezu und bilden eine unsichtbare Barriere zum Garten, der zwangsläufig eine gewisse Distanz wahrt.

Les fenêtres sont d'une telle pureté et simplicité qu'elles donnent l'impression de disparaître, formant une barrière invisible vers le jardin qui reste ainsi inéluctablement distant.

F87

Berlin, Germany, 2011

Address: n/a. Area: 130 m²
Client: BMVBS (Federal Ministry of Transport, Building and Urban Development
Cost: not disclosed

The Institute for Lightweight Structures and Conceptual Design (ILEK) at the University of Stuttgart, headed by Werner Sobek, won first prize in a competition called "Efficiency House Plus with Electromobility" organized by the German Federal Ministry of Transport, Building, and Urban Development. The design, developed under the direction of Sobek, "demonstrates the potential of actively coupling energy flows between an emerging fleet of electric vehicles and the built environment." The project involves a glass showcase in which the technical systems are prominently displayed to form a full-scale "living display." The project demonstrates the feasibility of future single-family homes that generate enough surplus energy to power the electric vehicles of their occupants. The concept also involves a design that can be completely disassembled and recycled after use. The architects state: "The holistic planning approach employed by the interdisciplinary design team takes the scope of 'sustainable design' to a new level, incorporating energy and material concepts which surpass the standards set by previous milestone projects such as the (US Department of Energy) Solar Decathlon competition."

Das von Werner Sobek geleitetete Institut für Leichtbau Entwerfen und Konstruieren (ILEK) an der Universität Stuttgart gewann den ersten Preis eines vom Bundesministerium für Verkehr, Bau und Stadtentwicklung ausgelobten Wettbewerbs für ein „Effizienzhaus Plus mit Elektromobilität". Der unter Leitung von Sobek entwickelte Entwurf „zeigt das Potenzial auf, welches aus der bisher ungekannten Verknüpfung der Energieströme zwischen der entstehenden Elektromobilität und unserer gebauten Umwelt erwächst". Das Projekt zeichnet sich durch einen gläsernen „Showcase" aus, in dem die haustechnischen Systeme prominent zur Schau gestellt werden, und das so zu einem „bewohnten Ausstellungsraum" wird. Das Haus stellt die reale Option unter Beweis, zukünftig Einfamilienhäuser zu bauen, die ausreichend Energieüberschuss produzieren, um die E-Mobile ihrer Bewohner mit Energie zu versorgen. Integraler Bestandteil des Konzepts ist die Möglichkeit, den Bau später vollständig rückzubauen und zu recyceln. Die Architekten erklären: „Die ganzheitliche Betrachtungsweise des interdisziplinären Planungsteams setzt ganz neue Maßstäbe für ‚nachhaltiges Entwerfen' und berücksichtigt Energie- und Materialkonzepte, die über bahnbrechende Projekte wie den Solar-Decathlon-Wettbewerb (der US-Energiebehörde) hinausgehen."

L'Institut des structures légères et de design conceptuel (ILEK) de l'université de Stuttgart, dirigé par Werner Sobek, a gagné le premier prix d'un concours organisé par le ministère fédéral allemand des Transports, de la Construction et du Développement urbain pour la construction d'une « maison à énergie positive combinée à l'électromobilité ». Le projet, développé sous la direction de Sobek, « met en évidence le potentiel du couplage actif de flux énergétiques entre le futur parc de véhicules électriques et l'environnement construit ». Il comprend une vitrine dans laquelle les appareillages sont exposés bien en vue comme un « tableau vivant » grandeur nature. L'ensemble apporte la preuve de la faisabilité de maisons individuelles qui génèrent un surplus énergétique suffisant pour alimenter les véhicules électriques de leurs habitants. Le concept fait également intervenir un design totalement démontable et recyclable après usage. Pour l'architecte : « L'approche de planification holistique adoptée par l'équipe interdisciplinaire de concepteurs étend la portée du "design durable" à un niveau encore jamais atteint, en prenant en compte des questions énergétiques et matérielles qui vont au-delà des standards mis en place par des projets antérieurs marquants, comme le concours Decathlon solaire (ministère américain de l'Énergie). »

Here, as in his other structures, Werner Sobek employs a strictly Euclidean vocabulary. The solidity of the F87 House is apparent in the photo above and in the section drawing to the right.

Werner Sobek setzt hier, wie auch bei anderen Bauten, konsequent auf euklidisches Vokabular. Die Massivität des F87 wird auf der Aufnahme oben und dem Querschnitt rechts deutlich.

Comme dans ses autres constructions, Werner Sobek emploie ici un vocabulaire strictement euclidien. La photo ci-dessus et la vue en coupe à droite mettent en évidence la solidité de la maison F87.

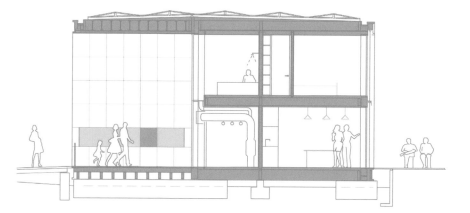

The exterior terrace and interior floors are in wood, contrasting with the large tiles seen in the entry area on the left.

Der Holzboden im Eingangsbereich und im Innern des Baus kontrastiert mit den großflächigen weißen Wandpaneelen in der Eingangszone (links).

La terrasse et les sols sont en bois, contrastant avec les grands carreaux que l'on voit à gauche dans l'entrée.

Sobek's strict adherence to white surfaces (with a bit of red every now and again) and full-height glazing makes the interior of the house bright and flexible in terms of potential use of spaces.

Sobeks strikte Vorliebe für weiße Oberflächen (mit roten Akzenten hier und dort), ebenso wie die geschosshohe Verglasung, machen das Interieur hell und flexibel nutzbar.

L'engagement strict de Sobek en faveur des surfaces blanches (avec un peu de rouge çà et là) et le vitrage pleine hauteur confèrent à l'intérieur de la maison clarté et souplesse en terme d'utilisation de l'espace.

TAO

TAO (Trace Architecture Office)
North 3rd Ring, West Road No. 43
Building No. 24
Beijing 100086
China

Tel: +86 10 8212 3535
Fax: +86 10 8212 3737
E-mail: t-a-o@vip.163.com
Web: www.t-a-o.cn

The founder and design Principal of TAO (Trace Architecture Office) **HUA LI** was born in 1972 in Lanzhou, China. He received his B.Arch degree from Tsinghua University in 1994 and an M.Arch degree from Yale University in 1999. He worked at Westfourth Architecture and Herbert Beckhard Frank Richlan & Associates in New York, before returning to China in 2003 to start his own practice in Beijing. He established TAO in 2009. Hua Li has also taught at the Central Academy of Fine Arts in Beijing as a Visiting Professor and been a visiting critic at the School of Architecture at Tsinghua University since 2005. Hua Li's completed projects include TAO Architect's Office, a refurbishment of a warehouse in Beijing (2009); Gaoligong Museum of Handcraft Paper (Tengchong, Yunnan, 2009–10, published here); Riverside Clubhouse (Yancheng, 2010); XiaoQuan Elementary School (Sichuan, 2011); and the sports center for Northeast Normal University (ChangChun, 2004–11), all in China.

HUA LI, Gründer und Direktor für Entwerfen bei TAO (Trace Architecture Office), wurde 1972 in Lanzhou, China, geboren. Er absolvierte seinen B.Arch 1994 an der Tsinghua University sowie 1999 einen M.Arch in Yale. Er arbeitete für Westfourth Architecture und Herbert Beckhard Frank Richlan & Associates in New York, bevor er 2003 nach China zurückkehrte und ein Büro in Peking gründete. 2009 folgte die Gründung von TAO. Hua Li war außerdem Gastdozent an der Zentralakademie für Bildende Künste in Peking und ist seit 2005 Gastkritiker an der Architekturfakultät der Tsinghua University. Zu seinen realisierten Projekten zählen das Büro von TAO in einem sanierten Speicher in Peking (2009), das Gaoligong Museum für Papierhandwerk (Tengchong, Yunnan, 2009–10, hier vorgestellt), das Riverside Clubhouse (Yancheng, 2010), die Grundschule in XiaoQuan (Sichuan, 2011) und die Sportanlagen für die Nordostchinesische Pädagogische Hochschule (ChangChun, 2004–11), alle in China.

Le fondateur et directeur du design de TAO (Trace Architecture Office), **HUA LI**, est né en 1972 à Lanzhou, en Chine Il est titulaire d'un B.Arch de l'université Tsinghua (1994) et d'un M.Arch de Yale (1999). Il a travaillé chez Westfourth Architecture et Herbert Beckhard Frank Richlan & Associates à New York avant de revenir en Chine en 2003 et d'ouvrir son cabinet à Pékin. Il a créé TAO en 2009. Il a également enseigné à l'Académie centrale des beaux-arts de Pékin en tant que professeur associé et il est critique invité à l'école d'architecture de l'université Tsinghua depuis 2005. Les projets déjà réalisés de Hua Li comprennent le cabinet d'architectes TAO, le réaménagement d'un entrepôt à Pékin (2009) ; le musée du Papier artisanal de Gaoligong (Tengchong, Yunnan, 2009–10, publié ici) ; le club Riverside (Yancheng, 2010) ; l'école élémentaire XiaoQuan (Sichuan, 2011) et le centre sportif de l'Université normale du Nord-Est (ChangChun, 2004–11), tous en Chine.

GAOLIGONG MUSEUM OF HANDCRAFT PAPER

Tengchong, Yunnan, China, 2009–10

Address: Tengchong, Yunnan, China. Area: 361 m²
Client: Committee of the Gaoligong Museum of Handcraft Paper
Cost: not disclosed

This museum is situated in a field next to the village of Xinzhuang, near Gaoligong Mountain in Yunnan, a world ecological preserve. The village has a long tradition of handcrafted papermaking. The museum includes a gallery, bookstore, work space, and guest rooms. The complex is conceived as a micro-village, or a cluster of several small buildings. The architect states: "The spatial concept is to create a visiting experience alternating between the interior of galleries and the landscape outside when visitors walk through the museum, so as to provoke an awareness of the inseparable relationship between papermaking and the environment." An emphasis has been placed on environmentally sustainable design, through the use of local craftsmanship (including farmers) and materials such as bamboo and handcrafted paper. Local volcanic stone is used for the exterior, roof, interior cladding, and floors. A traditional timber structural system that uses no nails called SunMao was employed.

Das Museum liegt in einem Feld in der Nähe des Dorfs Xinzhuang, nicht weit vom Gaoligongshan-Gebirge in Yunnan, einem internationalen Naturschutzgebiet. Das Dorf blickt auf eine lange Tradition des Papierhandwerks zurück. Zum Museum gehören eine Galerie, eine Buchhandlung, ein Werkstattbereich sowie Gästezimmer. Der Komplex wurde als Dorf im Kleinen, als Cluster mehrerer kleinerer Bauten konzipiert. Der Architekt führt aus: „Ziel des Raumkonzepts ist es, ein Besuchserlebnis zu ermöglichen, das im Wechsel zwischen Ausstellungsräumen und Landschaft durch das Museum führt und so ein Bewusstsein für die unauflösliche Wechselbeziehung von Papierhandwerk und Umwelt schafft." Besonderer Wert wurde auf nachhaltiges Design gelegt, etwa durch die Zusammenarbeit mit ortsansässigen Handwerkern (und Bauern) oder Baustoffen wie Bambus und handgeschöpftem Papier. Am Außenbau sowie für Dach, Innenverschalung und Böden kam lokaler Vulkanstein zum Einsatz. Gearbeitet wurde außerdem mit SunMao, einem traditionellen Holztragwerk.

Le musée se trouve dans un champ à proximité du village de Xinzhuang – qui possède une longue tradition papetière artisanale – et du mont Gaoligong, dans le Yunnan, une réserve écologique mondiale. Le musée comporte une galerie d'exposition, une librairie, un espace de travail et des chambres d'hôtes. Le complexe est conçu comme un micro-village, ou un groupe de petits bâtiments. Pour l'architecte : « Le concept spatial vise à faire vivre une véritable expérience aux visiteurs, entre l'intérieur des salles d'exposition et le paysage extérieur qu'on voit en parcourant le musée, afin de susciter une prise de conscience du lien indissociable entre la fabrication du papier et l'environnement. » L'accent a été mis sur le design écologiquement durable par le recours au savoir artisanal local (y compris agricole) et l'emploi de matériaux comme le bambou et le papier artisanal. De la pierre volcanique locale a été utilisée pour l'extérieur, le toit, le revêtement intérieur et les sols. Un système traditionnel de structure en bois sans clous, appelé SunMao, a également été utilisé.

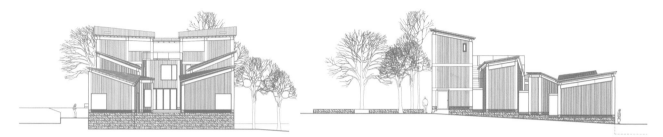

The architect has designed a series of elements that recall traditional village architecture while nonetheless remaining modern. The "village" aspect of the design can be seen in the drawings above—while the modernity is present in the large windows, for example.

Der Entwurf des Architekten zeigt Elemente, die an traditionelle Dorf-architektur erinnern, aber dennoch modern sind. Der „dörfliche" Charak-ter wird in den Zeichnungen oben deutlich, während die großen Fenster moderne Akzente setzen.

L'architecte a imaginé des éléments qui rappellent l'architecture villa-geoise traditionnelle, mais restent néanmoins modernes. On voit cet aspect « villageois » sur les schémas ci-dessus – tandis que la modernité est exprimée, par exemple, par les grandes fenêtres.

Wooden walls and ceilings are contrasted with gray tile floors. The large windows assure ample natural light inside.

Wände und Decken aus Holz kontrastieren mit den grauen Bodenfliesen. Die großen Fenster lassen reichlich Tageslicht einfallen.

Le bois des murs et des plafonds contraste avec les carreaux gris du sol. Les grandes fenêtres laissent largement pénétrer la lumière du jour à l'intérieur.

A drawing shows the pavilion structure with the scale of visitors vis-à-vis the architecture indicated. Above, another interior view with the rather complex angles and large openings of the design visible.

Die Zeichnung zeigt die Pavillonstruktur der Anlage im maßstäblichen Verhältnis. Auf einer weiteren Innenansicht (oben) sind die komplexen Winkel der Architektur und die großen Fensteröffnungen zu sehen.

Le schéma montre la structure pavillonnaire avec les visiteurs à l'échelle par rapport à l'architecture. Ci-dessus, une autre vue intérieure où l'on voit la structure anguleuse plutôt complexe et les larges ouvertures.

THAM & VIDEGÅRD

Tham & Videgård Arkitekter
Blekingegatan 46
116 62 Stockholm
Sweden

Tel: +46 8 702 00 46
Fax: +46 8 702 00 56
E-mail: info@tvark.se
Web: www.tvark.se

Tham & Videgård was created in 1999 in Stockholm. It is still directed by its cofounders and chief architects **BOLLE THAM** (born in 1970) and **MARTIN VIDEGÅRD** (born in 1968). Their work includes the Kalmar Museum of Art (Kalmar, 2004–08); the new Moderna Museet Malmö, the Swedish Museum of Modern Art (Malmö, 2009); along with the two projects published here: the Tellus Nursery (Telefonplan, Stockholm, 2009–10); and the Harads Tree Hotel (Harads, 2009–10), all in Sweden. They are currently working on the New School of Architecture at the Royal Institute of Technology (Valhallavägen, Stockholm, 2007–13) after winning the competition in 2007. Tham & Videgård is recognized as one of the significant newer firms on the international architecture scene and their involvement in the Harads Tree Hotel is a clear indication of the rising interest in architecture that is close to nature.

Tham & Videgård wurde 1999 in Stockholm gegründet. Das Büro arbeitet auch weiterhin unter Leitung seiner Gründer und leitenden Architekten **BOLLE THAM** (geboren 1970) und **MARTIN VIDEGÅRD** (geboren 1968). Zu ihren Projekten zählen das Kunstmuseum in Kalmar (Kalmar, 2004–08), das neue Moderna Museet Malmö – schwedisches Museum für moderne Kunst (Malmö, 2009) sowie zwei weitere, hier vorgestellte Projekte: der Tellus-Kindergarten (Telefonplan, Stockholm, 2009–10) sowie das Harads Tree Hotel (Harads, 2009–10), alle in Schweden. Aktuell arbeitet das Team an der neuen Architekturfakultät der Königlich-Technischen Hochschule (Valhallavägen, Stockholm, 2007–13), nachdem es 2007 den entsprechenden Wettbewerb für sich entscheiden konnte. Tham & Videgård haben sich als eines der interessantesten neuen Büros der internationalen Architekturszene etablieren können. Ihr Engagement für den Treehotel-Komplex in Harads ist ein deutliches Indiz für das wachsende Interesse an naturnaher Architektur.

Tham & Videgård a été fondée en 1999 à Stockholm. Aujourd'hui, l'agence est toujours dirigée par ses fondateurs et architectes en chef **BOLLE THAM** (né en 1970) et **MARTIN VIDEGÅRD** (né en 1968). Leurs réalisations comprennent le Musée d'art de Kalmar (Kalmar, 2004–08) ; le nouveau Moderna Museet Malmö, Musée suédois d'art moderne (Malmö, 2009) et les deux projets publiés ici : la crèche Tellus (Telefonplan, Stockholm, 2009–10) et un hôtel dans les arbres, le Harads Tree Hotel (Harads, 2009–10), toutes en Suède. Ils travaillent actuellement à la nouvelle École d'architecture de l'Institut royal de technologie (Valhallavägen, Stockholm, 2007–13) pour laquelle ils ont gagné un concours en 2007. Tham & Videgård est aujourd'hui reconnue comme l'une des jeunes agences les plus remarquables sur la scène architecturale internationale et leur implication dans le « Tree Hotel » de Harads constitue un signe clair de l'intérêt actuel croissant pour une architecture proche de la nature.

TELLUS NURSERY SCHOOL

Telefonplan, Stockholm, Sweden, 2009–10

*Address: Huvudfabriksgatan 18–20, 129 04 Hägersten, Stockholm, Sweden
Area: 1242 m². Client: Vasakronan, Renée Myrland
Cost: not disclosed. Collaboration: Eric Engström (Project Architect),
Mårten Nettelbladt, Andreas Helgesson*

This nursery school was built between a former urban and industrial development zone and a small forest where new housing is being developed. With façades made of sawed wood that filters direct sunlight, the building "complies with the highest standards for environmentally friendly and long-term sound construction" and was granted a 2011 Stockholm Urban Environment Award. A semi-enclosed entrance courtyard that allows parents and children space to meet or to depart is part of an "organic layout" that "encourages movement as space becomes continuous and creates both exterior and interior rooms of challenging shapes." Windows are placed at different heights to provide for the size of children and views of the area, while of course bringing natural light into the school. The unorthodox school plan provides for a section or "flat" reserved to each group of children, together with a common interior plaza where the groups interact. The main space is complemented with separate ateliers for water projects and art, as well as small secluded group rooms for rest and quiet activities.

Der Kindergarten wurde zwischen einem ehemaligen Stadt- und Industriegebiet und einem kleinen Waldgebiet realisiert, in dem ein neues Wohngebiet entsteht. Der Bau mit seiner Fassade aus Holzlatten, die zugleich als Sonnenschutz dienen, „wird höchsten Ansprüchen an umweltgerechtes und langlebiges, solides Bauen gerecht" und wurde 2011 mit dem Stadt-Umweltpreis der Stockholmer Handelskammer ausgezeichnet. Der in einem geschützten Innenhof gelegene Eingangsbereich, in dem sich Eltern und Kinder treffen können, ist Teil des „organischen Grundrisses", der „Bewegung fördert, indem er den Raum als Kontinuum definiert und Innen- und Außenräume in ungewöhnlichen Formen entstehen lässt". Fenster wurden in unterschiedlicher Höhe platziert, um der Größe der Kinder Rechnung zu tragen und den Blick in das Umfeld zu öffnen und natürlich Tageslicht in den Bau zu lassen. Durch den ungewöhnlichen Grundriss entsteht für die einzelnen Gruppenbereiche oder „Wohneinheiten" ein gemeinsam genutzter zentraler Spielbereich. Ergänzend zum Gemeinschaftsbereich gibt es Ateliers für Wasserspiele und Kunstprojekte sowie kleinere Gruppenräume für die Mittagsruhe und stille Beschäftigungen.

Le jardin d'enfants a été construit entre une ancienne zone urbaine et industrielle et un petit bois où de nouveaux logements sont actuellement aménagés. Avec ses façades en bois débité qui filtre l'ensoleillement direct, le bâtiment « répond aux normes les plus élevées en matière de construction respectueuse de l'environnement et rationnelle à long terme » et a reçu en 2011 un prix de la ville de Stockholm pour l'environnement urbain. La cour d'entrée pas entièrement fermée dans laquelle les parents et les enfants peuvent se retrouver ou se séparer fait partie d'une « disposition organique » qui « favorise le mouvement au fur et à mesure que la surface prend une forme continue et crée des espaces intérieurs et extérieurs aux formes stimulantes ». Les fenêtres sont placées à différentes hauteurs correspondant à la taille des enfants et leur permet de voir à l'extérieur tout en laissant pénétrer, bien sûr, la lumière du jour à l'intérieur. Le plan irrégulier prévoit une section ou « appartement » pour chaque groupe d'enfants et une aire intérieure commune où les groupes peuvent échanger. Des ateliers consacrés aux jeux d'eau et aux activités artistiques complètent l'espace principal, ainsi que des petites pièces à l'écart destinées au repos et aux activités calmes pour chaque groupe.

Above, façade elevations of the nursery school. Right page, view at night with the bright yellow façades and partially screened windows visible.

Oben Fassadenaufrisse des Kindergartens. Rechts abendliche Ansichten, auf denen die gelben Fassaden und die teilweise hinter Sichtschutz verborgenen Fenster zu sehen sind.

Ci-dessus, vues en élévation du jardin d'enfants. Page de droite, vue de nuit avec les façades jaunes lumineuses et les fenêtres partiellement occultées.

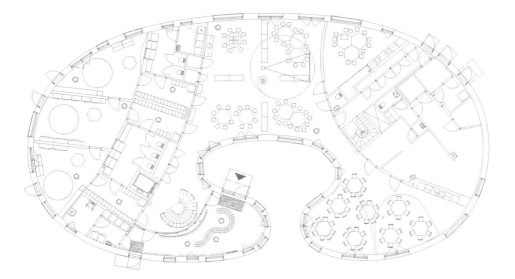

The amoeboid floor plan creates protected internal courtyard space seen in the photo below.

Der amöbenförmige Grundriss definiert einen geschützten Innenhof, der auch auf der Aufnahme unten zu sehen ist.

La forme amiboïde du plan de niveau crée la cour intérieure protégée qu'on voit sur la photo ci-dessous.

Bright colors are the rule as are
bright spaces for the children, as can
be seen in the photographs on this
page.

Leuchtende Farben und helle Räume
für Kinder sind hier die Regel, wie die
Ansichten auf dieser Seite belegen.

Les couleurs vives sont de rigueur,
ainsi que les espaces lumineux pour
les enfants, comme en témoignent
les photos de cette page.

HARADS TREE HOTEL (MIRRORCUBE)
Harads, Sweden, 2009–10

Address: Treehotel/Brittas Pensionat, Edeforsväg 2 A, 960 24 Harads, Sweden,
tel: +46 92 81 04 03, www.treehotel.se
Area: 16 m². Client: Brittas Pensionat. Cost: €90 680
Collaboration: Andreas Helgesson

The architects designed only one of several tree-house "rooms" at the Harads Tree Hotel—the Mirrorcube seen on this double page in its natural setting.

Die Architekten entwarfen nur eines der zahlreichen „Hotelzimmer" für das Harads Tree Hotel. Diese Doppelseite zeigt den Mirrorcube in seiner landschaftlichen Umgebung.

Les architectes n'ont créé que l'une des plusieurs « chambres » de l'hôtel dans les arbres de Harads – le cube miroir photographié dans son cadre naturel sur cette double page.

This tree-house hotel room, called Mirrorcube, is located in the north of Sweden. The structure designed by Tham & Videgård is made in good part of lightweight aluminum. Hung around a tree, it is 4 x 4 x 4 meters in size and is clad in mirrored glass. Plywood is employed for the interiors and the tree house offers a 360° view of the forest surroundings. The structure allows for a double bed, kitchenette, bath, living room, and a roof terrace. Intended for two people, the Mirrorcube can be acceded to by a rope ladder or a rope bridge. Managed by a small nearby hotel called Brittas Pensionat, the structure is meant as a prototype for at least 10 other similar tree-house hotel rooms, some of which have already been designed and built by other architects.

Der sogenannte Mirrorcube, ein Hotelzimmer in einem Baumhaus, liegt in Nordschweden. Der Entwurf von Tham & Videgård wurde weitgehend aus Leichtalumi-nium realisiert. Die 4 x 4 x 4 m große Konstruktion hängt an einem Baum und ist mit Spiegelglas verkleidet. Beim Innenausbau des Baumhauses kamen Sperrholzplatten zum Einsatz. Von hier aus bietet sich ein 360°-Ausblick in die waldige Umgebung. Das Haus bietet Platz für Doppelbett, Küchenzeile, Bad, Wohnbereich und eine Dachter-rasse. Das für zwei Personen geplante Baumhaus ist über eine Strickleiter oder eine Hängebrücke erreichbar. Der von Brittas Pensionat, einem kleinen Hotel in der Gegend, verwaltete Bau ist Prototyp für mindestens zehn weitere ähnliche Baumhaushotels von weiteren Architekten.

L'hôtel dans les arbres, baptisé Mirrorcube (cube de verre), se trouve dans le Nord de la Suède. La structure imaginée par Tham & Videgård est essentiellement faite d'aluminium léger. Le cube de 4 x 4 x 4 m accroché autour d'un arbre est revêtu de verre miroir. L'intérieur est en contreplaqué et les fenêtres permettent une vue à 360° de la forêt alentour. L'ensemble comprend un lit double, une kitchenette, une salle de bains, un salon et un toit en terrasse. Prévu pour loger deux personnes, le cube est accessible par une échelle de corde ou un pont de corde. Exploité par un petit hôtel du voisinage, la pension Brittas Pensionat, la structure est le prototype d'au moins dix autres chambres dans les arbres semblables, dont certaines ont été imaginées et construites par d'autres architectes.

Suspended in a tree with only relatively light wire to stabilize the structure, the Mirrorcube appears to almost hover in space, reflecting the trees and sky around it.

Der an einem Baum abgehängte Mirrorcube wird lediglich durch dünne Stahlkabel stabilisiert und scheint im Raum zu schweben. Im Kubus spiegeln sich Bäume und Himmel.

Accroché dans un arbre par des câbles assez légers pour stabiliser la structure, le cube semble flotter dans l'espace et reflète les arbres et le ciel alentour.

Left and below, the interiors of the Mirrorcube with a ladder leading up to the top level.

Links und unten Blicke in den Mirrorcube; eine Leiter führt zur oberen Ebene.

À gauche et ci-dessous, l'intérieur du cube et l'échelle qui mène au niveau supérieur.

At nightfall, with its interior lights on, the Mirrorcube glows from within at the same time as it continues to mimic its surroundings perfectly.

In der Abenddämmerung leuchtet der Mirrorcube, sobald das Licht eingeschaltet wird. Dabei ist er das (spiegelnde) Ebenbild seiner Umgebung.

À la tombée de la nuit, lorsque l'intérieur est éclairé, le cube brille de l'intérieur tout en continuant de reproduire parfaitement son environnement.

THREEFOLD ARCHITECTS

Threefold Architects
Great Western Studios
Studio 203
65 Alfred Road
London W2 5EU
UK

Tel: +44 20 89 69 23 23 / Fax: +44 20 75 04 87 04
E-mail: info@threefoldarchitects.com
Web: www.threefoldarchitects.com

JACK HOSEA was born in 1975 in Norwich, UK. He received his RIBA Part 1 B.Sc. in Architecture from the Bartlett School of Architecture, University College London (1995–98), and his Part 2 (2000–01), and Part 3 (2004) diplomas from the same school. He worked in the office of Michael Hopkins (London, 1999–2001), DMWR Architects (London, 2001–02), Big Brown Dog Architects (London, 2002–04), and was a founding Partner of Threefold Architects (2004). **MATTHEW DRISCOLL** was born in 1976 in London. He also received the RIBA Part 1, Part 2, and Part 3 qualifications from the Bartlett School of Architecture (1994–2004). He worked for Michael Hopkins and Partners (London, 1997–99), Sanei Hopkins Architects (London, 2000–01), and Niall McLaughlin Architects (London, 2001–04), before creating Threefold Architects with Jack Hosea. **RENEE SEARLE** was born in 1976 in Kuala Lumpur. Having studied at the Cooper Union (New York, 1999–2000) and the Bartlett (1995–2004), she joined Threefold as a Director, designer, and project leader in 2009. Their recent work includes Pure Groove (London, 2008); the Ladderstile House, a sustainable family home (Richmond, London, 2006–09, published here); the Apprentice Store, the conversion of Grade II listed structures into a family home (Bath, 2009); the mixed-use (office and residential) project in Turner Street, Whitechapel (London, 2010); and the ongoing Hurst Avenue House (London, 2009–), all in the UK.

JACK HOSEA wurde 1975 in Norwich, GB, geboren. Er absolvierte seinen RIBA-Abschluss in Architektur (Part 1) an der Bartlett School of Architecture am University College London (1995–98) sowie seine Diplome für Part 2 (2000–01) und Part 3 (2004) an derselben Hochschule. Er arbeitete für Michael Hopkins (London, 1999–2001), DMWR Architects (London, 2001–02) und Big Brown Dog Architects (London, 2002–04) und ist Gründungspartner bei Threefold Architects (2004). **MATTHEW DRISCOLL** wurde 1976 in London geboren. Auch er absolvierte seine Abschlüsse RIBA Part 1, Part 2 und Part 3 an der Bartlett School of Architecture (1994–2004). Er arbeitete für Michael Hopkins and Partners (London, 1997–99), Sanei Hopkins Architects (London, 2000–01), und Niall McLaughlin Architects (London, 2001–04), ehe er mit Jack Hosea Threefold Architects gründete. **RENEE SEARLE** wurde 1976 in Kuala Lumpur geboren. Nach ihrem Studium an der Cooper Union (New York, 1999–2000) und der Bartlett (1995–2004) schloss sie sich Threefold 2009 als Direktorin für Entwurf und Projektleiterin an. Zu ihren jüngeren Projekten zählen Pure Groove (London, 2008), das Ladderstile House, ein nachhaltiges Einfamilienhaus (Richmond, London, 2006–09, hier vorgestellt), Apprentice Store, der Umbau denkmalgeschützter Altbauten zu einem Einfamilienhaus (Bath, 2009), ein Büro- und Wohnhaus an der Turner Street, Whitechapel (London, 2010) sowie das aktuell in Planung befindliche Hurst Avenue House (London, 2009–), alle in Großbritannien.

JACK HOSEA est né en 1975 à Norwich, en Grande-Bretagne. Il est titulaire d'un B.Sc en architecture RIBA (partie 1) obtenu à l'École d'architecture Bartlett de l'University College de Londres (1995–98), ainsi que des diplômes des parties 2 (2000–01) et 3 (2004). Il a travaillé à l'agence Michael Hopkins (Londres, 1999–2001), chez DMWR Architects (Londres, 2001–02), Big Brown Dog Architects (Londres, 2002–04) et est l'un des partenaires fondateurs de Threefold Architects (2004). **MATTHEW DRISCOLL** est né en 1976 à Londres. Il a également obtenu les diplômes RIBA parties 1, 2 et 3 à l'École d'architecture Bartlett (1994–2004). Il a travaillé pour Michael Hopkins and Partners (Londres, 1997–99), Sanei Hopkins Architects (Londres, 2000–01) et Niall McLaughlin Architects (Londres, 2001–04) avant de créer Threefold Architects avec Jack Hosea. **RENEE SEARLE** est née en 1976 à Kuala Lumpur. Après des études à la Cooper Union (New York, 1999–2000) et Bartlett (1995–2004), elle a rejoint Threefold en tant que directrice, designer et chef de projet en 2009. Leurs dernières réalisations comprennent le siège de Pure Groove (Londres, 2008) ; la Ladderstile House, maison familiale durable (Richmond, Londres, 2006–09, publiée ici) ; l'Apprentice Store, reconversion en maison familiale de structures classées en catégorie II (Bath, 2009) ; le projet à usage mixte (bureau et résidentiel) de Turner Street, Whitechapel (Londres, 2010) et la maison en cours de construction de Hurst Avenue (Londres, 2009), toutes en Grande-Bretagne.

LADDERSTILE HOUSE
Richmond, London, UK, 2006–09

Address: n/a. Area: 444 m²
Client: Mr and Mrs Devoy. Cost: not disclosed

The architects clearly master the layering of materials and effects, as can be seen in this image of the swimming pool with its entirely open façade.

Wie meisterhaft die Architekten die Schichtung verschiedener Materialien und Effekte beherrschen, belegt unter anderem die Ansicht des Schwimmbads mit vollständig zu öffnender Glasfront.

Les architectes ont parfaitement maîtrisé la superposition de matériaux et d'effets, on le voit sur cette photo de la piscine et de sa façade complètement ouverte.

Wood is present in ample quantities, but there are also contrasts with metal and stone, brick and trees in this enclosed outdoor space.

Holz ist deutlich omnipräsent, kontrastiert in diesem geschützten Innenhof jedoch mit Metall und Stein, Ziegeln und Begrünung.

Le bois est présent en abondance, mais cet espace extérieur clos présente aussi des contrastes entre le métal et la pierre, les briques et les arbres.

This large, newly built residence, described as a "contemporary courtyard home," borders Richmond Park and is near Ladderstile Gate. Exposed timber beams span the site at the level of the first floor. The main living spaces are on the eastern side of the site beneath these beams, and are glazed along the side facing a 320-square-meter courtyard. The eastern elevation is clad in brick. An indoor swimming pool connects the two main wings of the house. A block facing south over the swimming pool contains two bedroom suites. Reusable materials, mainly bricks and rubble from the old house demolished on the site, were recycled. The buildings' superstructure is a prefabricated solid panel system; the walls, floors, roofs, and structural beams are made from sustainably sourced cross-laminated solid spruce. The prefabrication system employed allowed the house to be erected on site in under two weeks. Perforated screens and a planted wall system developed for the project also confirm its sustainable credentials. Rainwater is collected and stored in a 10 000-liter tank and is used to irrigate the green walls, sedum roof, and landscaped courtyards. Geothermal heating, heat exchangers, and high levels of insulation throughout underline the desire of the architects and the clients to create a sustainable residence.

Der große Neubau, ein als „zeitgenössisches Hofhaus" gestaltetes Einfamilienhaus, grenzt an Richmond Park und liegt nicht weit von Ladderstile Gate. Freilie-gende Holzträger überspannen das Grundstück auf Höhe des ersten Stocks. Die Hauptwohnräume liegen an der Ostseite des Grundstücks unterhalb dieser Träger und bieten dank verglaster Fronten den Blick in einen 320 m² großen Innenhof. Die Ostfassaden wurden verklinkert. Ein Innenpool verbindet die beiden Hauptflügel des Hau-ses. In einem Trakt über dem Pool, mit Blick nach Süden, liegen zwei Schlafzimmer mit Nebenräumen. Verwertbare Materialien wie Ziegel und Schutt vom abgerissenen Vorgängerbau wurden recycelt. Der Oberbau des Hauses wurde in Plattenbauweise realisiert, Wände, Böden, Decken und Träger aus massivem Fichten-Brettsperrholz aus nachhaltiger Forstwirtschaft gefertigt. Dank des Fertigbausystems konnte das Haus vor Ort in weniger als zwei Wochen errichtet werden. Perforierte Wandschirme und eine begrünte Wand unterstreichen die Nachhaltigkeit des Projekts. Regenwasser wird in einem 10 000-Liter-Tank gesammelt und dient zur Bewässerung der begrünten Wände sowie des mit Sedum begrünten Dachs und der begrünten Innenhöfe. Eine Erdwärmeheizung, Wärmetauscher und eine hohe Dämmung zeugen vom Engagement der Architekten und Bauherren für nachhaltiges Wohnen.

Cette grande résidence nouvellement construite et décrite comme une « maison contemporaine à cour » est située en bordure du Richmond Park, à proximité de Ladderstile Gate. Des poutres apparentes en bois enjambent l'ensemble au niveau du premier étage. Les principaux espaces à vivre sont situés du côté est, sous ces poutres, et sont vitrés sur le côté, face à une cour de 320 m². La façade est présente un revêtement de briques. Les deux ailes principales de la maison sont reliées par une piscine intérieure. Un bloc face au sud surplombe la piscine et abrite deux suites avec chambres. Des matériaux réutilisables ont été recyclés, surtout des briques et des gravats de l'ancienne maison démolie qui occupait auparavant le site. La superstructure est un système de solides panneaux préfabriqués, tandis que les murs, sols, toits et poutres de charpente sont en lamellé croisé d'épicéa massif issu de forêts gérées durablement. La préfabrication a permis à la maison d'être construite en moins de deux semaines. Des écrans perforés et un système de mur végétalisé développé pour le projet confirment également son caractère durable. L'eau de pluie est récupé-rée et stockée dans un réservoir de 10 000 l pour arroser la végétation des murs, le toit en sedum et les cours paysagères. Un chauffage géothermique, des échangeurs de chaleur et un niveau d'isolation élevé soulignent la volonté des architectes et de leurs clients de construire une maison durable.

The house is articulated around
layers and surfaces, wood, glass and
screens, as well as a vertical garden
seen to the right.

*Das Haus artikuliert sich in Schichten
und Oberflächen, Holz, Glas und
Wandschirmen sowie einem vertikalen
Garten rechts im Bild.*

*La maison s'articule en plusieurs
couches et surfaces autour du bois,
du verre et d'écrans perforés, sans
oublier le jardin vertical qu'on voit
à droite.*

Privacy is preserved in the bath area
in spite of the full-height glazing.
Wood is present in almost every
space.

Trotz geschosshoher Verglasung wird
auch im Bad Privatsphäre gewahrt.
Holz ist in fast allen Räumen präsent.

La salle de bains préserve l'intimité
malgré son vitrage sur toute la hauteur. Le bois est présent dans
presque toutes les pièces.

Glazed walls open entirely making the limit between inside and outside in this dining space ambiguous. Though straight lines dominate, the layering of materials and spaces gives a surprising variety to these spaces.

Glasfronten, die sich vollständig öffnen lassen, lassen die Grenzen von Innen und Außen verschwimmen, wie hier im Essbereich. Trotz ihrer Geradlinigkeit wirkt die Architektur dank der Schichtung verschiedener Materialien und Räume erstaunlich facettenreich.

Les parois vitrées s'ouvrent entièrement et rendent floues les limites entre intérieur et extérieur dans cette salle à manger. Si les lignes droites dominent, les matériaux et espaces superposés confèrent une étonnante diversité aux différentes pièces.

BERNARD TSCHUMI

Bernard Tschumi Architects
227 West 17th Street
New York, NY 10011
USA
Tel: +1 212 807 6340 / Fax: +1 212 242 3693
E-mail: nyc@tschumi.com / Web: www.tschumi.com

BERNARD TSCHUMI was born in Lausanne, Switzerland, in 1944. He studied in Paris and at the ETH, Zurich. He taught at the Architectural Association (AA), London (1970–79), and at Princeton (1976–80). He was Dean of the Graduate School of Architecture, Planning, and Preservation of Columbia University in New York from 1984 to 2003. He opened his own office, Bernard Tschumi Architects (Paris, New York), in 1981. Major projects include Second Prize in the Kansai International Airport Competition (Japan, 1988); the Video Gallery (Groningen, the Netherlands, 1990); Parc de la Villette (Paris, France, 1982–95); Le Fresnoy National Studio for Contemporary Arts (Tourcoing, France, 1991–97); the Lerner Student Center, Columbia University (New York, New York, USA, 1994–98); the School of Architecture (Marne-la-Vallée, France, 1994–98); the Interface Flon Train Station in Lausanne (Switzerland, 2001); the Vacheron Constantin Headquarters (Geneva, Switzerland, 2004); the Linder Athletic Center at the University of Cincinnati (Cincinnati, Ohio, USA, 2006); and the Zénith Concert Hall in Limoges (France, 2007). Among the firm's more recent projects are BLUE, a 17-story residential tower on the Lower East Side of New York (New York, USA, 2007); the New Acropolis Museum in Athens (Greece, 2004–09); a Cultural Center and Concert Hall in Bordeaux-Cenon (France, 2010); and the Alésia Museum and Archeological Park (Alésia, France, 2010–12, published here). Currently in progress are a museum for African-American Art and Culture in Prince George's County (Maryland, USA); and an expansion to the Tschumi-designed headquarters for the watch manufacturer Vacheron Constantin (Geneva, Switzerland).

BERNARD TSCHUMI wurde 1944 in Lausanne, Schweiz, geboren. Er studierte in Paris sowie an der ETH Zürich. Er lehrte an der Architectural Association (AA), London (1970–79) und der Princeton University (1976–80). Von 1984 bis 2003 war er Dekan der Graduiertenfakultät für Architektur, Stadtplanung und Denkmalschutz der Columbia University in New York. 1981 gründete er sein Büro Bernard Tschumi Architects (Paris, New York). Wichtige Projekte sind unter anderem der zweite Preis im Wettbewerb für den Internationalen Flughafen Kansai (Japan, 1988), die Video Gallery (Groningen, Niederlande, 1990), der Parc de la Villette (Paris, Frankreich, 1982–95), das Medienzentrum Le Fresnoy (Tourcoing, France, 1991–97), das Lerner Student Center, Columbia University (New York, USA, 1994–98), die Architekturhochschule Marne-la-Vallée (Frankreich, 1994–98), der Bahnhof Interface Flon in Lausanne (Schweiz, 2001), die Zentrale von Vacheron Constantin (Genf, Schweiz, 2004), das Linder-Athletikzentrum der University of Cincinnati (Cincinnati, Ohio, USA, 2006) und die Zénith-Konzerthalle in Limoges (Frankreich, 2007). Jüngere Projekte des Büros sind BLUE, ein 17-stöckiges Apartmenthochhaus an der Lower East Side in New York (2007), das neue Akropolis-Museum in Athen (2004–09), ein Kulturzentrum mit Konzerthalle in Bordeaux-Cenon (Frankreich, 2010) sowie der MuséoParc von Alésia (Alésia, France, 2010–12, hier vorgestellt). In Planung sind derzeit ein Museum für Afroamerikanische Kunst und Kultur in Prince George's County (Maryland, USA) und eine Erweiterung der von Tschumi entworfenen Zentrale für den Uhrenhersteller Vacheron Constantin (Genf, Schweiz).

BERNARD TSCHUMI est né à Lausanne en 1944. Il a fait ses études à Paris et à l'ETH de Zurich. Il a enseigné à l'Architectural Association (AA) de Londres (1970–79) et à Princeton (1976–80). Il a été doyen de la Graduate School of Architecture, Planning, and Preservation de l'université Columbia à New York entre 1984 et 2003. Il a ouvert son agence, Bernard Tschumi Architects (Paris, New York), en 1981. Ses projets principaux comprennent le deuxième prix du concours pour l'aéroport international du Kansai (Japon, 1988) ; la Video Gallery (Groningue, Pays-Bas, 1990) ; le parc de la Villette (Paris, 1982–95) ; le Studio national des arts contemporain Le Fresnoy (Tourcoing, France, 1991–97) ; le Centre étudiant Lerner de l'université Columbia (New York, 1994–98) ; l'École d'architecture (Marne-la-Vallée, France, 1994–98) ; la gare Interface Flon de Lausanne (2001) ; le siège de Vacheron Constantin (Genève, 2004) ; le Centre sportif Linder de l'université de Cincinnati (Cincinnati, Ohio, 2006) et la salle de concerts Zénith de Limoges (2007). Parmi les réalisations plus récentes de la société, on peut citer BLUE, une tour de logements de 17 étages du Lower East Side de New York (2007) ; le nouveau musée de l'Acropole d'Athènes (2004–09) ; un centre culturel et salle de concerts à Bordeaux-Cenon (2010) et le musée et parc archéologique d'Alésia (Alésia, France, 2010–12, publié ici). Bernard Tschumi travaille actuellement à un musée d'art et de culture afro-américains dans le comté de Prince George's (Maryland, États-Unis) et à une extension du siège de l'horloger Vacheron Constantin dont il est à l'origine (Genève).

ALÉSIA MUSEUM AND ARCHEOLOGICAL PARK

Alésia, France, 2010–12

Address: 1 Route des Trois Ormeaux, 21150 Alise-Sainte-Reine, Burgundy, France,
tel: +33 3 80 96 96 23, www.alesia.com
Area: 7000 m². Client: Bourgogne Region, France
Cost: not disclosed

Using a basic circular or cylindrical form, Bernard Tschumi succeeds in giving this structure a connection to its site and its history.

Ausgehend von einer schlichten Rundform gelingt es Bernard Tschumi, den Bau in seinen landschaftlichen und historischen Kontext einzubinden.

À l'aide d'une forme de base circulaire, ou cylindrique, Bernard Tschumi est parvenu à ancrer sa structure dans le site et son histoire.

The project marks an archeological site in central France and commemorates the history of the battle between Julius Caesar and the Gauls in 52 B.C. The concept involves the recreation of battlements and earthworks as they might have existed at the time. The partially buried stone circular museum itself is located on a hilltop near a medieval town. A rooftop deck allows visitors to survey the site, which remains much as it was more than 2000 years ago. The separate visitor center, a wooden building, is set nearly a kilometer away close to the position the Romans held below the town. The architects explain: "The roof of the round building is a garden planted with trees and grass, camouflaging the presence of the building when seen from the town above. Visitors may look onto reconstructions of the Roman battlements from the roof garden, or stroll down a path to experience the reconstitutions first-hand." Tschumi concludes: "Giving maximum presence to historical events and respecting the sensitive insertion of buildings into their natural environment responds to the ambition of the project while reflecting the imperative of 'modesty' demanded by archeologists. To be both visible and invisible is the paradox and challenge of the project."

Der MuséoParc-Komplex an einer Grabungsstätte in Zentralfrankreich folgt den Spuren der Schlacht zwischen Julius Caesar und den Galliern 52 v. Chr. Teil des Museumskonzepts ist unter anderem die historische Rekonstruktion von Befestigungen und Erdbauten der damaligen Zeit. Der teilweise im Boden versenkte Rundbau des Museums liegt auf einem Hügel in der Nähe einer mittelalterlichen Stadt. Von einer Dachterrasse haben die Besucher Blick über das gesamte Gelände, das weitgehend so aussieht wie vor über 2000 Jahren. Das separate Besucherzentrum, ein Holzbau, liegt rund einen Kilometer von den historischen römischen Stellungen unterhalb der Stadt. Die Architekten führen aus: „Das Dach des Rundbaus ist als Garten mit Rasen und Bäumen gestaltet, was den Bau aus Sicht der höher gelegenen Stadt fast im Umfeld verschwinden lässt. Besucher können vom Dachgarten aus die rekonstruierten römischen Befestigungsanlagen sehen oder auf einem schmalen Weg direkt durch die Rekonstruktion laufen." Tschumi schließt: „Die Entscheidung, den historischen Ereignissen absolute Priorität einzuräumen und die Bauten sensibel in ihr landschaftliches Umfeld einzufügen, entspricht dem ambitionierten Projekt und darüber hinaus der von den Archäologen gewünschten ‚Bescheidenheit'. Sichtbar und zugleich unsichtbar zu sein ist Paradox und Herausforderung dieses Projekts."

Le projet marque un site archéologique dans le Centre de la France et commémore l'histoire de la bataille entre Jules César et les Gaulois en 52 av. J.-C. Le concept comprend la reconstruction de fortifications et d'ouvrages de terrassement tels qu'ils ont pu exister à l'époque. Le musée circulaire construit en pierre, en partie enterré, occupe le sommet d'une colline non loin d'une ville médiévale. Une galerie autour du toit permet aux visiteurs d'observer le site, en grande partie inchangé depuis plus de 2000 ans. Le centre d'accueil des visiteurs, en bois, se trouve à un kilomètre, près de la position que les Romains tenaient alors en contrebas de la ville. Les architectes expliquent que « le toit du bâtiment rond est un jardin planté d'arbres et de pelouse qui dissimulent sa présence depuis la ville en contrebas. Les visiteurs peuvent observer les fortifications romaines reconstruites depuis le jardin ou descendre un sentier pour vivre les reconstitutions de première main ». Tschumi conclut par ces mots : « L'ambition de ce projet est de donner une présence maximale aux événements historiques et de respecter l'intégration délicate des bâtiments dans la nature environnante tout en tenant compte des impératifs de "modestie" exigés par les archéologues. Être à la fois visible et invisible, c'est le paradoxe et le défi de ce projet. »

Trees on the upper level and terraces below encircle the building, giving it a rapport with the trees on the site and allowing visitors to view the area from any point.

Bäume auf der Dachterrasse und umlaufende Balkone in den Geschossen darunter stellen den Bezug zum Baumbestand auf dem Gelände her und erlauben den Besuchern, die Gegend allseitig zu überblicken.

Les arbres à l'étage supérieur et les terrasses en dessous encerclent le bâtiment et répondent aux arbres du site tout en permettant aux visiteurs de l'admirer de toutes parts.

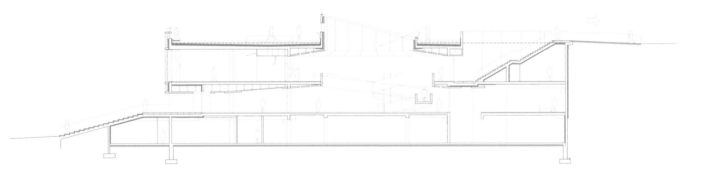

Plans (below) show the perfectly circular plan of the museum. The center of Tschumi's cylinder is the suspended disk and the large open space beneath it.

Grundrisse (unten) zeigen die kompromisslose Rundform des Museums. Herzstück des von Tschumi geplanten „Zylinders" ist eine schwebende Scheibe über einem großzügigen offenen Foyer.

Les plans (ci-dessous) montrent la forme parfaitement circulaire du musée. Au centre du cylindre imaginé par Tschumi se trouve le disque suspendu au-dessus du vaste espace ouvert.

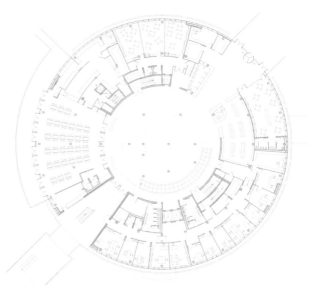

UNSANGDONG

Unsandong
GF Penta House
163–43 Haewha, Jongno
Seoul 110–530
South Korea

Tel: +82 2 764 8401
Fax: +82 2 764 8403
E-mail: usdspace@hanmail.net
Web: www.usdspace.com

Born in 1964, **JANG YOON GYOO** received his B.S. (1987) and M.Arch (1990) degrees from Seoul National University. He was a Project Designer for Seoul Architecture Consultants (1990–94) and a Partner with Artech Architects & Partners (1995–96), before founding his own office, Jang Yoon Gyoo Experimental Studio (1995–2001). He has been a Principal of Unsangdong since 2001. He also directs the JungMiso Art Gallery. **SHIN CHANG HOON** was born in 1970, and graduated in Architectural Engineering from Yeungnam University. He has an M.Arch degree from the University of Seoul. Their work includes Kring, Kumho Compound Culture Complex (Seoul, 2008); Thousand Palace, an installation for the Hi Seoul Festival Stage (Seoul, 2009); E+ Green Home, Jeon Dae (Cheo In, Po Gok, Yong In, Kyeong Gi, 2010–11, published here); and they are currently completing the Hyundai Motor Group Pavilion for the 2012 Yeosu Exhibition, all in South Korea.

JANG YOON GYOO, geboren 1964, absolvierte seinen B.S. (1987) und seinen M.Arch (1990) an der Seoul National University. Er war Projektplaner bei Seoul Architecture Consultants (1990–94) und Partner bei Artech Architects & Partners (1995–96), bevor er sein eigenes Büro Jang Yoon Gyoo Experimental Studio (1995–2001) gründete. Seit 2001 ist er Geschäftsführer bei Unsangdong und leitet darüber hinaus die JungMiso Art Gallery. **SHIN CHANG HOON**, geboren 1970, schloss sein Studium der Architektur und Bauplanung an der Yeungnam University ab. Seinen M.Arch absolvierte er an der University of Seoul. Zu den Projekten des Büros zählen der Kring-Kumho-Kulturkomplex (Seoul, 2008), Thousand Palace, eine Bühneninstallation für das Hi Seoul Festival (Seoul, 2009), E+ Green Home, Jeon Dae (Cheo In, Po Gok, Yong In, Kyeong Gi, 2010–11, hier vorgestellt). Aktuell arbeiten sie an der Fertigstellung des Pavillons der Hyundai-Gruppe für die Messe in Yeosu 2012, alle in Südkorea.

Né en 1964, **JANG YOON GYOO** est titulaire d'un B.S. (1987) et d'un M.Arch (1990) de l'université nationale de Séoul. Il a été concepteur de projets pour Seoul Architecture Consultants (1990–94) et partenaire d'Artech Architects & Partners (1995–96) avant de fonder son agence, Jang Yoon Gyoo Experimental Studio (1995–2001). Il dirige Unsangdong depuis 2001. Il est aussi directeur de la galerie d'art JungMiso. **SHIN CHANG HOON** est né en 1970, il est diplômé en génie du bâtiment de l'université Yeungnam et possède un M.Arch de l'université de Séoul. Leurs travaux comprennent le Kring, centre culturel du groupe Kumho (Séoul, 2008); Thousand Palace, une installation pour la scène du festival Hi Seoul (Séoul, 2009); E+ Green Home, Jeon Dae (Cheo In, Po Gok, Yong In, Kyeong Gi, 2010–11, publiée ici), tous en Corée-du-Sud. Ils sont en train d'achever le pavillon du groupe Hyundai pour l'exposition de Yeosu en 2012.

E+ GREEN HOME

Jeon Dae, Cheo In, Po Gok, Yong In, Kyeong Gi, South Korea, 2010–11

Address: n/a. Area: 344 m²
Client: Kolon E&C. Cost: not disclosed

This **E+ GREEN HOME** located south of Seoul uses a synthesis of optimized green technology and an "intelligent energy-saving system." The architects state: "Our aim was not to juxtapose green technologies with just a mindless architectural shape, we made a stringent effort to combine technology and architecture in a subtle way." The roof system, dubbed "Rooftecture" by Unsangdong, minimizes energy loss and solar gain while maximizing rainwater recovery. They compare it to a mountain that "efficiently uses natural resources such as the sun, water, earth, and wind." The house uses the StoTherm Classic external wall insulation system made with EPS board and cement-free components, Stellac thermally treated wood, building-integrated photovoltaics, which are materials that are used to replace conventional building materials in parts of the building envelope, high-efficiency solar thermal collectors, a wind turbine, and a geothermal heat pump. This is the first PHI (Passive House Institute)–certified residence in South Korea.

Das **E+ GREEN HOME** im Süden von Seoul kombiniert optimierte grüne Technologien und ein „intelligentes Energiesparsystem". Die Architekten erklären: „Uns ging es darum, grüne Technologien nicht einfach in eine nichtssagende architektonische Hülle zu stecken, stattdessen haben wir uns konsequent bemüht, Technik und Architektur fast unmerklich miteinander zu verbinden." Das Dachsystem, von Unsangdong „Rooftecture" genannt, minimiert Energieverluste und Solargewinn und maximiert zugleich die Regenwassernutzung. Die Architekten ziehen den Vergleich zu einem Berg, der „effizient natürliche Ressourcen nutzt, wie etwa Sonne, Wasser, Erde und Wind". Zum Einsatz kam ein aufwendiges Dämmsystem (StoTherm) – eine Außendämmung aus EPS-Platten und zementfreien Komponenten – sowie Thermoholz nach dem Stellac-Verfahren, integrierte Photovoltaik-Elemente (alles Materialien, die teilweise konventionelle Baustoffe in der Gebäudehülle ersetzen), hocheffiziente Sonnenkollektoren, eine Windturbine und eine Erdwärmepumpe. Das Haus wurde vom PHI (Passivhaus Institut) als erstes Passivhaus Südkoreas zertifiziert.

Située au Sud de Séoul, la **E+ GREEN HOME** a recours à une synthèse de technologie verte optimisée et d'un « système d'économies d'énergie intelligent ». Les architectes expliquent : « Nous ne voulions pas simplement juxtaposer des technologies vertes dans une forme architecturale sans caractère, nous avons fait un gros effort pour combiner subtilement technologie et architecture. » Le toit, baptisé « Rooftecture » par Unsangdong, permet de minimiser les pertes d'énergie et l'apport solaire, tout en maximisant la récupération de l'eau de pluie. Il est comparé à une montagne qui « exploite efficacement des ressources naturelles telles que le soleil, l'eau, la terre et le vent ». La maison est équipée du système d'isolation extérieure StoTherm Classic avec panneaux PSE et composants sans ciment, de bois thermo-traité Stellac, d'éléments photovoltaïques intégrés – des matériaux utilisés en lieu et place des matériaux de construction traditionnels à certains endroits de l'enveloppe du bâtiment, de capteurs thermiques solaires haute efficacité, d'une éolienne et d'une pompe à chaleur géothermique. C'est la première maison certifiée PHI (Passivhaus Institut) en Corée-du-Sud.

The house appears very different depending on the angle of view—with solar panels and angled surfaces on one elevation (left page) and a white, schematic profile on the other (this page).

Je nach Blickwinkel zeigt das Haus verschiedene Gesichter – Solarmodule und Schrägen zur einen Seite (links) oder ein weißes, schematisches Profil zur anderen Seite (nebenstehend).

La maison prend une apparence très différente selon l'angle sous lequel elle est observée – panneaux solaires et surfaces anguleuses sur une vue en élévation (page de gauche) ou profil blanc graphique sur l'autre (page de droite).

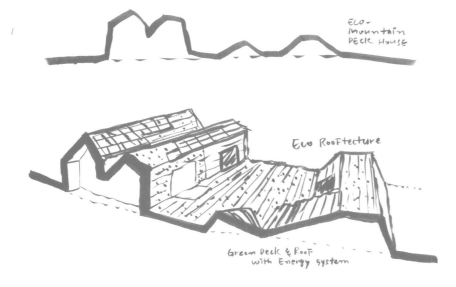

ECO-
Mountain
DECK House

Eco Rooftecture

Green Deck & Roof
with Energy System

Sketches reveal the undulating form
of the house, which assumes an
almost organic profile. Interiors are
functional with natural light permit-
ting the reduction of energy use.

*Skizzen visualisieren die gefaltete
Form des Hauses, das ein fast organi-
sches Profil zeigt. Die Innenräume
sind funktional gehalten. Einfallendes
Tageslicht senkt den Energieverbrauch.*

*Les croquis mettent en évidence la
forme ondulée de la maison qui lui
confère un profil presque organique.
L'intérieur est fonctionnel et la
lumière naturelle permet de réduire
la consommation d'énergie.*

The point of the architects seems to be that interiors can be attractive and functional even when they are conceived to be energy efficient.

Die Architekten stellen unter Beweis, dass auch energieeffizient geplante Interieurs attraktiv und funktional sein können.

Les architectes semblent avoir voulu montrer que des intérieurs pouvaient être agréables et fonctionnels, même lorsqu'ils sont conçus avant tout pour leur efficacité énergétique.

VECTOR ARCHITECTS

Vector Architects
Rm 1903 South Tower, SOHO Shangdu
No. 8 Dongdaqiao Road
Chaoyang District
100020 Beijing
China

Tel: +86 10 5869 9706 / Fax: +86 10 5869 8319
E-mail: info@vectorarchitects.com
Web: www.vectorarchitects.com

GONG DONG received M.Arch degrees from Tsinghua University (Beijing, 1999) and the University of Illinois at Urbana Champaign (2001). During the year 2000, he was an exchange student at the Technische Universitat München (Germany). He worked in the offices of Richard Meier (New York, 2004–05) and Steven Holl (New York, 2005–07), before becoming a founding Partner of Vector Architects (Bejing, 2008). **CHIEN-HO HSU** received his B.Arch degree from Chuanyuan Christian University, Department of Architecture (1992) and his M.Arch from Harvard GSD (1997). He worked for Eisenman Architects (New York, 1997–98 and 2000–01), Gwathmey Siegel (New York, 1998–2000), Pei Cobb Freed (New York, 2001–02), and Thomas Phifer (New York, 2003–06), before joining Vector Architects as a Partner in 2010. Their projects include Apartment E3 (Beijing, 2008); CR Land Guanganmen Green Technology Showroom (Beijing, 2008, published here); CR Land Hefei Dongdajie Sales Pavilion (Hefei, 2009); Zhangjiawo Elementary School (Tianjin, 2008–10); the Chongqing Taoyuanju Community Center (Chongqing, 2010); and the Kunshan Pavilion (Shanghai, 2010–11), all in China.

GONG DONG absolvierte seinen M.Arch an der Tsinghua University (Peking, 1999) und der University of Illinois at Urbana Champaign (2001). 2000 war er Austauschstudent an der Technischen Universität München (Deutschland). Er arbeitete in den Büros von Richard Meier (New York, 2004–05) und Steven Holl (New York, 2005–07), ehe er Gründungspartner bei Vector Architects (Peking, 2008) wurde. **CHIEN-HO HSU** absolvierte seinen B.Arch an der Architekturfakultät der Christlichen Universität Chuanyuan (1992) und seinen M.Arch an der Harvard GSD (1997). Er arbeitete für Eisenman Architects (New York, 1997–98 und 2000–01), Gwathmey Siegel (New York, 1998–2000), Pei Cobb Freed (New York, 2001–02) und Thomas Phifer (New York, 2003–06), bevor er 2010 als Partner zu Vector Architects kam. Zu den Projekten des Büros zählen das Apartment E3 (Peking, 2008), der Showroom für Grüne Technologien in Guanganmen für CR Land (Peking, 2008, hier vorgestellt), ein Verkaufspavillon für CR Land in Hefei Dongdajie (Hefei, 2009), eine Grundschule in Zhangjiawo (Tianjin, 2008–10), ein Gemeindezentrum in Chongqing Taoyuanju (Chongqing, 2010) sowie der Kunshan-Pavillon (Shanghai, 2010–11), alle in China.

GONG DONG a obtenu un M.Arch à l'université Tsinghua (Pékin, 1999) et un autre à l'université de l'Illinois à Urbana Champaign (2001). Il a participé à un échange à l'Université technique de Munich en 2000. Il a travaillé dans les agences de Richard Meier (New York, 2004–05) et Steven Holl (New York, 2005–07) avant de devenir partenaire fondateur de Vector Architects (Pékin, 2008). **CHIEN-HO HSU** est titulaire d'un B.Arch de l'université chrétienne Chuanyuan, département d'architecture (1992) et d'un M.Arch de la Harvard GSD (1997). Il a travaillé pour Eisenman Architects (New York, 1997–98 et 2000–01), Gwathmey Siegel (New York, 1998–2000), Pei Cobb Freed (New York, 2001–02) et Thomas Phifer (New York, 2003–06) avant de rejoindre Vector Architects en tant que partenaire en 2010. Leurs projets comprennent l'appartement E3 (Pékin, 2008) ; l'espace d'exposition de technologies vertes de CR Land à Guanganmen (Pékin, 2008, publié ici) ; le pavillon Hefei Dongdajie de CR Land (Hefei, 2009) ; l'école élémentaire Zhangjiawo (Tianjin, 2008–10) ; le Centre communautaire Taoyuanju de Chongqing (Chongqing, 2010) et le pavillon Kunshan (Shanghai, 2010–11), tous en Chine.

CR LAND GUANGANMEN GREEN TECHNOLOGY SHOWROOM

Beijing, China, 2008

Address: Beijing, China
Area: 450 m². Client: CR Land
Cost: not disclosed

This is a temporary Green Technology Showroom slated for a three-year period of use in connection with one of CR Land's residential projects in Beijing. CR Land (Beijing) Co., Ltd. engages in property development and is a subsidiary of China Resources Land Ltd. The architects aimed to create a "floating installation in a garden which could be built, demolished, and recycled through an easy and straightforward way with the least impact to the planned site." A vertical grass wall and roof were used to improve thermal efficiency and reduce storm-water runoff. Grass panels with an integrated irrigation system were employed on the roof. The architects also sought to visually harmonize the structure with the garden where it was placed. The building was elevated off the ground, greatly reducing excavation and foundation work and facilitating demolition.

Der temporäre Showroom für Grüne Technologien ist zunächst für drei Jahre geplant und wurde im Rahmen einer von CR Land entwickelten Wohnanlage realisiert. CR Land (Peking) ist ein Bauunternehmen und Tochterunternehmen der China Resources Land. Die Architekten wollten eine „schwebende Installation in einem Garten realisieren, die leicht und unkompliziert zu bauen, rückzubauen und recyceln ist und dabei minimale Auswirkungen auf den geplanten Standort hat". Eine vertikale Graswand und ein mit Gras begrüntes Dach tragen zur Energieeffizienz des Baus bei und reduzieren den Regenwasserabfluss. Bei der Dachbegrünung kamen Grassoden und ein Bewässerungssystem zum Einsatz. Den Architekten ging es nicht zuletzt auch darum, den Bau harmonisch in die Grünanlage zu integrieren, in der er liegt. Da der Pavillon über dem Boden aufgeständert wurde, konnten Aushub und Fundamentarbeiten erheblich reduziert werden, was wiederum den Rückbau erleichtert.

Cet espace d'exposition temporaire de technologies vertes est conçu pour être utilisé pendant trois ans, associé à l'un des projets résidentiels de CR Land à Pékin. CR Land (Pékin) Co., Ltd. est une filiale de China Resources Land Ltd. engagée dans la promotion immobilière. Les architectes ont voulu créer une « installation flottante dans un jardin susceptible d'être construite, démolie et recyclée de manière simple et directe, avec un impact réduit au minimum sur le site qui l'accueille ». Un mur vertical et un toit de gazon permettent une meilleure efficacité thermique et réduisent l'écoulement des eaux pluviales. Des panneaux de gazon à système d'irrigation intégré ont été utilisés pour le toit. Les architectes ont aussi cherché à intégrer harmonieusement la structure dans le jardin où elle a été placée. Le bâtiment a été surélevé par rapport au sol, ce qui a permis de réduire considérablement les travaux d'excavation et de fondations, et en facilitera la démolition.

Lifted off the ground, the showroom is covered on three sides by vegetation that serves as an efficient insulator. It is more of a rectangular, elevated tube than an anchored, "permanent" building.

Der über dem Boden aufgeständerte Showroom wurde an drei Seiten begrünt, was zugleich als effiziente Dämmung wirkt. Die Konstruktion wirkt eher wie eine schwebende Röhre als ein „permanenter", im Boden verankerter Bau.

Surélevé par rapport au sol, l'espace d'exposition est recouvert sur trois côtés d'une végétation qui constitue également une isolation efficace. C'est plus un tube rectangulaire surélevé qu'un bâtiment « permanent » arrimé au sol.

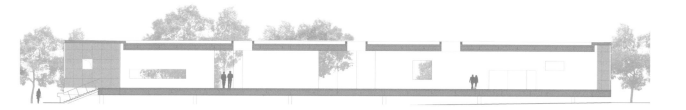

Right, a site plan showing the long, rectangular form of the showroom. The green vertical faces of the building cede to ample glazing and openings so large that the difference between interior and exterior is blurred.

Rechts ein Grundstücksplan, auf dem das gestreckte Rechteck des Showrooms zu erkennen ist. Die vertikal begrünte Fassade wird von großflächiger Verglasung und Fassadenöffnungen unterbrochen: Die Grenzen von Innen- und Außenraum verschwimmen.

À droite, un plan du site montre la forme allongée et rectangulaire de la construction. Les surfaces verticales de végétation cèdent la place à de larges vitrages et des ouvertures si importantes qu'elles gomment la distinction entre intérieur et extérieur.

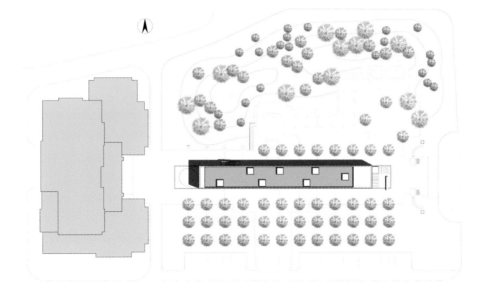

Layered screens of different types divide the space and enliven it, while allowing natural light to be present throughout.

Mehrere Wandschirme verschiedener Machart gliedern und beleben den Raum und lassen zugleich Tageslicht ungehindert in den Raum.

Différents types d'écrans superposés divisent l'espace et l'animent en permettant à la lumière naturelle d'être partout présente.

VO TRONG NGHIA

Vo Trong Nghia Co., Ltd.
85 Bis Phan Ke Binh, Dakao, District 1
Ho Chi Minh City
Vietnam

Tel: +84 8 3829 7763 / Fax: +84 8 3911 0103
E-mail: info@votrongnghia.com
Web: www.votrongnghia.com

VO TRONG NGHIA was born in Quang Binh Province, Vietnam, in 1976. He attended Ha Noi Architecture University (1994) and received a B.Arch degree from the Nagoya Institute of Technology (Japan, 2002), followed by a Master of Civil Engineering from Tokyo University (2004). His major works are the Ho Chi Minh City University of Architecture (HUA) (with Kazuhiro Kojima and Daisuke Sanuki, Ho Chi Minh City, Mekong Delta, 2006), won by an international design competition in 2006; the wNw Café (Binh Duong, 2006); wNw Bar (Binh Duong, 2008); Trung Nguyen Coffee Culture Center (Hanoi, 2008); Bamboo Wing (Dai Lai, Vinh Phuc Province, 2009, published here); the Vietnam Pavilion for Shanghai Expo (Shanghai, China, 2010); Stacking Green (Ho Chi Minh City, 2011, also published here); and Stone Villa (Quangninh, 2011), all in Vietnam unless stated otherwise. The Stacking Green project was designed in collaboration with **DAISUKE SANUKI**, born in 1975 in Japan and educated at the Tokyo University of Science (degrees in 1998 and 2000), and **SHUNRI NISHIZAWA**, born in 1980 in Japan and educated at Tokyo University (B.Arch 2003, M.Arch 2005) before working in the office of Tadao Ando (Osaka, 2005–09). Both Sanuki and Nishizawa were Partners in the firm of Vo Trong Nghia from 2009 to 2011.

VO TRONG NGHIA wurde 1976 in der Provinz Quang Binh, Vietnam, geboren. Er studierte an der Architekturhochschule von Hanoi (1994) und absolvierte zunächst einen B.Arch an der Technischen Universität Nagoya (Japan, 2002) sowie anschließend einen Master in Bauingenieurwesen an der University of Tokyo (2004). Zu seinen wichtigsten Arbeiten zählen die Architekturhochschule in Ho Chi Minh City (HUA) (mit Kazuhiro Kojima und Daisuke Sanuki, Ho Chi Minh City, Mekong-Delta, 2006), Preisträger eines Entwurfswettbewerbs 2006, das wNw Café (Binh Duong, 2006), die wNw Bar (Binh Duong, 2008), das Trung Nguyen Coffee Culture Center (Hanoi, 2008), der Bamboo Wing (Dai Lai, Provinz Vinh Phuc, 2009, hier vorgestellt), der Vietnamesische Pavillon für die Expo Shanghai (Shanghai, China, 2010), Stacking Green (Ho Chi Minh City, 2011, ebenfalls hier vorgestellt) und die Stone Villa (Quangninh, 2011), alle in Vietnam, sofern nicht anders angegeben. Stacking Green entstand in Kollaboration mit **DAISUKE SANUKI**, geboren 1975 in Japan, Studium an der Naturwissenschaftlichen University of Tokyo (Abschlüsse 1998 und 2000), und **SHUNRI NISHIZAWA**, 1980 in Japan geboren, Studium an der University of Tokyo (B.Arch 2003, M.Arch 2005), anschließend tätig bei Tadao Ando (Osaka, 2005–09). Sowohl Sanuki als auch Nishizawa waren von 2009 bis 2011 Partner im Büro von Vo Trong Nghia.

VO TRONG NGHIA, né dans la province de Quang Binh (Viêtnam) en 1976, a étudié à l'Université d'architecture d'Hanoï (1994). Il a obtenu son B.Arch à l'Institut de technologie de Nagoya (Japon, 2002) et un master en ingénierie civile à l'université de Tokyo (2004). Ses réalisations les plus importantes sont l'Université d'architecture d'Hô Chi Minh-Ville (HUA) (avec Kazuhiro Kojima et Daisuke Sanuki, Hô Chi Minh-Ville, delta du Mékong, 2006), projet remporté lors d'un concours international de design en 2006 ; le café wNw (Binh Duong, 2006) ; le bar wNw (Binh Duong, 2008) ; le Centre de la culture du café Trung Nguyen (Hanoï, 2008) ; Bamboo Wing (Dai Lai, province de Vinh Phuc, 2009, publiée ici) ; le pavillon du Viêtnam pour l'Expo de Shanghai (2010) ; la maison Stacking Green (Hô Chi Minh-Ville, 2011, également publiée ici) et la Villa de pierre (Quangninh, 2011), toutes au Viêtnam sauf si spécifié. Le projet Stacking Green a été créé en collaboration avec **DAISUKE SANUKI**, né en 1975 au Japon, qui a fait ses études à l'Université des sciences de Tokyo (diplômes en 1998 et 2000), et **SHUNRI NISHIZAWA**, né en 1980 au Japon, qui a fait ses études à l'université de Tokyo (B.Arch 2003, M.Arch 2005) avant de travailler dans l'agence de Tadao Ando (Osaka, 2005–09). Sanuki comme Nishizawa ont été partenaires dans la société de Vo Trong Nghia de 2009 à 2011.

BAMBOO WING

Dai Lai, Vinh Phuc Province, Vietnam, 2009

Address: Dai Lai, Vinh Phuc Province, Vietnam. Area: 1600 m²
Client: Hong Hac Dai Lai Jsc. Cost: not disclosed

The architects sought to use bamboo both as a finishing material and in structural applications. This building is a pure bamboo structure, using "no steel or other man-made structural materials." A 12-meter open space proves the strength and resilience of the material and is used for wedding parties, live music concerts, and ceremonies. Inspired by bird wings, the structure "is good for capturing the wind." The architect writes: "Inspired by nature, **BAMBOO WING** takes the form of bird wings and floats over the natural landscape of its site situated near Hanoi… With its deep eaves and the water in the open spaces, people feel as if they are living in nature."

Dem Architekten ging es darum, Bambus sowohl als Verblendmaterial als auch als Tragwerk zu nutzen. Der Bau ist eine reine Bambuskonstruktion, die gänzlich auf „Stahl oder künstliche Baumaterialien" verzichtet. Ein offener, 12 m tiefer, überbauter Bereich zeugt von der Stärke und Belastbarkeit des Materials: Genutzt wird der Raum für Hochzeiten, Live-Konzerte und andere Feierlichkeiten. Das an die Flügel eines Vogels erinnernde Bauwerk ist darüber hinaus ideal geeignet, „Wind einzufangen". Der Architekt schreibt: „Inspiriert von der Natur, ist der **BAMBOO WING** den Schwingen eines Vogels nachempfunden und schwebt über der Naturlandschaft in der Nähe von Hanoi … Mit seinem tief vorgezogenen Dach und dem Wasser auf den Freiflächen fühlt man sich hier, als würde man mitten in der Natur wohnen."

Les architectes ont cherché à utiliser le bambou comme matériau de finition ainsi que dans des applications structurelles. Le bâtiment se compose d'une structure entièrement en bambou « sans acier, ni aucun autre matériau de construction artificiel ». Un espace ouvert de 12 m, utilisé pour célébrer des mariages, pour des concerts en direct et des cérémonies, atteste de la solidité et de la résistance du matériau. Inspiré par les ailes des oiseaux, la construction « est bonne pour capter le vent ». L'architecte déclare : « Inspirée par la nature, **BAMBOO WING** prend la forme d'ailes d'oiseaux et flotte au-dessus du paysage naturel de son site, près d'Hanoï. […] Avec ses profonds avant-toits et l'eau des espaces ouverts, les visiteurs ont l'impression de se trouver en pleine nature. »

The basic forms of the building are visible in the plan above—a semicircular covering arches over spaces for guests of the events organized under the Bamboo Wing.

Die Grundform des Gebäudes ist am Grundriss oben ablesbar – ein Halbrund erhebt sich bogenförmig über einem Gastbereich für Veranstaltungen im Bamboo Wing.

On voit sur le plan ci-dessus les formes de base du bâtiment : des arches couvertes semi-circulaires au-dessus d'espaces pour les spectateurs des manifestations organisées sous la Bamboo Wing.

A basin, whose level is actually higher than that of the seating area, arcs around the bamboo structure. The arcing forms of the building are stunning, as seen in these images.

Ein Wasserbecken, dessen Pegel über Bodenniveau des Gastbereichs liegt, folgt bogenförmig den Konturen des Bambusbaus. Die Bogenkonstruktion ist eindrucksvoll, wie hier zu sehen.

Un bassin, dont le niveau est plus haut que le sol où sont placées les chaises, sinue autour de la structure en bambou. Les formes arquées de la structure que l'on voit ici sont impressionnantes.

P 390

The resilience and strength of bamboo are used to their utmost in this structure—which might easily have been imagined in steel or other metals, but the architect has taken pride in avoiding "man-made" materials.

Der Bau lotet die Grenzen der Belastbarkeit und Stabilität von Bambus aus. Der Entwurf wäre leicht in Stahl oder Metall zu realisieren gewesen, doch der Architekt legte besonderen Wert darauf, auf „künstliche" Materialien zu verzichten.

La structure tire un parti optimal de la résistance et de la force du bambou – elle aurait facilement pu être créée en acier ou dans un autre métal, mais les architectes tirent une grande fierté d'avoir évité les matériaux « artificiels ».

STACKING GREEN

Ho Chi Minh City, Vietnam, 2011

Address: n/a. Area: 65 m². Client: Hoang Thi Thu Ha
Cost: not disclosed. Collaboration: Daisuke Sanuki, Shunri Nishizawa,
Thuan Viet JSC, Wind and Water House JSC

This house, designed for a couple in their 30s and their mother, was built in a narrow lot—20 meters deep and just four meters wide. The front and back façades are entirely composed of layers of concrete planters cantilevered from two side walls. The distance between the planters and the height of the planters are adjusted according to the height of the plants, which varies from 25 to 40 centimeters. An automatic irrigation system inside the planters provides humidity. There are few partition walls to assure interior fluidity and views of the green façades. Both the green façades and the rooftop garden are intended to shield residents from street noise and pollution. Natural ventilation is provided through the façades and two top openings. The architect states: "We observed the bioclimatic principles of the traditional Vietnamese courtyard house."

Das für ein Paar in den Dreißigern und dessen Mutter entworfene Haus wurde auf einem schmalen Grundstück gebaut, das 20 m tief und nur 4 m breit ist. Die Fassaden des Wohnbaus wurden an Vorder- und Rückseite mit übereinander gestaffelten Pflanzkästen aus Beton realisiert, die zwischen den beiden Seitenwänden auskragen. Der Abstand zwischen den Pflanzkästen und deren Höhe orientiert sich an der Höhe der Pflanzen, die von 25 bis 40 cm reicht. Ein automatisches Bewässerungssystem sorgt für ausreichende Feuchtigkeit. Durch nur wenige Trennwände wird der Raumfluss und der Blick auf die grünen Fassaden gewahrt. Grüne Fassaden und ein Dachgarten dienen nicht zuletzt auch der Abschirmung der Bewohner vom Straßenlärm und der Luftverschmutzung. Eine natürliche Durchlüftung ist durch die offenen Fassaden und zwei Dachöffnungen gegeben. Der Architekt erklärt: „Wir haben uns von den bioklimatischen Prinzipien des vietnamesischen Hofhauses anregen lassen."

La maison, créée pour un couple de trentenaires et leur mère, a été construite sur une parcelle très étroite – 20 m de profondeur pour à peine 4 m de largeur. Les façades avant et arrière sont entièrement composées de jardinières en béton empilées en porte à faux par rapport aux deux murs latéraux. L'écart entre les jardinières et leur hauteur est ajusté selon la taille des plantes, qui varie de 25 à 40 cm. Un système automatique d'irrigation à l'intérieur des jardinières apporte de l'humidité. Les cloisons séparatrices sont peu nombreuses afin de garantir une fluidité intérieure et des vues des façades de verdure. Les façades végétalisées et le jardin sur le toit doivent abriter les habitants de la maison des bruits de la rue et de la pollution. Les façades et deux ouvertures en haut fournissent une ventilation naturelle. L'architecte explique « avoir observé les principes bioclimatiques dans les maisons vietnamiennes traditionnelles à cour ».

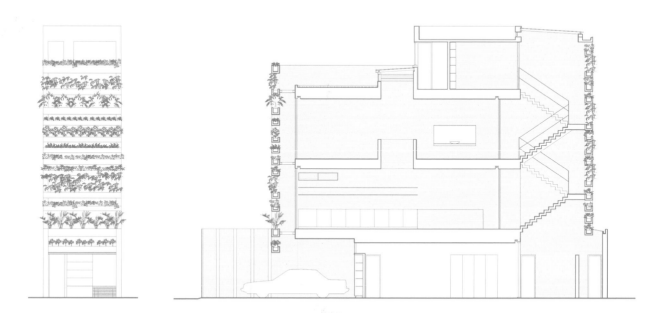

An elevation drawing of the façade (above) and a section show that the building is relatively narrow and deep. To the right, the façade is decidedly "green" due to the numerous plants at each level.

Ein Aufriss der Fassade (oben) und ein Querschnitt machen deutlich, wie schmal und tief das Gebäude ist. Die Fassade wirkt durch eine Vielzahl von Pflanzen auf den verschiedenen Ebenen auffällig „grün" (rechts).

Le schéma en élévation de la façade (ci-dessus) et la vue en coupe montrent l'étroitesse et la profondeur du bâtiment. À droite, la façade est résolument « verte » avec ses nombreuses plantes à tous les niveaux.

A drawing (below) shows the relation
of the building to sunlight: plants are
omnipresent, be it on the "stacked"
façade or on the green roof seen left.

Eine Zeichnung (unten) veranschaulicht Sonnenstand und Gebäudeposi-
tion. Die Begrünung ist allgegenwär-
tig, ob nun in Form der gestaffelten
Fassadenbepflanzung oder eines
begrünten Dachs links im Bild.

Le schéma (ci-dessous) montre le
bâtiment par rapport à l'ensoleillement : les plantes sont omnipré-
sentes, sur la façade « empilée »
ou sur le toit végétalisé que l'on
voit à gauche.

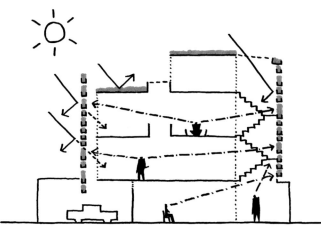

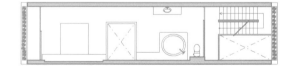

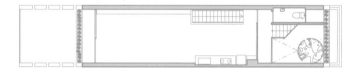

Plans show the long, rectangular
shape of the building. Interior spaces
are influenced in their light and color
by the continuous screen of plants
outside.

Auf den Grundrissen ist die gestreckte
Rechteckform des Gebäudes zu erkennen. Lichtverhältnisse und Farbein-
druck der Innenräume sind vom
durchgängigen „Grünschirm" der Fassadenbepflanzung geprägt.

Les plans montrent la forme allongée
et rectangulaire du bâtiment. La luminosité et la coloration des espaces
intérieurs sont modifiées par l'écran
continu de plantes à l'extérieur.

WOHA

WOHA
29 Hong Kong Street
Singapore 059668
Singapore

Tel: +65 642 4555 / Fax: +65 6423 4666
E-mail: admin@woha.net
Web: www.woha.net

RICHARD HASSELL received his B.Arch degree from the University of Western Australia (Perth, 1989) and his M.Arch from the Royal Melbourne Institute of Technology (Melbourne, 2002). **WONG MUN SUMM** was born in Singapore and received his B.A. degree in architectural studies from the National University of Singapore (1986), followed by a B.Arch degree from the same institution in 1989. They founded WOHA in 1994 in Singapore. Their work includes Moulmein Rise (Singapore, 2003, winner of a 2007 Aga Khan Award); The Met (Bangkok, Thailand, 2005–09, published here); Alila Villas Uluwatu (Bali, Indonesia, 2005–09, also published here); the School of Arts (Singapore, 2010); Stadium Mass Rapid Transit Station (Singapore, 2011); Bras Basah Mass Rapid Transit Station (Singapore, 2011); the InterContinental Sanya Resort (Sanya, Hainan Island, China, 2011); and the Park Royal on Pickering (Singapore, 2012), all in Singapore unless stated otherwise.

RICHARD HASSELL absolvierte seinen B.Arch an der University of Western Australia (Perth, 1989) und seinen M.Arch am Royal Melbourne Institute of Technology (Melbourne, 2002). **WONG MUN SUMM** wurde in Singapur geboren und absolvierte seinen B.A. in Architektur an der National University of Singapore (1986) sowie einen B.Arch an derselben Hochschule (1989). Gemeinsam gründeten sie 1994 ihr Büro WOHA in Singapur. Zu ihren Projekten zählen Moulmein Rise (Singapur, 2003, Gewinner des Aga Khan Award 2007), The Met (Bangkok, Thailand, 2005–09, hier vorgestellt), Alila Villas Uluwatu (Bali, Indonesien, 2005–09, ebenfalls hier vorgestellt), die Hochschule der Künste in Singapur (2010), der MRT-Bahnhof Stadium (Singapur, 2011), der MRT-Bahnhof Bras Basah (Singapur, 2011), das InterContinental Sanya Resort (Sanya, Insel Hainan, China, 2011) und das Hotel Park Royal on Pickering (Singapur, 2012), alle in Singapur, sofern nicht anders vermerkt.

RICHARD HASSELL a obtenu son B.Arch à l'université d'Australie-Occidentale (Perth, 1989) et son M.Arch à l'Institut royal de technologie de Melbourne (2002). **WONG MUN SUMM** est né à Singapour et a obtenu son B.A. en études architecturales à l'université nationale de Singapour (1986), puis un B.Arch en 1989. Ils ont fondé WOHA en 1994 à Singapour. Leurs réalisations comprennent la tour Moulmein Rise (Singapour, 2003, lauréate d'un prix Aga Khan 2007) ; The Met (Bangkok, 2005 –09, publié ici) ; les villas Alila d'Uluwatu (Bali, Indonésie, 2005–09, également publiées ici) ; l'École d'art (Singapour, 2010) ; la station Stade du Mass Rapid Transit (Singapour, 2011) ; la station Bras Basah du Mass Rapid Transit (Singapour, 2011) ; l'InterContinental Sanya Resort (Sanya, île de Hainan, Chine, 2011) et l'hôtel Park Royal on Pickering (Singapour, 2012).

THE MET
Bangkok, Thailand, 2005–09

Address: 123 South Salthorn Road, Thungmahamek, Salthorn, Bangkok 10120, Thailand,
tel: +66 662 287 3883, www.met-bangkok.com
Area: 124 884 m². Client: Pebble Bay Thailand Co. Ltd. Cost: not disclosed

This naturally ventilated "green" tower proposes an alternative to the more typical sealed, glazed curtain-wall buildings generally erected in tropical regions. The cross-ventilated apartments have breezeways, outdoor living areas, planters, "high-rise gardens," and open-air community terraces with barbecues, libraries, spas, and other facilities. Every available horizontal surface, including private balconies, is planted, with vertical faces shaded by "creeper screens." Cladding is an attempt to "reinterpret Thai temple tiles." The architects state: "The orderly, elegant building makes an attractive addition to the chaotic skyline of Bangkok. With its openings to the sky behind, and planted façades, balconies, and sky gardens, **THE MET** weaves nature into the concrete jungle of central Bangkok."

Das natürlich belüftete „grüne" Hochhaus versteht sich als Alternative zu konventionell geschlossenen und verglasten Curtain-Wall-Bauten, die üblicherweise in den Tropen gebaut werden. Zur Ausstattung der querdurchlüfteten Apartments zählen offene „Windkorridore", Loggien, Pflanzkästen, „Hochgärten" und Gemeinschafts-terrassen mit Grill, Bibliothek, Spas sowie anderen Einrichtungen. Alle verfügbaren horizontalen Flächen, einschließlich der privaten Loggien, wurden bepflanzt. „Bodende-ckerwandschirme" spenden den vertikalen Flächen Schatten. Die Verblendstruktur ist eine „Neuinterpretation thailändischer Tempelfliesen". Die Architekten erklären: „Das klar gegliederte, elegante Gebäude ist eine attraktive Bereicherung der chaotischen Skyline von Bangkok. Dank der Öffnungen, durch die der Himmel aufscheint, der begrünten Fassaden, Loggien und Dachgärten webt **THE MET** Natur in den Betondschungel des Stadtzentrums von Bangkok."

La tour « verte » naturellement ventilée constitue une alternative aux immeubles plus classiques, étanches et à façade rideau vitrée, qui sont généralement construits dans les zones tropicales. Les appartements à ventilation transversale présentent des passages couverts, des séjours extérieurs, des jardinières, des « tours jardins » et des terrasses communes avec barbecues, bibliothèques, spas ou autres équipements. La moindre surface horizontale disponible est plantée, balcons privés compris, et les faces verticales du bâtiment sont ombragées par des « écrans de plantes rampantes ». Le revêtement est une tentative de « réinterprétation des carreaux des temples thaïs ». Pour les architectes, « le bâtiment régulier et élégant constitue un point d'attraction supplémentaire dans la ligne d'horizon plutôt désordonnée de Bangkok. Avec ses ouvertures sur le ciel, ses façades plantées, ses balcons et jardins en hauteur, **THE MET** introduit la nature dans la jungle de béton du centre-ville ».

Below, plans for the 28th floor (left)
and the 55th floor (right). Though its
forms are the result of an accumulation of rectangles, The Met shows its
green face in the image above.

Unten die Etagengrundrisse für den
28. Stock (links) und den 55. Stock
(rechts). Obwohl der Entwurf auf
rechteckigen Modulen basiert, zeigt
The Met nach außen eine grüne
Fassade (oben).

Ci-dessous, plans du 28ᵉ étage (à
gauche) et du 55ᵉ étage (à droite).
Bien que sa forme résulte d'une
accumulation de rectangles,
The Met montre sa face verte
sur la photo ci-dessus.

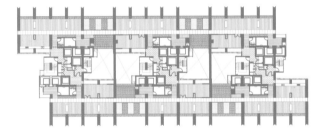

Double-height spaces and a play on materials, such as wood, water, or gravel, characterize these interior views.

Innenansichten, die sich durch doppelte Geschosshöhe und ein Spiel mit verschiedenen Materialien auszeichnen, darunter Holz, Wasser und Kies.

Des espaces double hauteur et le jeu avec des matériaux tels que le bois, l'eau ou les graviers marquent ces vues intérieures.

ALILA VILLAS ULUWATU

Bali, Indonesia, 2005–09

Address: Jl Belimbing Sari, Banjar Tambiyak, Desa Pecatu 80364, Bali, Indonesia,
tel: 62 361 848 2166, www.alilahotels.com/uluwatu
Area: 26 595 m². Client: PT Bukit Uluwatu Villa. Cost: not disclosed

Long horizontal lines where the distinction between interior and exterior, or even the pool and the ocean beyond, becomes difficult to ascertain.

Gestreckte horizontale Linien dominieren diese Ansicht, auf der Übergänge zwischen Innen und Außen und sogar zwischen Pool und Meer kaum noch auszumachen sind.

Les longues lignes horizontales rendent difficile toute distinction entre intérieur et extérieur, ou même entre la piscine et l'océan au-delà.

This complex including a 50-suite hotel and 35 villas located on the Bukit Peninsula is "a Green Globe 21–rated ecologically sustainable development." Local farmers' terraces inspire the design. The roofs make use of Balinese volcanic pumice rock as a natural insulating material. Set into the terraced site in a conscious attempt to avoid modifying the natural landscape, the villas are linked by bridges that cross water gardens. Local dry savannah plants are used for landscaping, avoiding the need for excessive irrigation. The architects explain: "Materials are all sourced locally—the walls use stones from the actual site from the road cuttings, while all other materials are either from Bali or Java. Only recycled Ulin timber and bamboo was used. Craftsmen in Java and Bali made the furniture, lamps, and accessories."

Der Komplex, eine Hotelanlage mit 50 Suiten und 35 Villen, liegt auf der Halbinsel Bukit und ist „ein ökologisch nachhaltiges Bauprojekt mit Green-Globe-21-Zertifikat". Angeregt wurde der Entwurf von den Terrassenfeldern der lokalen Bauern. Die Dächer aus balinesischem Vulkangestein (Bimsstein) dienen zugleich der natürlichen Dämmung. Die bewusst in die Terrassen des Grundstücks eingebetteten Villen stören die natürliche Landschaft nicht und sind durch Brücken miteinander verbunden, die Wassergärten überspannen. Begrünt wurde mit heimischen Savannengewächsen, die Trockenheit vertragen, sodass sich übermäßige Bewässerung erübrigt. Die Architekten erklären: „Baumaterialien wurden vollständig lokal beschafft – in den Mauern wurde Stein vom Grundstück verbaut, der beim Abriss von Straßenwegen anfiel, während sämtliche weiteren Baustoffe von Bali oder Java stammen. Ausschließlich recyceltes Ulin-Holz und Bambus kamen zum Einsatz. Handwerker aus Java und Bali fertigten Möbel, Leuchten und Accessoires."

Le complexe, composé d'un hôtel de 50 suites et de 35 villas sur la péninsule de Bukit, est un exemple de « développement durable écologique labellisé Green Globe 21 ». La conception s'inspire des cultures en terrasses locales. Les toits sont en pierre ponce volcanique de Bali qui isole naturellement. Disposées sur le site en terrasses avec l'intention délibérée de ne pas modifier le paysage, les villas sont reliées par des passerelles qui enjambent des jardins aquatiques. Des plantes locales de savane sèche ont été utilisées pour l'aménagement paysager afin d'éviter tout besoin excessif d'irrigation. Les architectes expliquent que « tous les matériaux sont d'origine locale – les murs sont en pierres récupérées sur le site en creusant les tranchées pour la route, tous les autres matériaux viennent de Bali ou de Java. Seuls du bois ulin recyclé et du bambou ont été utilisés. Les meubles, lampes et accessoires ont été réalisés par des artisans de Java et Bali.

Locally quarried volcanic pumice stone is seen used in walls in the image to the right. Plants and wood from the region contribute to the ecological aspect of this project.

Der Vulkanstein der Mauern rechts im Bild stammt aus Steinbrüchen vor Ort. Ökologische Aspekte sind unter anderem der Rückgriff auf regionale Pflanzen und Holzvorkommen.

On voit sur la photo de droite la pierre ponce volcanique extraite sur place et utilisée pour les murs. Les plantes et le bois d'origine locale apportent une contribution écologique de plus au projet.

The horizontality of the design connects it more fully to the ocean and
the sky, evoking Bali's traditions of
decorative art at the same time.

Die horizontalen Linien des Entwurfs
stellen den Bezug zu Meer und Himmel her und sind zugleich eine
Hommage an die balinesische Kunst-
handwerkstradition.

L'horizontalité du concept le
rapproche plus de l'océan et du
ciel, tout en évoquant la tradition
balinaise des arts décoratifs.

Below, a plan of a hotel villa. Above, a rooftop suspended between ocean and sky.

Unten der Grundriss einer Villa. Oben eine Dachterrasse zwischen Himmel und Meer.

Ci-dessous, un plan d'une villa de l'hôtel. En haut, un toit suspendu entre ciel et océan.

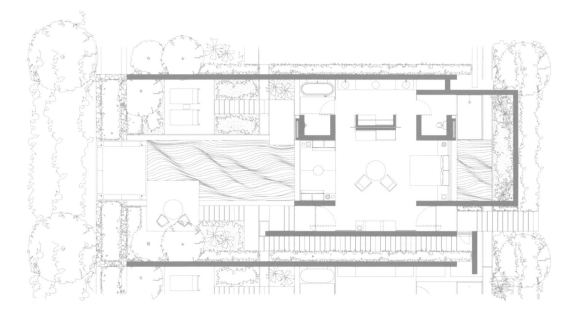

Above, the master plan of the com-
plex with a section drawing above
indicating the steep drop-off of the
site.

Oben der Masterplan des Komplexes.
Darüber ein Querschnitt des steil
abfallenden Küstengrundstücks.

Ci-dessus, le plan directeur du com-
plexe et une vue en coupe indiquant
la forte déclivité du site.

INDEX OF BUILDINGS, NAMES AND PLACES

INDEX OF BUILDINGS, NAMES AND PLACES

CREDITS

PHOTO CREDITS — **2** © Oki Hiroyuki / **7** © Iwan Baan / **8** © Gulf Coast Community Design Studio / **11** © Oki Hiroyuki / **12** © Kalle Sanner / **13** © Marcel van der Burg / **14** © Thies Wachter / **15** © Autostadt Wolfsburg, DE / **16** © Andrew Meredith / **17** © Filip Dujardin / **19** © Albert Lim / **21** © Christopher Charles Benninger Architects / **22** © Oki Hiroyuki / **24** © Zooey Braun / **25** © BIG&Glessner / **26** © Adrian Smith + Gordon Gill Architecture / **28** © Jardin Botanico Culiacan / **29** © H. G. Esch / **33** © Robert Such/Arcaid / **35** © Takumi Ota Photography / **36** © Ulrich Schwarz / **39** © Graphix-images, Augusto da Silva / **41** © H. G. Esch / **42** © vaneetveldt+nyhuis / **43** © Eriksson Architects LTD / **44** © Ateliers 115 Architectes / **45, 47, 49-51** © Graphix-images, Augusto da Silva / **46** © Ateliers 115 Architectes / **48** © Image Sol'Air, Jean-Lou Peyromaure / **52** © Belzberg Architects / **53-57, 58 bottom, 60-63** © Iwan Baan / **58 top, 59** © Benny Chan / **64-71** © Ben Wood Studio Shanghai / **72-79** © BIG&Glessner / **80** © BNIM / **81-85** © Assassi / **86** © Brooks + Scarpa / **87-91** © John Linden/Brooks + Scarpa / **92** © Centerbrook Architects and Planners / **93-95** © Peter Aaron/OTTO / **96-101** © Centerbrook Architects and Planners / **102-103, 106-109** © Déca Laage – Groupe H / **104-105** deca-laage©gudrun bergdahl / **110** © dekleva gregoric arhitekti / **111-119** © Cristóbal Palma / **120-125** © Miran Kambic / **126** © Djuric Tardio Architectes / **127-133** © Clément Guillaume / **134** © ecosistema urbano architects ltd / **135, 137, 143 bottom-144 top, 145** © Javier de Paz / **136, 138-143 top, 144 bottom** © Emilio P. Doiztúa / **146** © Studio Olafur Eliasson GmbH / **147-151** © Autostadt Wolfsburg, DE / **152-155** © Jardin Botanico Culiacan / **156** © Xander Remkes / **157-163** © Marcel van der Burg / **164** © Christian Scholz / **165-167** © Antje Quiram / **168-171** © Thies Wachter / **172** © Gulf Coast Community Design Studio / **173, 176 top, 177** © Alan Karchmer / **174-175, 176 bottom** © Gulf Coast Community Design Studio / **178** © HMC Architects / **179-185** © Ryan Beck Photography / **186-191** © Hopkins Architects / **192** © import export Architecture / **193-199** © Filip Dujardin / **200** © vaneetveldt+nyhuis / **201-205** © Stijn Bollaert / **206** © ingenhoven architects / **207 top, 209-213** © H. G. Esch / **207 bottom** © Andreas Keller / **208** © ingenhoven architects / **214-221** © Jensen & Skodvin Architects / **222** © Johnsen Schmaling Architects / **223-229** © John J. Macaulay / **230-235** © Doug Edmunds / **236** © k-Studio / **237-241** © Yiorgos Kordakis / **242** © Architekturbüro Wolfgang Kergassner / **243-247** © Roland Halbe / **248** © Malin Hedman / **249-253** © Kalle Sanner / **254** © Mathias Klotz's Studio / **255-263** © Cristóbal Palma / **264** © Kengo Kuma and Associates / **265-273** © Takumi Ota Photography / **274** © Lake|Flato Architects / **275-279** © Frank Ooms / **280-285** © Hester + Hardaway / **286** © Leapfactory / **287, 290-291** © Francesco Mattuzzi / **288, 292** © Marco Destefanis / **289, 293** © Gughi Fassino / **294-301** © SKM Architects / **302-307** © realities:united, studio for art and architecture / **308** © Jan Lillebø/Bergens Tidende / **309-317** © Bent René Synnevåg / **318-323** © Adrian Smith + Gordon Gill Architecture / **324** © A.T. Schaefer / **325-329** © Zooey Braun / **330-331** © Matthias Koslik / **332-333** © Ulrich Schwarz / **334** © TAO / **335-339** © Shu He / **340** © Mikael Olsson / **341-351** © Åke E:son Lindman / **352** © Threefold Architects / **353-355, 359** © Nick Kane / **356-358** © Jon Holland / **360** © Martin Mai / **361-367** © Iwan Baan / **3368** © Unsangdong Architects / **369-375** © Sergio Pirrone / **376** © Vector Architects/Gong Dong / **377-383** © Shu He / **384** © Votrongnghia Co., Ltd / **385-397** © Oki Hiroyuki / **398** © WOHA / **399** © Kirsten Bucher / **400-411** © Patrick Bingham-Hall

CREDITS FOR PLANS / DRAWINGS / CAD DOCUMENTS — **47-50** © Ateliers 115 Architectes / **55-56** © Belzberg Architects / **67-70** © Ben Wood Studio Shanghai / **72-79** © BIG&Glessner / **83-85** © BNIM / **89, 91** © Brooks + Scarpa / **97-98, 101** © Centerbrook Architects and Planners / **106-108** © Déca Laage – Groupe H / **112, 114, 116-117** © dekleva gregoric arhitekti / **129, 132** © Djuric Tardio Architectes / **137, 140** © ecosistema urbano architects ltd / **158, 160, 162** © Dick van Gameren architecten / **168, 171** © Gigon/Guyer / **175, 177** © Gulf Coast Community Design Studio / **181-182, 184** © HMC Architects / **188, 191** © Hopkins Architects / **198-199, 201, 203, 205** © import export Architecture / **209, 210, 213** © ingenhoven architects / **217, 220** © Jensen & Skodvin Architects / **225-227, 229-230** © Johnsen Schmaling Architects / **239** © k-Studio / **245-246** © Architekturbüro Wolfgang Kergassner / **250-251** © Kjellgren Kaminsky Architecture AB / **266-267, 269** © Kengo Kuma and Associates / **277, 279, 283, 285** © Lake|Flato Architects / **289, 291-292** © Leapfactory / **299-300** © SKM Architects / **302-307** © realities:united, studio for art and architecture / **311** © Saunders Architects / **318-323** © Adrian Smith + Gordon Gill Architecture / **327, 331** © Werner Sobek / **336, 339** © TAO / **342, 344** © Tham & Videgård Arkitekter / **365-366** © Bernard Tschumi Architects / **372** © Unsangdong Architects / **379, 381, 383** © Vector Architects/Gong Dong / **386, 390, 392, 394, 396** © Votrongnghia Co., Ltd / **401, 410-411** © WOHA